Oh My Goddess! 4

ああっ女神さまっ

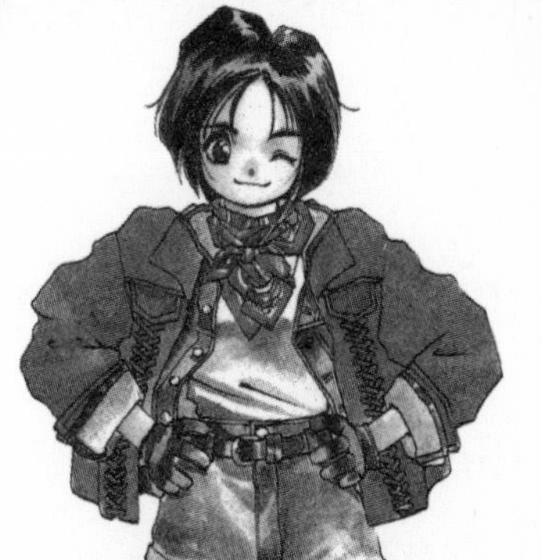

STORY AND ART BY
Kosuke Fujishima

TRANSLATION BY
Dana Lewis, Alan Gleason,
AND Toren Smith

LETTERING AND TOUCH-UP BY
Susie Lee AND Betty Dong
WITH Tom2K

DARK HORSE MANGA™

CHAPTER 24
The Flying Motor Club...........3

CHAPTER 25
Let's Take the Love Seeds......29

CHAPTER 26
The Nemesis....................57

CHAPTER 27
Mara's Counterattack...........81

CHAPTER 28
Balance-Ball Amour..........107

CHAPTER 29
The Worst Day
of a Demon....................133

CHAPTER 30
Engine O' Mystery............157

Letters to the Enchantress....183

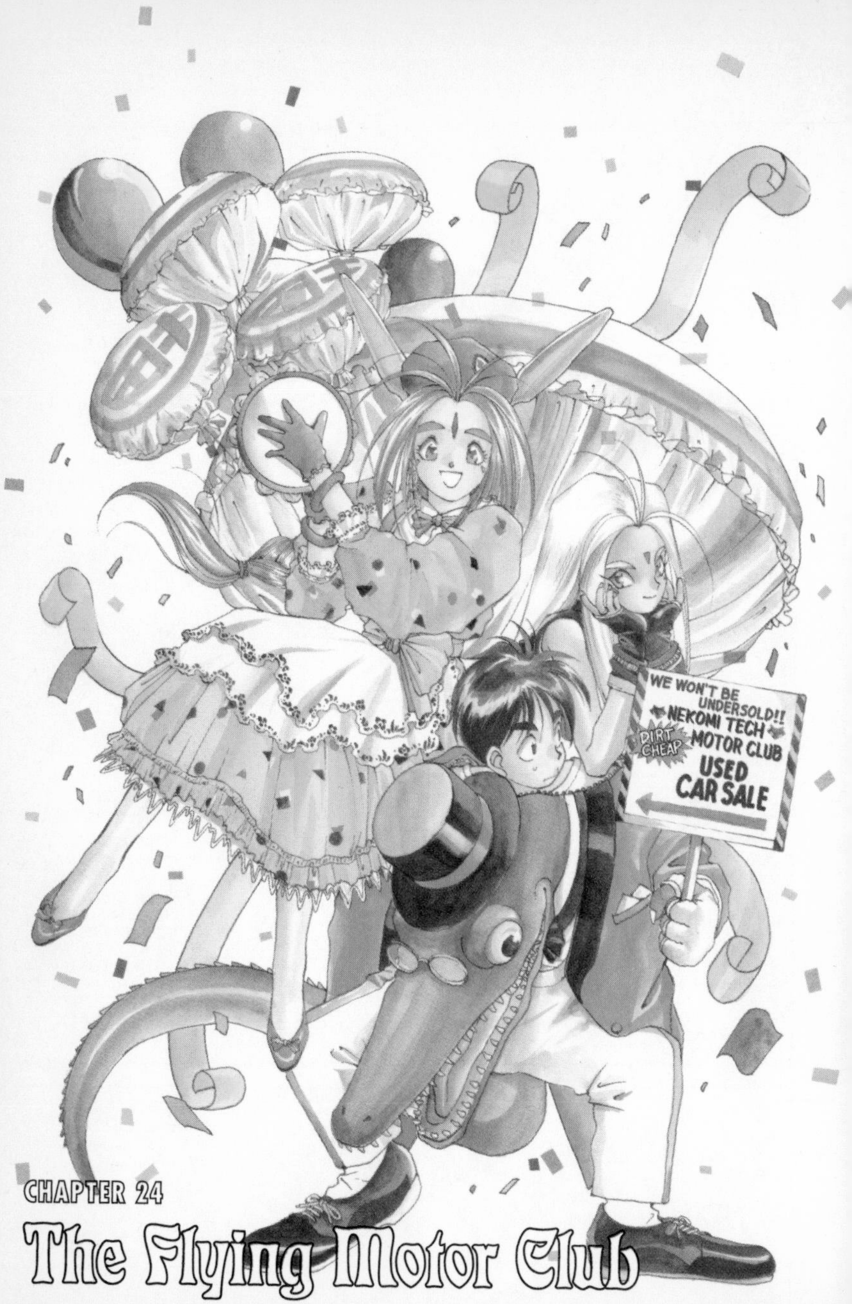
WE WON'T BE UNDERSOLD!!
NEKOMI TECH MOTOR CLUB
DIRT CHEAP
USED CAR SALE

CHAPTER 24

The Flying Motor Club

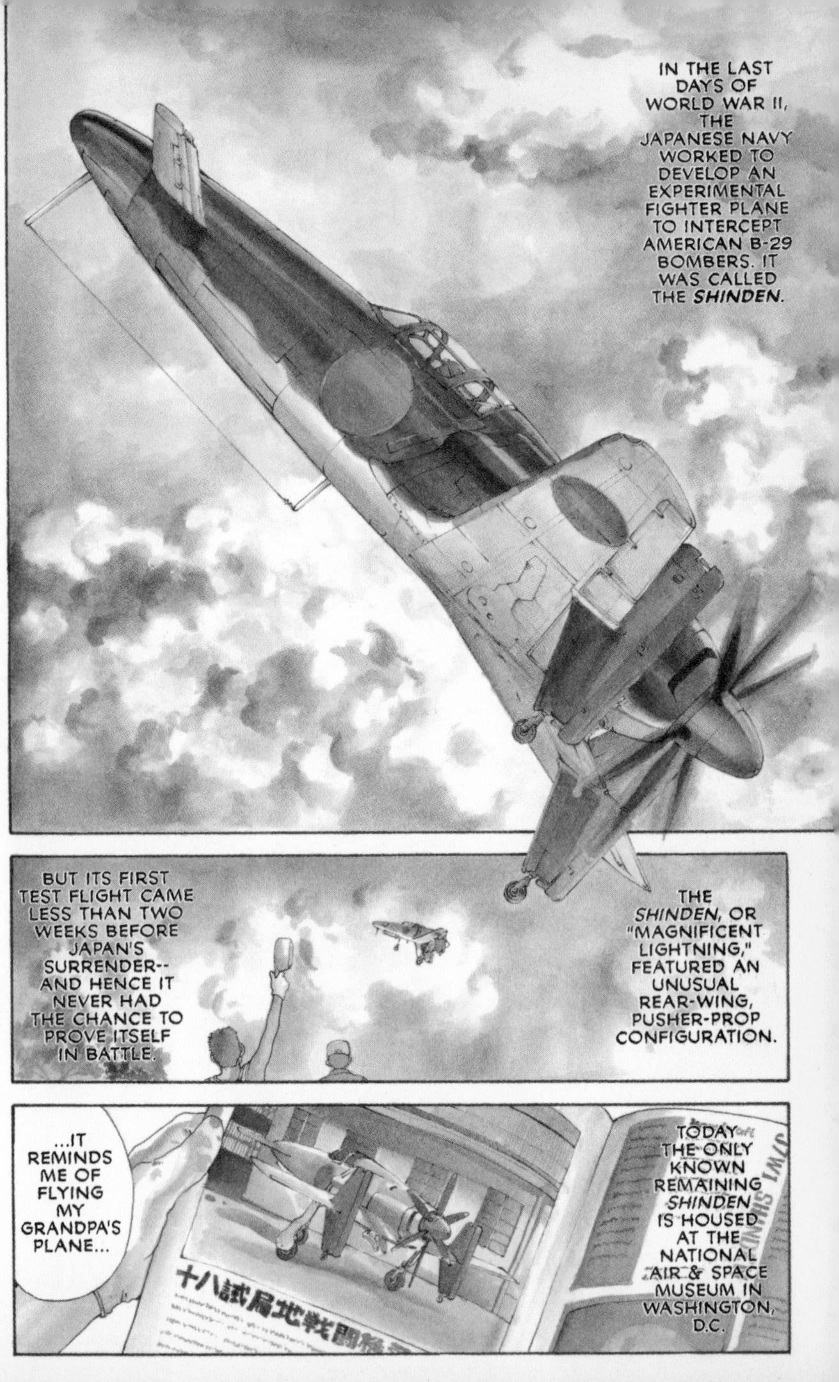
IN THE LAST DAYS OF WORLD WAR II, THE JAPANESE NAVY WORKED TO DEVELOP AN EXPERIMENTAL FIGHTER PLANE TO INTERCEPT AMERICAN B-29 BOMBERS. IT WAS CALLED THE *SHINDEN*.
THE *SHINDEN*, OR "MAGNIFICENT LIGHTNING," FEATURED AN UNUSUAL REAR-WING, PUSHER-PROP CONFIGURATION.
BUT ITS FIRST TEST FLIGHT CAME LESS THAN TWO WEEKS BEFORE JAPAN'S SURRENDER-- AND HENCE IT NEVER HAD THE CHANCE TO PROVE ITSELF IN BATTLE.
TODAY THE ONLY KNOWN REMAINING *SHINDEN* IS HOUSED AT THE NATIONAL AIR & SPACE MUSEUM IN WASHINGTON, D.C.
十八試局地戦闘
...IT REMINDS ME OF FLYING MY GRANDPA'S PLANE...

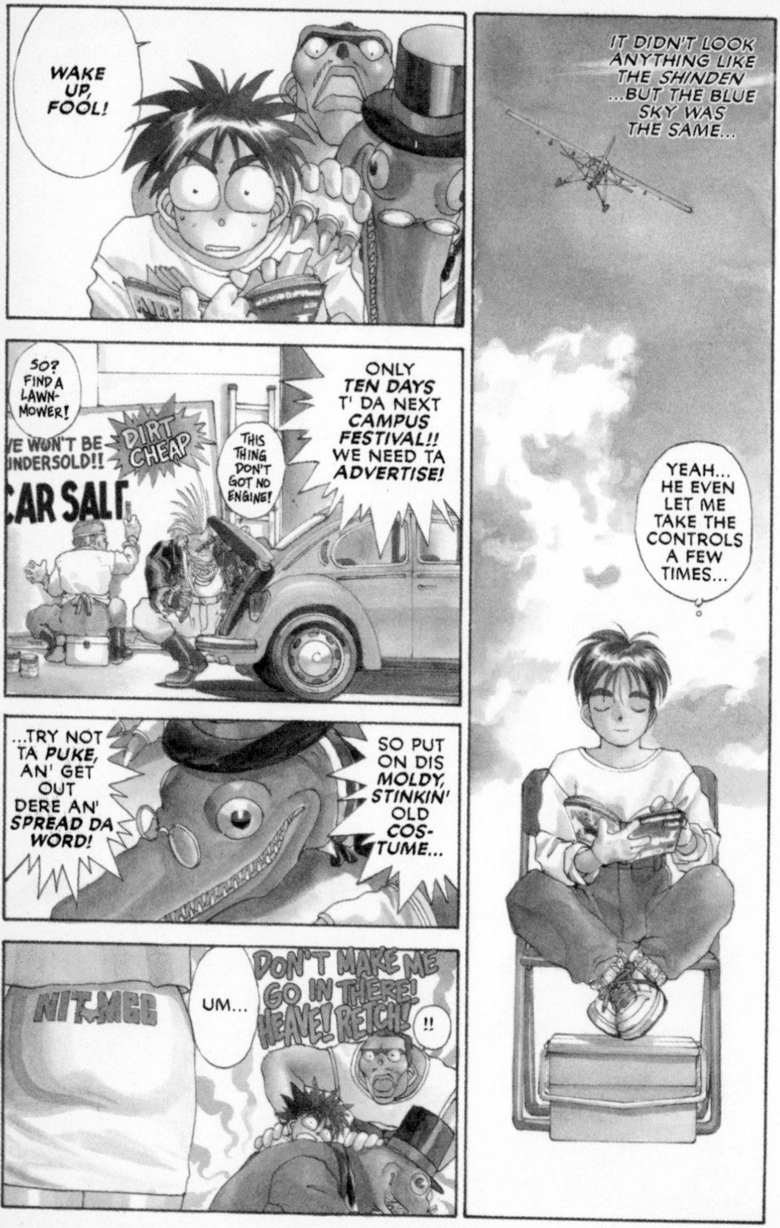
IT DIDN'T LOOK ANYTHING LIKE THE SHINDEN ...BUT THE BLUE SKY WAS THE SAME...
YEAH... HE EVEN LET ME TAKE THE CONTROLS A FEW TIMES...
WAKE UP, FOOL!
ONLY TEN DAYS T' DA NEXT CAMPUS FESTIVAL!! WE NEED TA ADVERTISE!
THIS THING DON'T GOT NO ENGINE!
DIRT CHEAP
SO? FIND A LAWN-MOWER!
E WON'T BE UNDERSOLD!!
CAR SAL
SO PUT ON DIS MOLDY, STINKIN' OLD COS-TUME...
...TRY NOT TA PUKE, AN' GET OUT DERE AN' SPREAD DA WORD!
!!
DON'T MAKE ME GO IN THERE! HEAVE! RETCH!
UM...

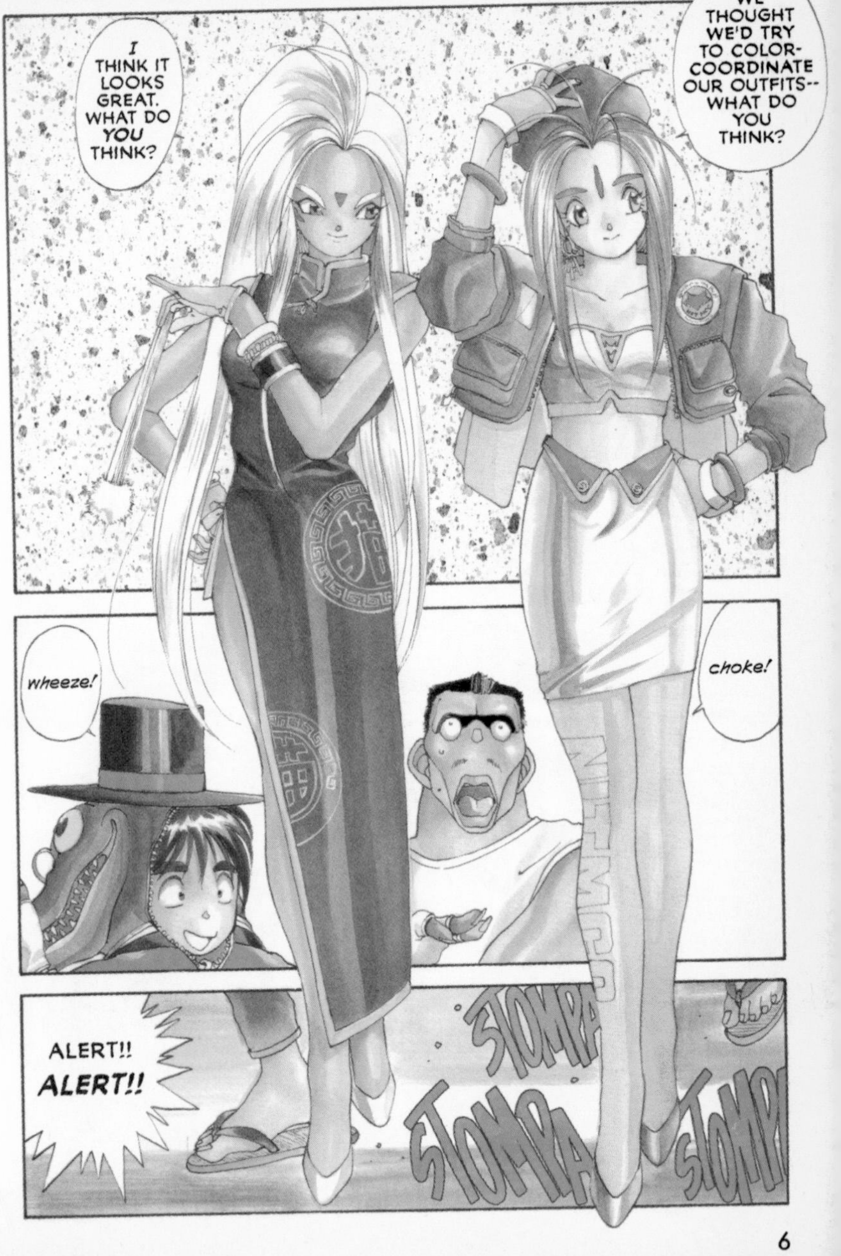
WE THOUGHT WE'D TRY TO COLOR-COORDINATE OUR OUTFITS--WHAT DO YOU THINK?
I THINK IT LOOKS GREAT. WHAT DO *YOU* THINK?
choke!
wheeze!
STOMPA
STOMPA
STOMPA
STOMPA
ALERT!!
ALERT!!

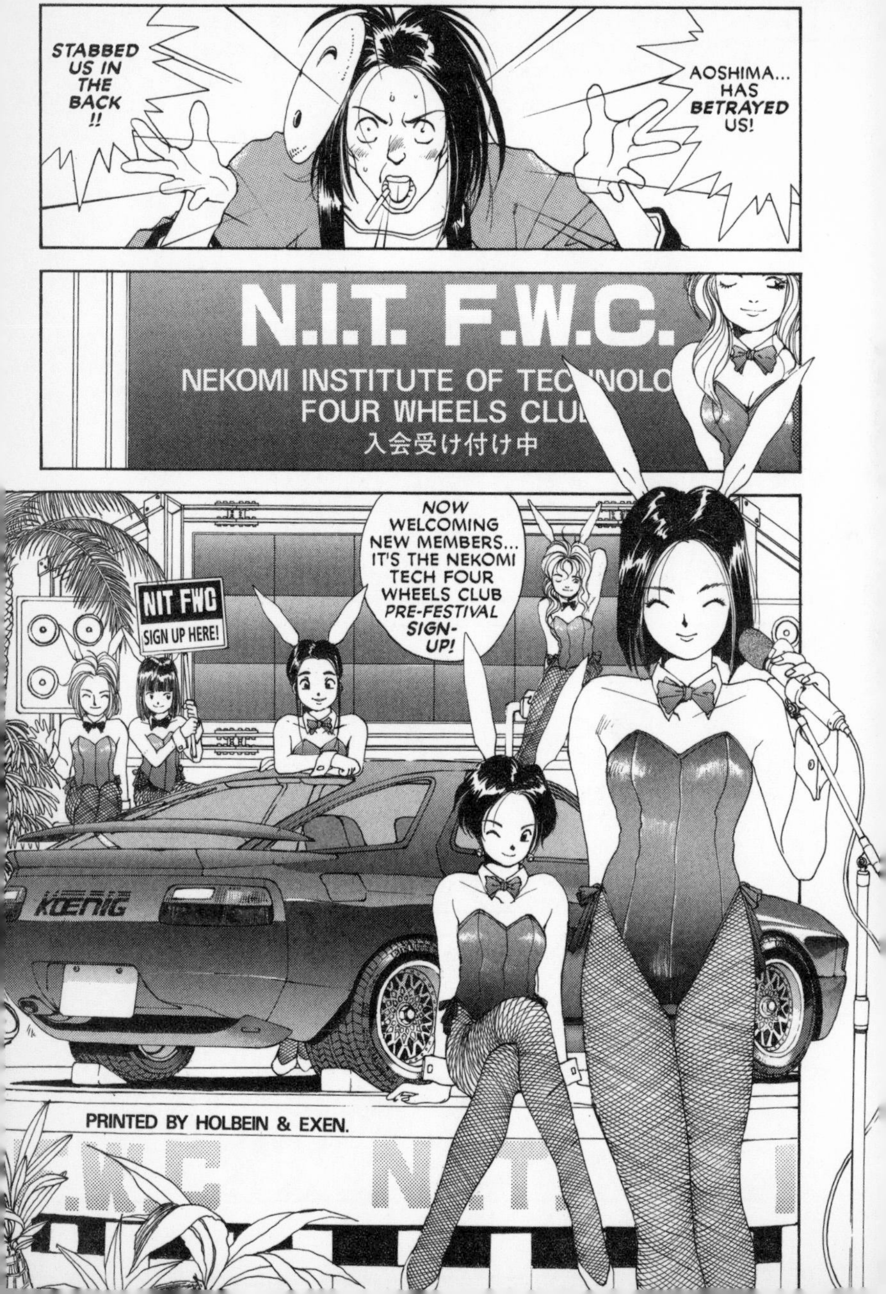
AOSHIMA... HAS BETRAYED US!
STABBED US IN THE BACK !!
N.I.T. F.W.C.
NEKOMI INSTITUTE OF TEC NOLO
FOUR WHEELS CLUB
入会受け付け中
NOW WELCOMING NEW MEMBERS... IT'S THE NEKOMI TECH FOUR WHEELS CLUB *PRE-FESTIVAL SIGN-UP!*
NIT FWC
SIGN UP HERE!
KOENIG
PRINTED BY HOLBEIN & EXEN.

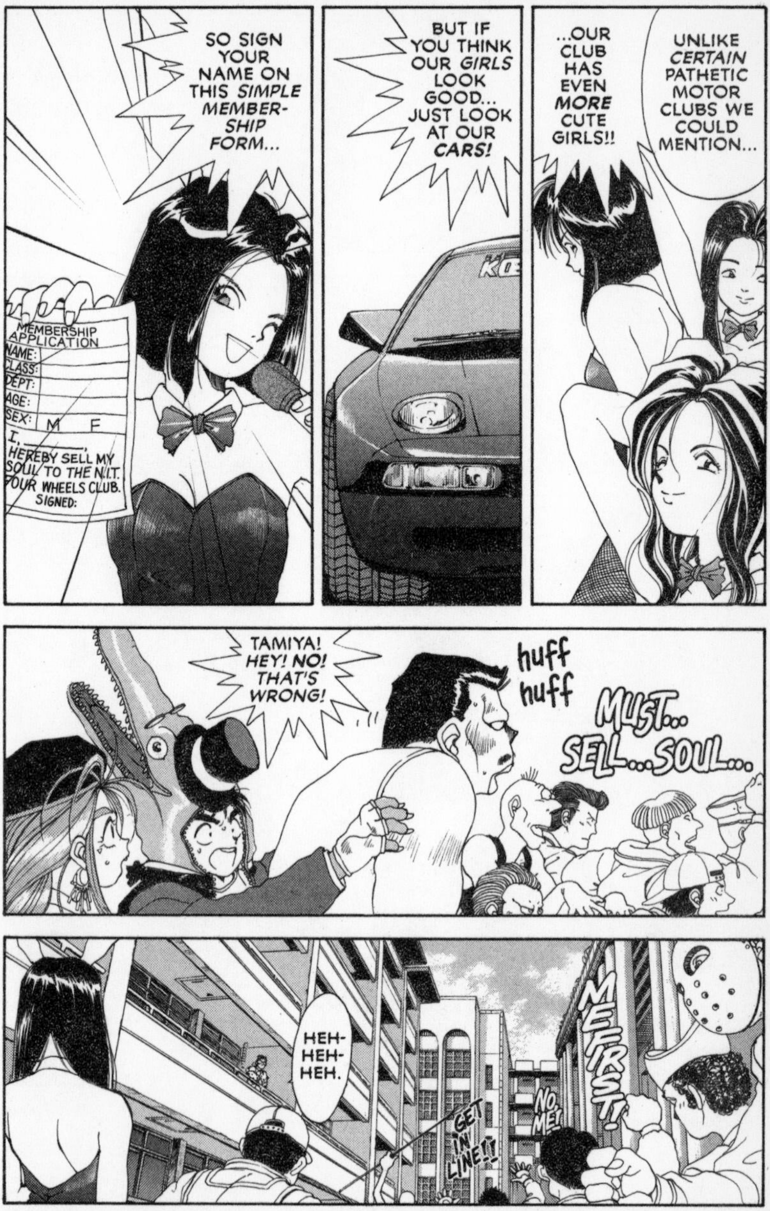
UNLIKE CERTAIN PATHETIC MOTOR CLUBS WE COULD MENTION...
...OUR CLUB HAS EVEN MORE CUTE GIRLS!!
BUT IF YOU THINK OUR GIRLS LOOK GOOD... JUST LOOK AT OUR CARS!
SO SIGN YOUR NAME ON THIS SIMPLE MEMBERSHIP FORM...
MEMBERSHIP APPLICATION
NAME:
CLASS:
DEPT:
AGE:
SEX: M F
I, ______, HEREBY SELL MY SOUL TO THE N.I.T. FOUR WHEELS CLUB.
SIGNED:
huff huff
MUST... SELL...SOUL...
TAMIYA! HEY! NO! THAT'S WRONG!
ME FIRST!
NO ME!
GET IN LINE!!
HEH-HEH-HEH.

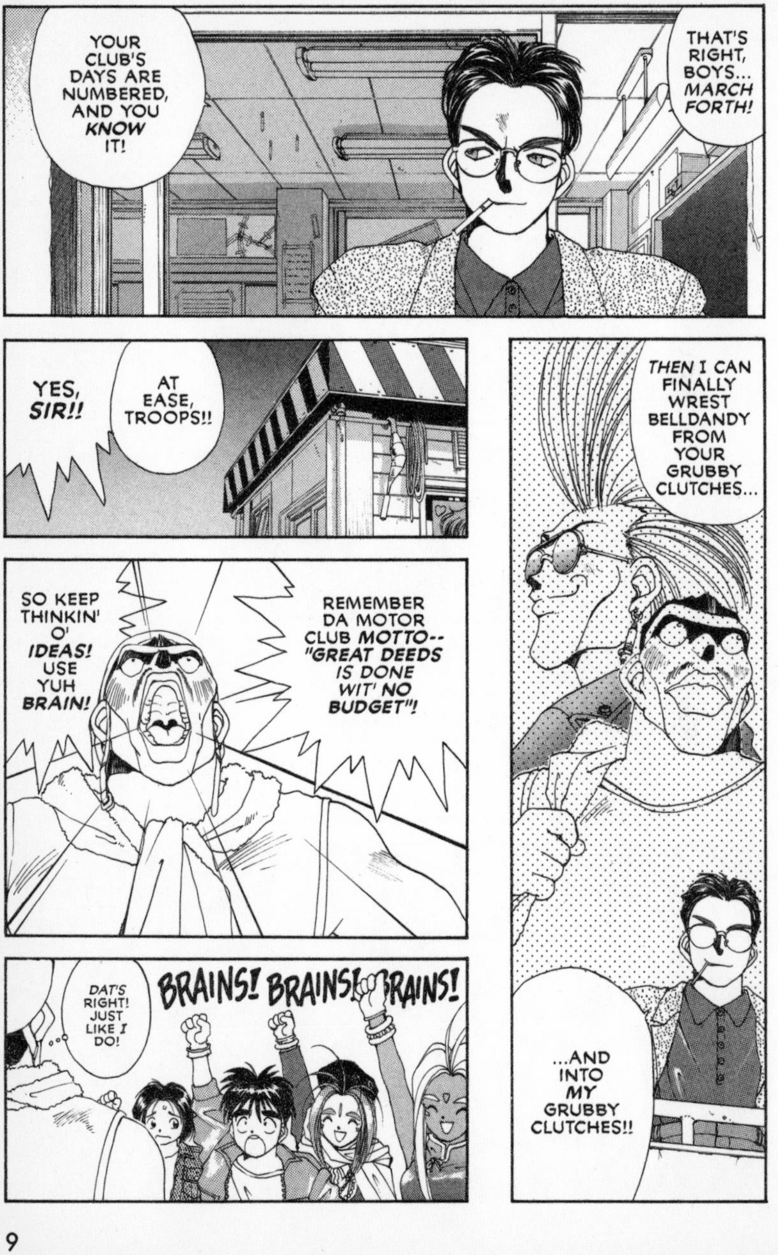
THAT'S RIGHT, BOYS... *MARCH FORTH!*
YOUR CLUB'S DAYS ARE NUMBERED, AND YOU *KNOW* IT!
THEN I CAN FINALLY WREST BELLDANDY FROM YOUR GRUBBY CLUTCHES...
...AND INTO *MY* GRUBBY CLUTCHES!!
AT EASE, TROOPS!!
YES, *SIR!!*
REMEMBER DA MOTOR CLUB *MOTTO-- "GREAT DEEDS IS DONE WIT' NO BUDGET"!*
SO KEEP THINKIN' O' *IDEAS!* USE YUH *BRAIN!*
BRAINS! BRAINS! BRAINS!
DAT'S RIGHT! JUST LIKE *I* DO!

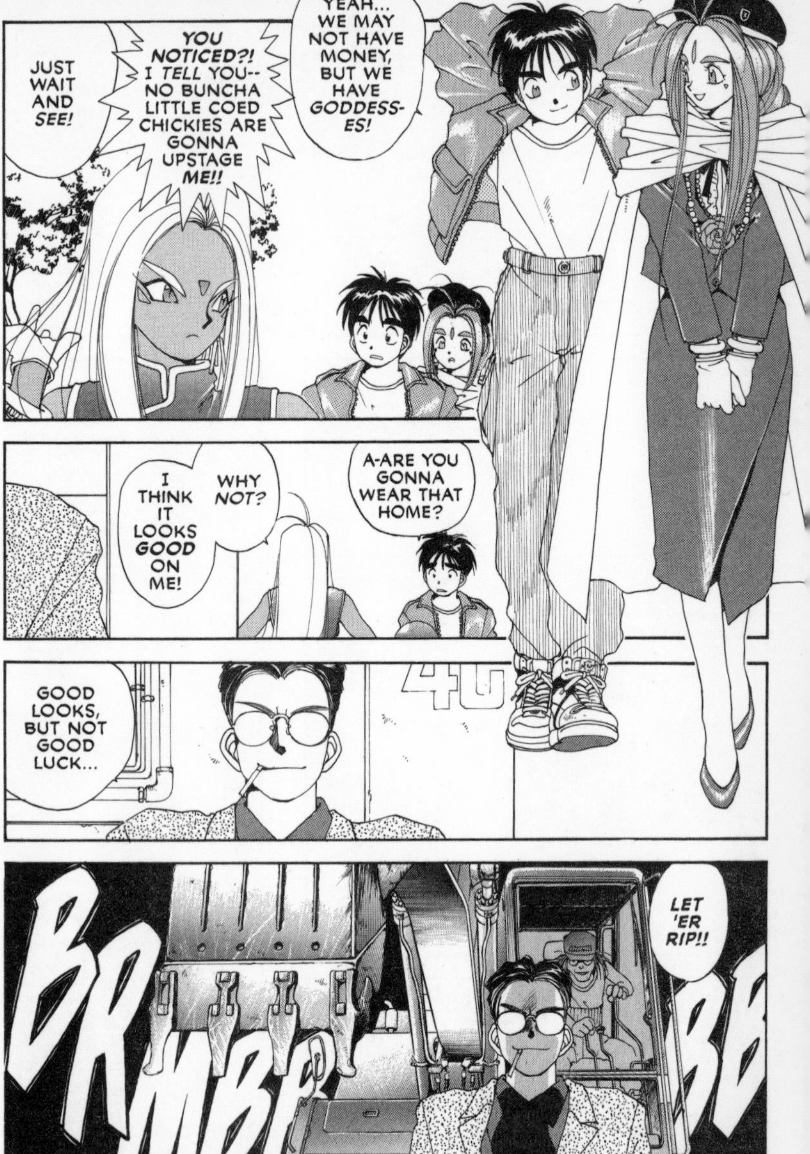
YEAH... WE MAY NOT HAVE MONEY, BUT WE HAVE *GODDESSES!*
YOU NOTICED?! I *TELL* YOU-- NO BUNCHA LITTLE COED CHICKIES ARE GONNA UPSTAGE *ME!!*
JUST WAIT AND *SEE!*
A-ARE YOU GONNA WEAR THAT HOME?
WHY *NOT?*
I THINK IT LOOKS *GOOD* ON ME!
GOOD LOOKS, BUT NOT GOOD LUCK...
LET 'ER RIP!!
BRMBB
BB

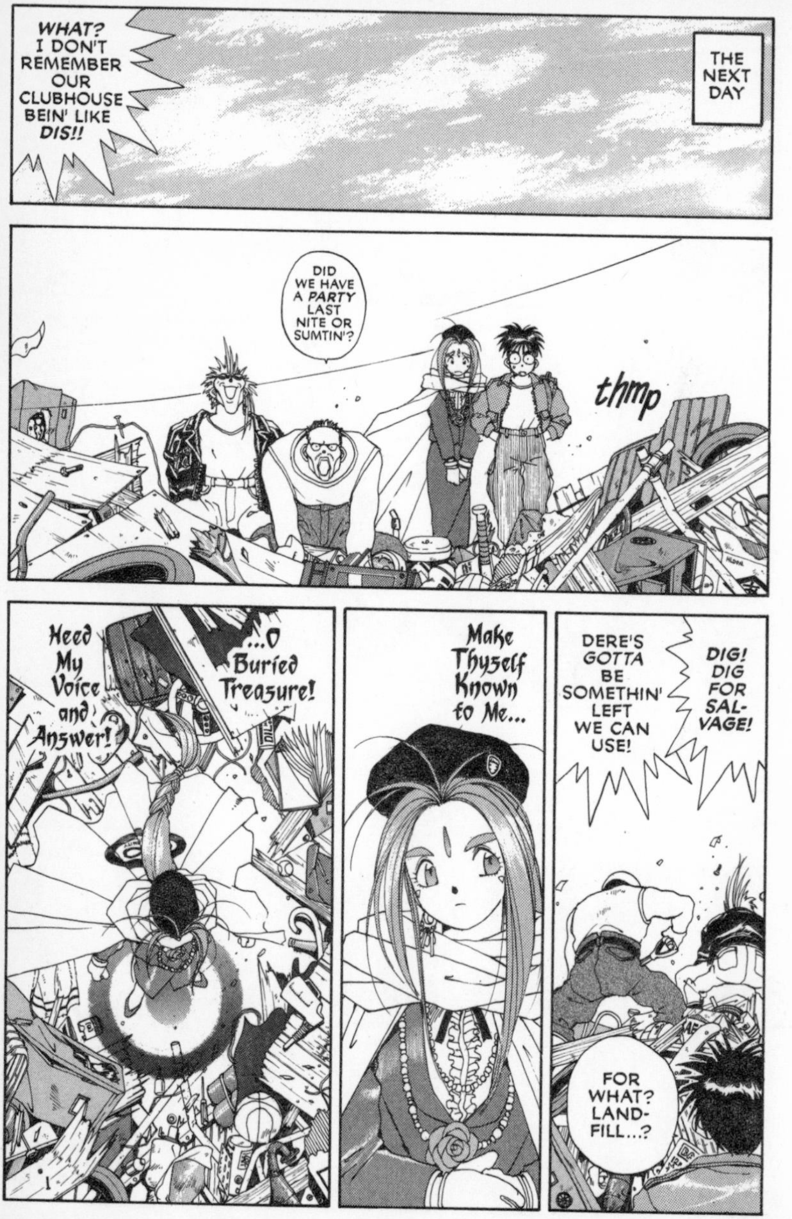
THE NEXT DAY
WHAT? I DON'T REMEMBER OUR CLUBHOUSE BEIN' LIKE DIS!!
DID WE HAVE A PARTY LAST NITE OR SUMTIN'?
thmp
DIG! DIG FOR SALVAGE!
DERE'S GOTTA BE SOMETHIN' LEFT WE CAN USE!
FOR WHAT? LANDFILL...?
Make Thyself Known to Me...
...O Buried Treasure!
Heed My Voice and Answer!

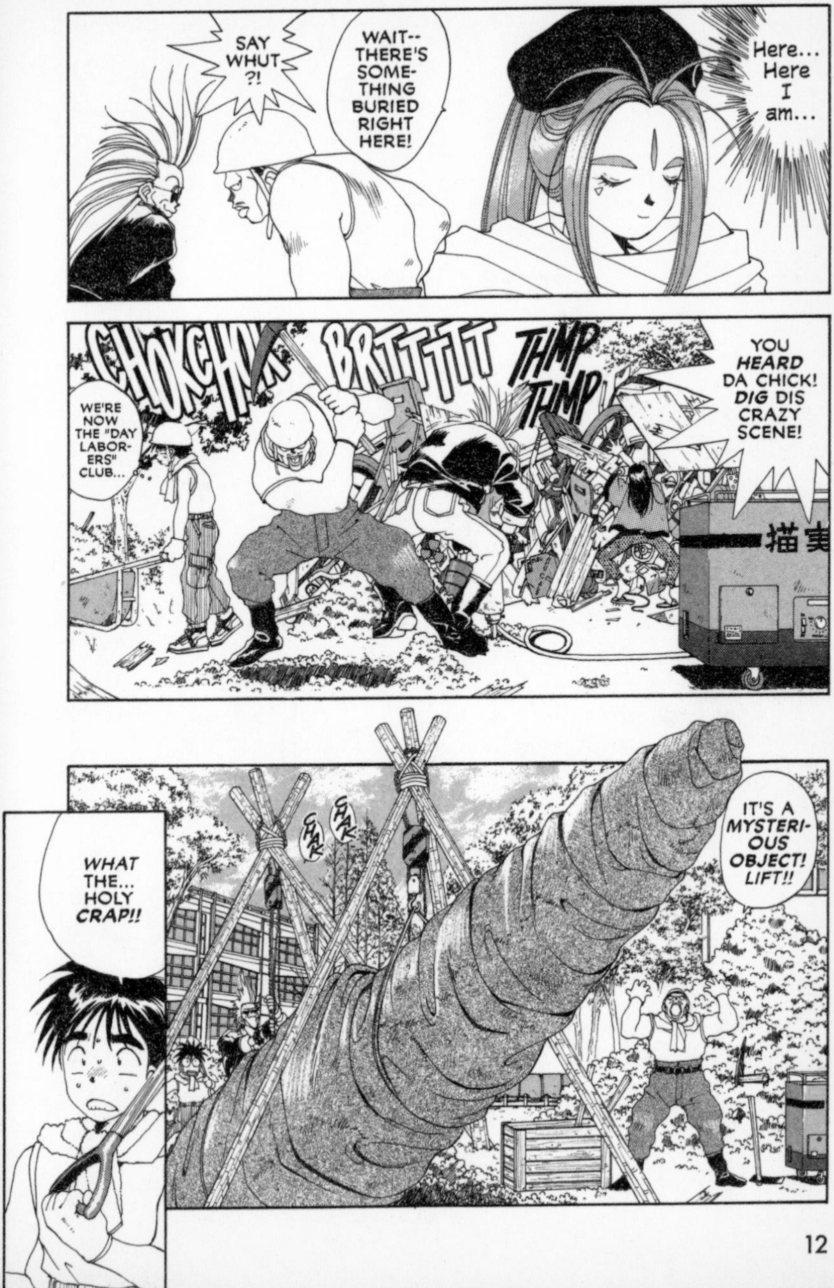
Here... Here I am...
WAIT-- THERE'S SOME-THING BURIED RIGHT HERE!
SAY WHUT?!
YOU HEARD DA CHICK! DIG DIS CRAZY SCENE!
猫実
THMP THMP
BRTTTTT
CHOKCHOK
WE'RE NOW THE "DAY LABORERS" CLUB...
IT'S A MYSTERIOUS OBJECT! LIFT!!
CHAK CHAK
WHAT THE... HOLY CRAP!!

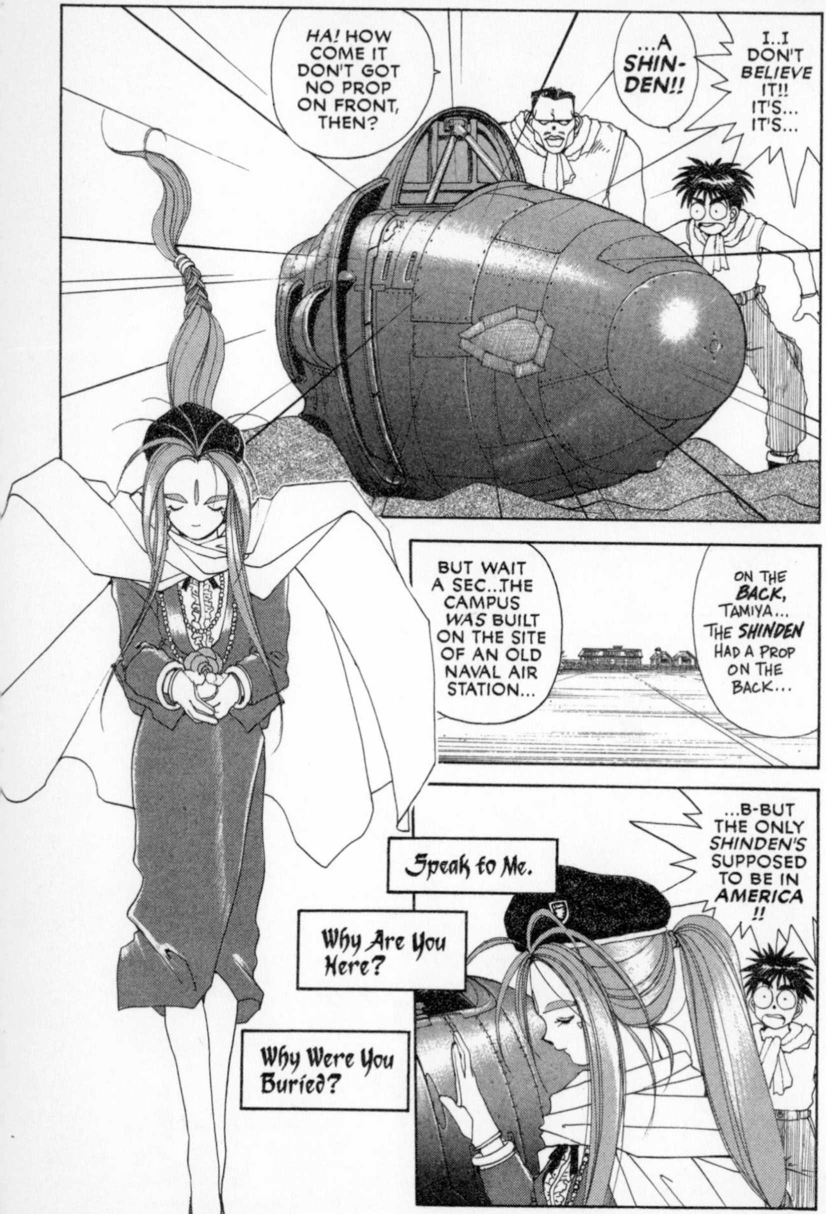
I..I DON'T BELIEVE IT!! IT'S... IT'S...
...A SHIN-DEN!!
HA! HOW COME IT DON'T GOT NO PROP ON FRONT, THEN?
ON THE BACK, TAMIYA... THE SHINDEN HAD A PROP ON THE BACK...
BUT WAIT A SEC...THE CAMPUS WAS BUILT ON THE SITE OF AN OLD NAVAL AIR STATION...
...B-BUT THE ONLY SHINDEN'S SUPPOSED TO BE IN AMERICA !!
Speak to Me.
Why Are You Here?
Why Were You Buried?

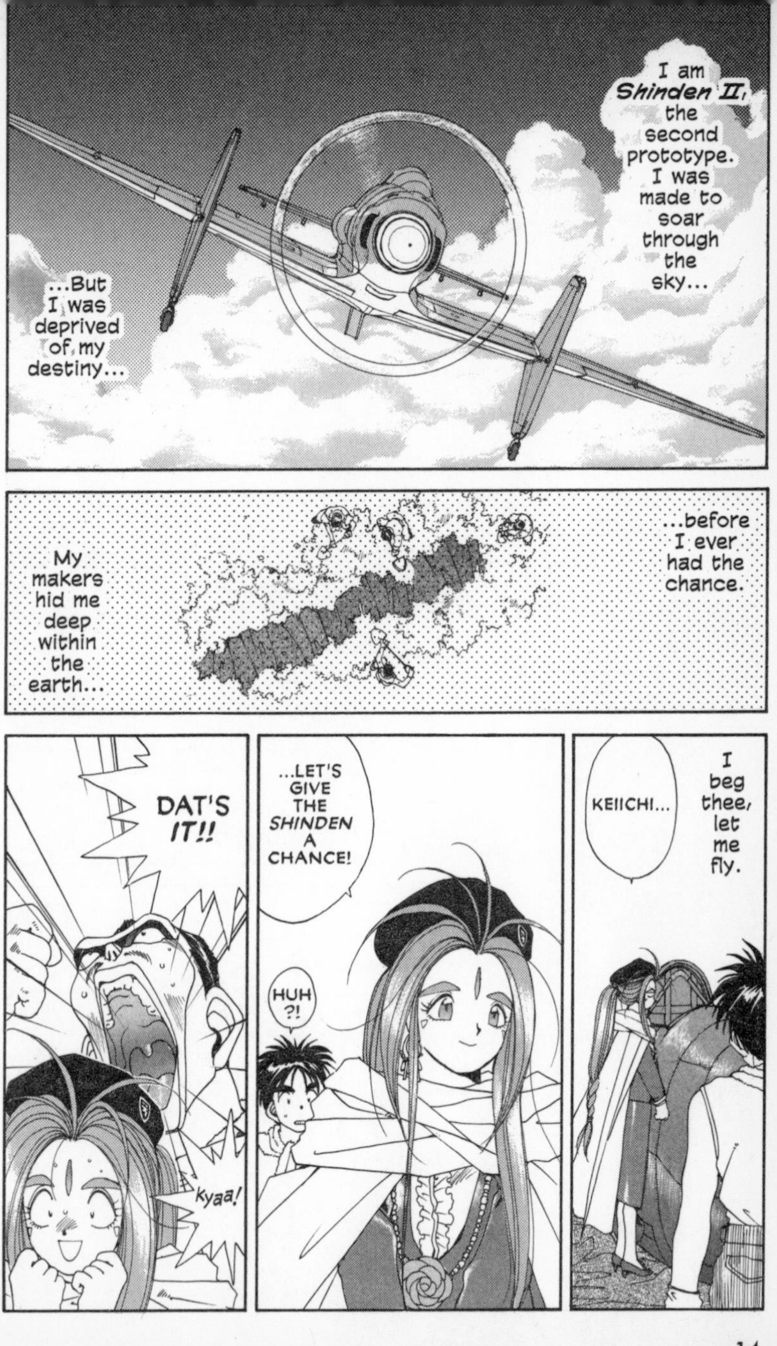
I am *Shinden II*, the second prototype. I was made to soar through the sky...
...But I was deprived of my destiny...
...before I ever had the chance.
My makers hid me deep within the earth...
I beg thee, let me fly.
KEIICHI...
...LET'S GIVE THE *SHINDEN* A CHANCE!
HUH ?!
DAT'S *IT!!*
Kyaa!

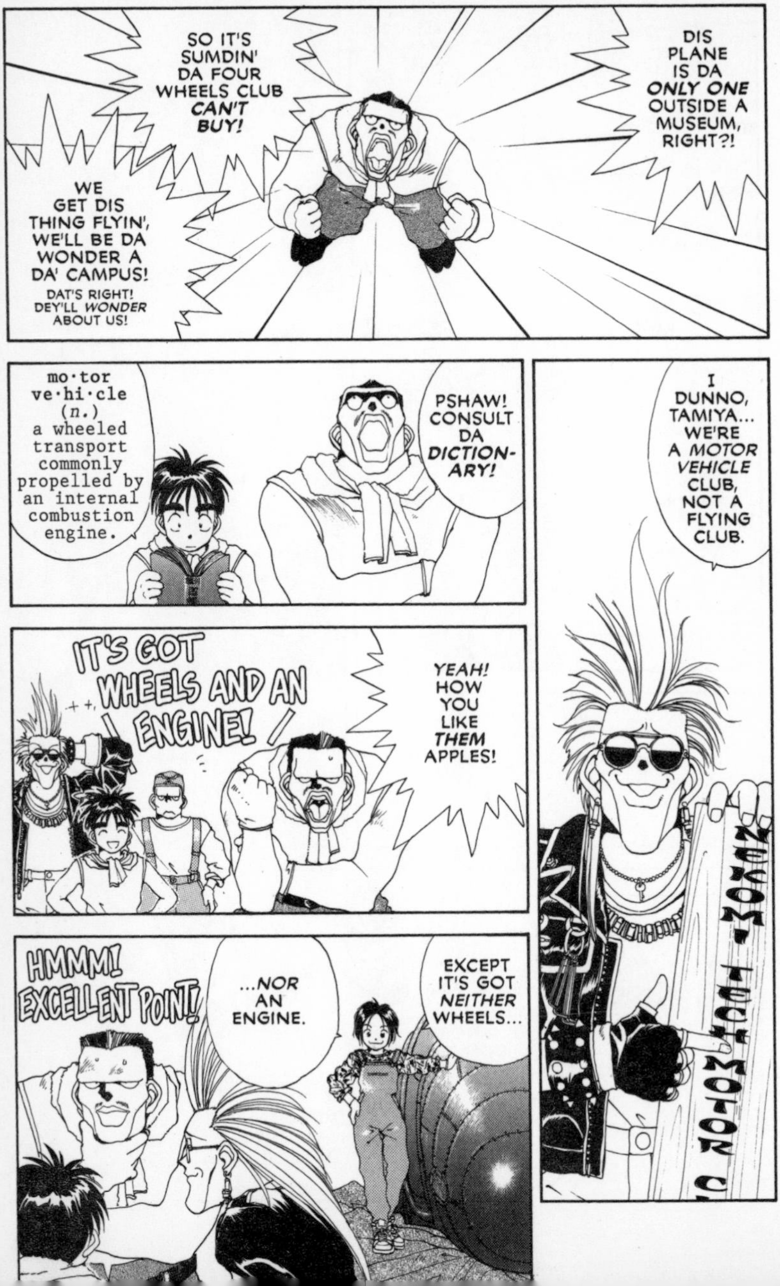
DIS PLANE IS DA *ONLY ONE* OUTSIDE A MUSEUM, RIGHT?!
SO IT'S SUMDIN' DA FOUR WHEELS CLUB *CAN'T BUY!*
WE GET DIS THING FLYIN', WE'LL BE DA WONDER A DA' CAMPUS!
DAT'S RIGHT! DEY'LL *WONDER* ABOUT US!
I DUNNO, TAMIYA... WE'RE A *MOTOR VEHICLE* CLUB, NOT A FLYING CLUB.
NEKOMI TECH MOTOR C
PSHAW! CONSULT DA *DICTION-ARY!*
mo·tor ve·hi·cle (*n.*) a wheeled transport commonly propelled by an internal combustion engine.
YEAH! HOW YOU LIKE *THEM* APPLES!
IT'S GOT WHEELS AND AN ENGINE!
EXCEPT IT'S GOT *NEITHER* WHEELS...
...*NOR* AN ENGINE.
HMMM! EXCELLENT POINT!

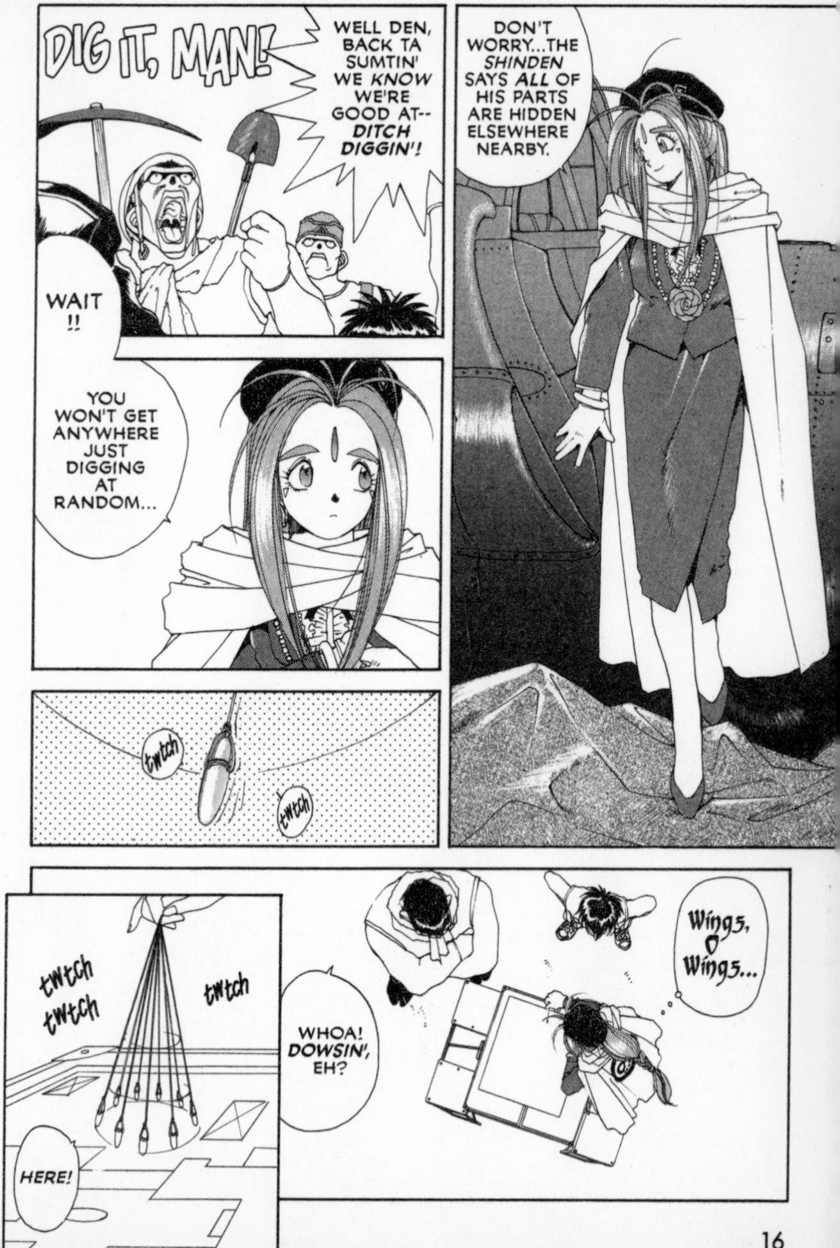
DON'T WORRY...THE *SHINDEN* SAYS *ALL* OF HIS PARTS ARE HIDDEN ELSEWHERE NEARBY.
WELL DEN, BACK TA SUMTIN' WE *KNOW* WE'RE GOOD AT-- *DITCH DIGGIN'*!
DIG IT, MAN!
WAIT !!
YOU WON'T GET ANYWHERE JUST DIGGING AT RANDOM...
twtch
twtch
Wings, O Wings...
WHOA! *DOWSIN'*, EH?
twtch
twtch twtch
HERE!

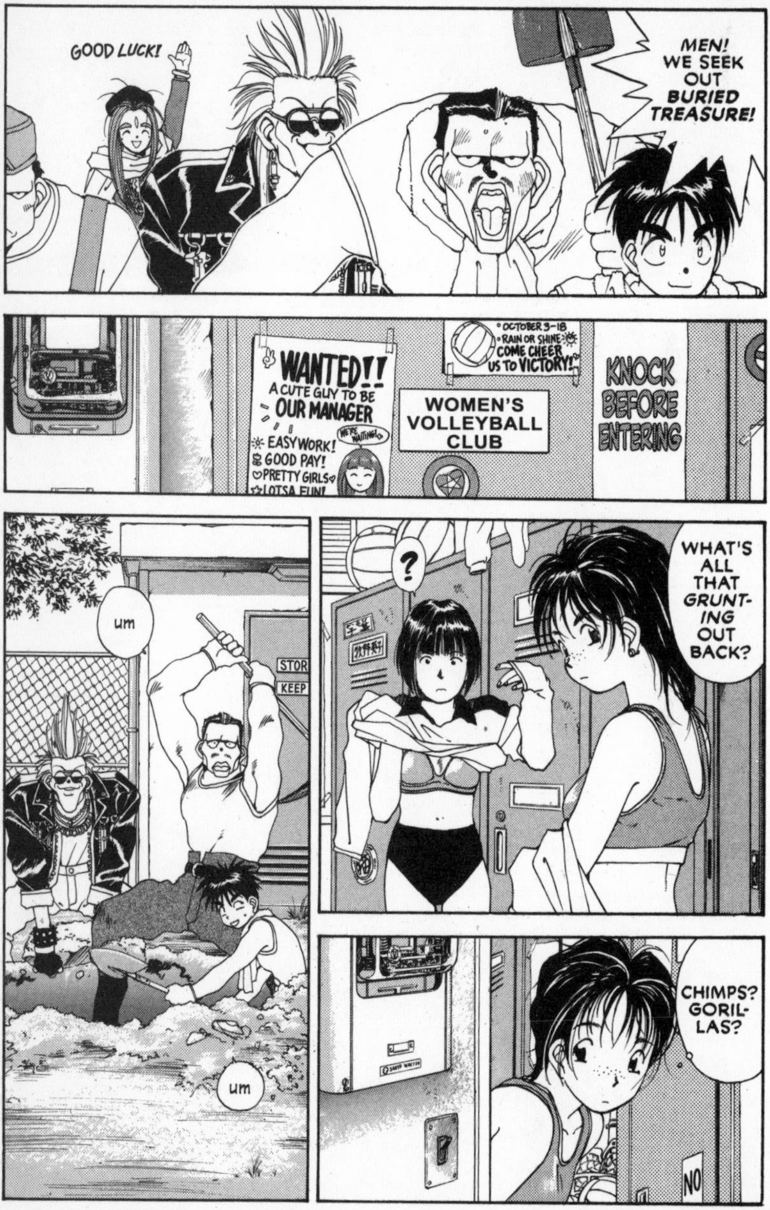
MEN! WE SEEK OUT BURIED TREASURE!
GOOD LUCK!
KNOCK BEFORE ENTERING
• OCTOBER 3-18 • RAIN OR SHINE • COME CHEER US TO VICTORY!
WOMEN'S VOLLEYBALL CLUB
WANTED!! A CUTE GUY TO BE OUR MANAGER
WE'RE WAITING!
EASY WORK! GOOD PAY! PRETTY GIRLS LOTSA FUN!
WHAT'S ALL THAT GRUNTING OUT BACK?
?
CHIMPS? GORILLAS?
NO
um
STOR
KEEP
um

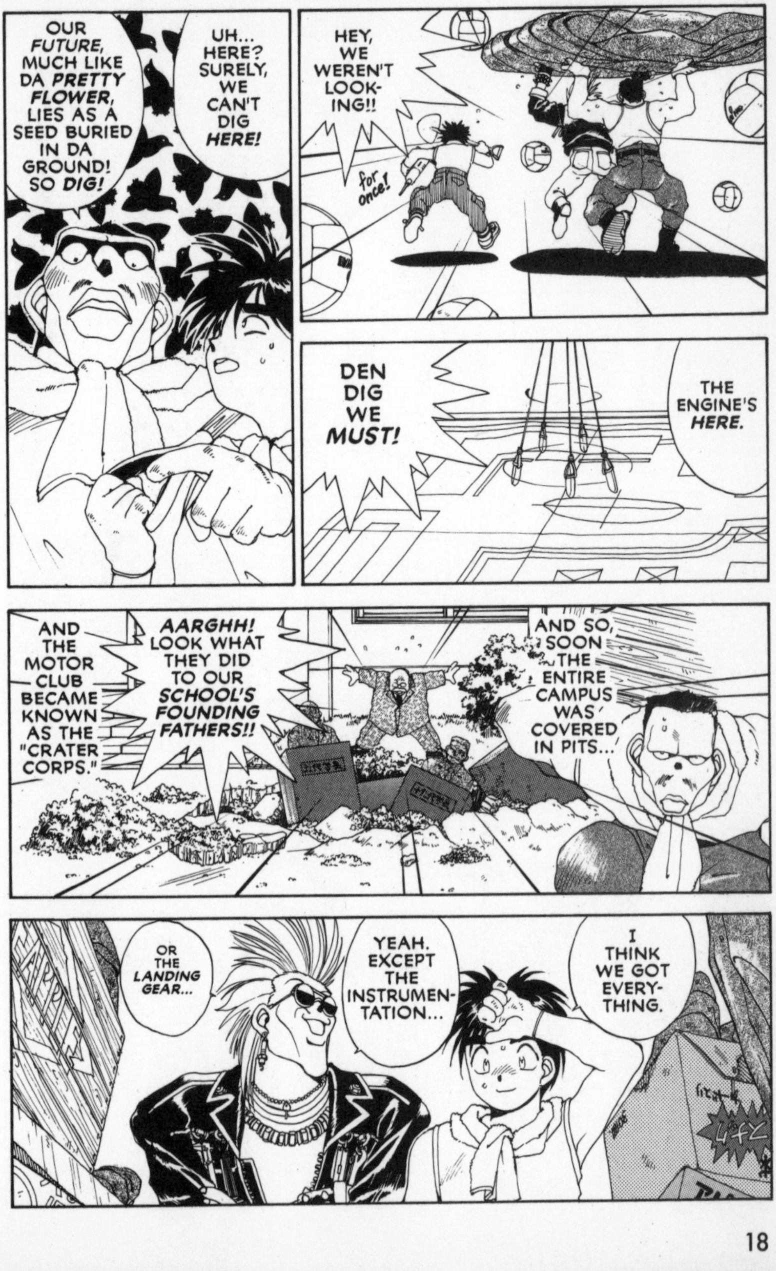
HEY, WE WEREN'T LOOKING!!
for once!
THE ENGINE'S HERE.
DEN DIG WE MUST!
UH... HERE? SURELY, WE CAN'T DIG HERE!
OUR FUTURE, MUCH LIKE DA PRETTY FLOWER, LIES AS A SEED BURIED IN DA GROUND! SO DIG!
AND SO, SOON THE ENTIRE CAMPUS WAS COVERED IN PITS...
AARGHH! LOOK WHAT THEY DID TO OUR SCHOOL'S FOUNDING FATHERS!!
AND THE MOTOR CLUB BECAME KNOWN AS THE "CRATER CORPS."
I THINK WE GOT EVERYTHING.
YEAH. EXCEPT THE INSTRUMENTATION...
OR THE LANDING GEAR...

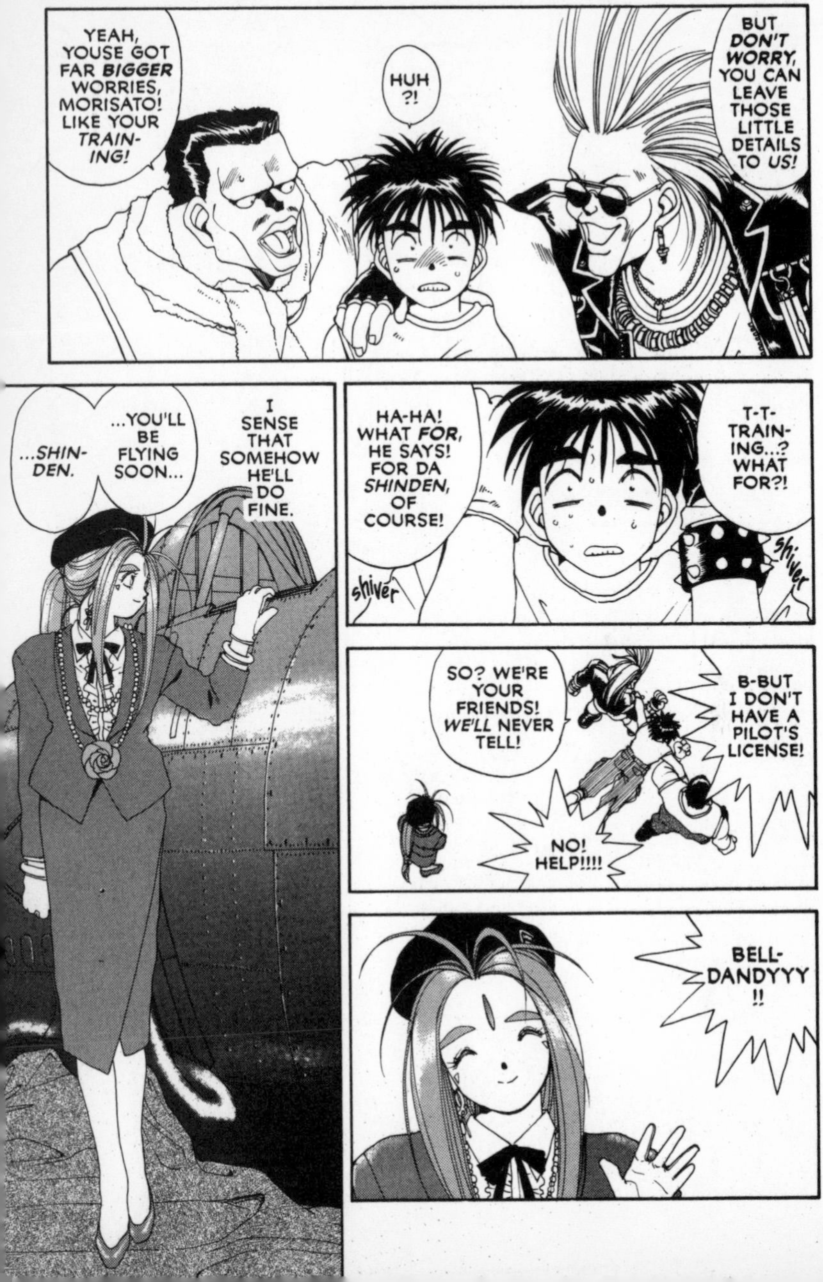
BUT DON'T WORRY, YOU CAN LEAVE THOSE LITTLE DETAILS TO US!
HUH ?!
YEAH, YOUSE GOT FAR BIGGER WORRIES, MORISATO! LIKE YOUR TRAIN-ING!
T-T-TRAIN-ING...? WHAT FOR?!
HA-HA! WHAT FOR, HE SAYS! FOR DA SHINDEN, OF COURSE!
shiver
shiver
B-BUT I DON'T HAVE A PILOT'S LICENSE!
SO? WE'RE YOUR FRIENDS! WE'LL NEVER TELL!
NO! HELP!!!!
BELL-DANDYYY !!
I SENSE THAT SOMEHOW HE'LL DO FINE.
...YOU'LL BE FLYING SOON...
...SHIN-DEN.

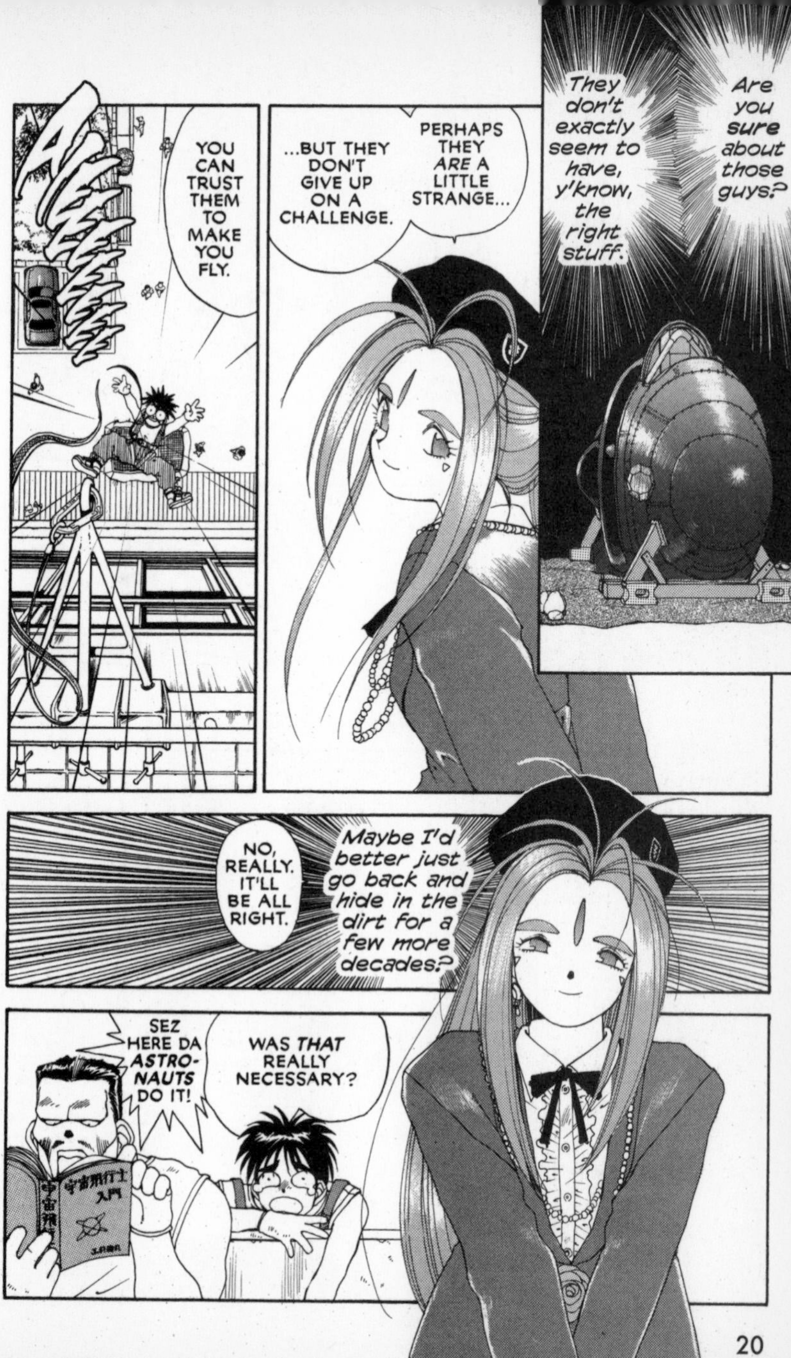
Are you sure about those guys?
They don't exactly seem to have, y'know, the right stuff.
PERHAPS THEY ARE A LITTLE STRANGE...
...BUT THEY DON'T GIVE UP ON A CHALLENGE.
YOU CAN TRUST THEM TO MAKE YOU FLY.
Maybe I'd better just go back and hide in the dirt for a few more decades?
NO, REALLY. IT'LL BE ALL RIGHT.
WAS THAT REALLY NECESSARY?
SEZ HERE DA ASTRONAUTS DO IT!

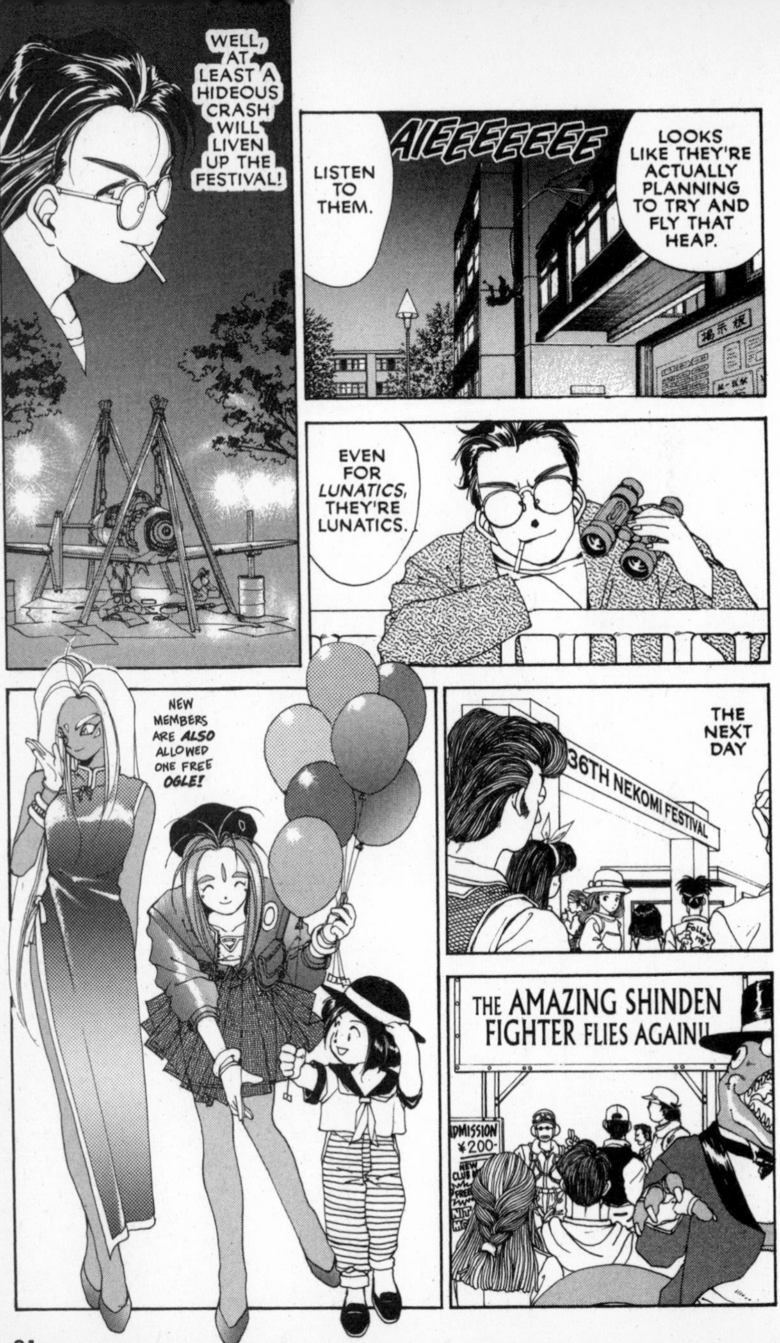
LOOKS LIKE THEY'RE ACTUALLY PLANNING TO TRY AND FLY THAT HEAP.
AIEEEEEEEE
LISTEN TO THEM.
EVEN FOR LUNATICS, THEY'RE LUNATICS.
WELL, AT LEAST A HIDEOUS CRASH WILL LIVEN UP THE FESTIVAL!
THE NEXT DAY
36TH NEKOMI FESTIVAL
THE AMAZING SHINDEN FIGHTER FLIES AGAIN!!
ADMISSION ¥200-
NEW MEMBERS ARE ALSO ALLOWED ONE FREE OGLE!

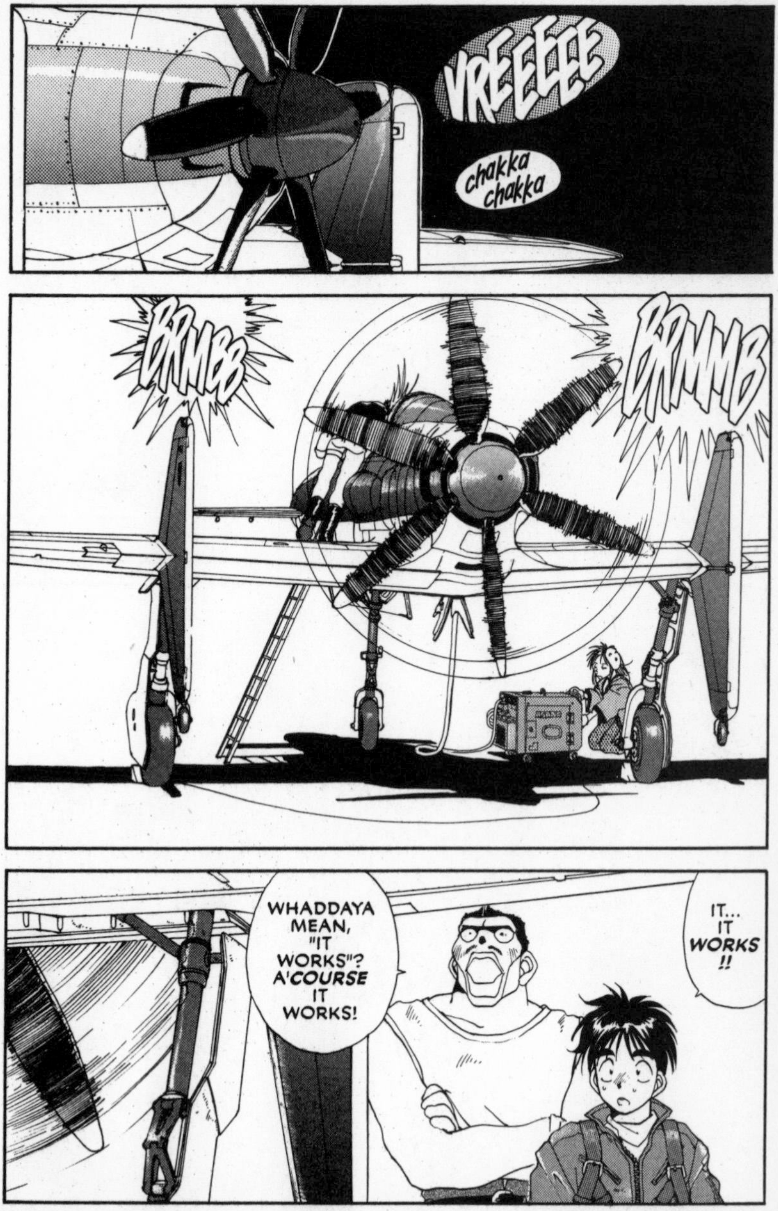
VREEEEE
chakka chakka
BRMMB
BRMBB
IT... IT WORKS!!
WHADDAYA MEAN, "IT WORKS"? A'COURSE IT WORKS!

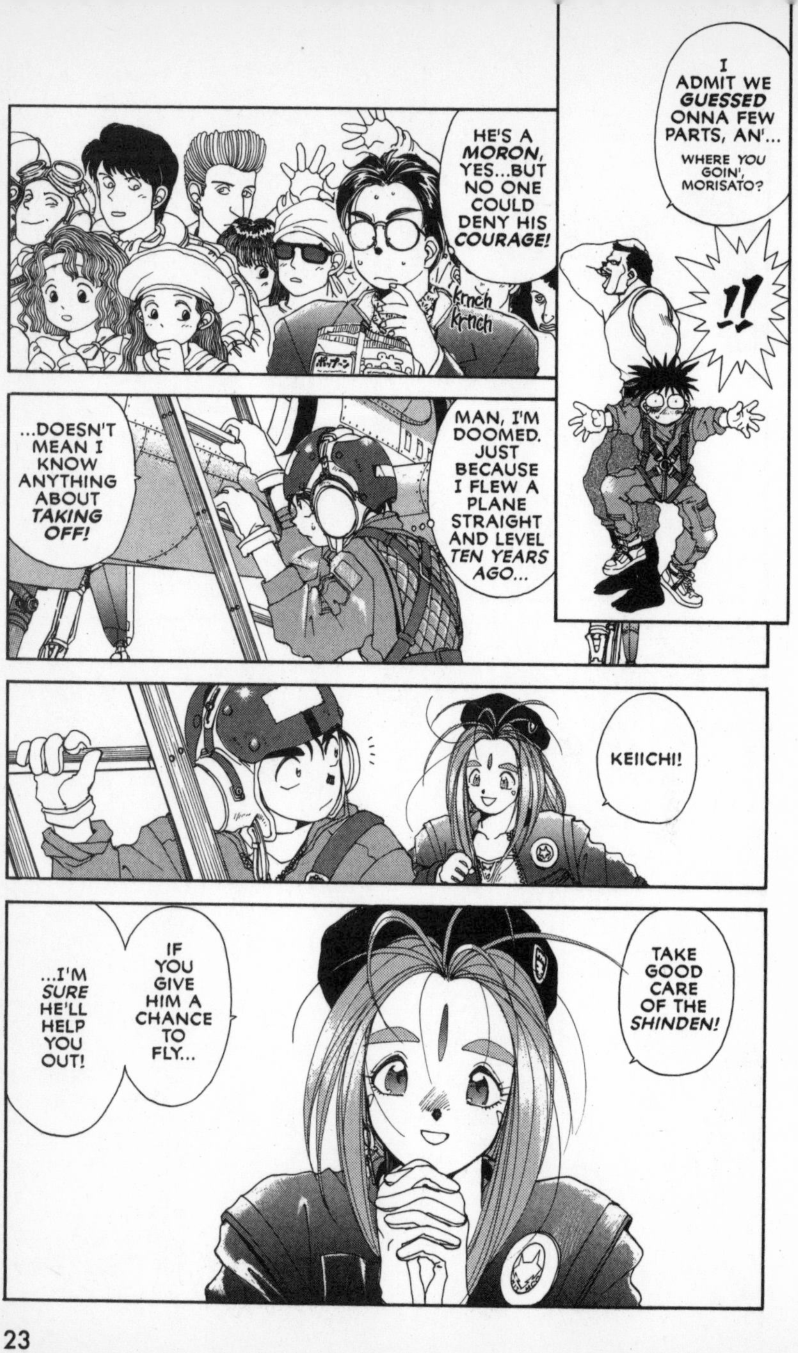
I ADMIT WE GUESSED ONNA FEW PARTS, AN'...
WHERE YOU GOIN', MORISATO?
!!
HE'S A MORON, YES...BUT NO ONE COULD DENY HIS COURAGE!
krnch krnch
MAN, I'M DOOMED. JUST BECAUSE I FLEW A PLANE STRAIGHT AND LEVEL TEN YEARS AGO...
...DOESN'T MEAN I KNOW ANYTHING ABOUT TAKING OFF!
KEIICHI!
TAKE GOOD CARE OF THE SHINDEN!
IF YOU GIVE HIM A CHANCE TO FLY...
...I'M SURE HE'LL HELP YOU OUT!

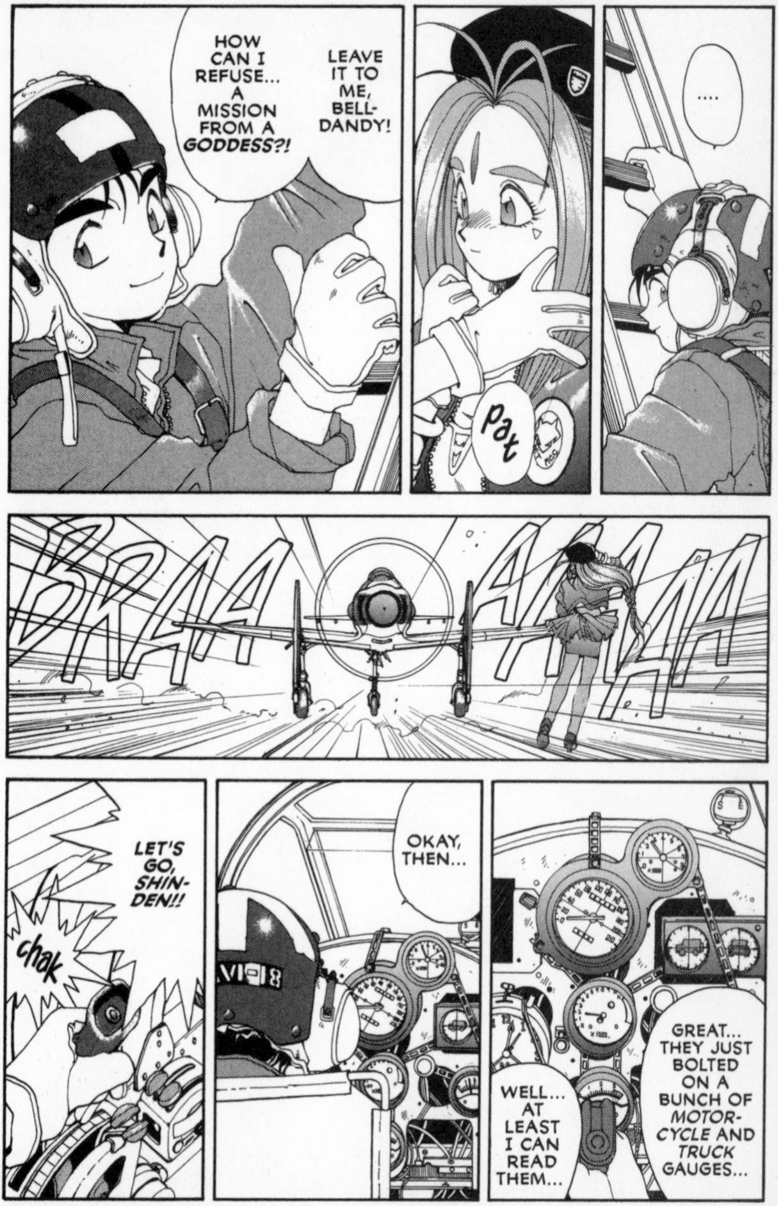
....
pat
HOW CAN I REFUSE... A MISSION FROM A GODDESS?! LEAVE IT TO ME, BELL-DANDY!
BRAAAAAAA
GREAT... THEY JUST BOLTED ON A BUNCH OF MOTORCYCLE AND TRUCK GAUGES...
WELL... AT LEAST I CAN READ THEM...
OKAY, THEN...
LET'S GO, SHIN-DEN!!
chak

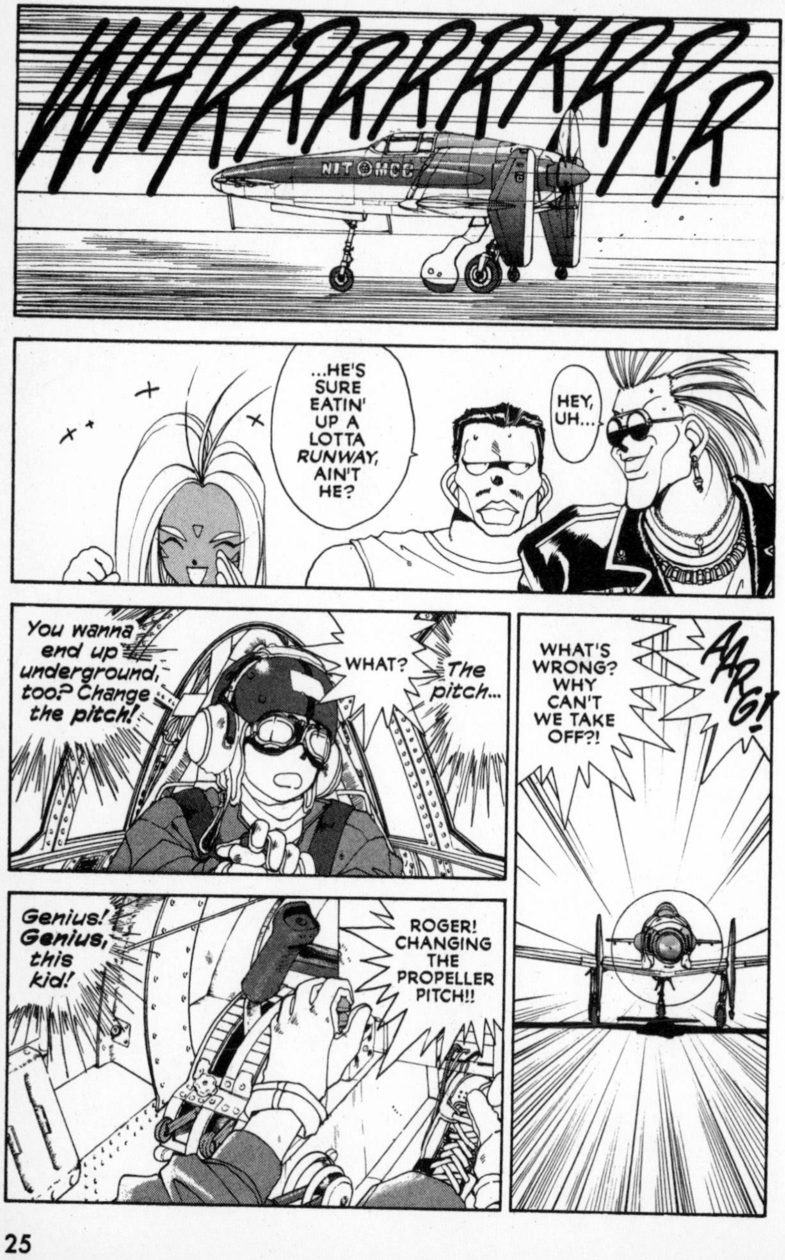
WHRRRRRRRRRR
HEY, UH...
...HE'S SURE EATIN' UP A LOTTA *RUNWAY*, AIN'T HE?
WHAT'S WRONG? WHY CAN'T WE TAKE OFF?!
AARG!
The pitch...
WHAT?
You wanna end up underground, too? Change the pitch!
ROGER! CHANGING THE PROPELLER PITCH!!
Genius! Genius, this kid!

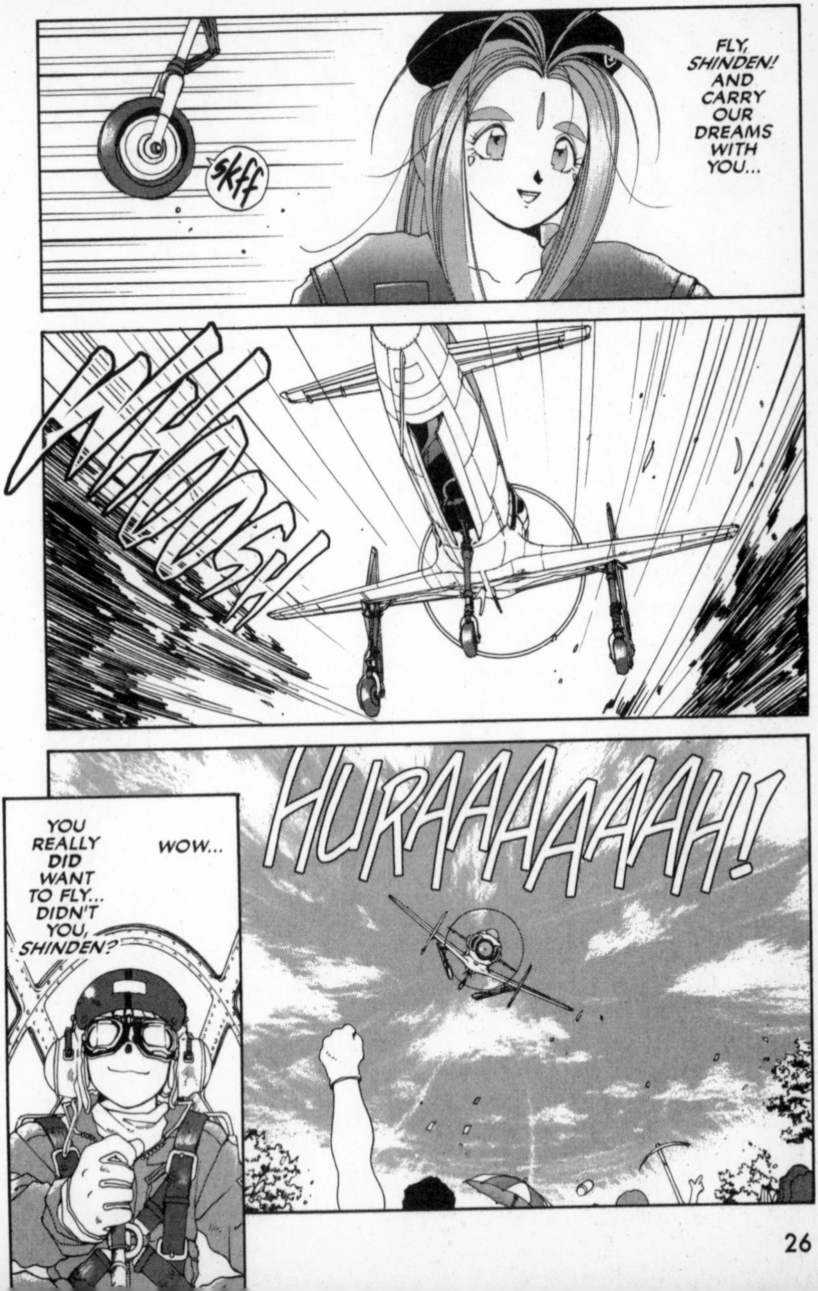
FLY, SHINDEN! AND CARRY OUR DREAMS WITH YOU...
skff
WHOOSH
HURAAAAAAAH!
WOW...
YOU REALLY DID WANT TO FLY... DIDN'T YOU, SHINDEN?

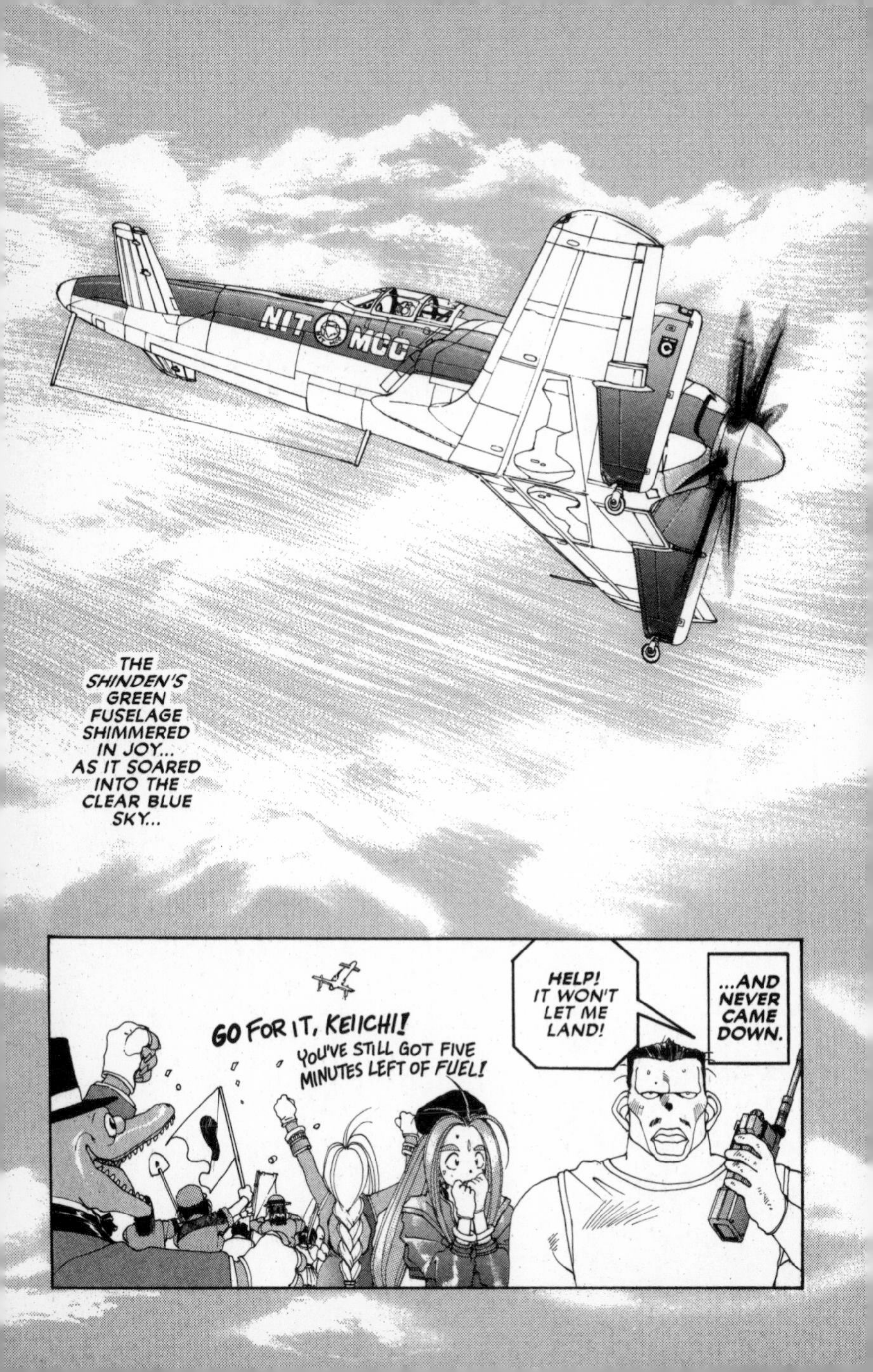
NIT MCC
THE SHINDEN'S GREEN FUSELAGE SHIMMERED IN JOY... AS IT SOARED INTO THE CLEAR BLUE SKY...
...AND NEVER CAME DOWN.
HELP! IT WON'T LET ME LAND!
GO FOR IT, KEIICHI!
YOU'VE STILL GOT FIVE MINUTES LEFT OF FUEL!

THE ADVENTURES OF MINI-URD

PART 2

1/24

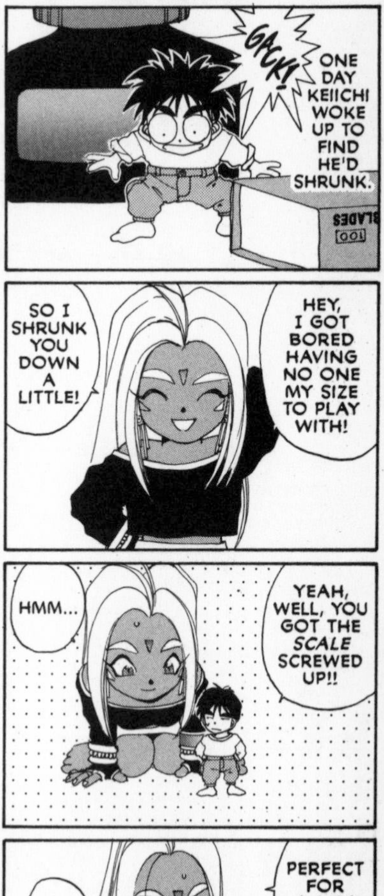
GACK!
ONE DAY KEIICHI WOKE UP TO FIND HE'D SHRUNK.
HEY, I GOT BORED HAVING NO ONE MY SIZE TO PLAY WITH!
SO I SHRUNK YOU DOWN A LITTLE!
YEAH, WELL, YOU GOT THE *SCALE* SCREWED UP!!
HMM...
PERFECT FOR A 1/24 SCALE DIO-RAMA!
LET ME OUT OF HERE...

1/35

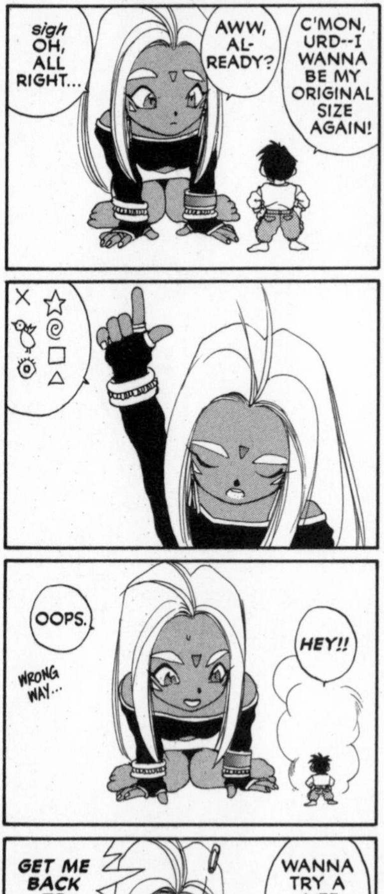
C'MON, URD--I WANNA BE MY ORIGINAL SIZE AGAIN!
AWW, AL-READY?
sigh OH, ALL RIGHT...
HEY!!
OOPS.
WRONG WAY...
WANNA TRY A *1/35* SCALE DIORA--
GET ME BACK TO NORMAL!

SEE YOU NEXT TIME!

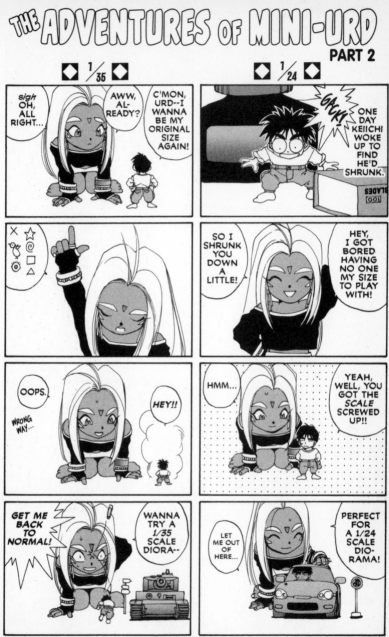

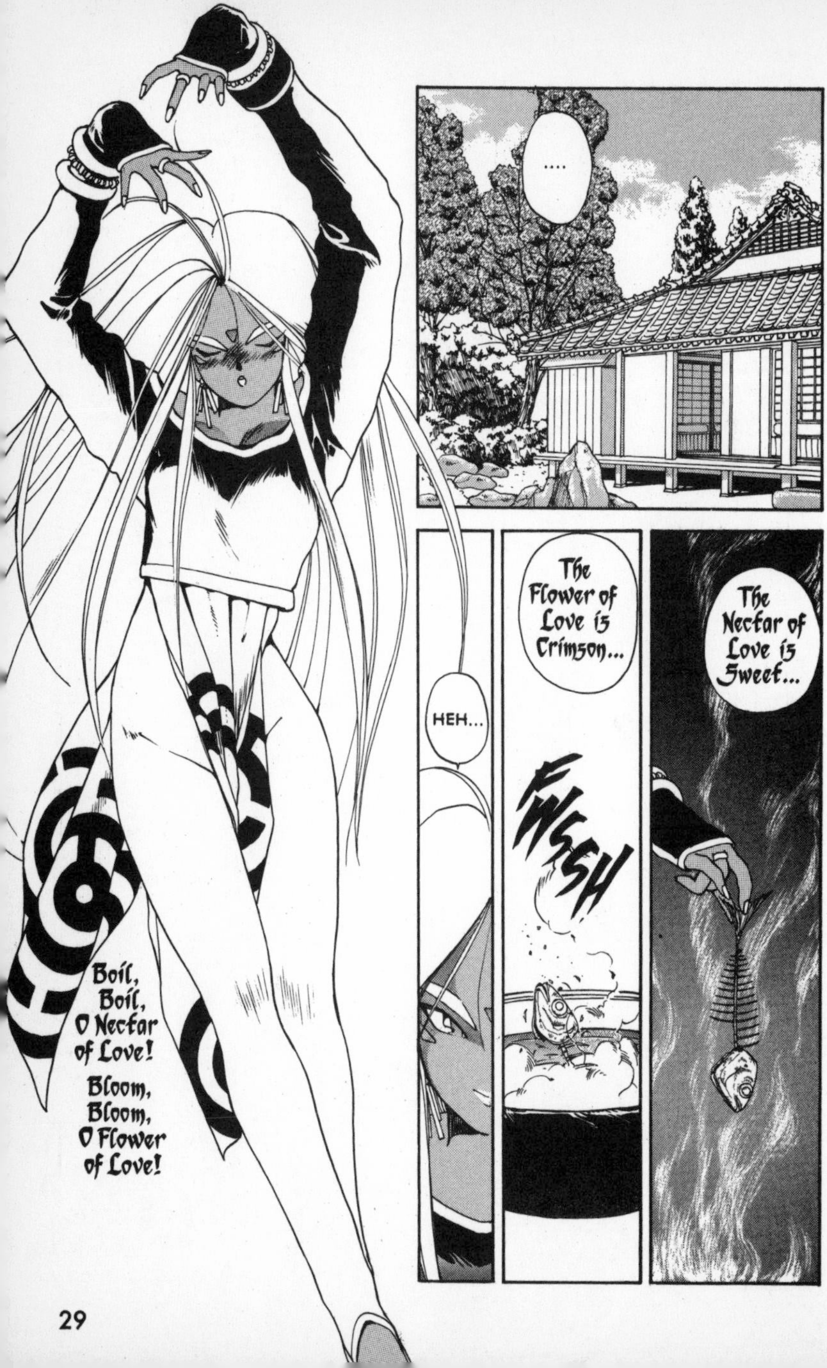

....
The Nectar of Love is Sweet...
The Flower of Love is Crimson...
FWSSH
HEH...
Boil, Boil, O Nectar of Love!
Bloom, Bloom, O Flower of Love!

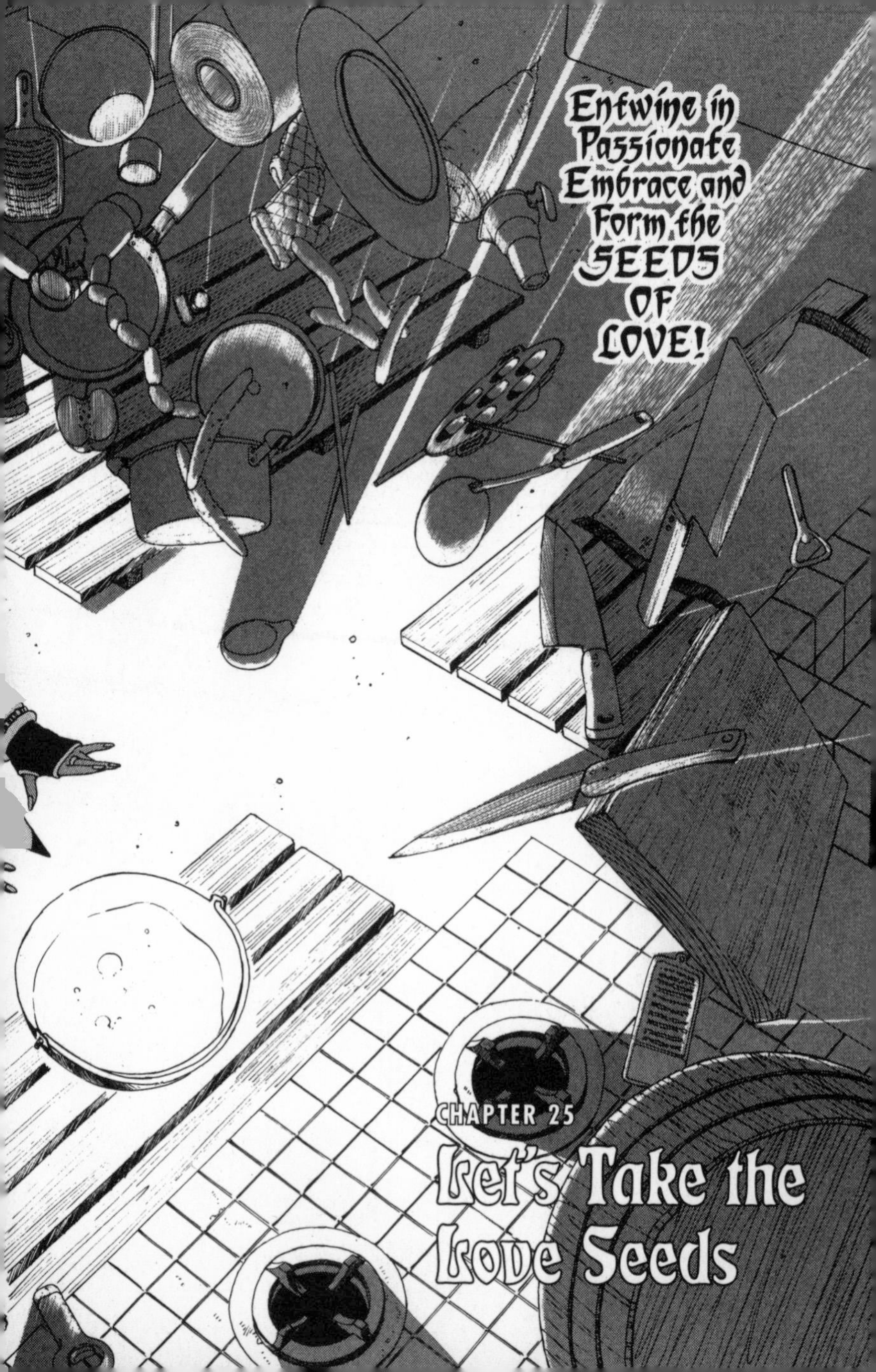
Entwine in Passionate Embrace and Form the SEEDS OF LOVE!
CHAPTER 25
Let's Take the Love Seeds

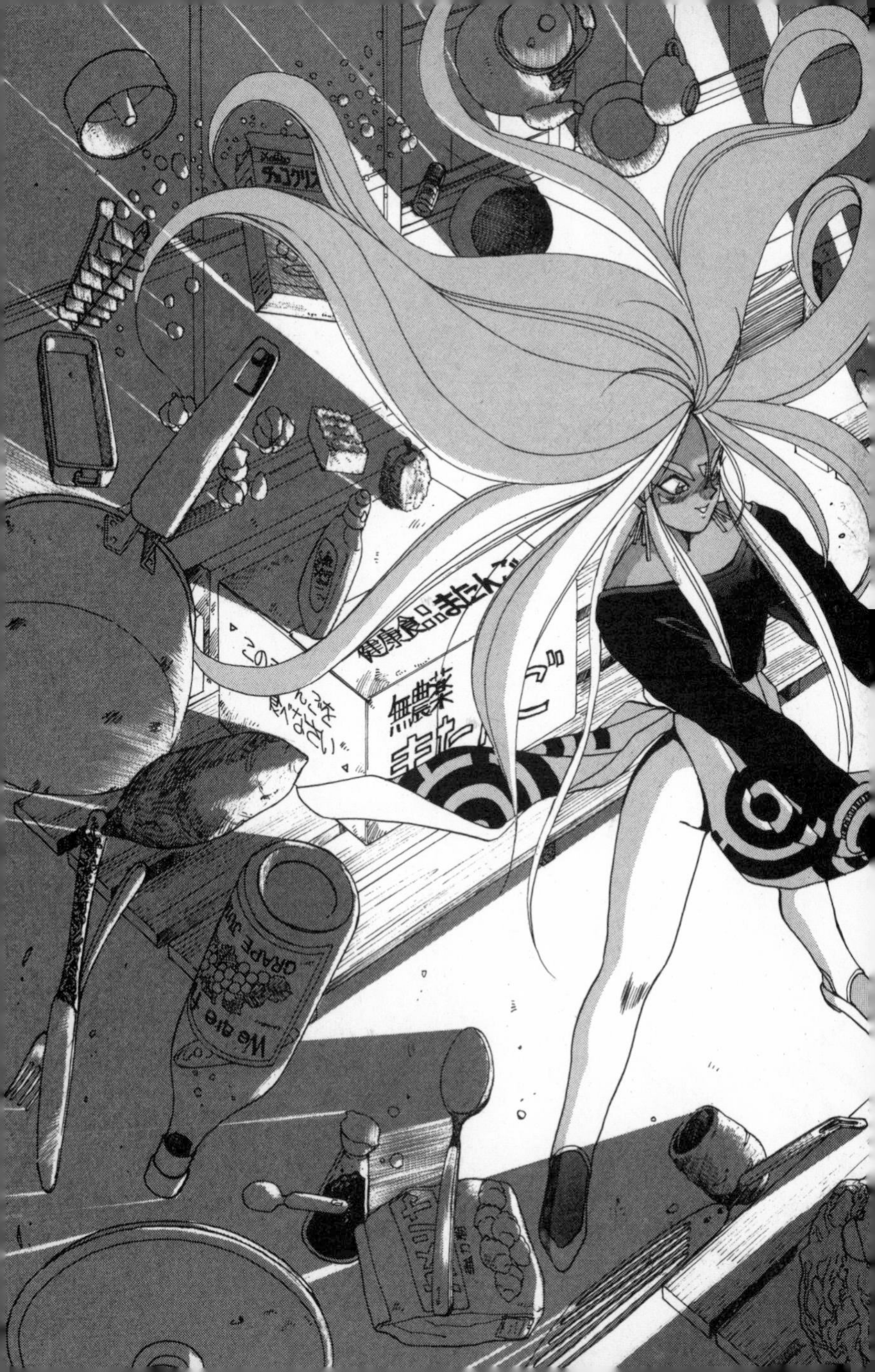
健康食品またんご
無農薬
GRAPE
We are

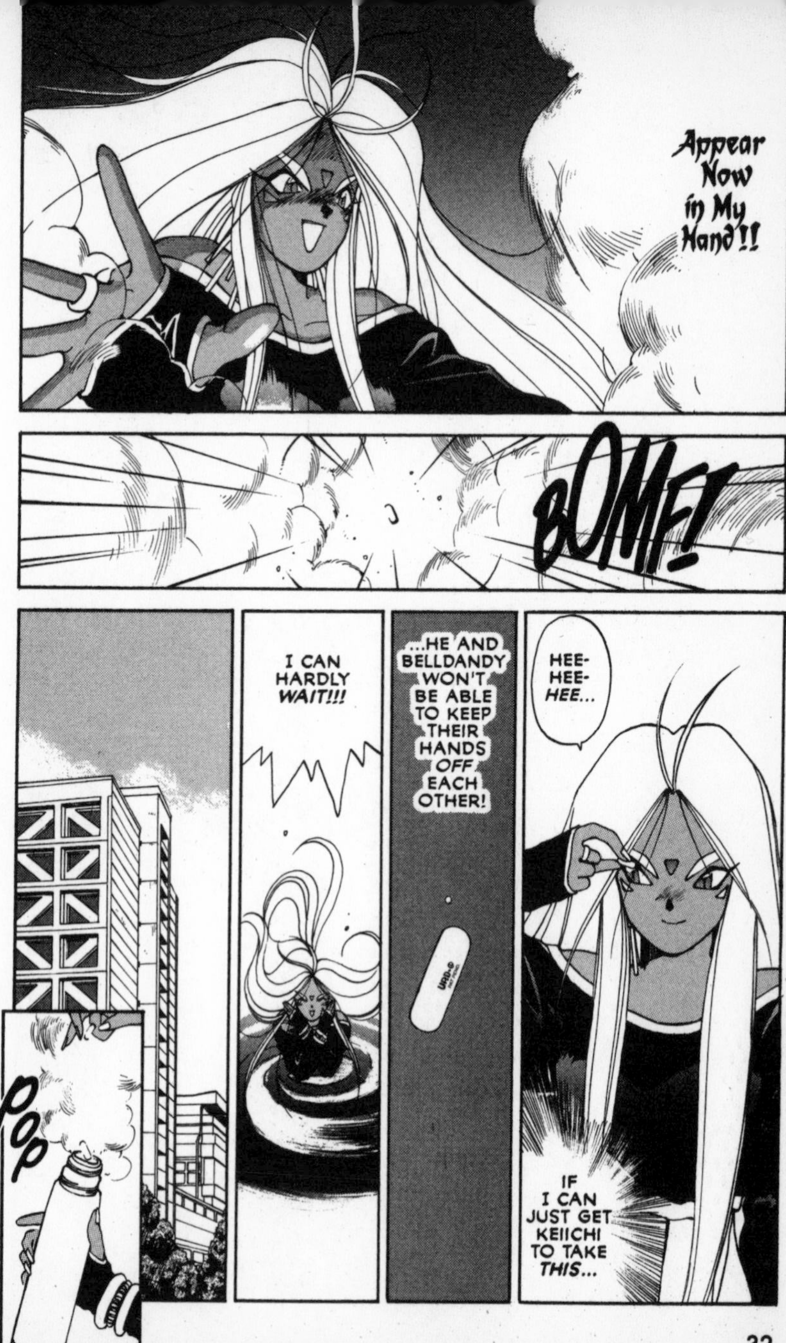
Appear Now in My Hand!!
BOMF!
HEE-HEE-HEE...
IF I CAN JUST GET KEIICHI TO TAKE THIS...
...HE AND BELLDANDY WON'T BE ABLE TO KEEP THEIR HANDS OFF EACH OTHER!
I CAN HARDLY WAIT!!!
POP

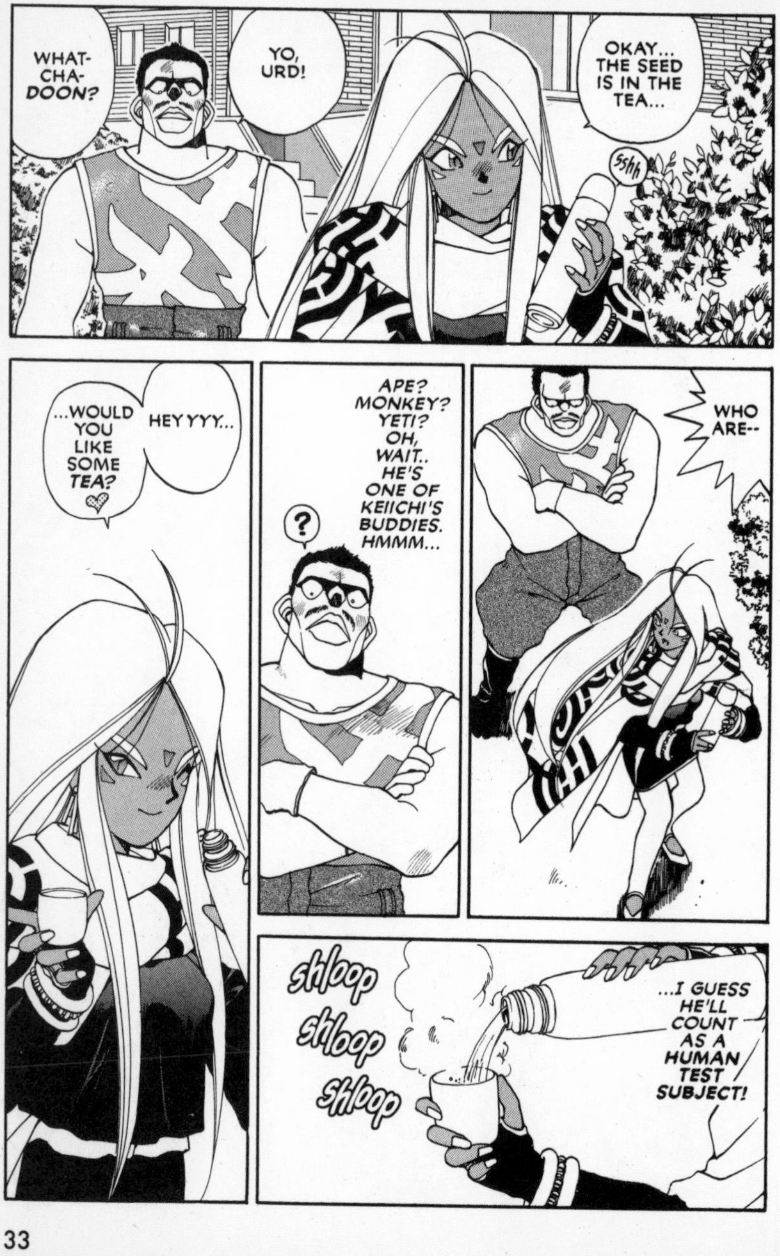

OKAY... THE SEED IS IN THE TEA...
sshh
YO, URD!
WHAT-CHA-DOON?
WHO ARE--
APE? MONKEY? YETI? OH, WAIT.. HE'S ONE OF KEIICHI'S BUDDIES. HMMM...
?
...I GUESS HE'LL COUNT AS A HUMAN TEST SUBJECT!
shloop
shloop
shloop
HEY YYY...
...WOULD YOU LIKE SOME TEA?

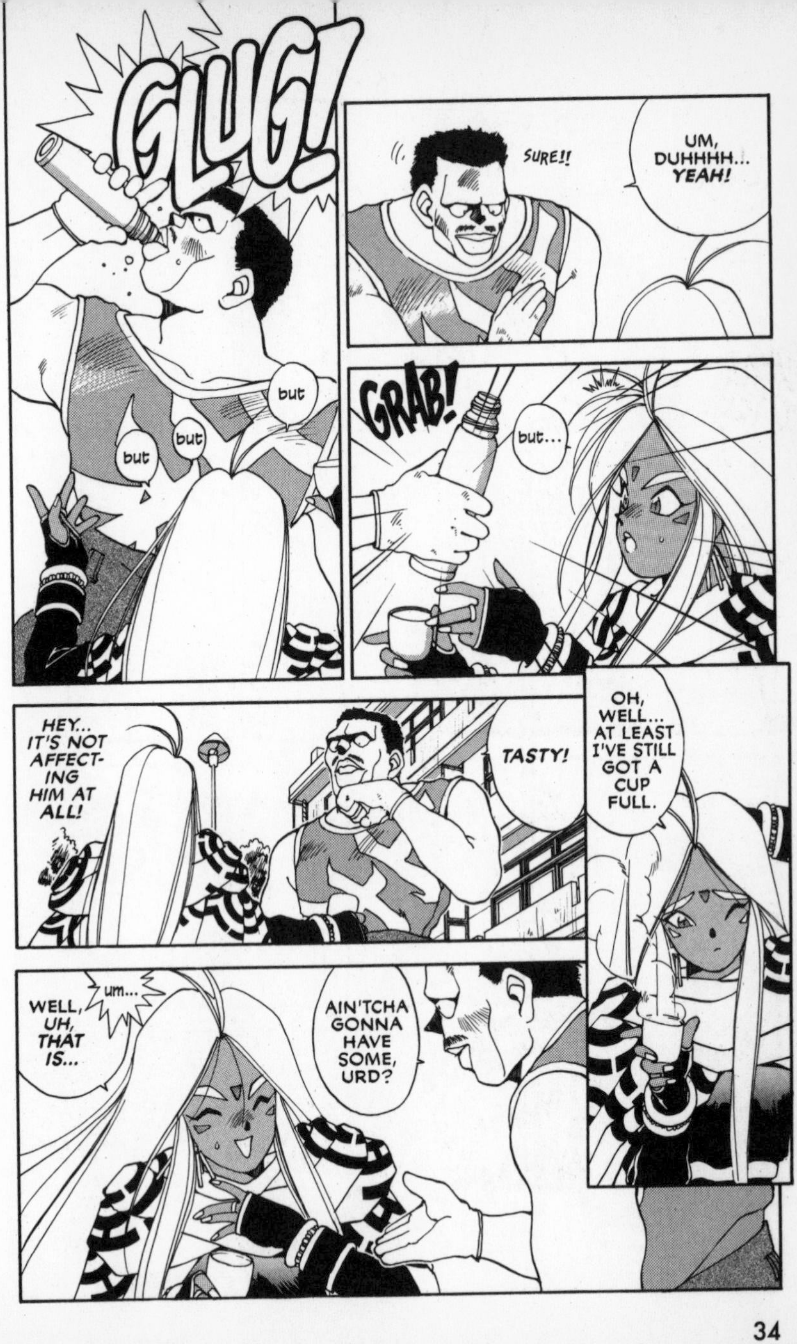

UM, DUHHHH... YEAH!
SURE!!
GRAB!
but...
GLUG!
but
but
but
OH, WELL... AT LEAST I'VE STILL GOT A CUP FULL.
TASTY!
HEY... IT'S NOT AFFECT-ING HIM AT ALL!
AIN'TCHA GONNA HAVE SOME, URD?
um...
WELL, UH, THAT IS...

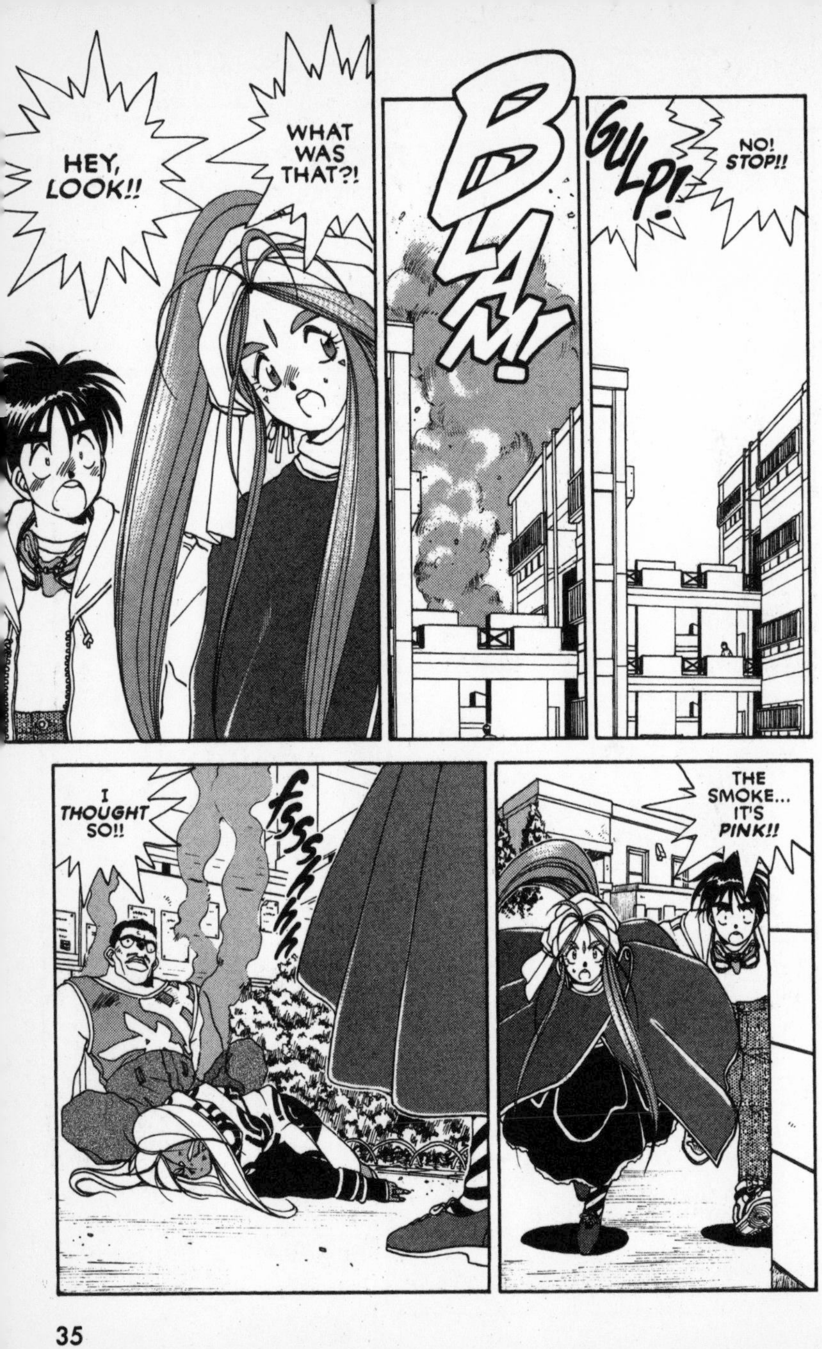
NO! STOP!!
GULP!
BLAM!
WHAT WAS THAT?!
HEY, LOOK!!
THE SMOKE... IT'S PINK!!
fssshhh
I THOUGHT SO!!

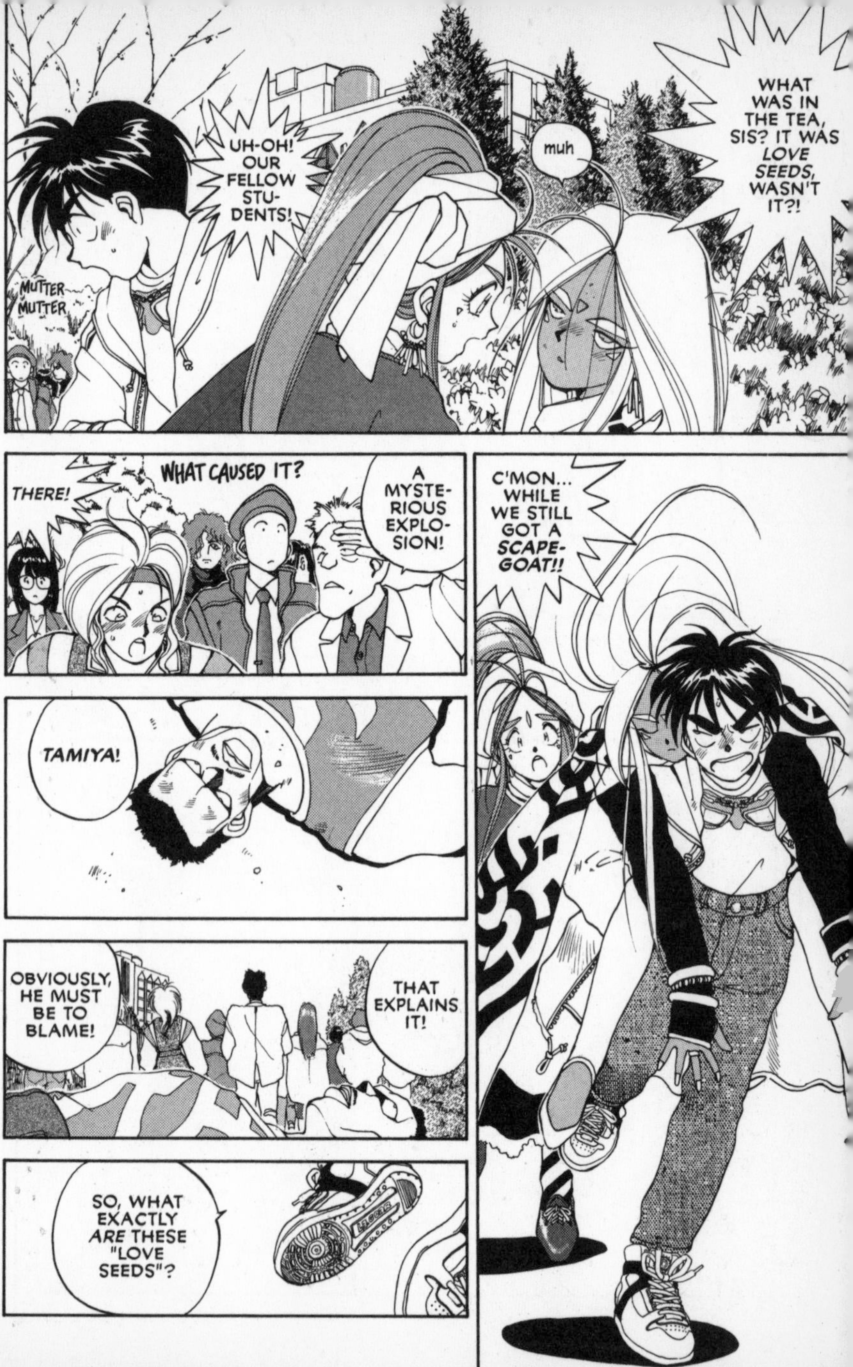

WHAT WAS IN THE TEA, SIS? IT WAS *LOVE SEEDS,* WASN'T IT?!
muh
UH-OH! OUR FELLOW STU-DENTS!
MUTTER MUTTER
C'MON... WHILE WE STILL GOT A *SCAPE-GOAT!!*
A MYSTE-RIOUS EXPLO-SION!
WHAT CAUSED IT?
THERE!
TAMIYA!
THAT EXPLAINS IT!
OBVIOUSLY, HE MUST BE TO BLAME!
SO, WHAT EXACTLY *ARE* THESE "LOVE SEEDS"?

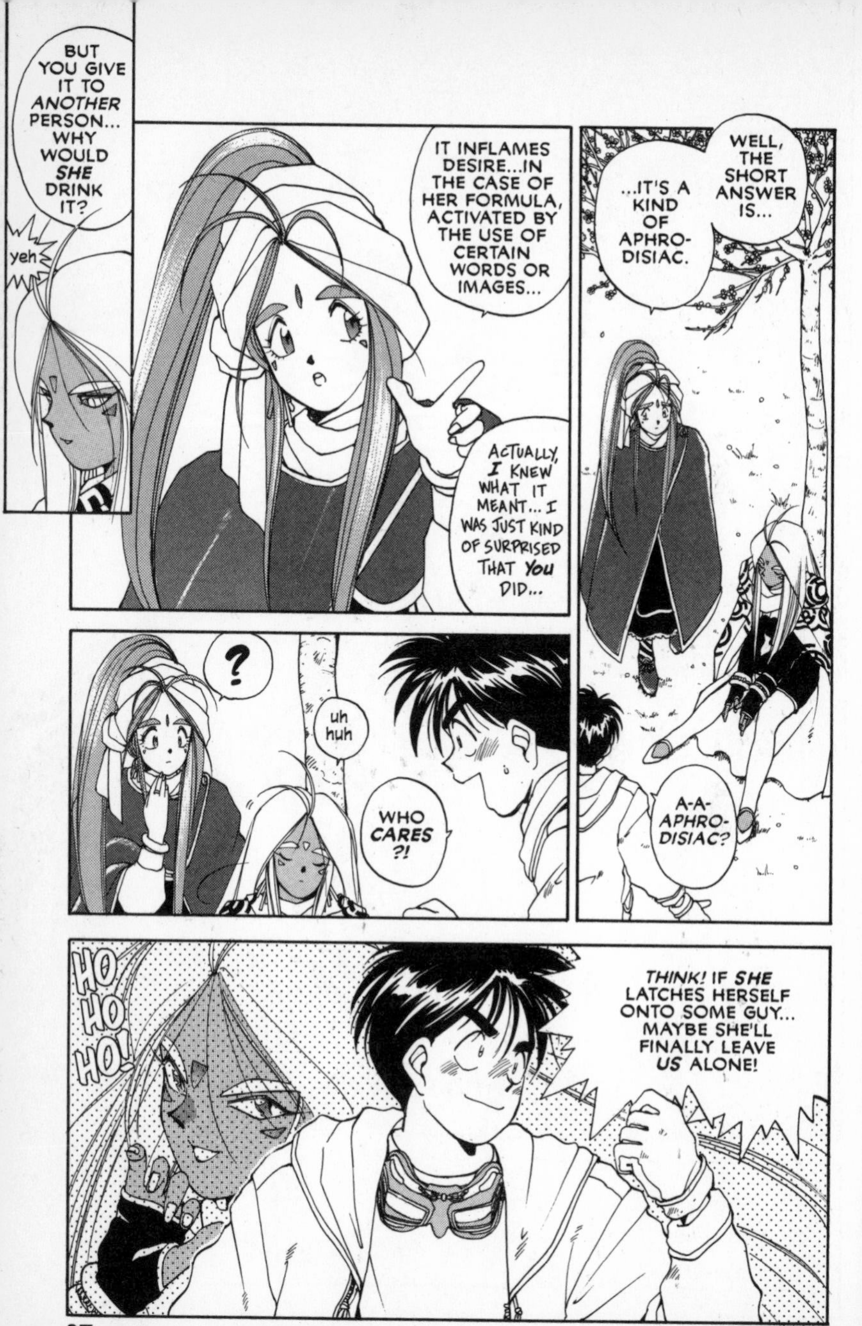
WELL, THE SHORT ANSWER IS...
...IT'S A KIND OF APHRODISIAC.
A-A-APHRODISIAC?
IT INFLAMES DESIRE...IN THE CASE OF HER FORMULA, ACTIVATED BY THE USE OF CERTAIN WORDS OR IMAGES...
ACTUALLY, I KNEW WHAT IT MEANT... I WAS JUST KIND OF SURPRISED THAT YOU DID...
BUT YOU GIVE IT TO ANOTHER PERSON... WHY WOULD SHE DRINK IT?
yeh
?
uh huh
WHO CARES ?!
THINK! IF SHE LATCHES HERSELF ONTO SOME GUY... MAYBE SHE'LL FINALLY LEAVE US ALONE!
HO HO HO!

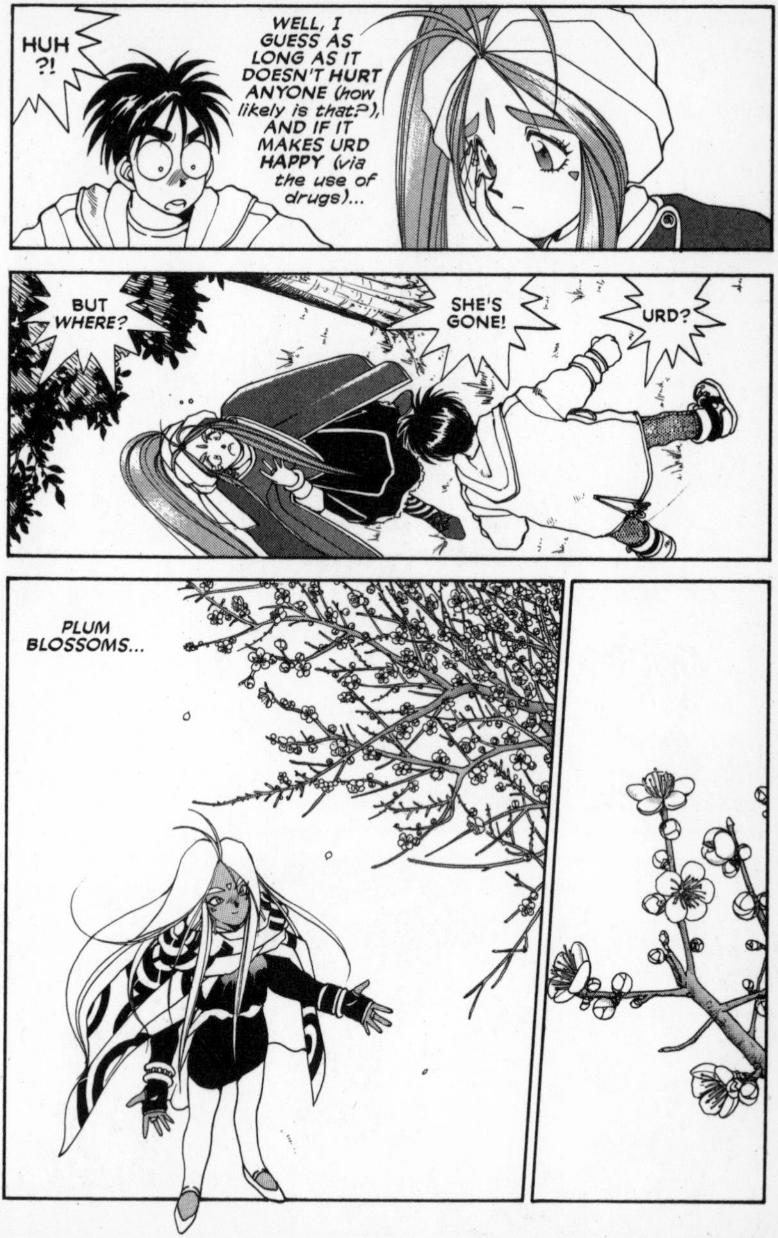
WELL, I GUESS AS LONG AS IT DOESN'T HURT ANYONE (how likely is that?), AND IF IT MAKES URD HAPPY (via the use of drugs)...
HUH ?!
URD?
SHE'S GONE!
BUT WHERE?
PLUM BLOSSOMS...

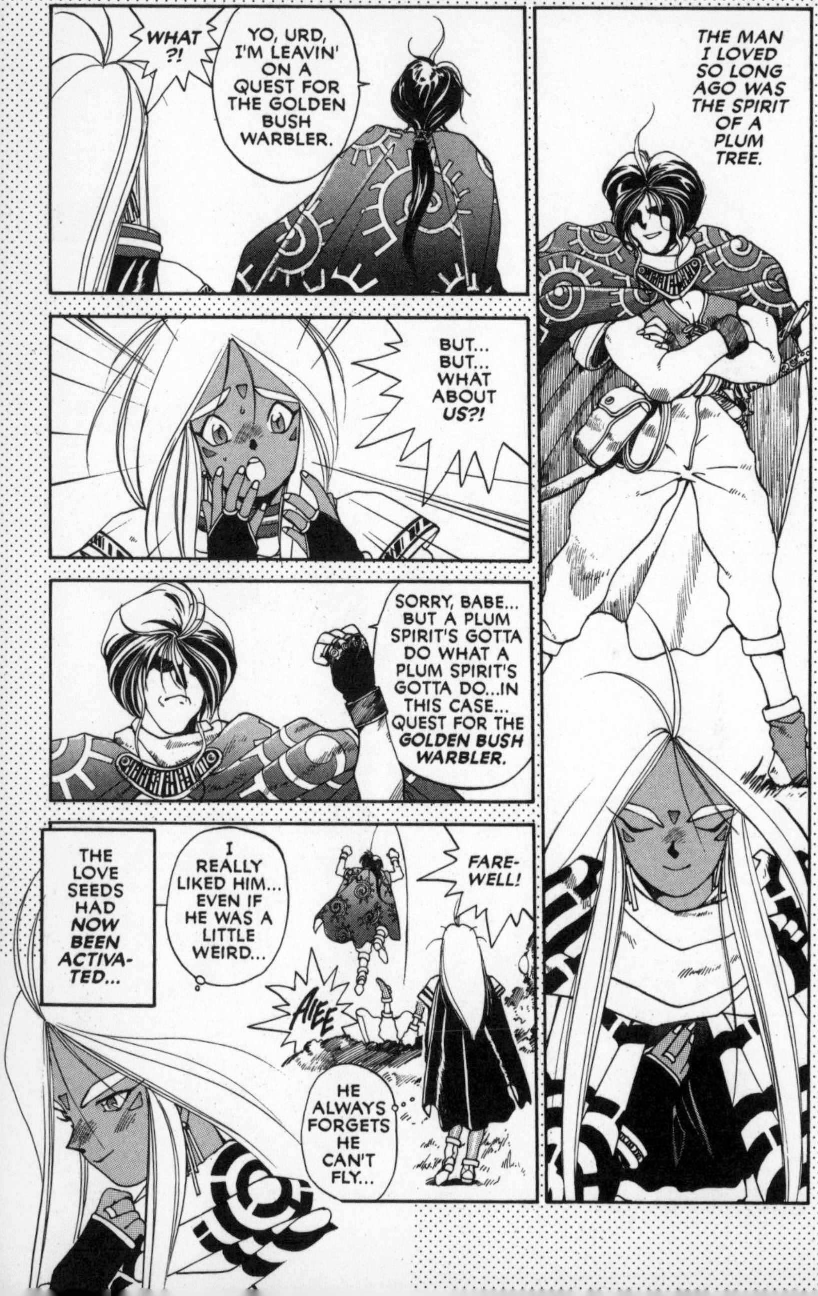
THE MAN I LOVED SO LONG AGO WAS THE SPIRIT OF A PLUM TREE.
YO, URD, I'M LEAVIN' ON A QUEST FOR THE GOLDEN BUSH WARBLER.
WHAT?!
BUT... BUT... WHAT ABOUT *US?!*
SORRY, BABE... BUT A PLUM SPIRIT'S GOTTA DO WHAT A PLUM SPIRIT'S GOTTA DO...IN THIS CASE... QUEST FOR THE *GOLDEN BUSH WARBLER.*
FARE-WELL!
AIEE
HE ALWAYS FORGETS HE CAN'T FLY...
I REALLY LIKED HIM... EVEN IF HE WAS A LITTLE WEIRD...
THE LOVE SEEDS HAD *NOW BEEN ACTIVATED...*

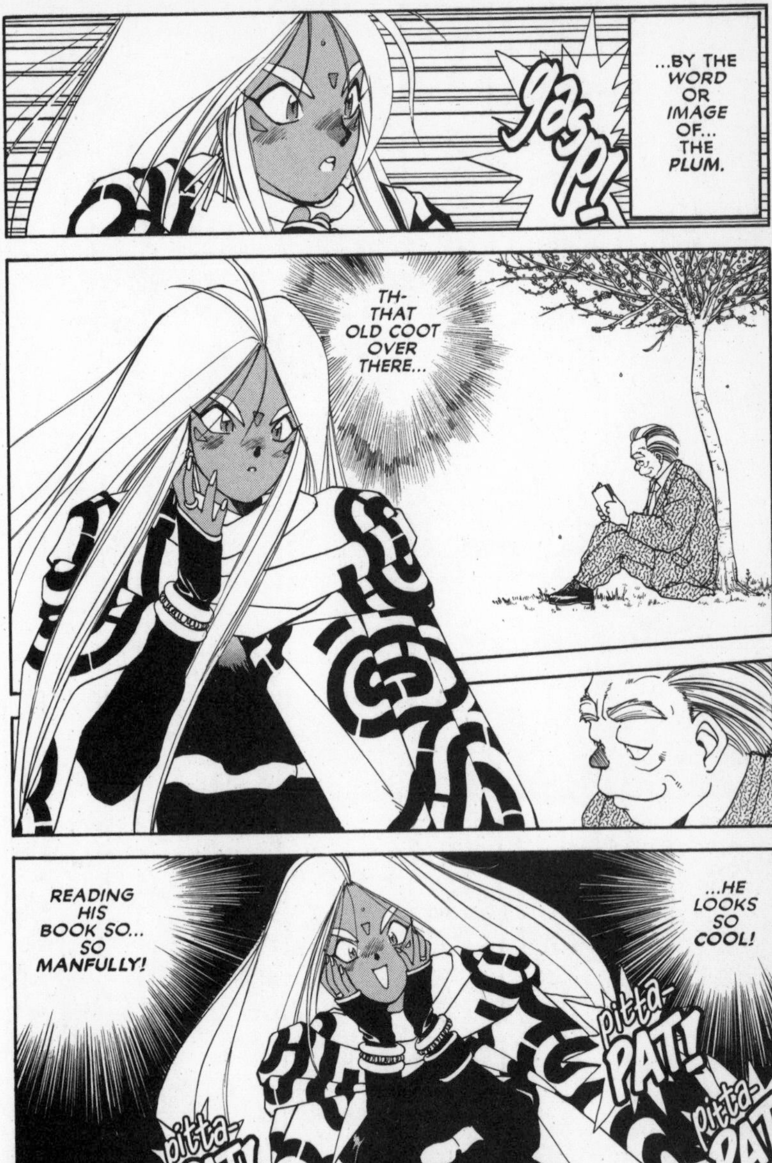
...BY THE WORD OR IMAGE OF... THE PLUM.
gasp!
TH-THAT OLD COOT OVER THERE...
...HE LOOKS SO COOL!
READING HIS BOOK SO... SO MANFULLY!
pitta-PAT!
pitta-PAT!
pitta-PAT!

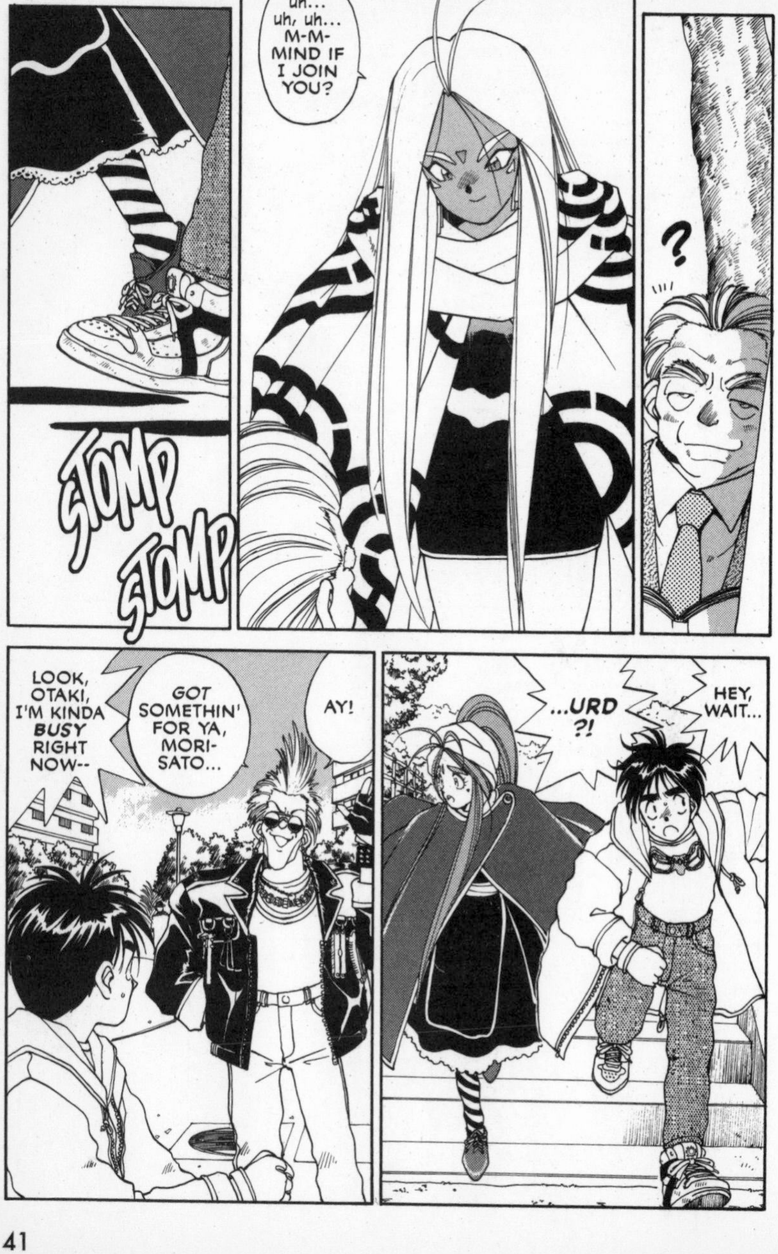
?
uh... uh, uh... M-M-MIND IF I JOIN YOU?
STOMP STOMP
HEY, WAIT...
...URD ?!
AY!
GOT SOMETHIN' FOR YA, MORI-SATO...
LOOK, OTAKI, I'M KINDA BUSY RIGHT NOW--

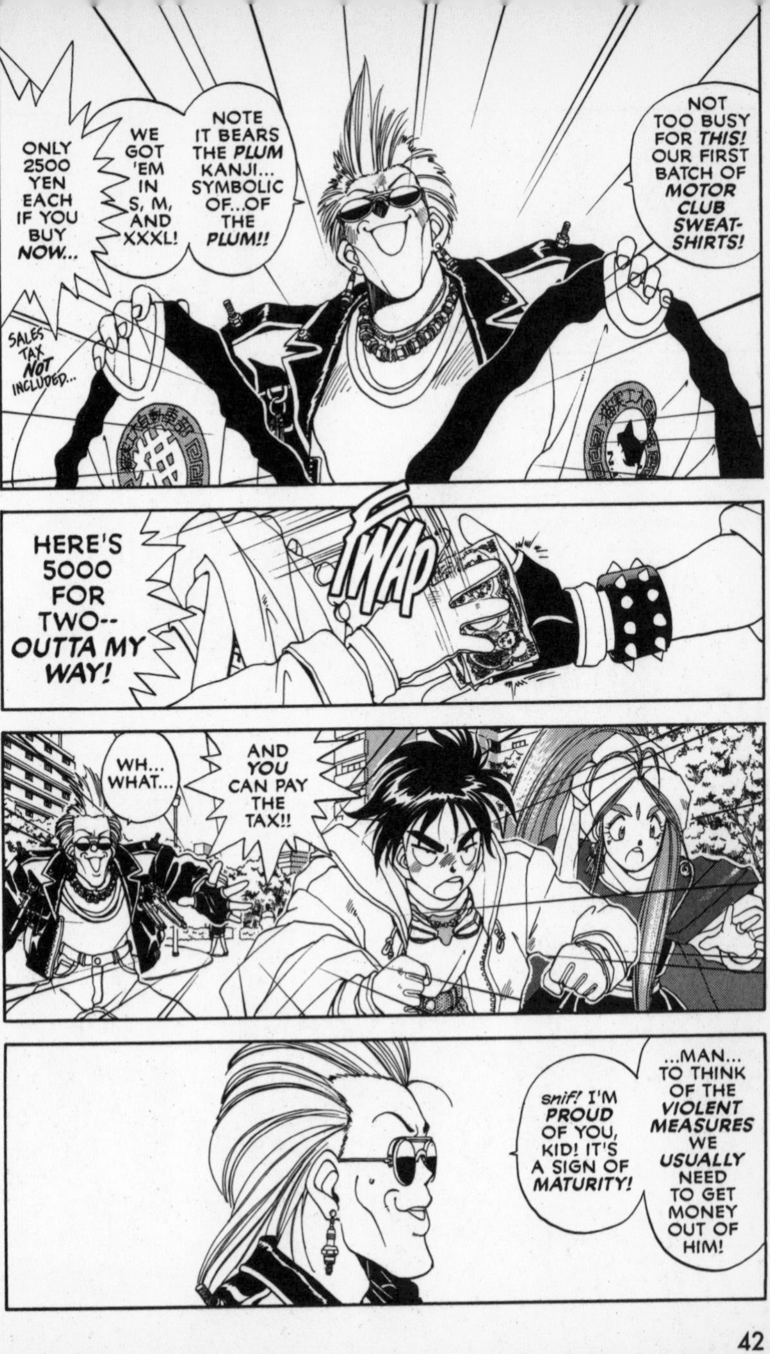
NOT TOO BUSY FOR THIS! OUR FIRST BATCH OF MOTOR CLUB SWEAT-SHIRTS!
NOTE IT BEARS THE PLUM KANJI... SYMBOLIC OF...OF THE PLUM!!
WE GOT 'EM IN S, M, AND XXXL!
ONLY 2500 YEN EACH IF YOU BUY NOW...
SALES TAX NOT INCLUDED...
FWAP
HERE'S 5000 FOR TWO-- OUTTA MY WAY!
AND YOU CAN PAY THE TAX!!
WH... WHAT...
...MAN... TO THINK OF THE VIOLENT MEASURES WE USUALLY NEED TO GET MONEY OUT OF HIM!
snif! I'M PROUD OF YOU, KID! IT'S A SIGN OF MATURITY!

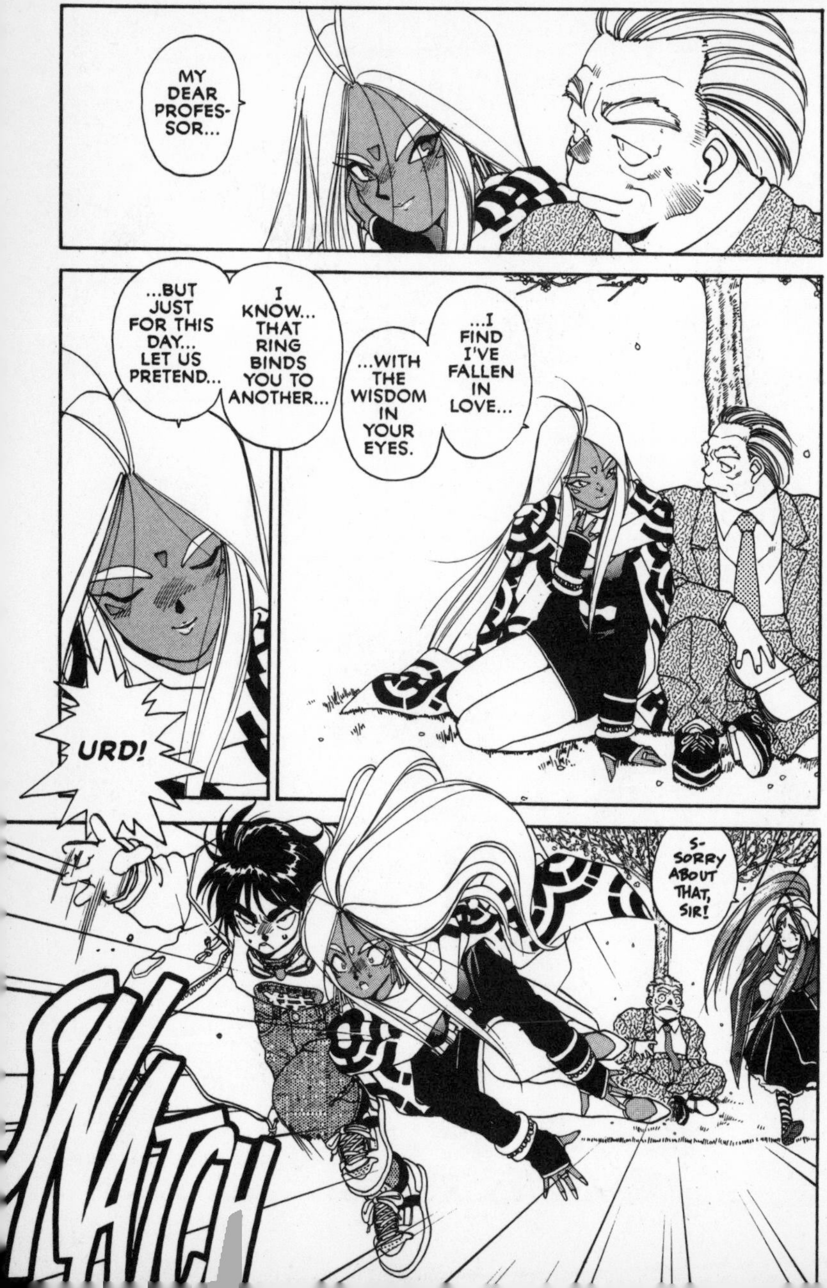
MY DEAR PROFESSOR...
...I FIND I'VE FALLEN IN LOVE...
...WITH THE WISDOM IN YOUR EYES.
I KNOW... THAT RING BINDS YOU TO ANOTHER...
...BUT JUST FOR THIS DAY... LET US PRETEND...
URD!
S-SORRY ABOUT THAT, SIR!
SNATCH

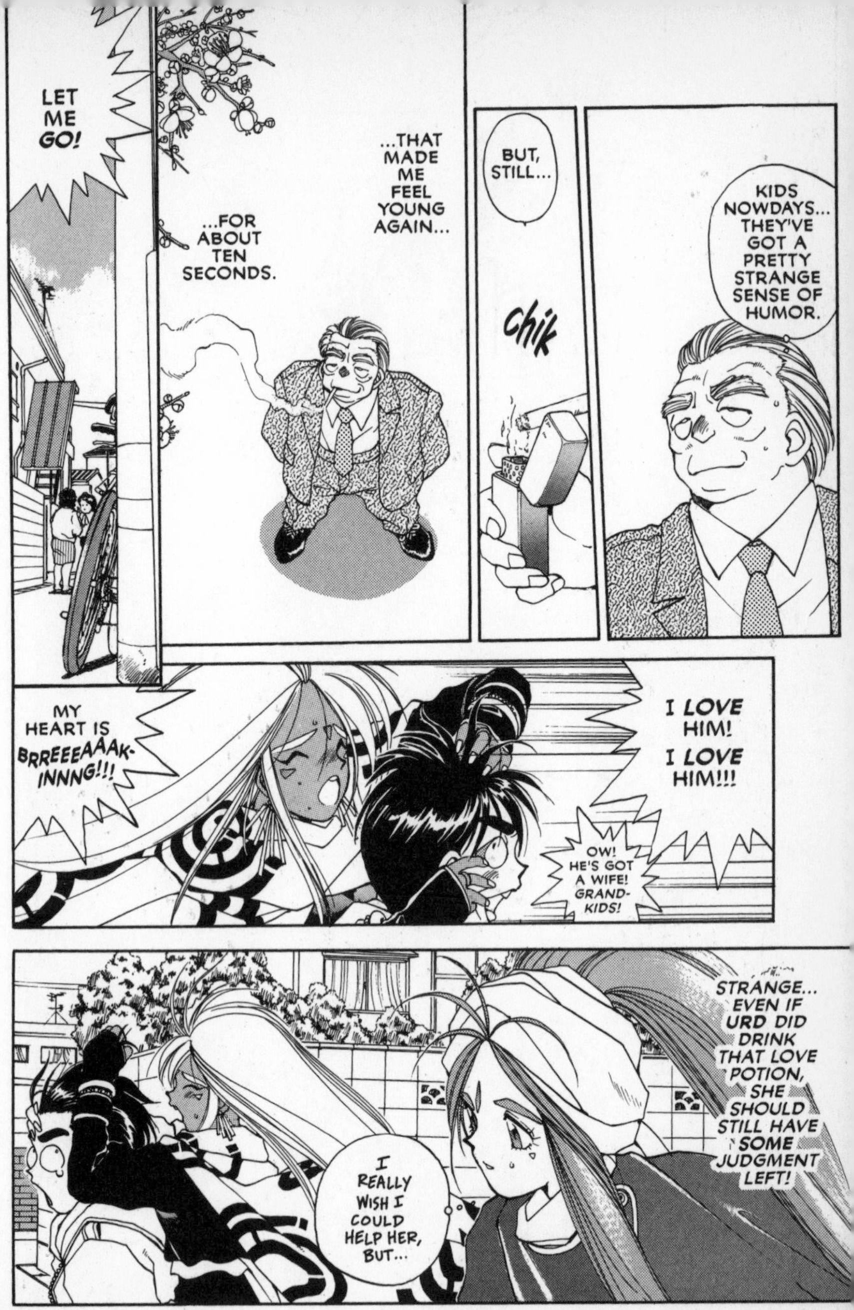
KIDS NOWDAYS... THEY'VE GOT A PRETTY STRANGE SENSE OF HUMOR.
BUT, STILL...
Chik
...THAT MADE ME FEEL YOUNG AGAIN...
...FOR ABOUT TEN SECONDS.
LET ME GO!
I LOVE HIM! I LOVE HIM!!!
MY HEART IS BRREEEAAAK-INNNG!!!
OW! HE'S GOT A WIFE! GRAND-KIDS!
STRANGE... EVEN IF URD DID DRINK THAT LOVE POTION, SHE SHOULD STILL HAVE SOME JUDGMENT LEFT!
I REALLY WISH I COULD HELP HER, BUT...

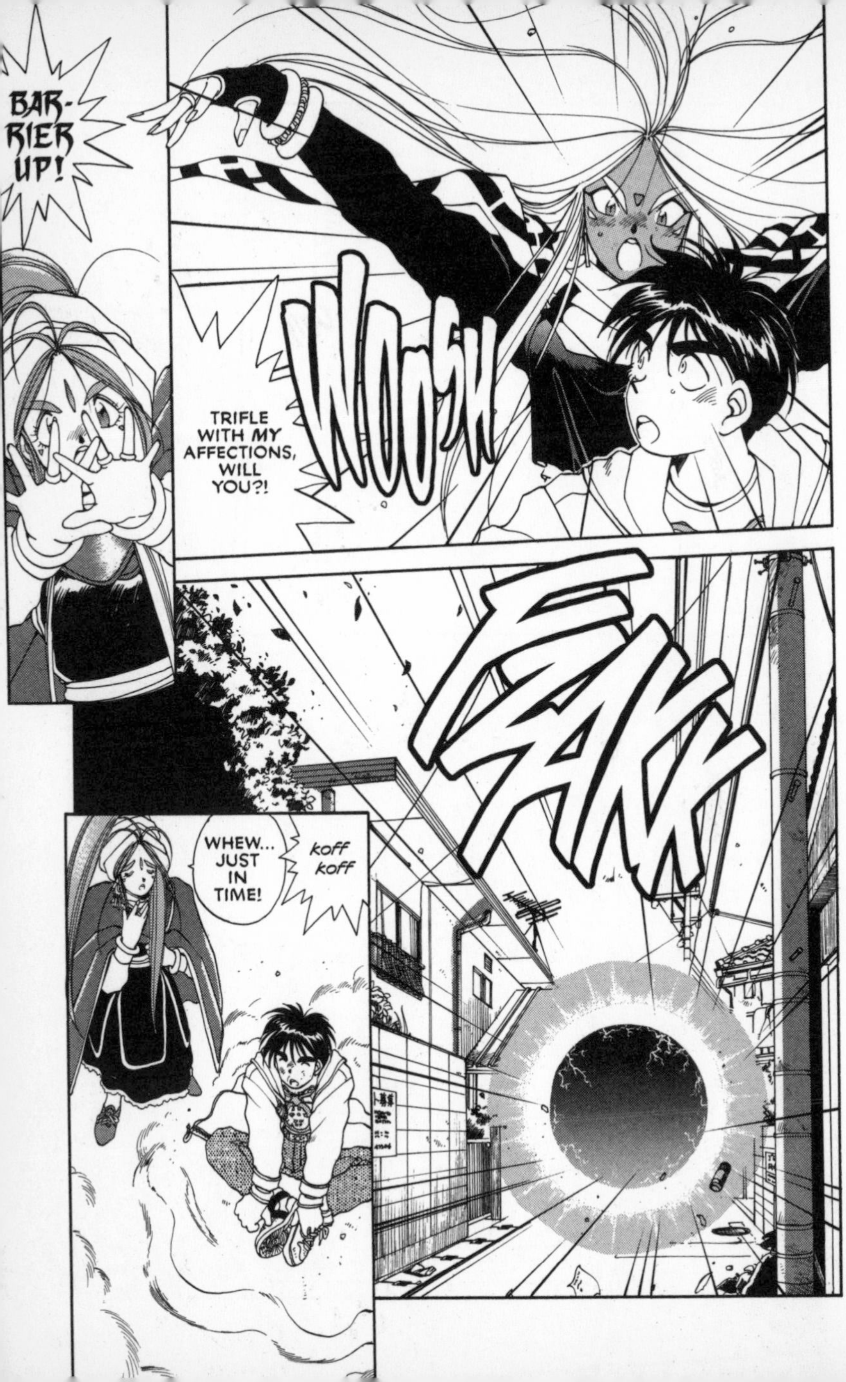
WOOSH
TRIFLE WITH MY AFFECTIONS, WILL YOU?!
BAR-RIER UP!
WHEW... JUST IN TIME!
koff koff

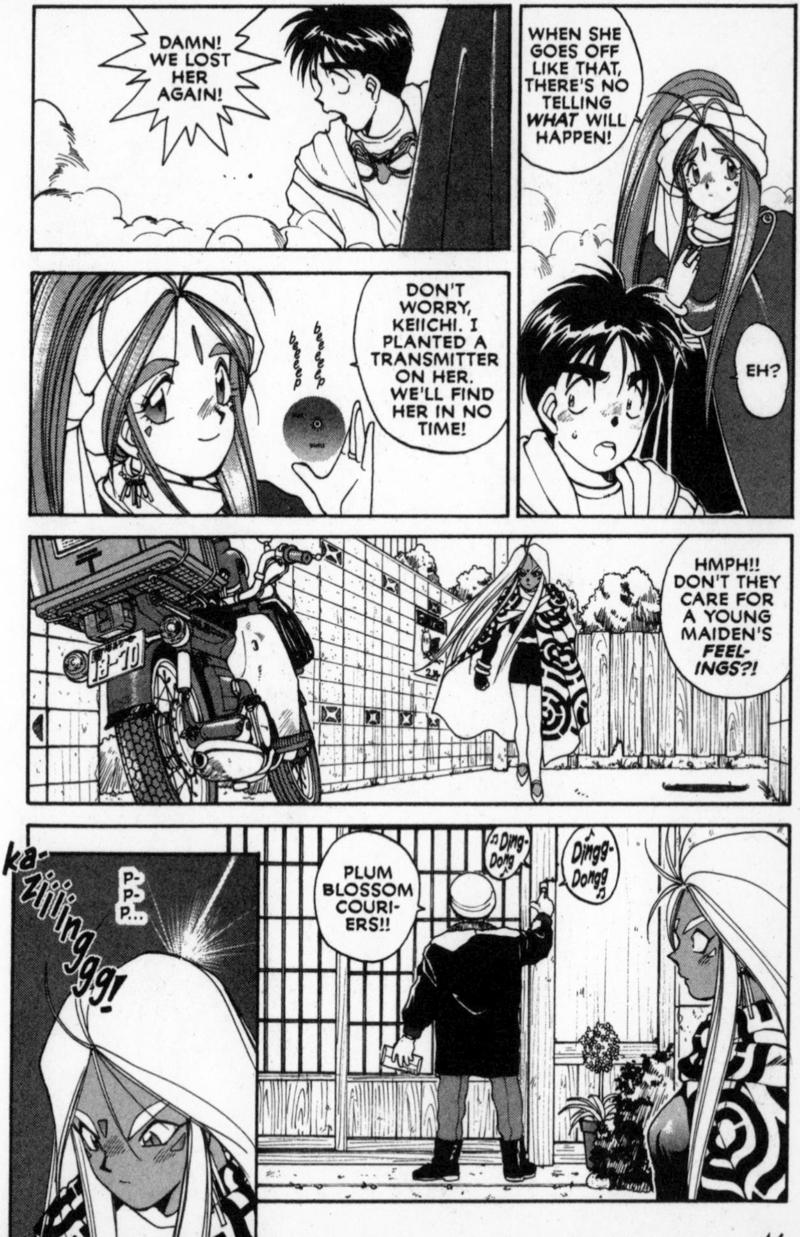
WHEN SHE GOES OFF LIKE THAT, THERE'S NO TELLING *WHAT* WILL HAPPEN!
EH?
DAMN! WE LOST HER AGAIN!
beeeep
beeeep
DON'T WORRY, KEIICHI. I PLANTED A TRANSMITTER ON HER. WE'LL FIND HER IN NO TIME!
HMPH!! DON'T THEY CARE FOR A YOUNG MAIDEN'S *FEEL-INGS?!*
Dingg-Dongg
Ding-Dong
PLUM BLOSSOM COURI-ERS!!
P-P-P...
ka-ziiiingg!

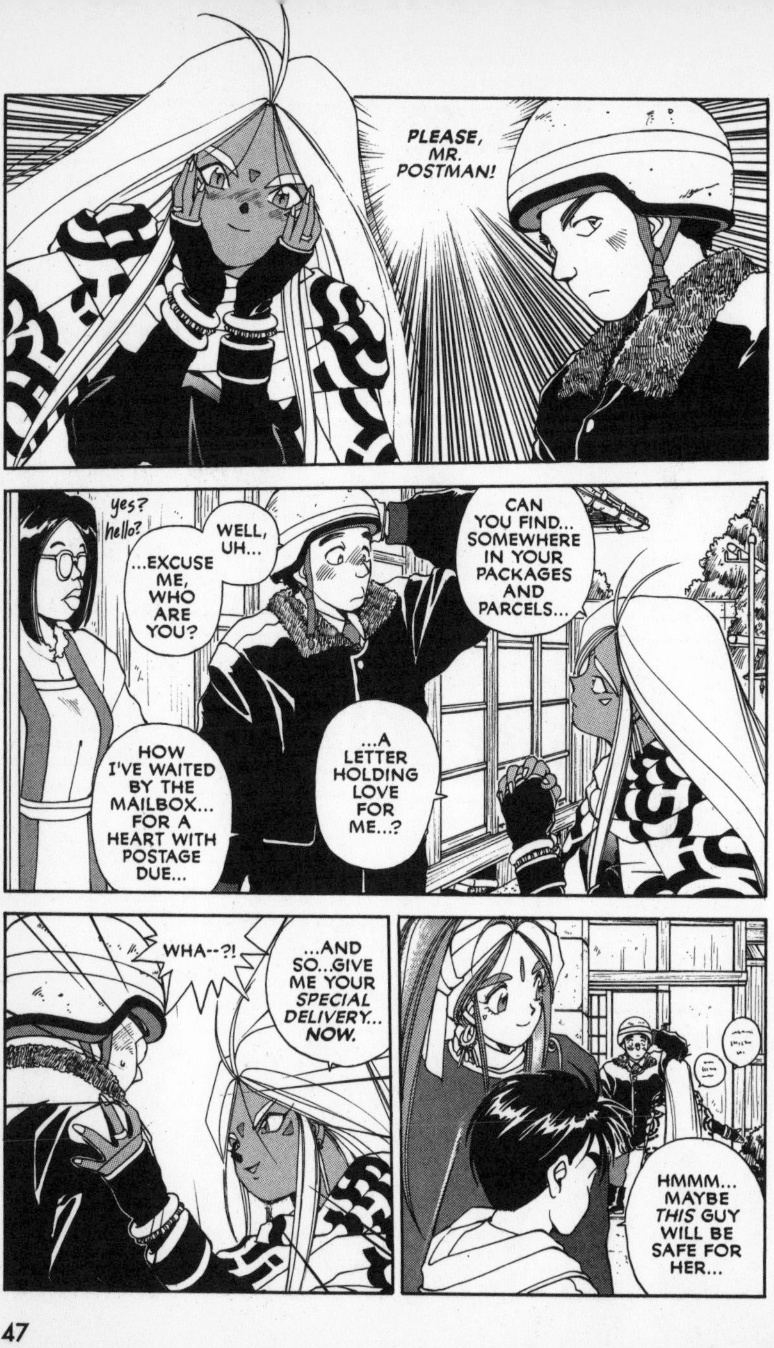
PLEASE, MR. POSTMAN!
CAN YOU FIND... SOMEWHERE IN YOUR PACKAGES AND PARCELS...
WELL, UH...
...EXCUSE ME, WHO ARE YOU?
yes? hello?
...A LETTER HOLDING LOVE FOR ME...?
HOW I'VE WAITED BY THE MAILBOX... FOR A HEART WITH POSTAGE DUE...
HMMM... MAYBE *THIS* GUY WILL BE SAFE FOR HER...
...AND SO...GIVE ME YOUR *SPECIAL DELIVERY*... NOW.
WHA--?!

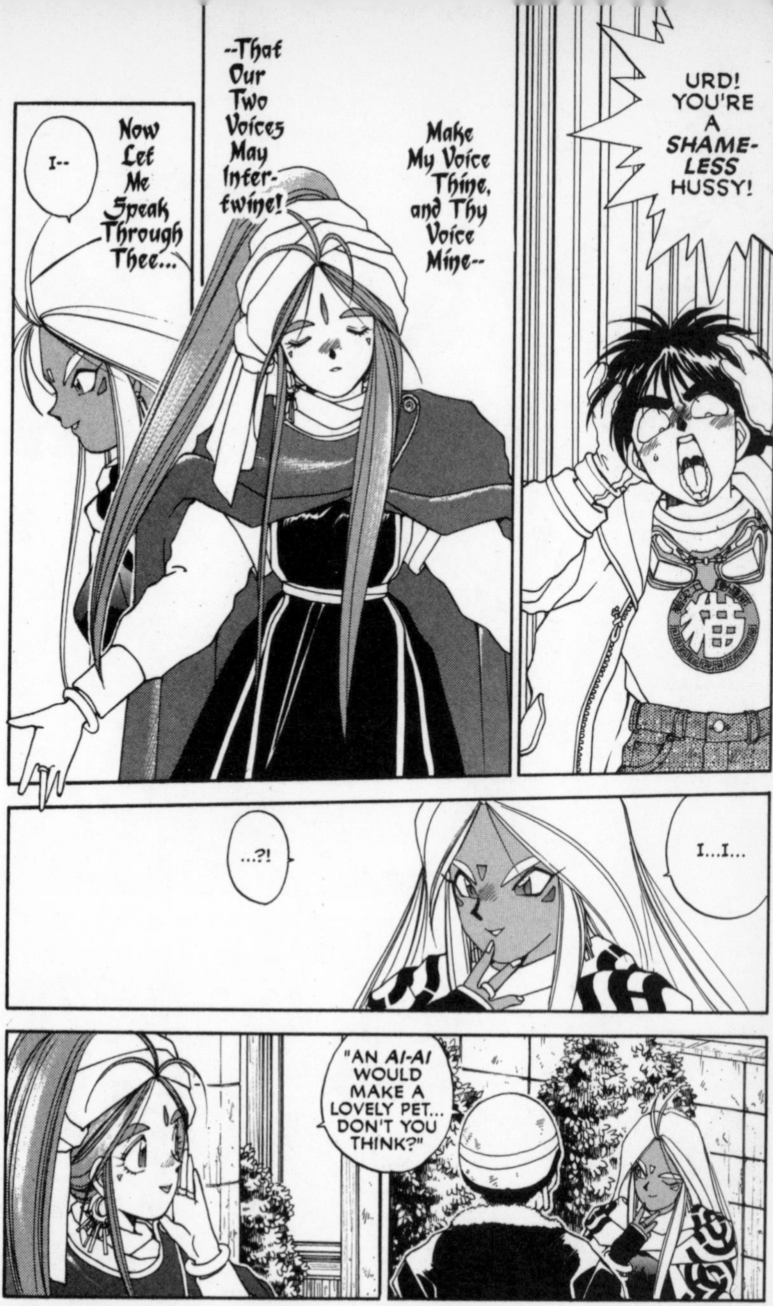
URD! YOU'RE A SHAME-LESS HUSSY!
Make My Voice Thine, and Thy Voice Mine--
--That Our Two Voices May Inter-twine!
Now Let Me Speak Through Thee...
I--
I...I...
...?!
"AN AI-AI WOULD MAKE A LOVELY PET... DON'T YOU THINK?"

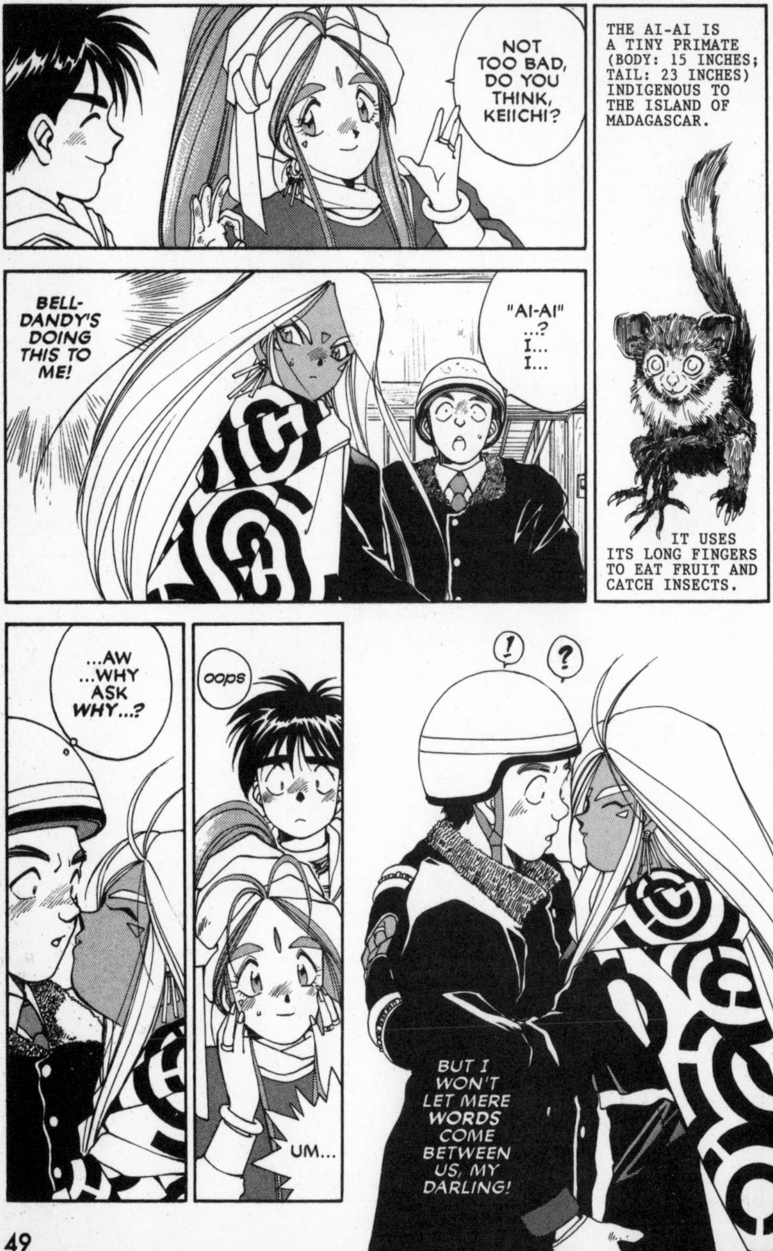
THE AI-AI IS A TINY PRIMATE (BODY: 15 INCHES; TAIL: 23 INCHES) INDIGENOUS TO THE ISLAND OF MADAGASCAR.
IT USES ITS LONG FINGERS TO EAT FRUIT AND CATCH INSECTS.
NOT TOO BAD, DO YOU THINK, KEIICHI?
"AI-AI" ...? I... I...
BELL-DANDY'S DOING THIS TO ME!
!
?
BUT I WON'T LET MERE WORDS COME BETWEEN US, MY DARLING!
oops
UM...
...AW ...WHY ASK WHY...?

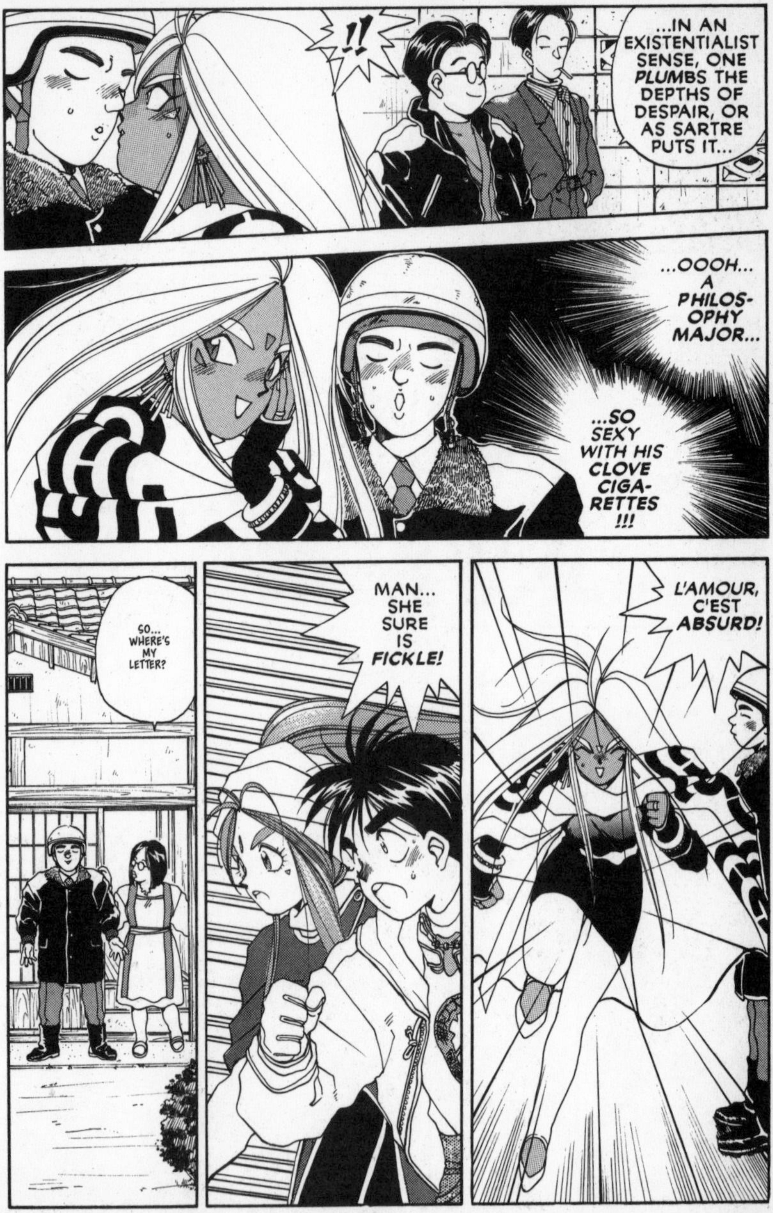
...IN AN EXISTENTIALIST SENSE, ONE PLUMBS THE DEPTHS OF DESPAIR, OR AS SARTRE PUTS IT...
!!
...OOOH... A PHILOS-OPHY MAJOR...
...SO SEXY WITH HIS CLOVE CIGA-RETTES !!!
L'AMOUR, C'EST ABSURD!
MAN... SHE SURE IS FICKLE!
SO... WHERE'S MY LETTER?

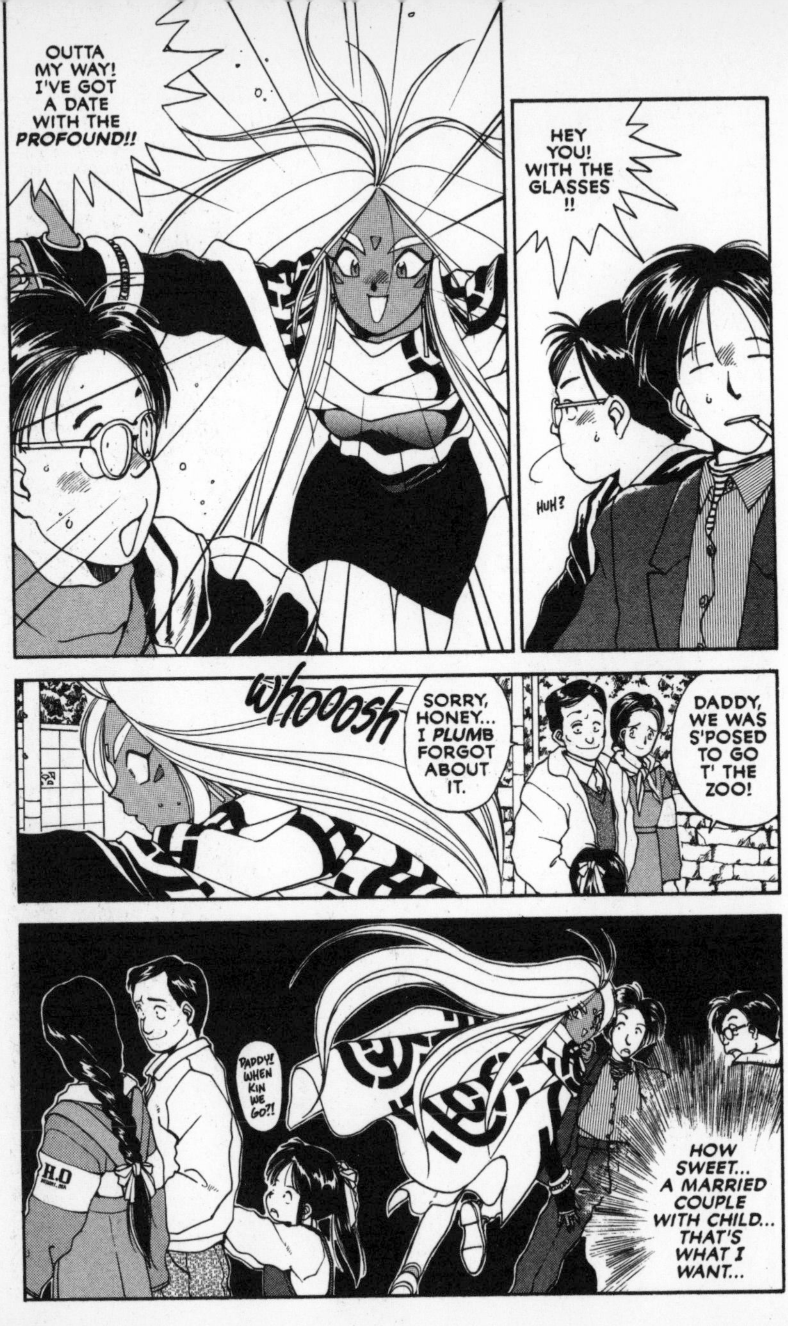
HEY YOU! WITH THE GLASSES !!
HUH?
OUTTA MY WAY! I'VE GOT A DATE WITH THE *PROFOUND!!*
DADDY, WE WAS S'POSED TO GO T' THE ZOO!
SORRY, HONEY... I *PLUMB* FORGOT ABOUT IT.
WHOOOSH
HOW SWEET... A MARRIED COUPLE WITH CHILD... THAT'S WHAT I WANT...
DADDY! WHEN KIN WE GO?!

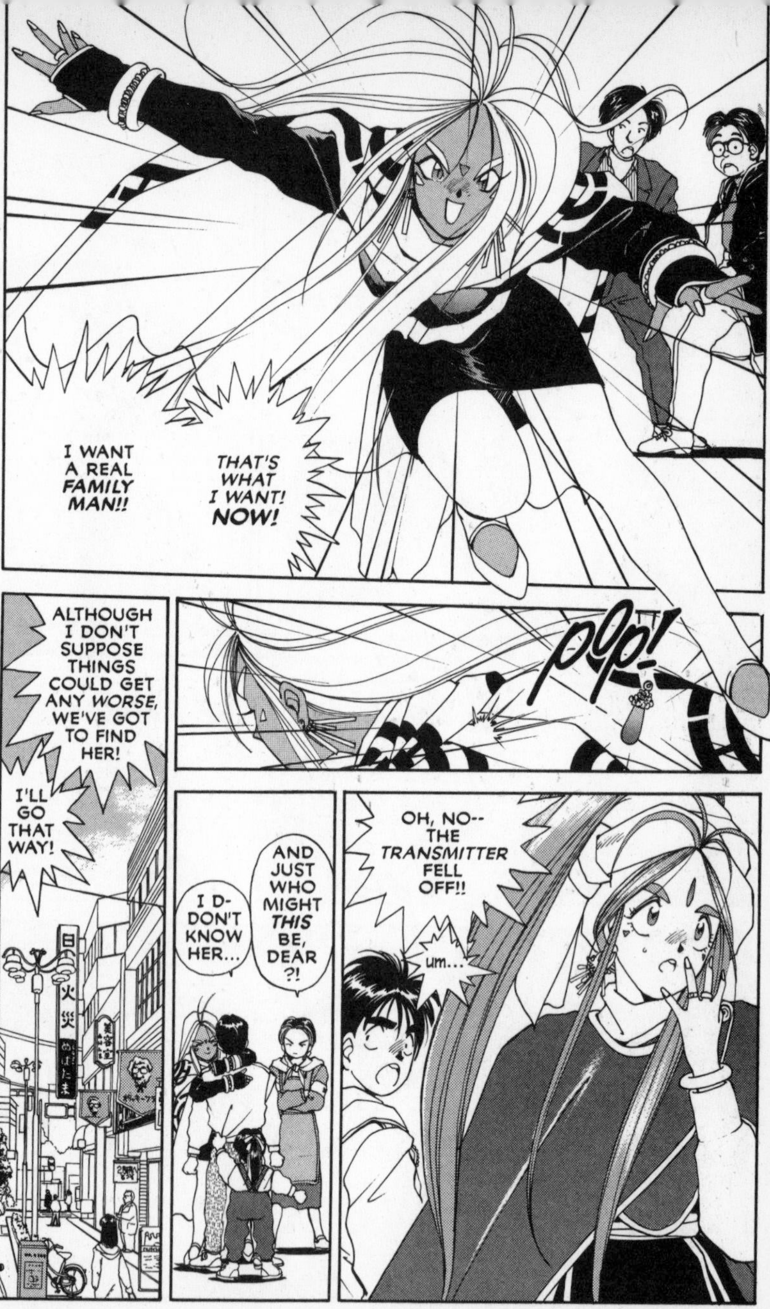
THAT'S WHAT I WANT! NOW!
I WANT A REAL FAMILY MAN!!
plop!
OH, NO-- THE TRANSMITTER FELL OFF!!
um...
AND JUST WHO MIGHT THIS BE, DEAR ?!
I D- DON'T KNOW HER...
ALTHOUGH I DON'T SUPPOSE THINGS COULD GET ANY WORSE, WE'VE GOT TO FIND HER!
I'LL GO THAT WAY!

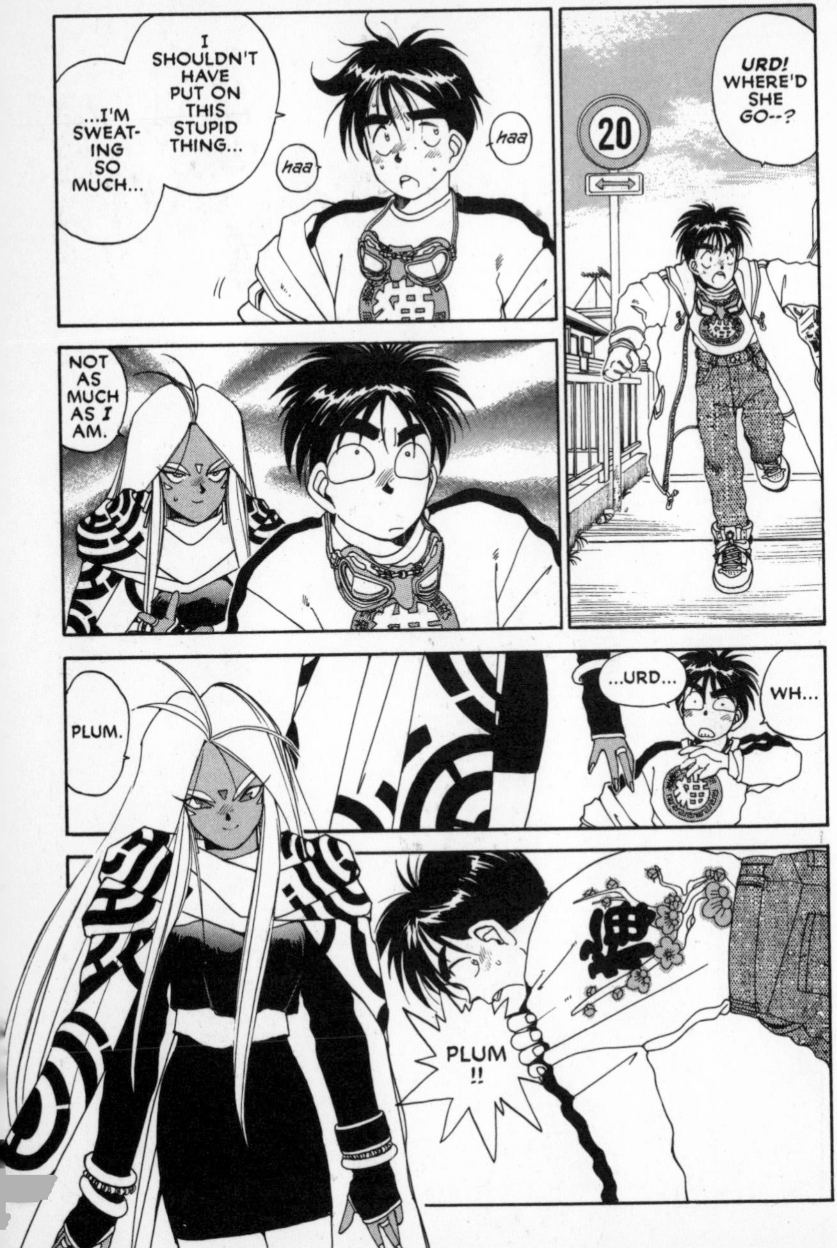

20
URD! WHERE'D SHE GO--?
haa
haa
I SHOULDN'T HAVE PUT ON THIS STUPID THING...
...I'M SWEAT-ING SO MUCH...
NOT AS MUCH AS I AM.
WH...
...URD...
PLUM.
PLUM !!

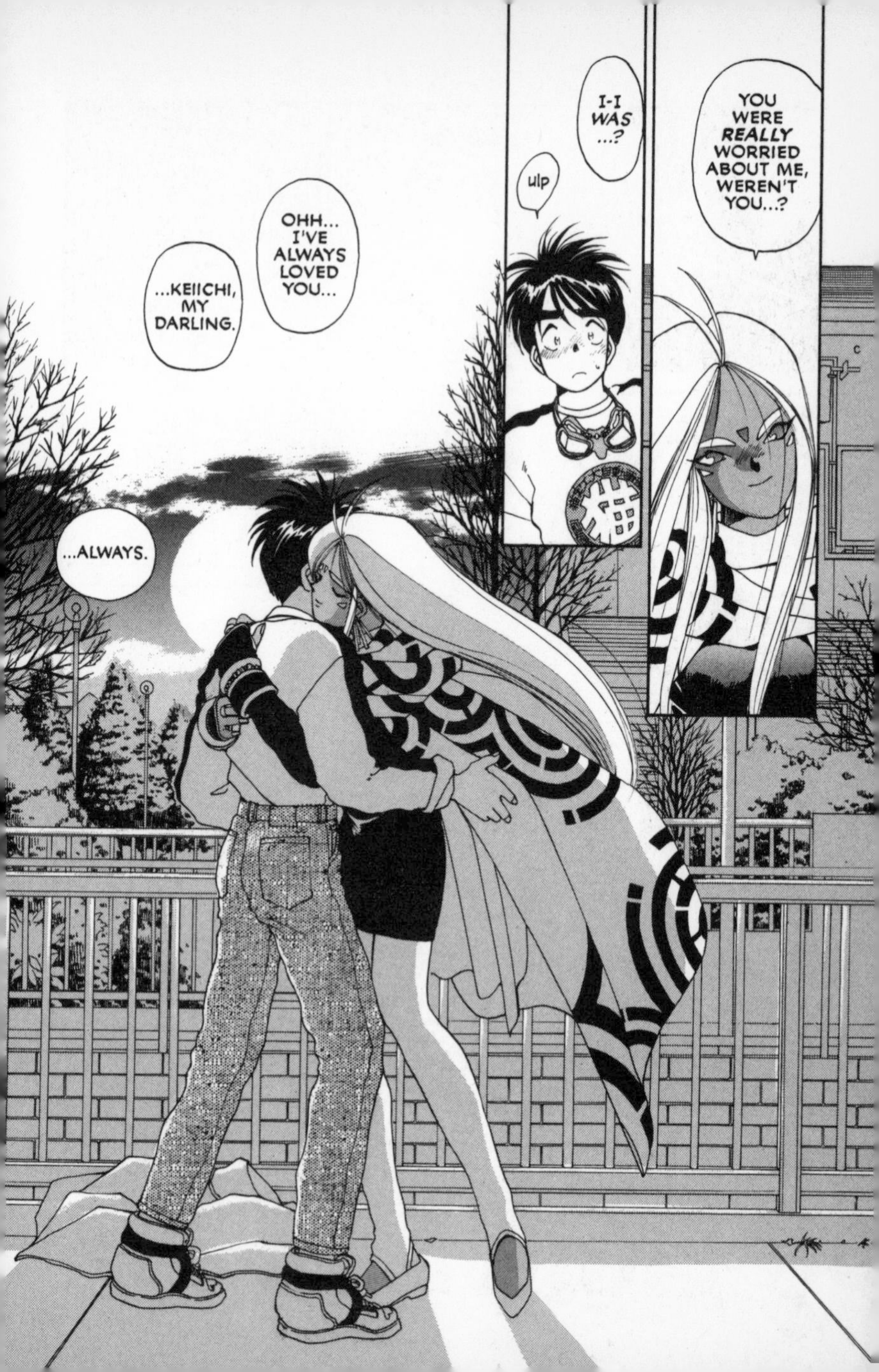
YOU WERE *REALLY* WORRIED ABOUT ME, WEREN'T YOU...?
I-I *WAS* ...?
ulp
OHH... I'VE ALWAYS LOVED YOU...
...KEIICHI, MY DARLING.
...ALWAYS.

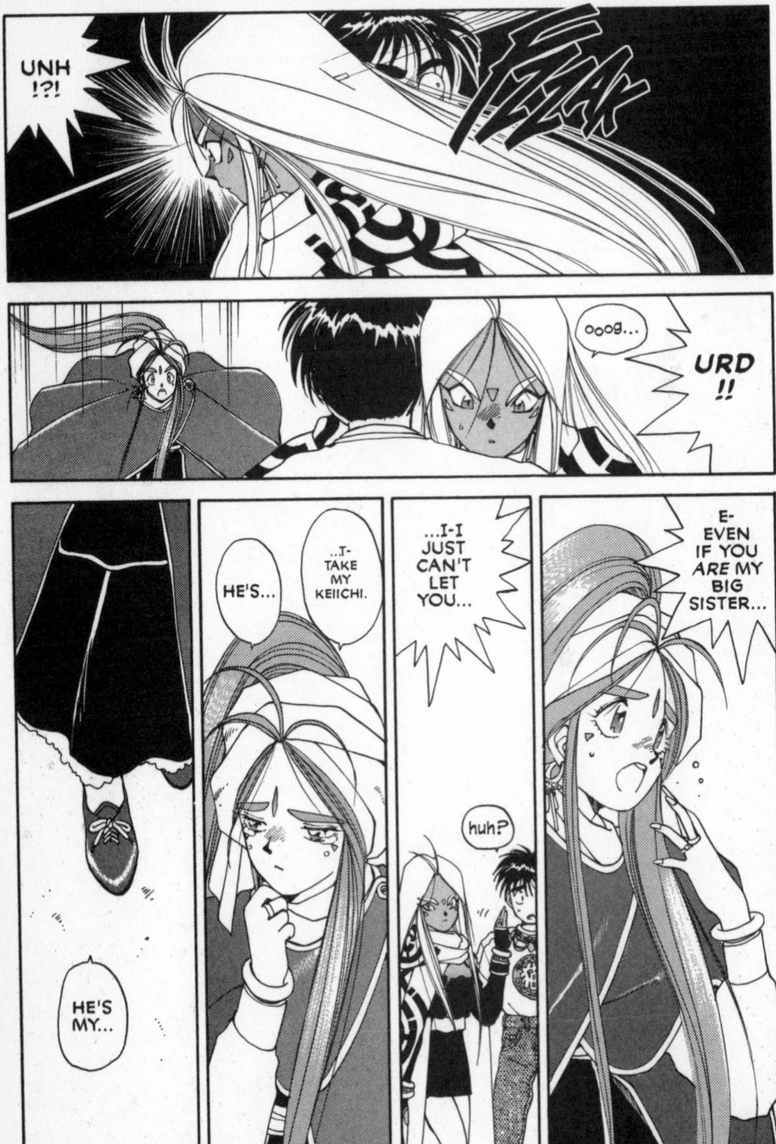
FZZAK
UNH !?!
URD !!
ooog...
E- EVEN IF YOU ARE MY BIG SISTER...
...I-I JUST CAN'T LET YOU...
huh?
...T- TAKE MY KEIICHI.
HE'S...
HE'S MY...

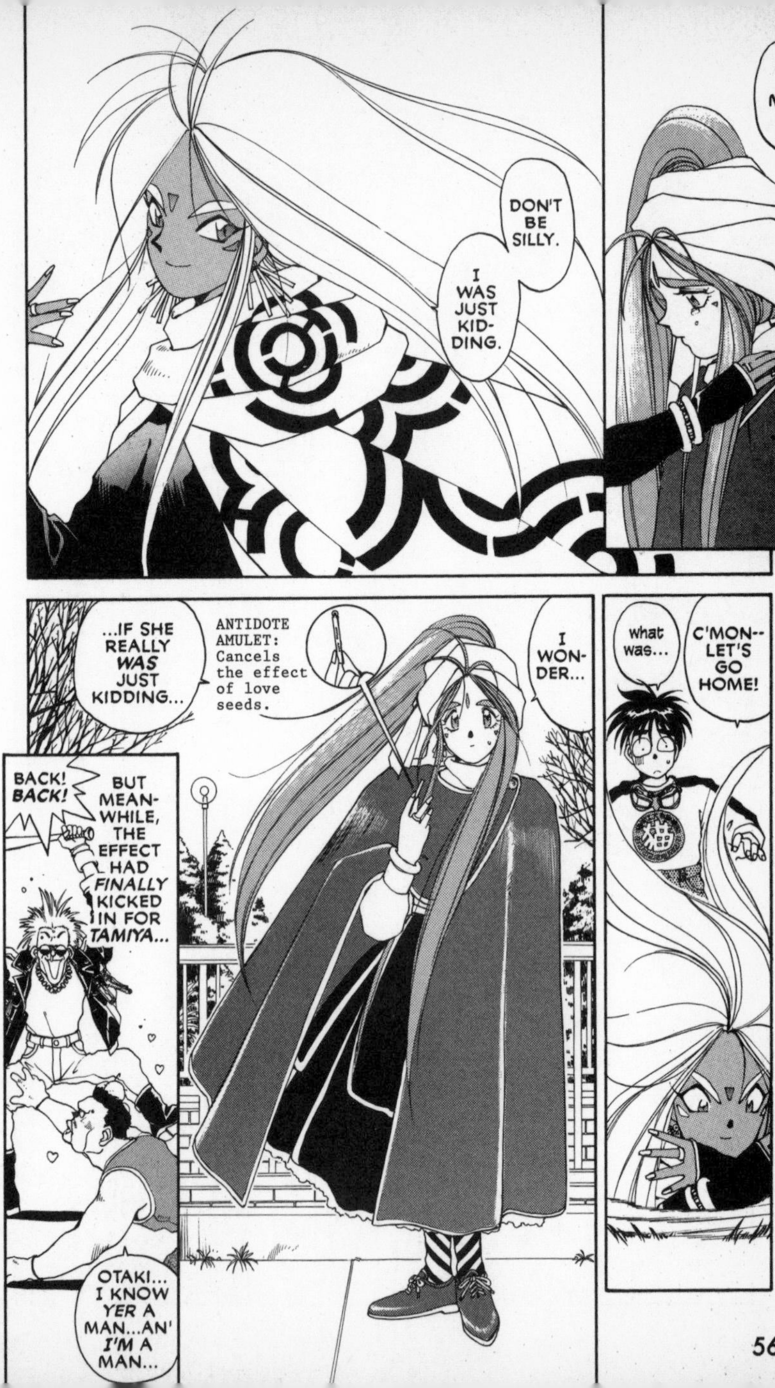
MY...
pat
DON'T BE SILLY.
I WAS JUST KIDDING.
C'MON-- LET'S GO HOME!
what was...
I WONDER...
ANTIDOTE AMULET: Cancels the effect of love seeds.
...IF SHE REALLY *WAS* JUST KIDDING...
BUT MEANWHILE, THE EFFECT HAD *FINALLY* KICKED IN FOR *TAMIYA*...
BACK! *BACK!*
OTAKI... I KNOW *YER* A MAN...AN' *I'M* A MAN...

CHAPTER 26

The Nemesis

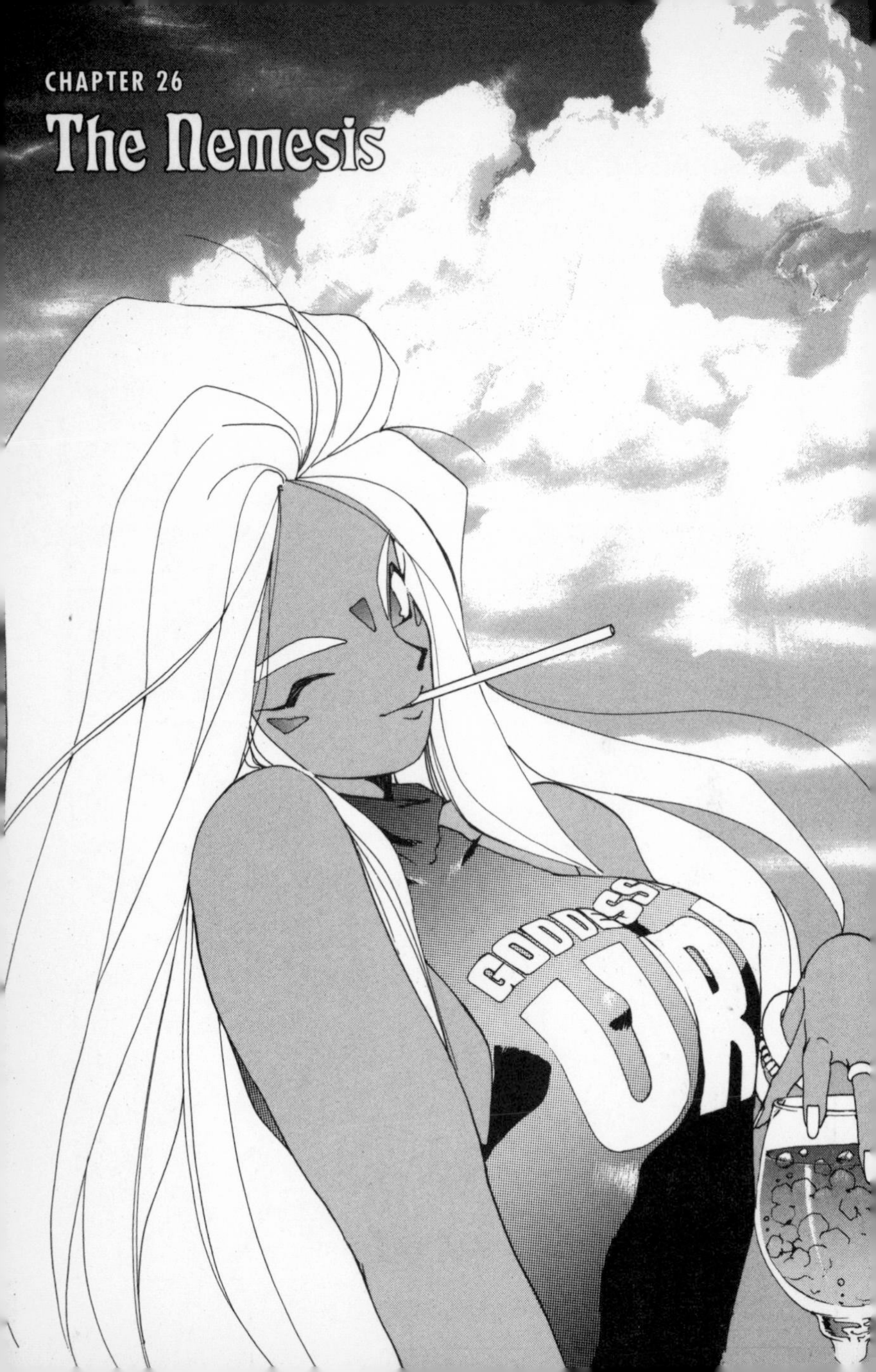
GODDESS

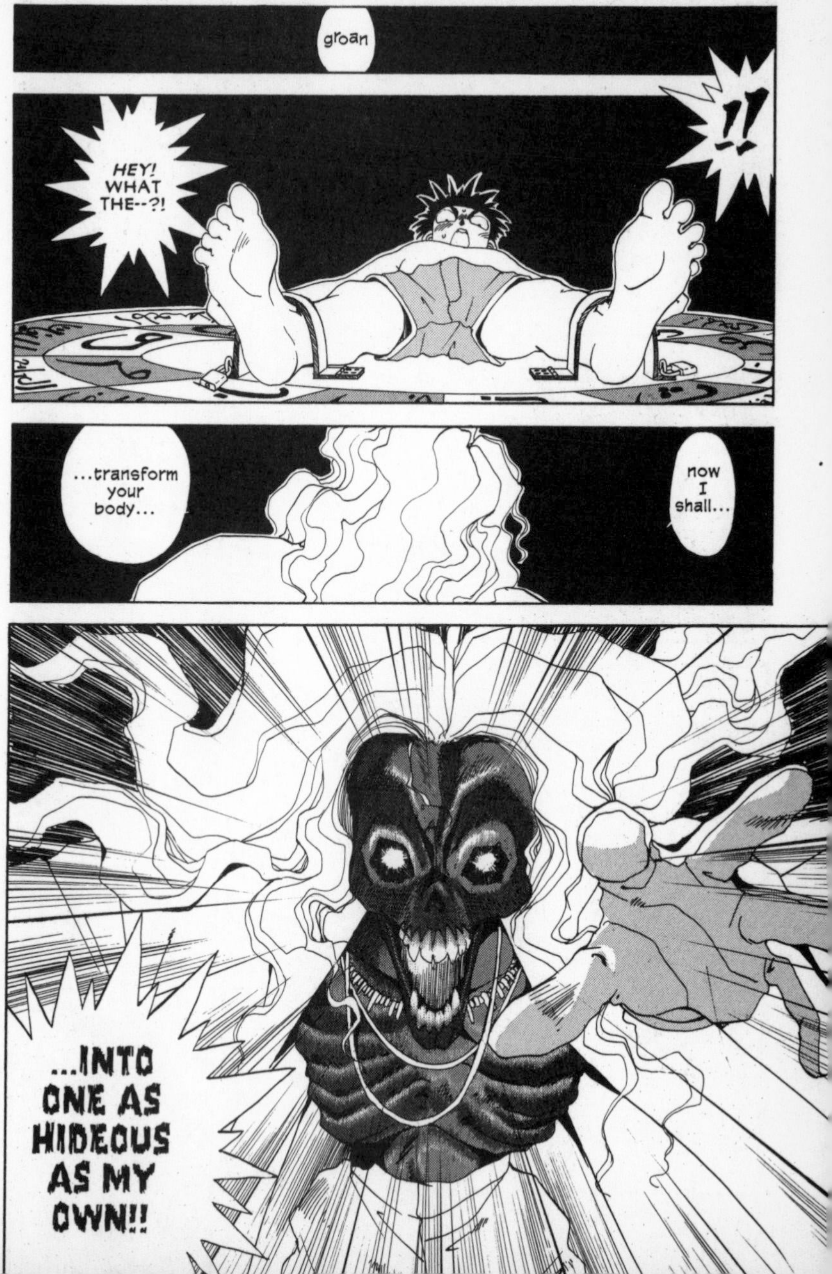
groan
!!
HEY! WHAT THE--?!
now I shall...
...transform your body...
...INTO ONE AS HIDEOUS AS MY OWN!!

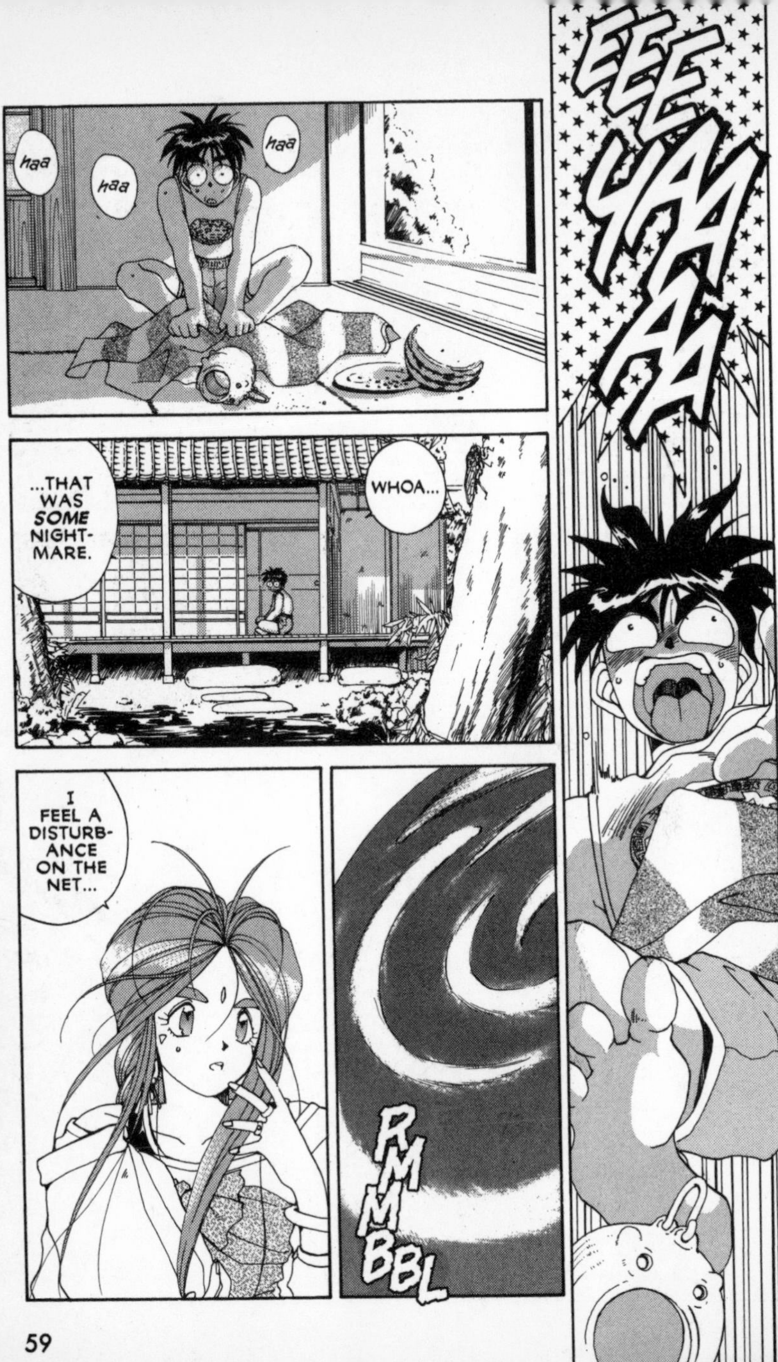
EEEYAAAAA
haa
haa
haa
WHOA...
...THAT WAS SOME NIGHT-MARE.
RMMBBL
I FEEL A DISTURB-ANCE ON THE NET...

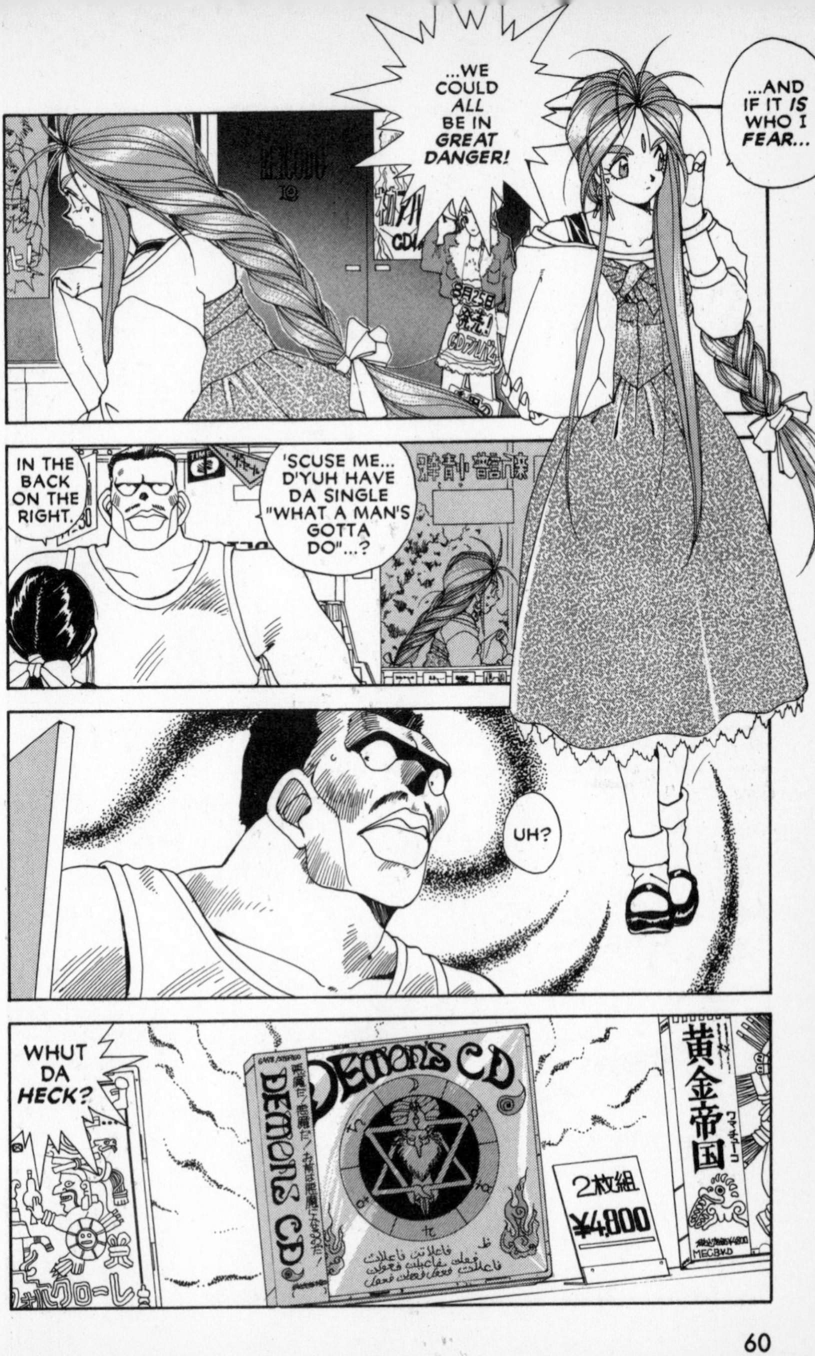
...AND IF IT *IS* WHO I *FEAR*...
...WE COULD *ALL* BE IN *GREAT DANGER!*
'SCUSE ME... D'YUH HAVE DA SINGLE "WHAT A MAN'S GOTTA DO"...?
IN THE BACK ON THE RIGHT.
UH?
WHUT DA *HECK?*
DEMON'S CD
2枚組
¥4,800
黄金帝国

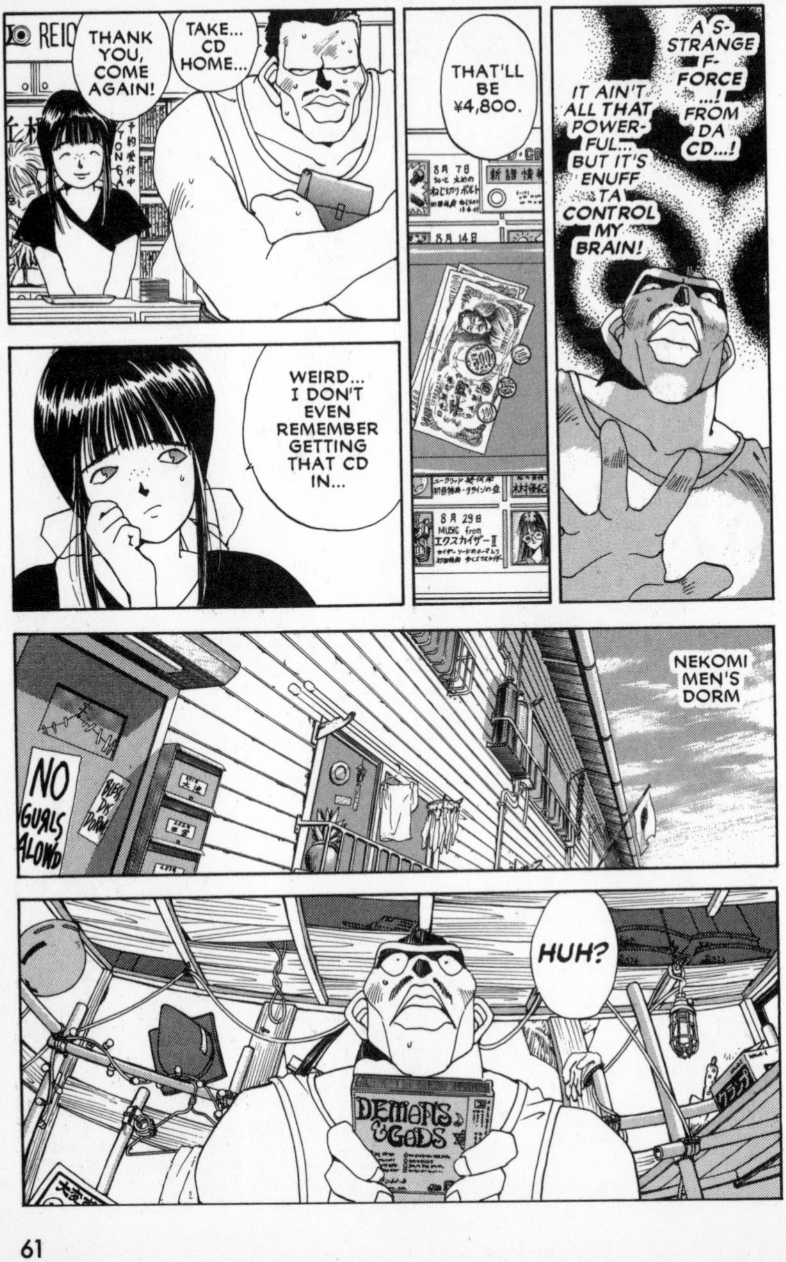
A S-STRANGE F-FORCE ...! FROM DA CD...!
IT AIN'T ALL THAT POWERFUL... BUT IT'S ENUFF TA CONTROL MY BRAIN!
THAT'LL BE ¥4,800.
TAKE... CD HOME...
THANK YOU, COME AGAIN!
REIO
WEIRD... I DON'T EVEN REMEMBER GETTING THAT CD IN...
NEKOMI MEN'S DORM
NO GURLS ALOWD
HUH?
DEMONS & GODS

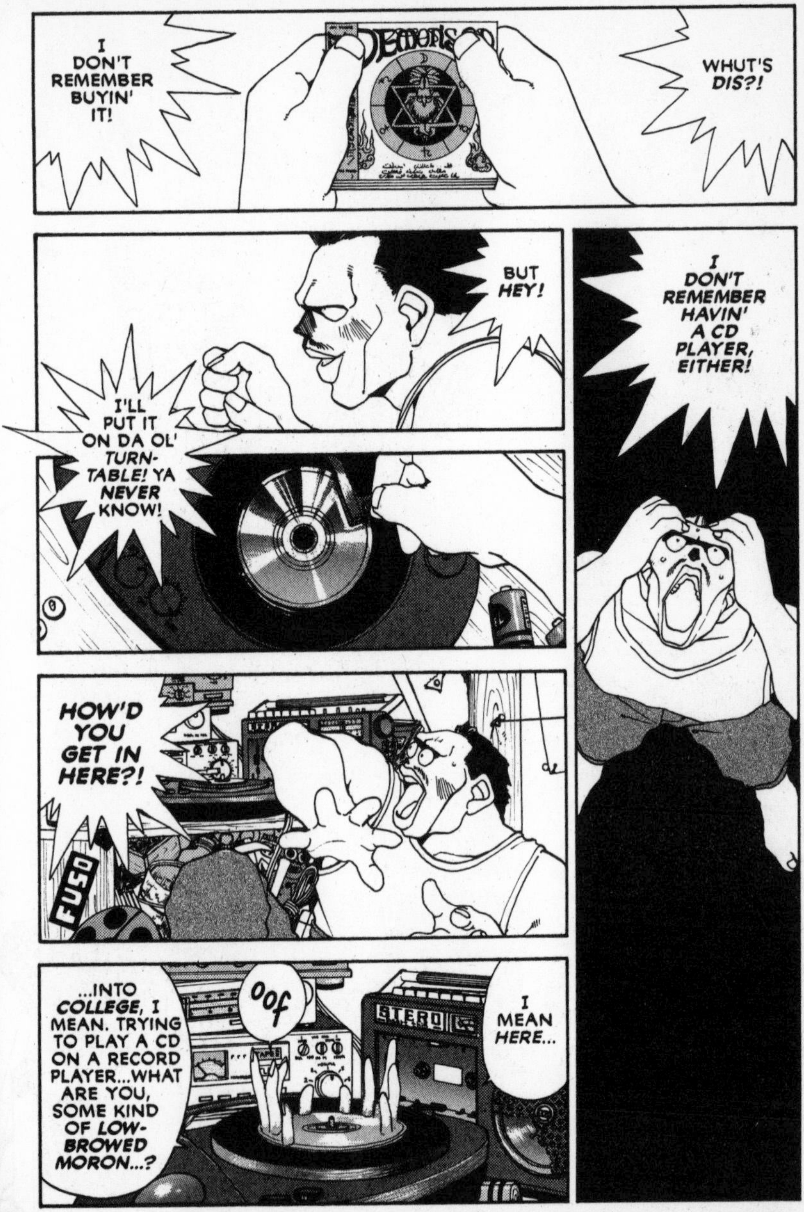
WHUT'S *DIS?!*
I DON'T REMEMBER BUYIN' IT!
I DON'T REMEMBER HAVIN' A CD PLAYER, EITHER!
BUT *HEY!*
I'LL PUT IT ON DA OL' *TURN-TABLE!* YA *NEVER* KNOW!
HOW'D YOU GET IN HERE?!
FUSO
I MEAN *HERE...*
oof
...INTO *COLLEGE*, I MEAN. TRYING TO PLAY A CD ON A RECORD PLAYER...WHAT ARE YOU, SOME KIND OF *LOW-BROWED MORON...?*

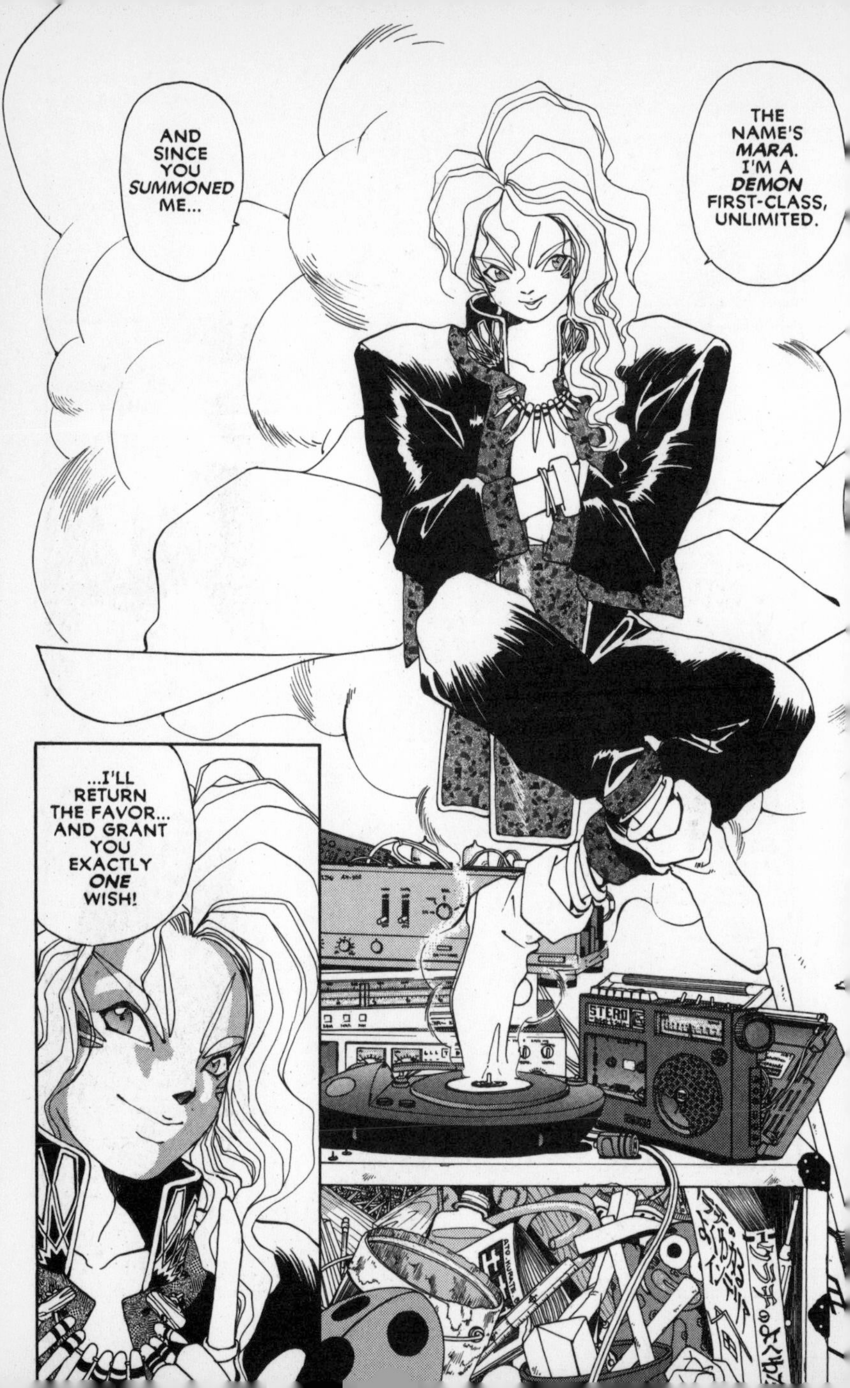
THE NAME'S *MARA*. I'M A *DEMON* FIRST-CLASS, UNLIMITED.
AND SINCE YOU *SUMMONED* ME...
...I'LL RETURN THE FAVOR... AND GRANT YOU EXACTLY *ONE* WISH!

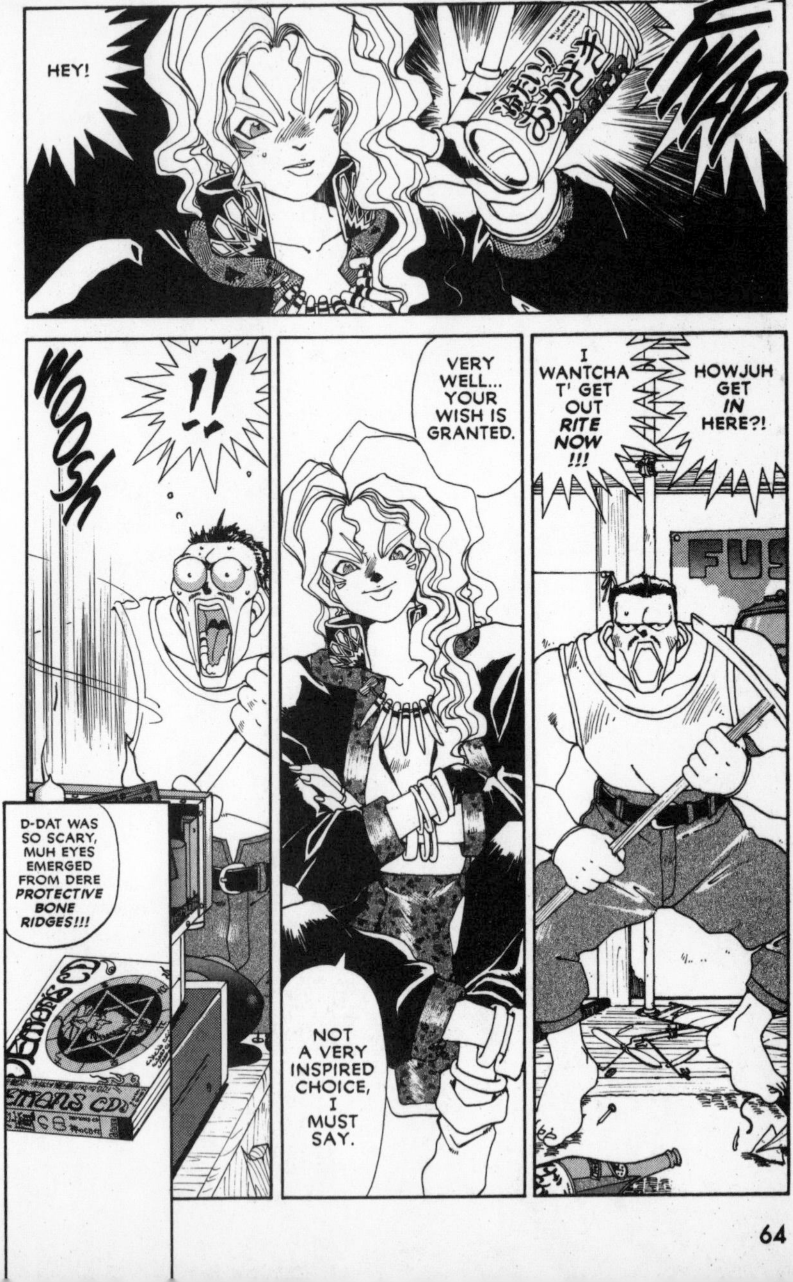
HEY!
FWAP
HOWJUH GET *IN* HERE?!
I WANTCHA T' GET OUT *RITE NOW* !!!
FUS
VERY WELL... YOUR WISH IS GRANTED.
NOT A VERY INSPIRED CHOICE, I MUST SAY.
!!
WOOSH
D-DAT WAS SO SCARY, MUH EYES EMERGED FROM DERE *PROTECTIVE BONE RIDGES!!!*

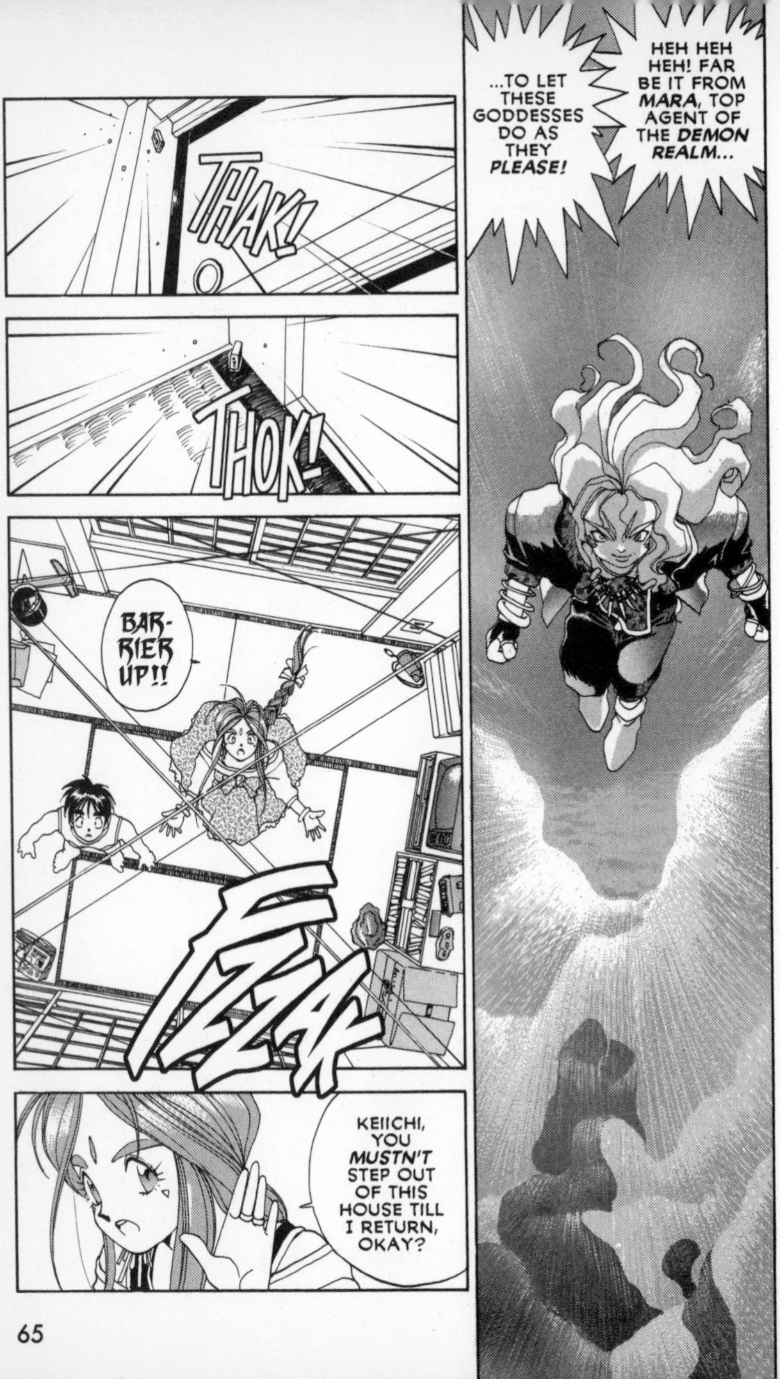
HEH HEH HEH! FAR BE IT FROM *MARA*, TOP AGENT OF THE *DEMON REALM*...
...TO LET THESE GODDESSES DO AS THEY *PLEASE!*
THAK!
THOK!
BAR-RIER UP!!
FZZAK
KEIICHI, YOU *MUSTN'T* STEP OUT OF THIS HOUSE TILL I RETURN, OKAY?

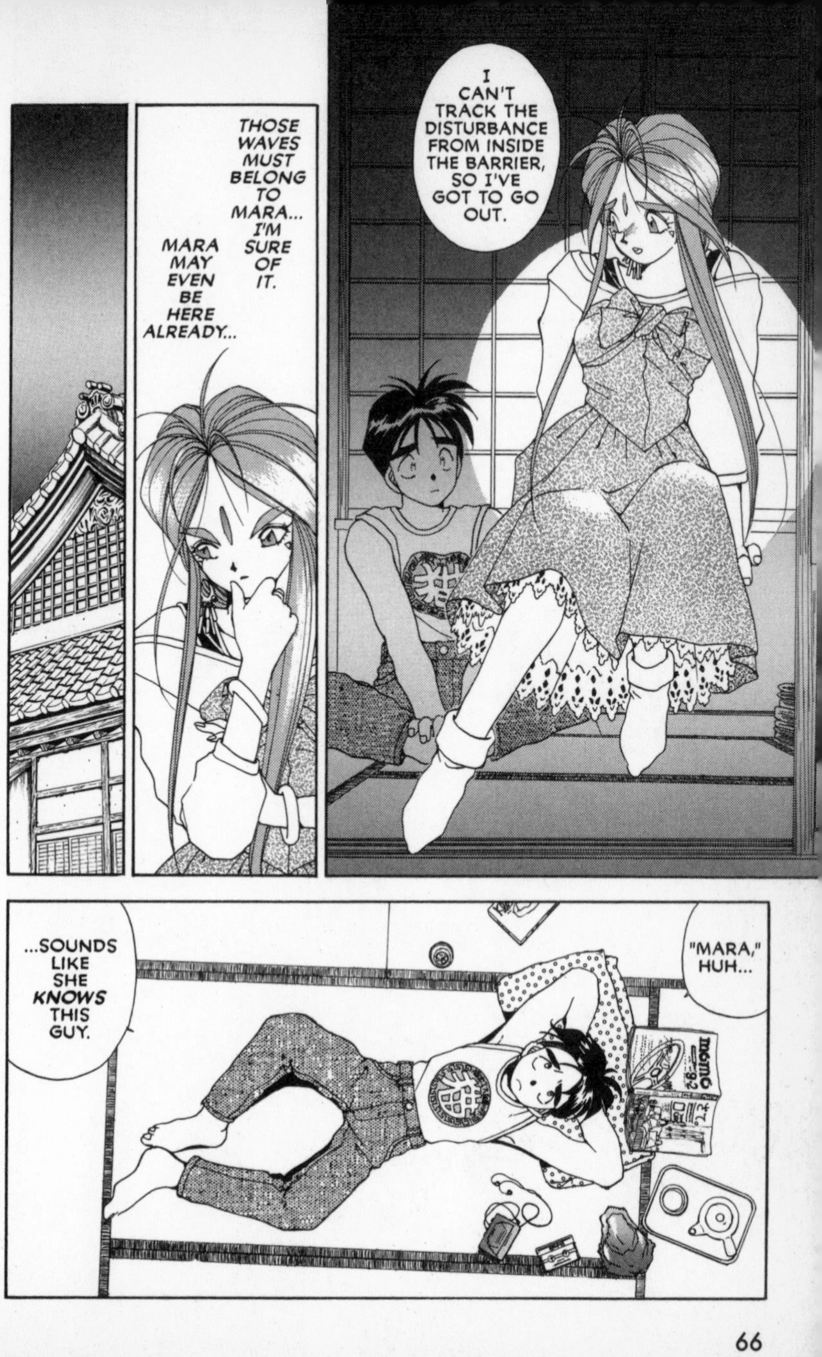
I CAN'T TRACK THE DISTURBANCE FROM INSIDE THE BARRIER, SO I'VE GOT TO GO OUT.
THOSE WAVES MUST BELONG TO MARA... I'M SURE OF IT.
MARA MAY EVEN BE HERE ALREADY...
"MARA," HUH...
...SOUNDS LIKE SHE *KNOWS* THIS GUY.

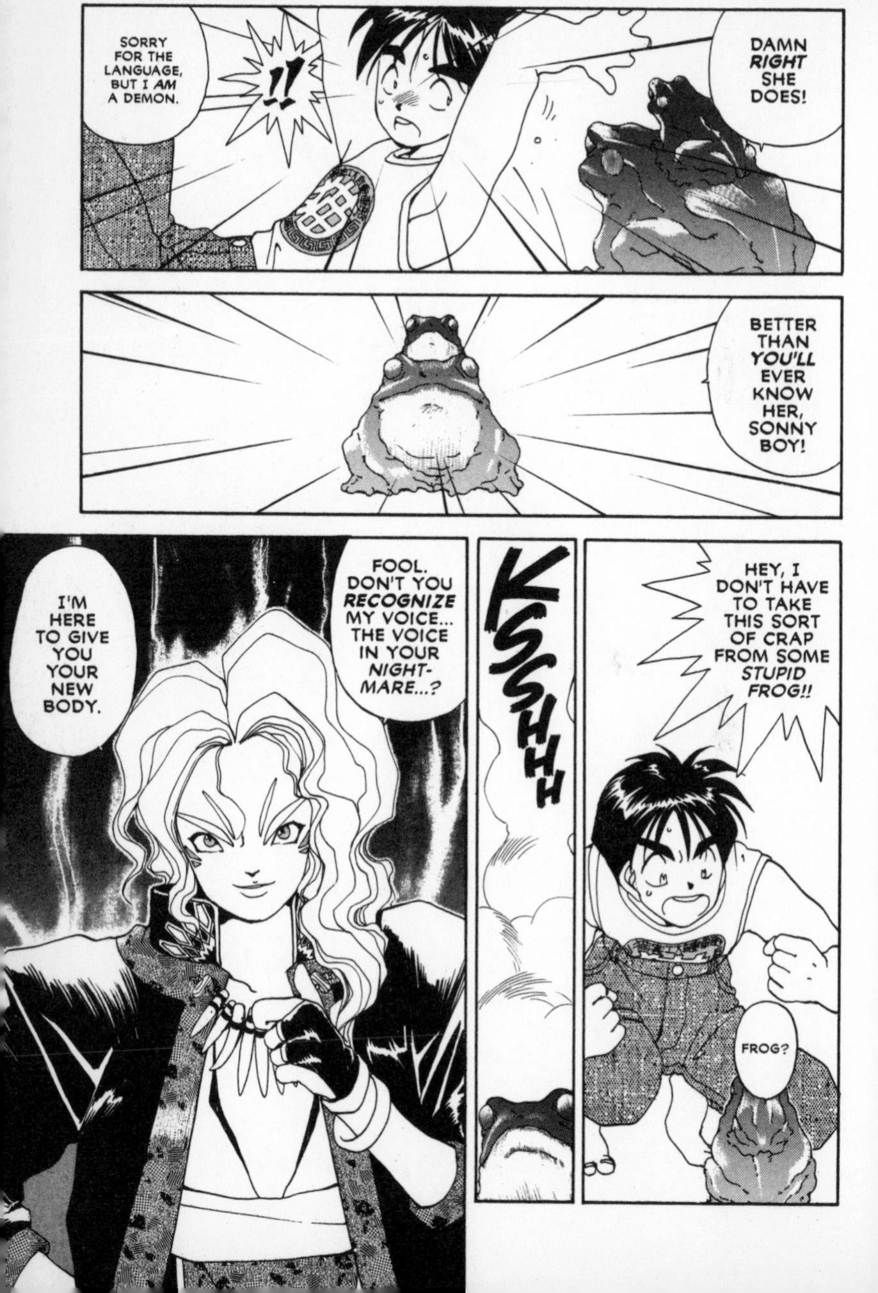
DAMN RIGHT SHE DOES!
!!
SORRY FOR THE LANGUAGE, BUT I AM A DEMON.
BETTER THAN YOU'LL EVER KNOW HER, SONNY BOY!
HEY, I DON'T HAVE TO TAKE THIS SORT OF CRAP FROM SOME STUPID FROG!!
FROG?
KSSHHH
FOOL. DON'T YOU RECOGNIZE MY VOICE... THE VOICE IN YOUR NIGHT-MARE...?
I'M HERE TO GIVE YOU YOUR NEW BODY.

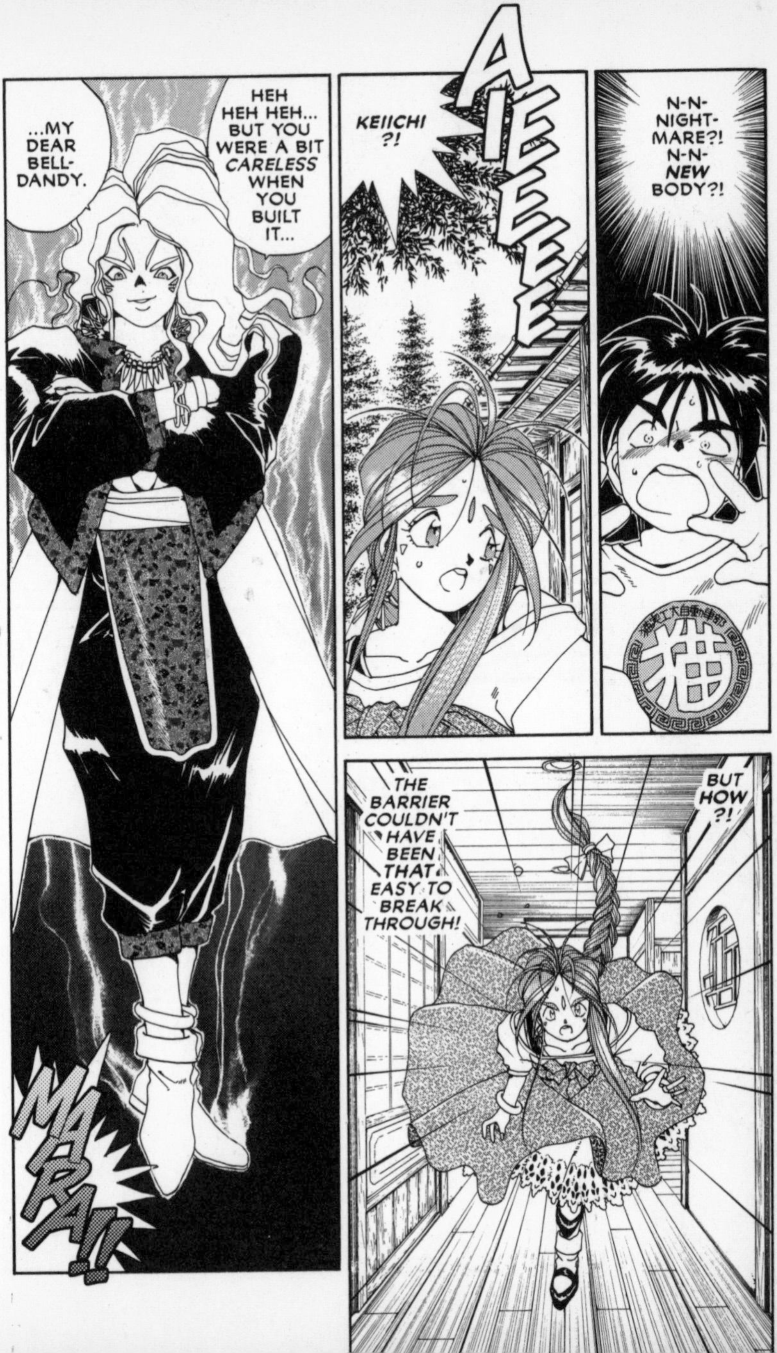
N-N-NIGHTMARE?! N-N-NEW BODY?!
AIEEEEE
KEIICHI?!
BUT HOW?!
THE BARRIER COULDN'T HAVE BEEN THAT EASY TO BREAK THROUGH!
HEH HEH HEH... BUT YOU WERE A BIT CARELESS WHEN YOU BUILT IT...
...MY DEAR BELLDANDY.
MARA!!

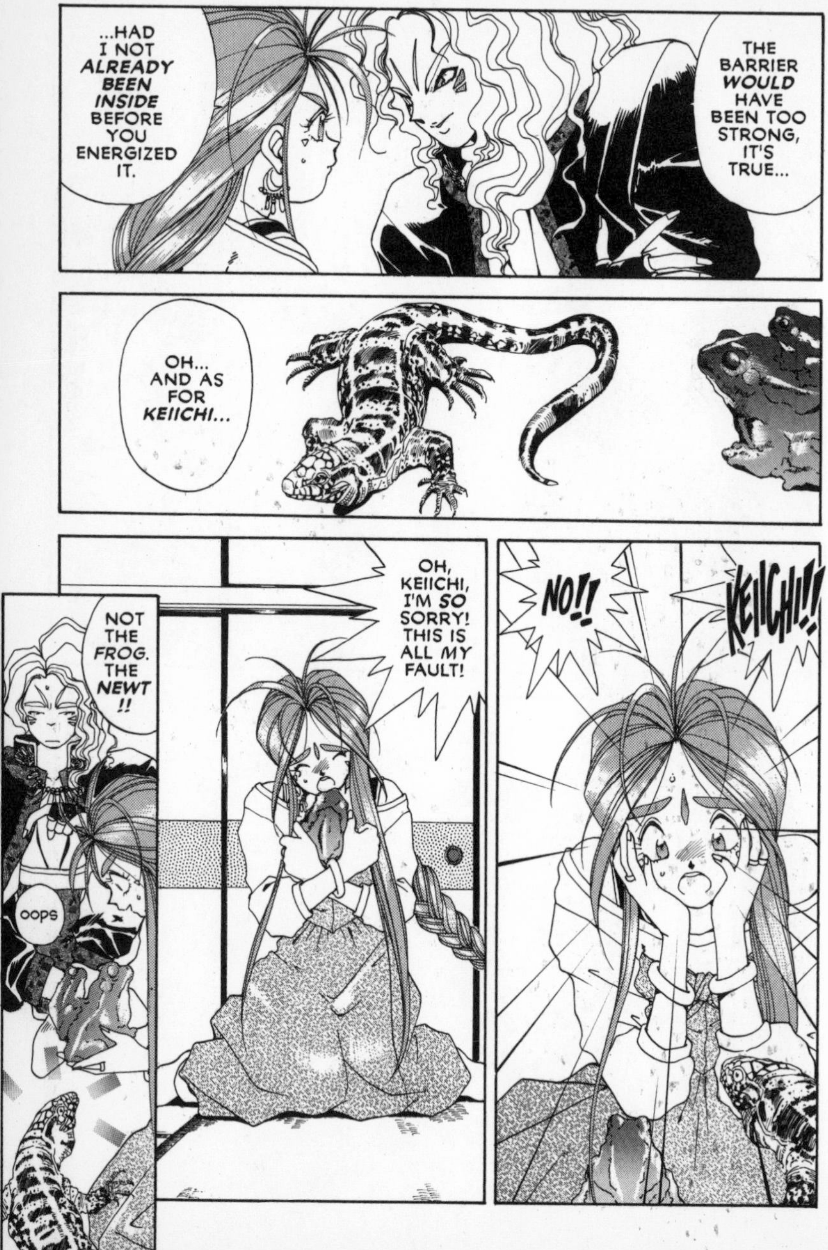
THE BARRIER WOULD HAVE BEEN TOO STRONG, IT'S TRUE...
...HAD I NOT ALREADY BEEN INSIDE BEFORE YOU ENERGIZED IT.
OH... AND AS FOR KEIICHI...
KEIICHI!!
NO!!
OH, KEIICHI, I'M SO SORRY! THIS IS ALL MY FAULT!
NOT THE FROG. THE NEWT!!
oops

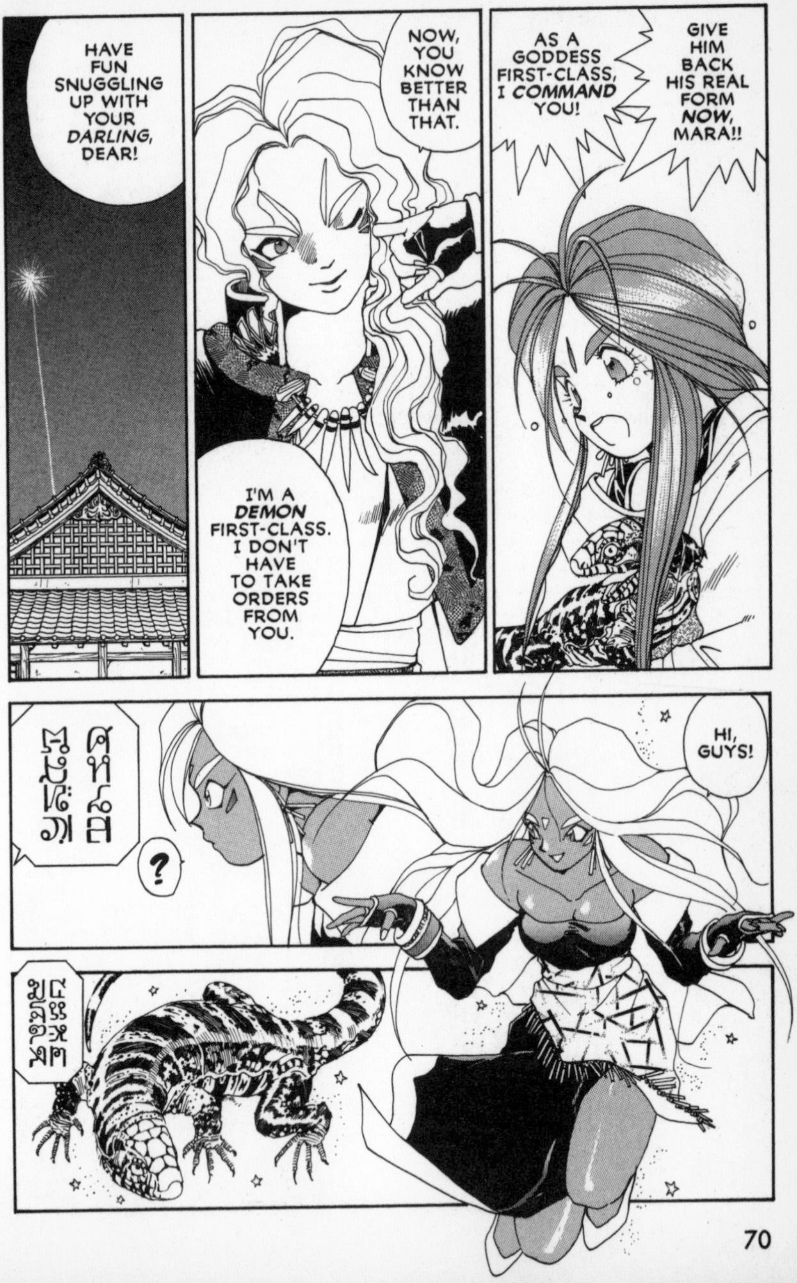
GIVE HIM BACK HIS REAL FORM *NOW*, MARA!!
AS A GODDESS FIRST-CLASS, I *COMMAND* YOU!
NOW, YOU KNOW BETTER THAN THAT.
I'M A ***DEMON*** FIRST-CLASS. I DON'T HAVE TO TAKE ORDERS FROM YOU.
HAVE FUN SNUGGLING UP WITH YOUR *DARLING*, DEAR!
HI, GUYS!
?

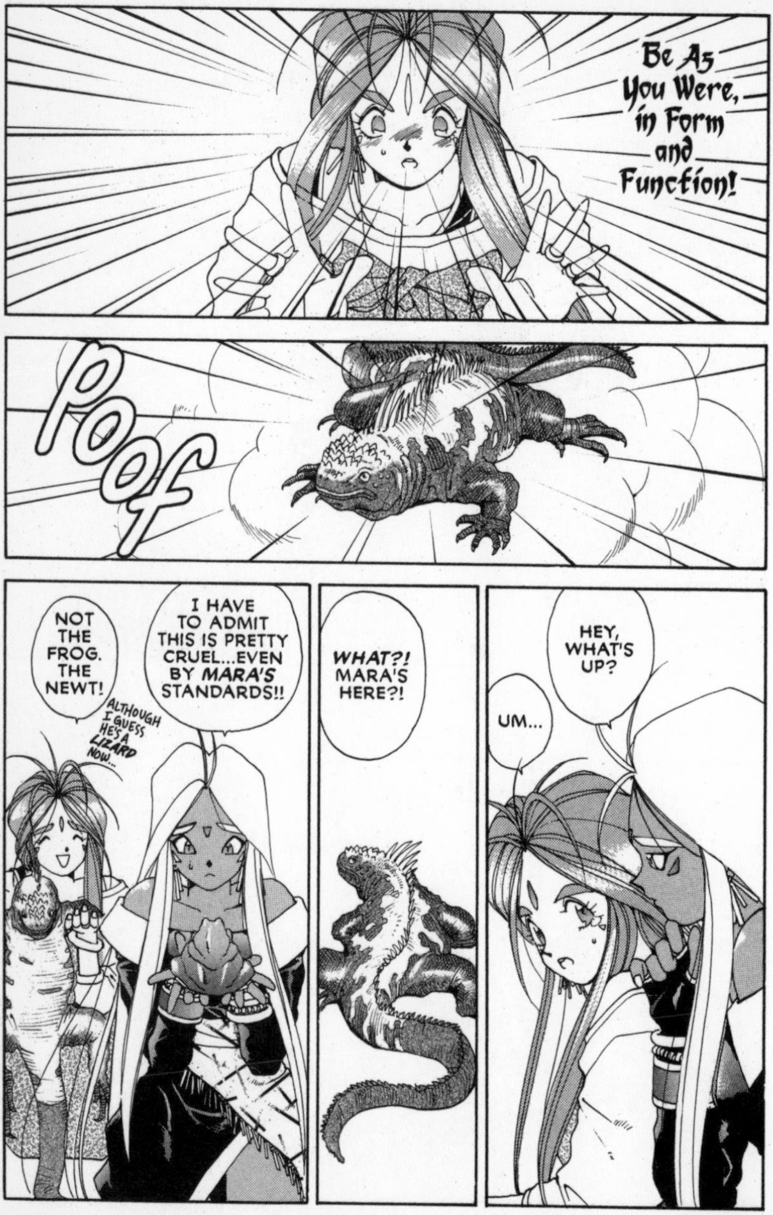

Be As You Were, in Form and Function!
poof
HEY, WHAT'S UP?
UM...
WHAT?! MARA'S HERE?!
I HAVE TO ADMIT THIS IS PRETTY CRUEL...EVEN BY *MARA'S* STANDARDS!!
NOT THE FROG. THE NEWT!
ALTHOUGH I GUESS HE'S A *LIZARD* NOW...

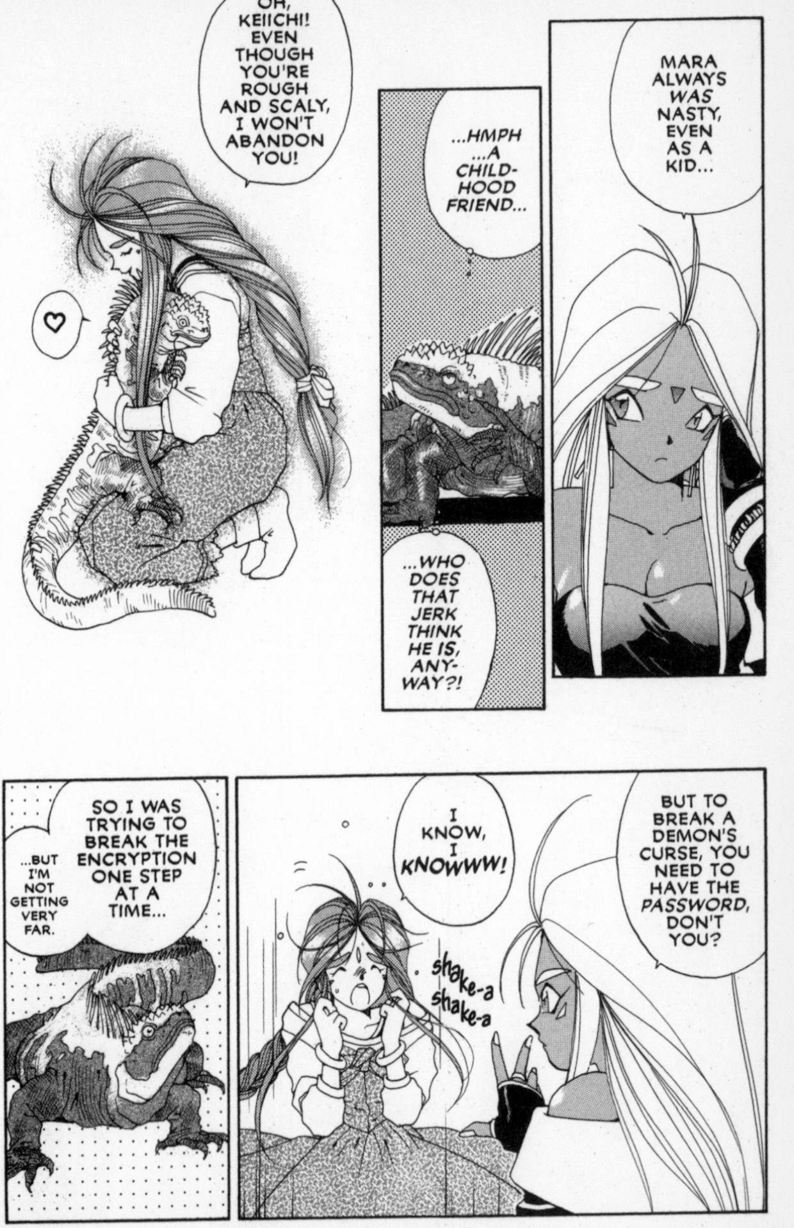
MARA ALWAYS *WAS* NASTY, EVEN AS A KID...
...*HMPH* ...*A CHILD-HOOD FRIEND...*
...*WHO DOES THAT JERK THINK HE IS, ANY-WAY?!*
OH, KEIICHI! EVEN THOUGH YOU'RE ROUGH AND SCALY, I WON'T ABANDON YOU!
♡
BUT TO BREAK A DEMON'S CURSE, YOU NEED TO HAVE THE *PASSWORD,* DON'T YOU?
I KNOW, I *KNOWWW!*
shake-a shake-a
SO I WAS TRYING TO BREAK THE ENCRYPTION ONE STEP AT A TIME...
...BUT I'M NOT GETTING VERY FAR.

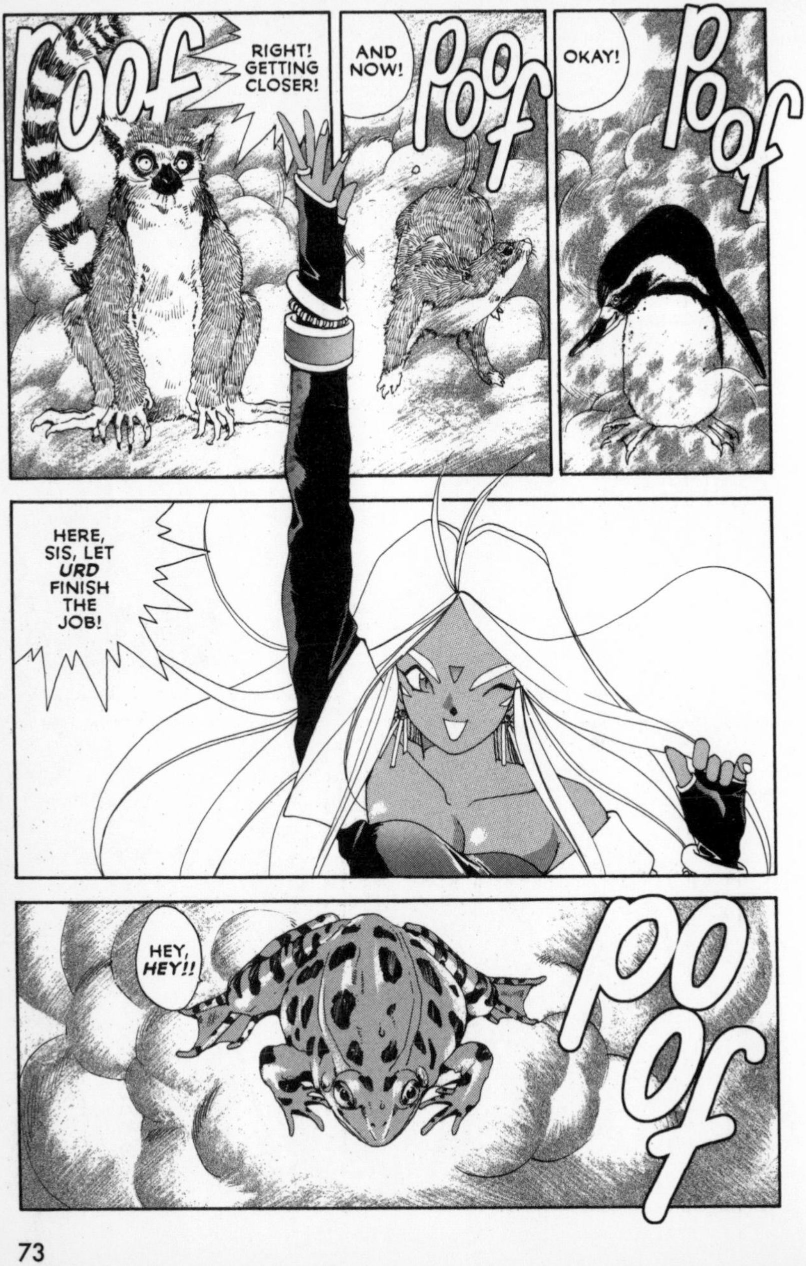
poof
OKAY!
poof
AND NOW!
RIGHT! GETTING CLOSER!
poof
HERE, SIS, LET URD FINISH THE JOB!
poof
HEY, HEY!!

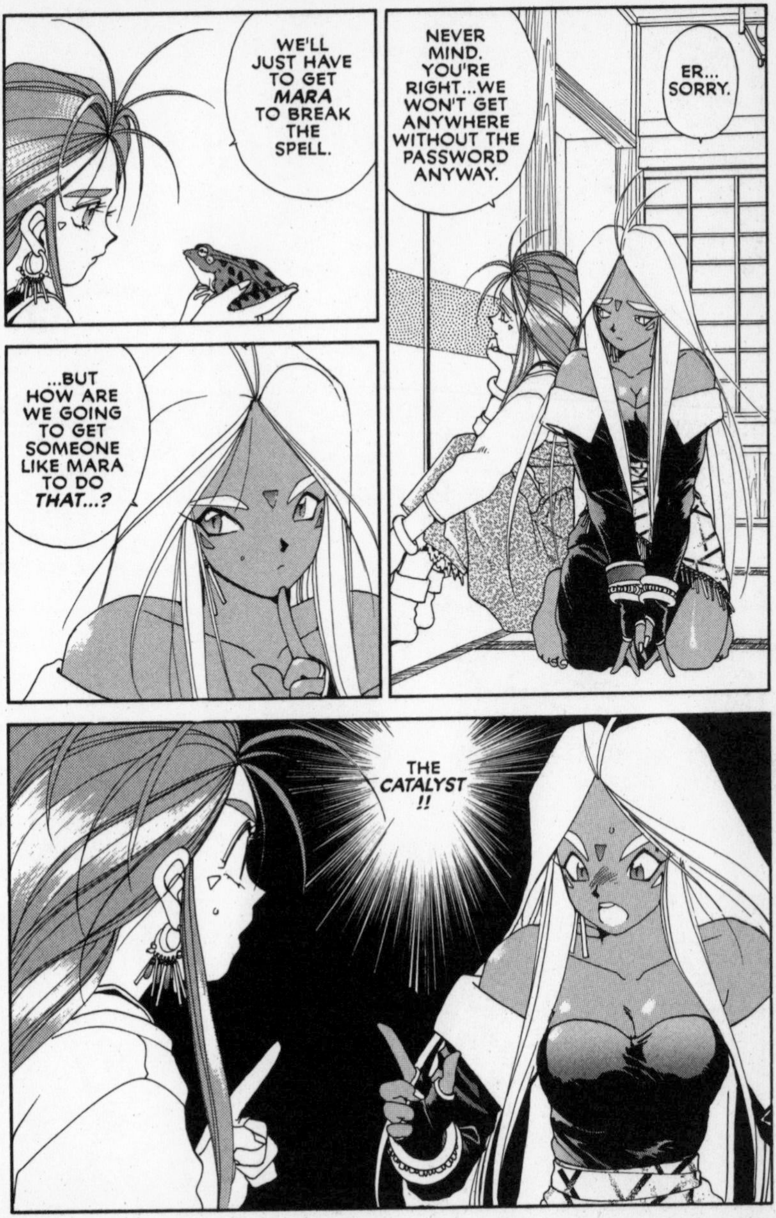
ER... SORRY.
NEVER MIND. YOU'RE RIGHT...WE WON'T GET ANYWHERE WITHOUT THE PASSWORD ANYWAY.
WE'LL JUST HAVE TO GET *MARA* TO BREAK THE SPELL.
...BUT HOW ARE WE GOING TO GET SOMEONE LIKE MARA TO DO *THAT...?*
THE *CATALYST* *!!*

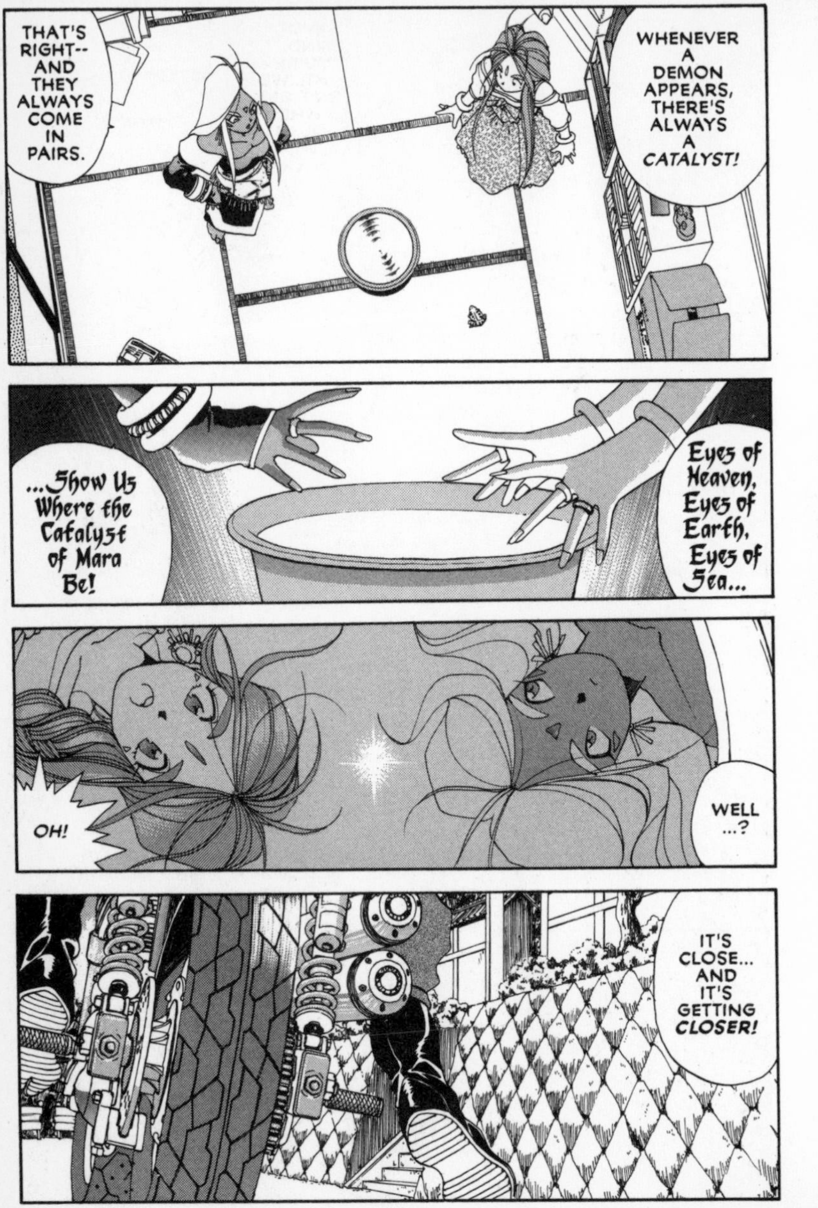
WHENEVER A DEMON APPEARS, THERE'S ALWAYS A *CATALYST!*
THAT'S RIGHT-- AND THEY ALWAYS COME IN PAIRS.
Eyes of Heaven, Eyes of Earth, Eyes of Sea...
...Show Us Where the Catalyst of Mara Be!
WELL ...?
OH!
IT'S CLOSE... AND IT'S GETTING *CLOSER!*

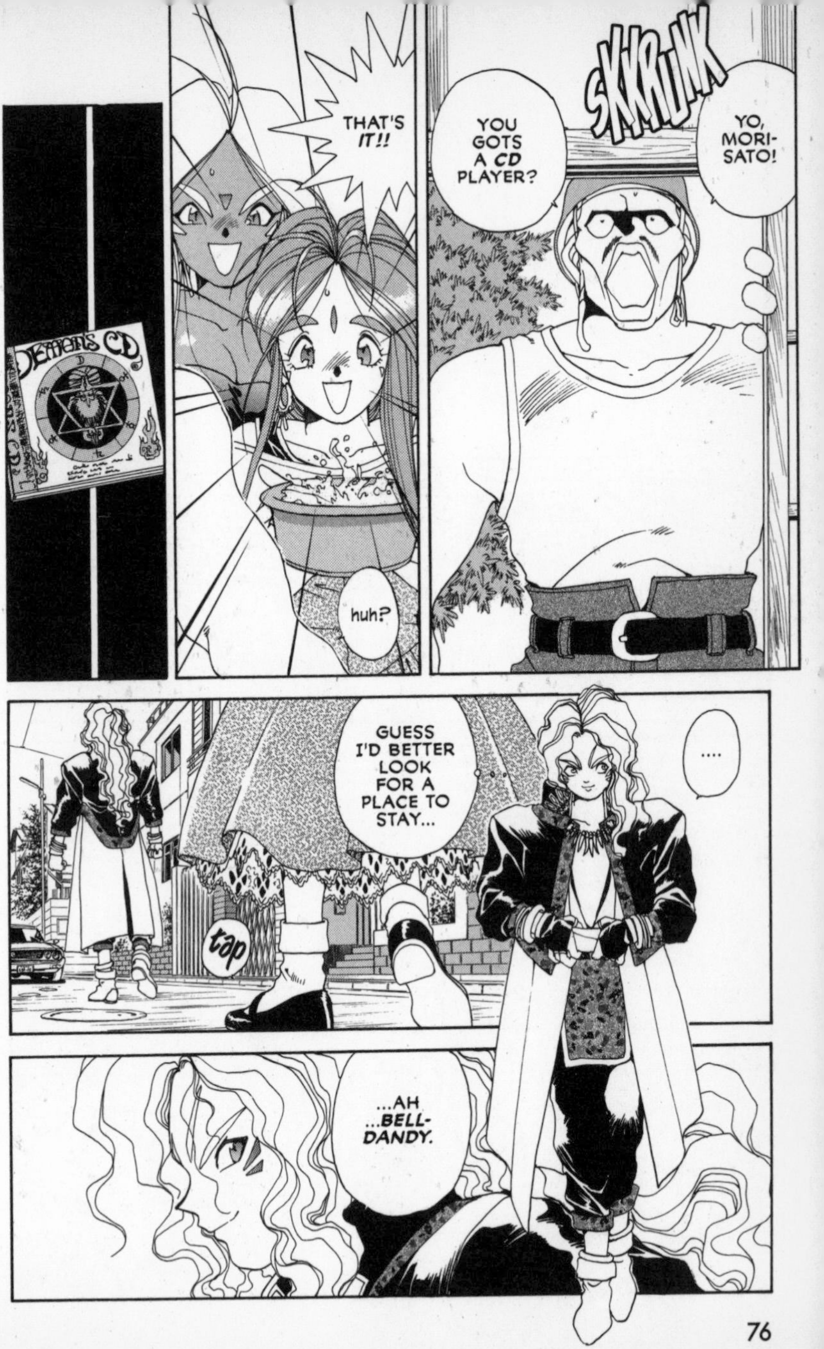
YO, MORI-SATO!
SKKRUNK
YOU GOTS A *CD* PLAYER?
THAT'S *IT!!*
huh?
DEMON'S CD
....
GUESS I'D BETTER LOOK FOR A PLACE TO STAY...
tap
...AH ...*BELL-DANDY.*

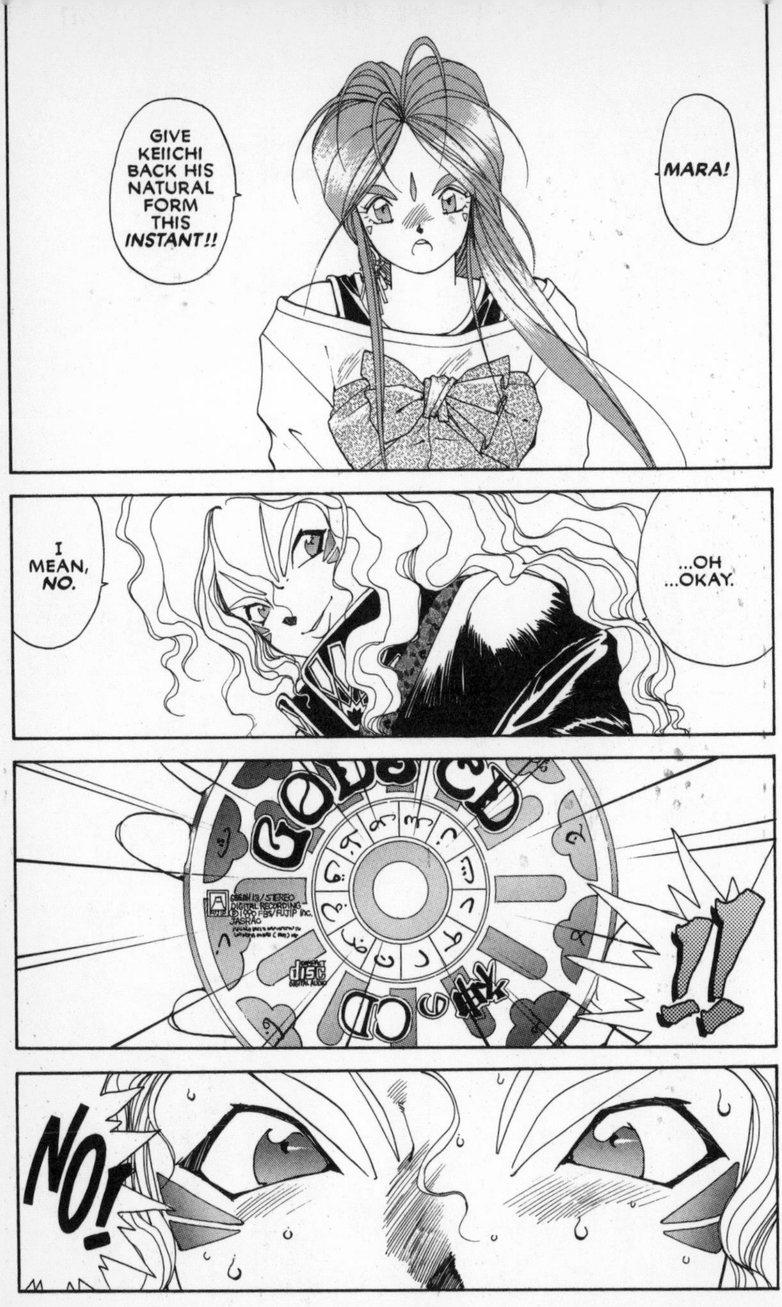
MARA!
GIVE KEIICHI BACK HIS NATURAL FORM THIS INSTANT!!
...OH ...OKAY.
I MEAN, NO.
!!
NO!

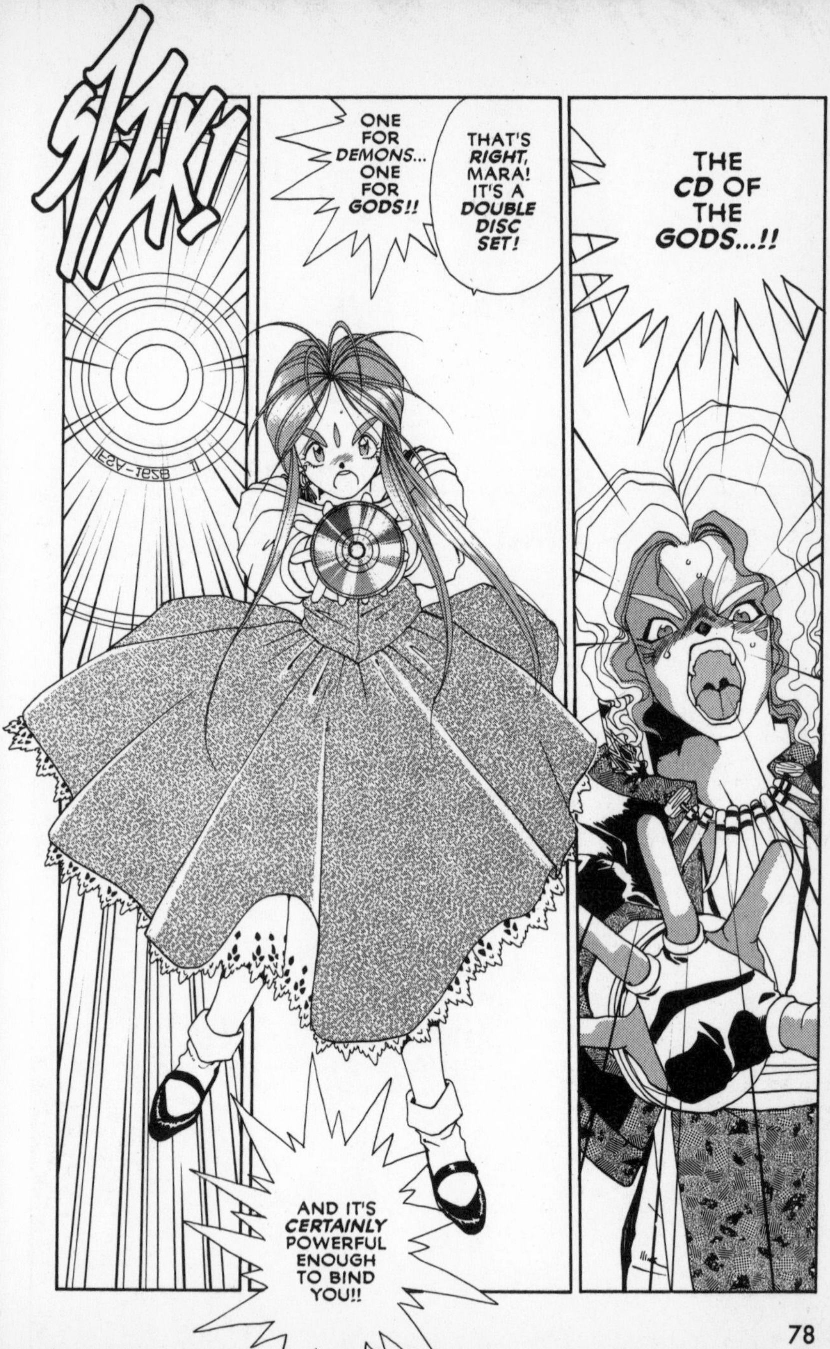
THE CD OF THE GODS...!!
ONE FOR DEMONS... ONE FOR GODS!!
THAT'S RIGHT, MARA! IT'S A DOUBLE DISC SET!
AND IT'S CERTAINLY POWERFUL ENOUGH TO BIND YOU!!
SHAKI!

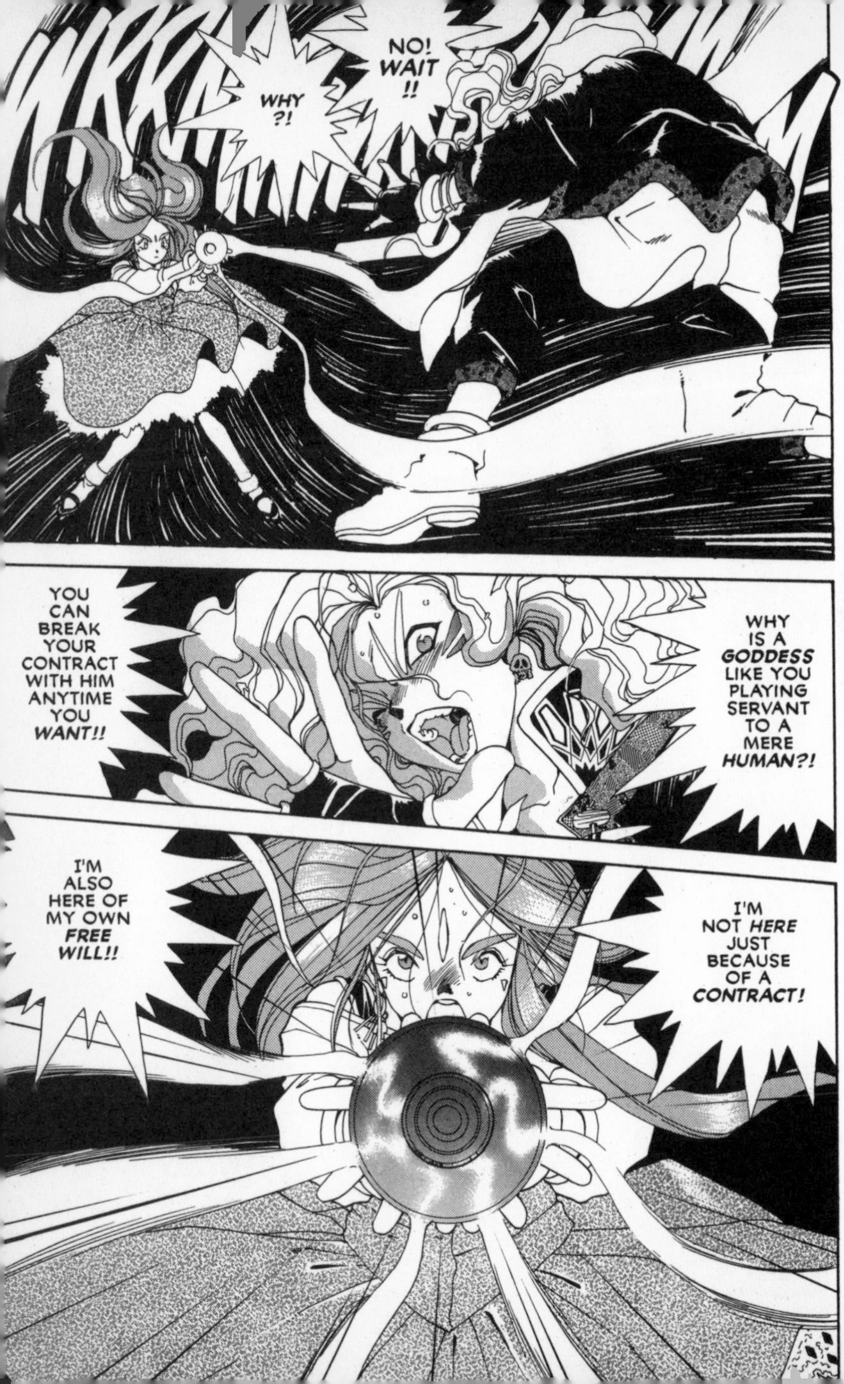
NO! WAIT!!
WHY?!
WHY IS A GODDESS LIKE YOU PLAYING SERVANT TO A MERE HUMAN?!
YOU CAN BREAK YOUR CONTRACT WITH HIM ANYTIME YOU WANT!!
I'M NOT HERE JUST BECAUSE OF A CONTRACT!
I'M ALSO HERE OF MY OWN FREE WILL!!

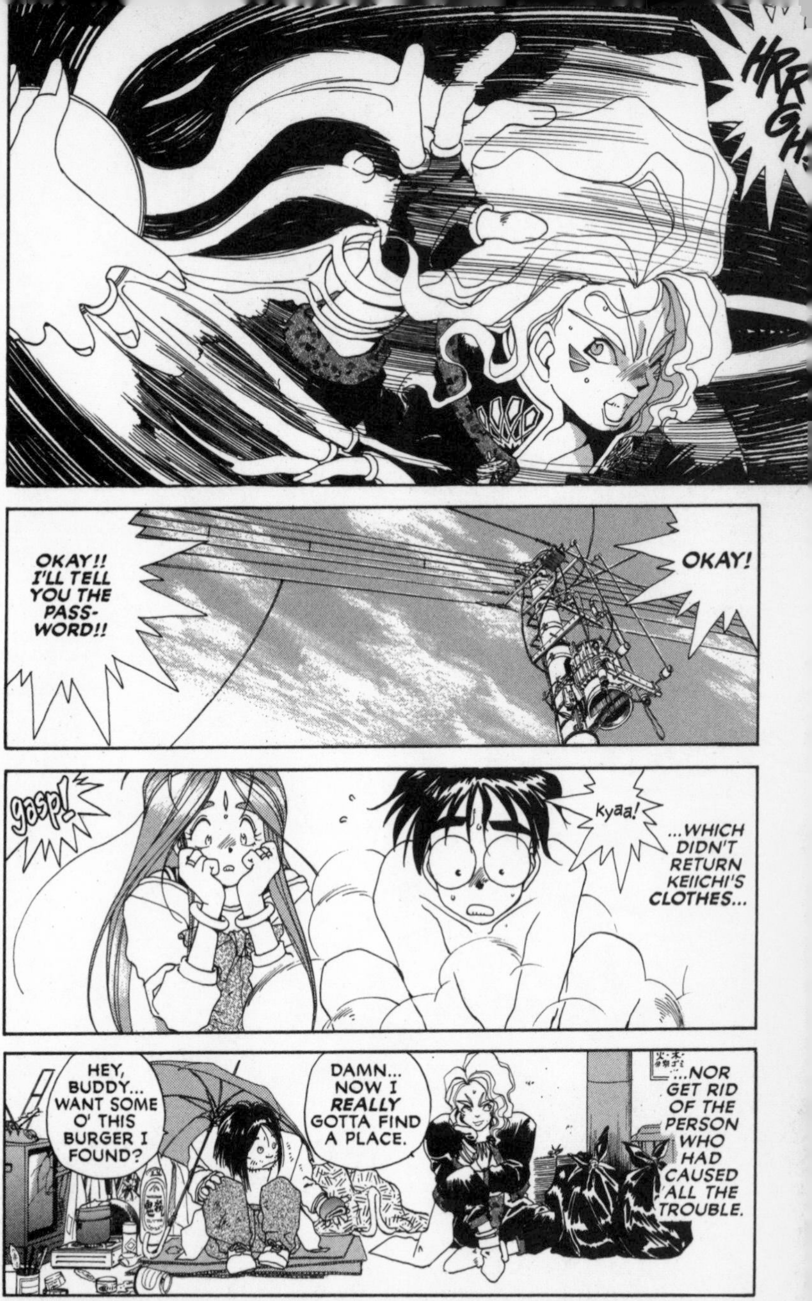
HRRRGH!
OKAY!
OKAY!! I'LL TELL YOU THE PASS-WORD!!
...WHICH DIDN'T RETURN KEIICHI'S CLOTHES...
kyaa!
gasp!
...NOR GET RID OF THE PERSON WHO HAD CAUSED ALL THE TROUBLE.
DAMN... NOW I *REALLY* GOTTA FIND A PLACE.
HEY, BUDDY... WANT SOME O' THIS BURGER I FOUND?

CHAPTER 27

Mara's Counterattack

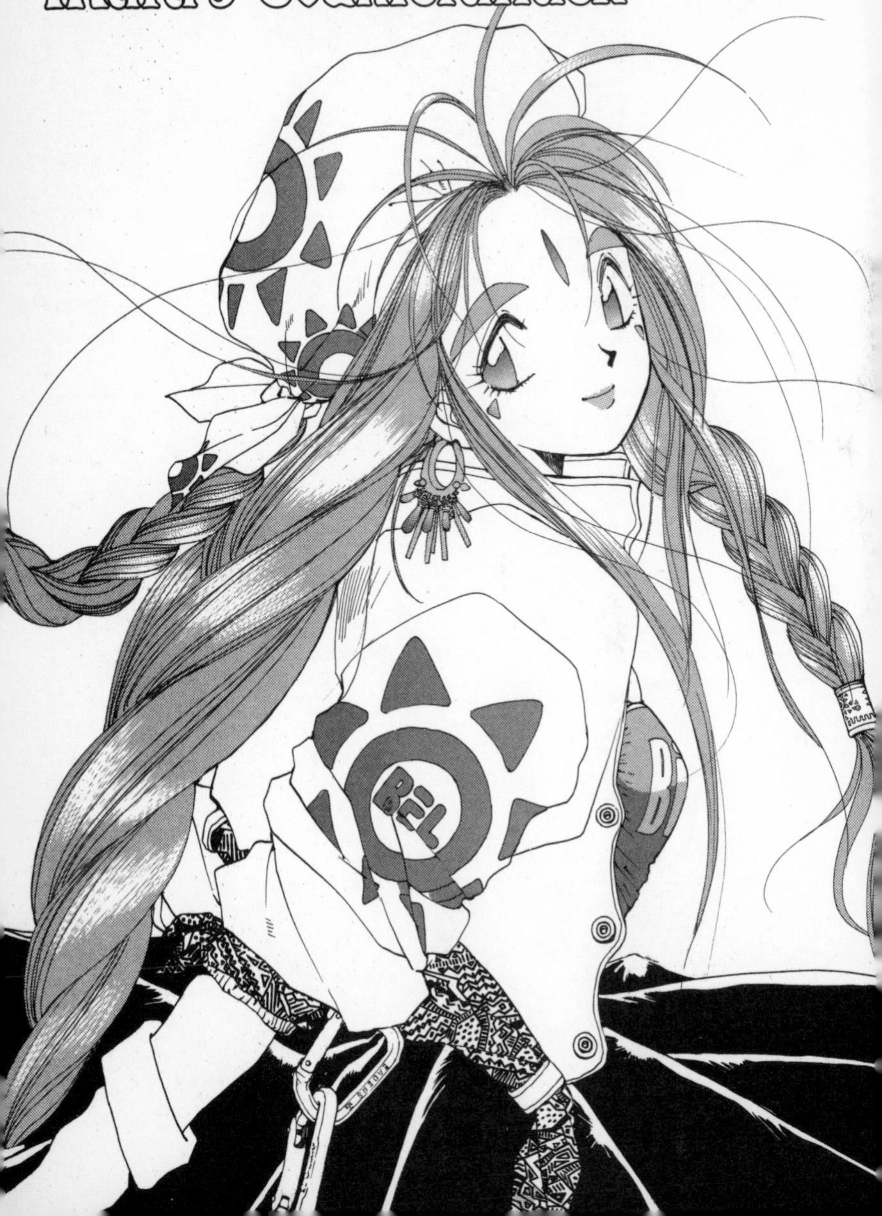

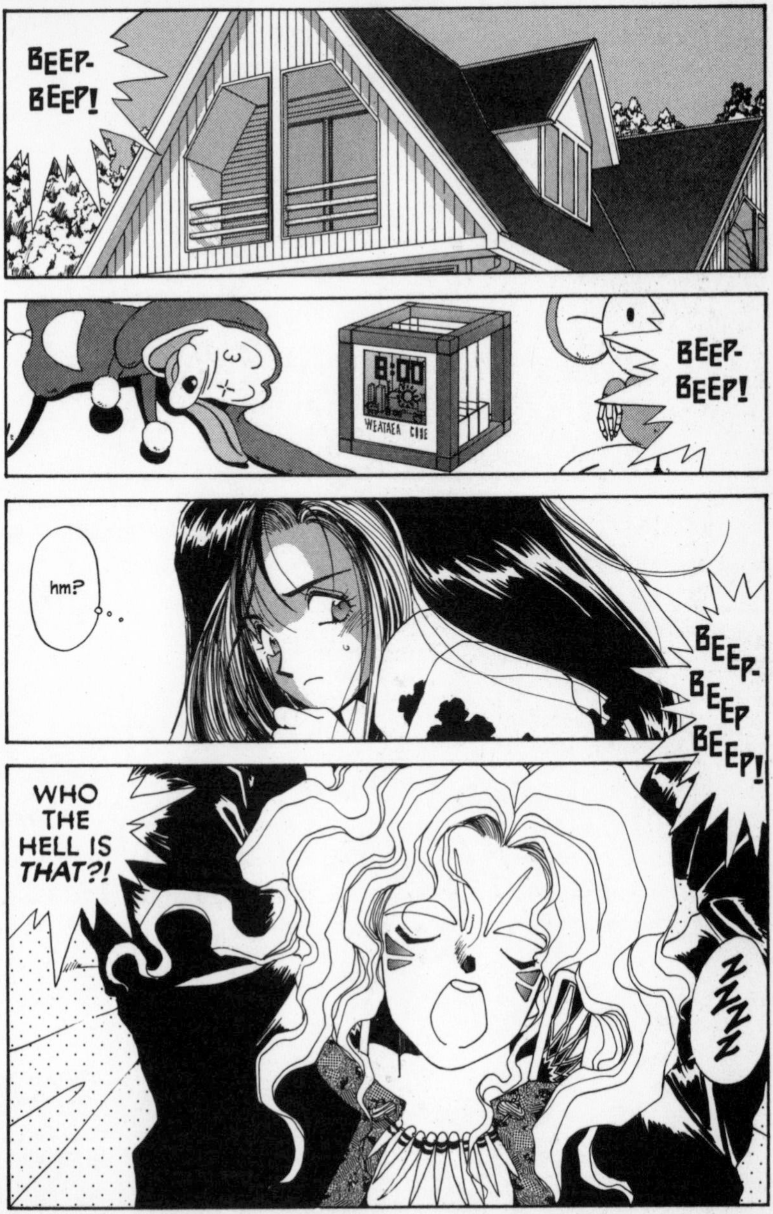
BEEP-BEEP!
BEEP-BEEP!
hm?
BEEP-BEEP BEEP BEEP!
ZZZZ
WHO THE HELL IS *THAT?!*

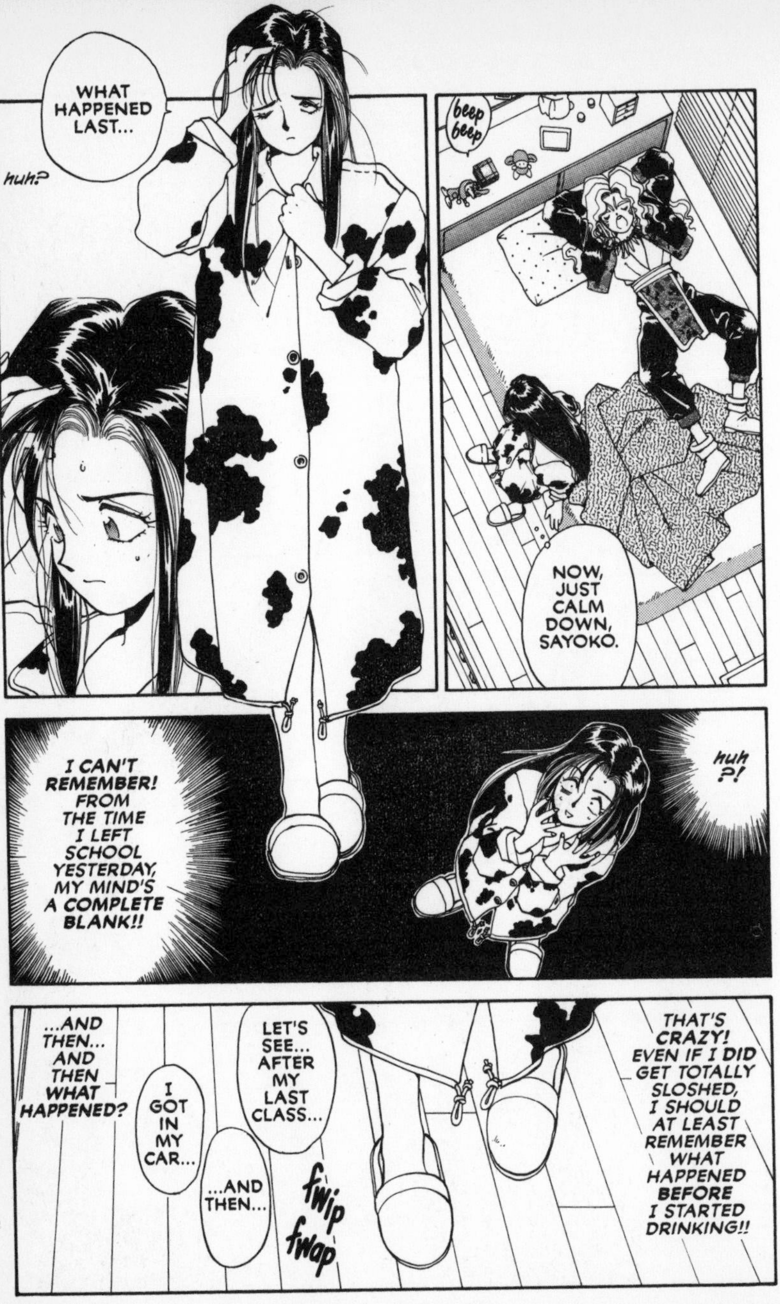
beep beep
NOW, JUST CALM DOWN, SAYOKO.
WHAT HAPPENED LAST...
huh?
huh ?!
I CAN'T REMEMBER! FROM THE TIME I LEFT SCHOOL YESTERDAY, MY MIND'S A COMPLETE BLANK!!
THAT'S CRAZY! EVEN IF I DID GET TOTALLY SLOSHED, I SHOULD AT LEAST REMEMBER WHAT HAPPENED BEFORE I STARTED DRINKING!!
fwip fwap
LET'S SEE... AFTER MY LAST CLASS...
I GOT IN MY CAR...
...AND THEN...
...AND THEN... AND THEN WHAT HAPPENED?

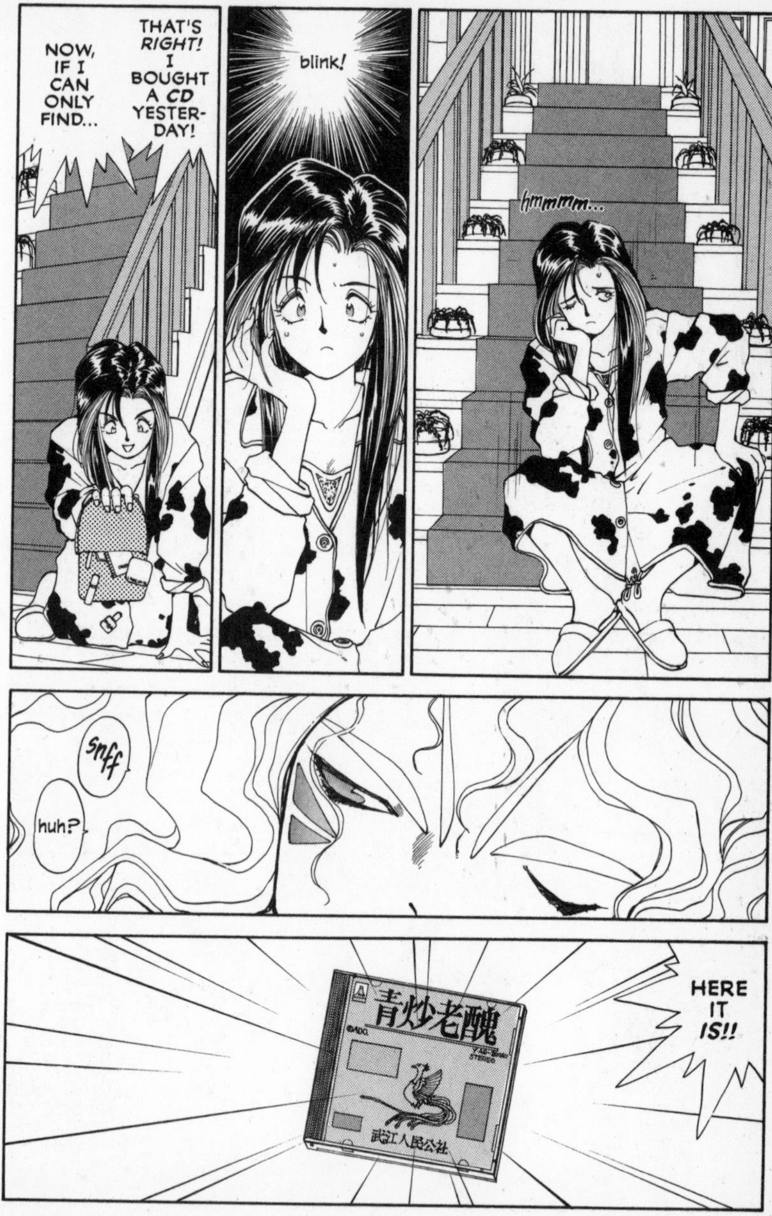
hmmmm...
blink!
THAT'S RIGHT! I BOUGHT A CD YESTER-DAY!
NOW, IF I CAN ONLY FIND...
snff
huh?
HERE IT IS!!
青炒老醜
武江人民公社

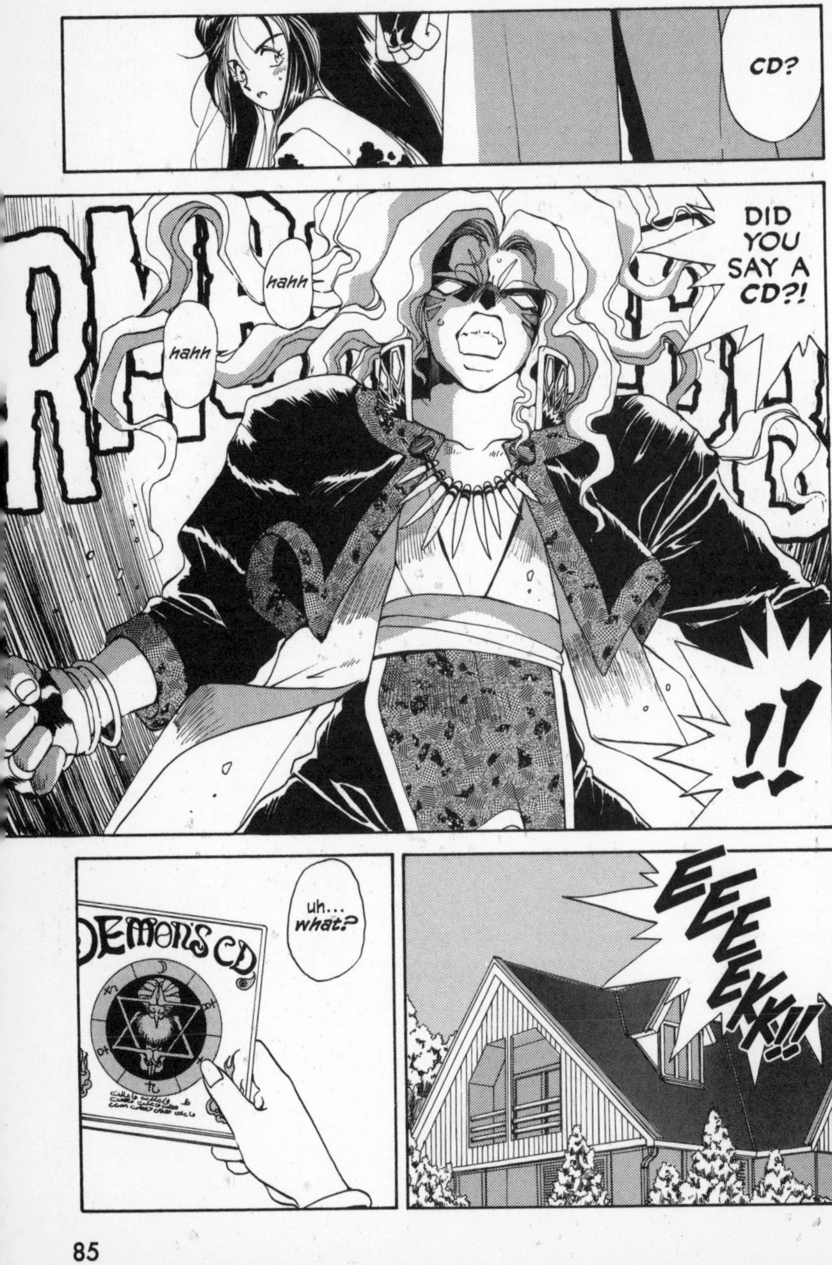
CD?
DID YOU SAY A CD?!
hahh
hahh
!!
EEEEKK!!
uh... what?
DEMON'S CD

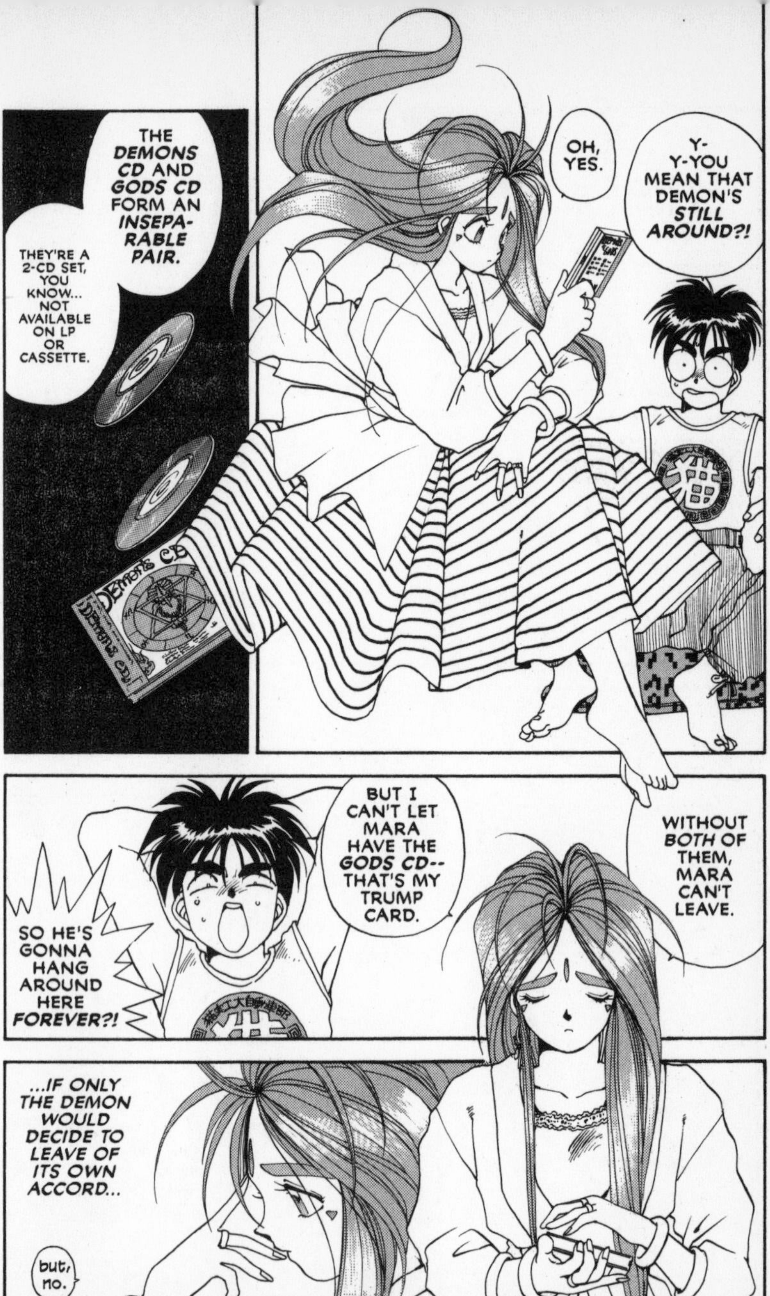
Y-Y-YOU MEAN THAT DEMON'S STILL AROUND?!
OH, YES.
THE DEMONS CD AND GODS CD FORM AN INSEPARABLE PAIR.
THEY'RE A 2-CD SET, YOU KNOW... NOT AVAILABLE ON LP OR CASSETTE.
WITHOUT BOTH OF THEM, MARA CAN'T LEAVE.
BUT I CAN'T LET MARA HAVE THE GODS CD-- THAT'S MY TRUMP CARD.
SO HE'S GONNA HANG AROUND HERE FOREVER?!
...IF ONLY THE DEMON WOULD DECIDE TO LEAVE OF ITS OWN ACCORD...
but, no.

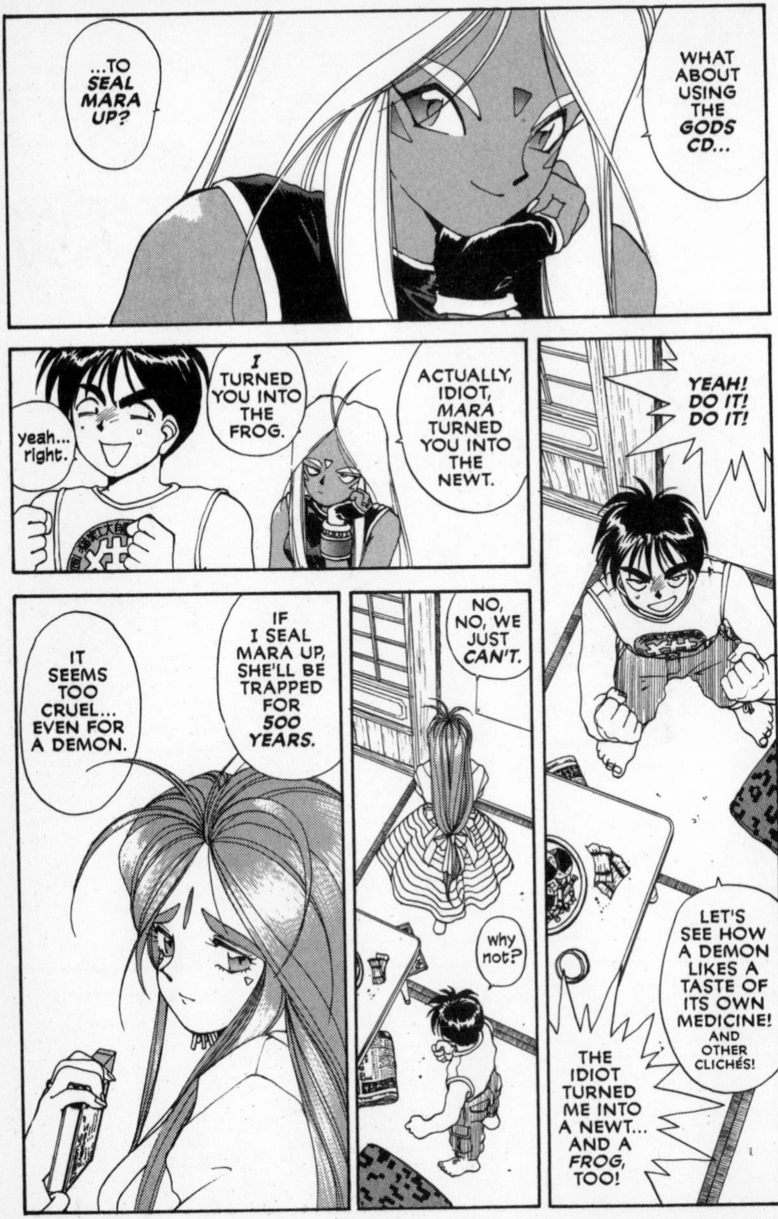
WHAT ABOUT USING THE GODS CD...
...TO SEAL MARA UP?
YEAH! DO IT! DO IT!
LET'S SEE HOW A DEMON LIKES A TASTE OF ITS OWN MEDICINE! AND OTHER CLICHÉS!
THE IDIOT TURNED ME INTO A NEWT... AND A FROG, TOO!
ACTUALLY, IDIOT, MARA TURNED YOU INTO THE NEWT.
I TURNED YOU INTO THE FROG.
yeah... right.
NO, NO, WE JUST CAN'T.
why not?
IF I SEAL MARA UP, SHE'LL BE TRAPPED FOR 500 YEARS.
IT SEEMS TOO CRUEL... EVEN FOR A DEMON.

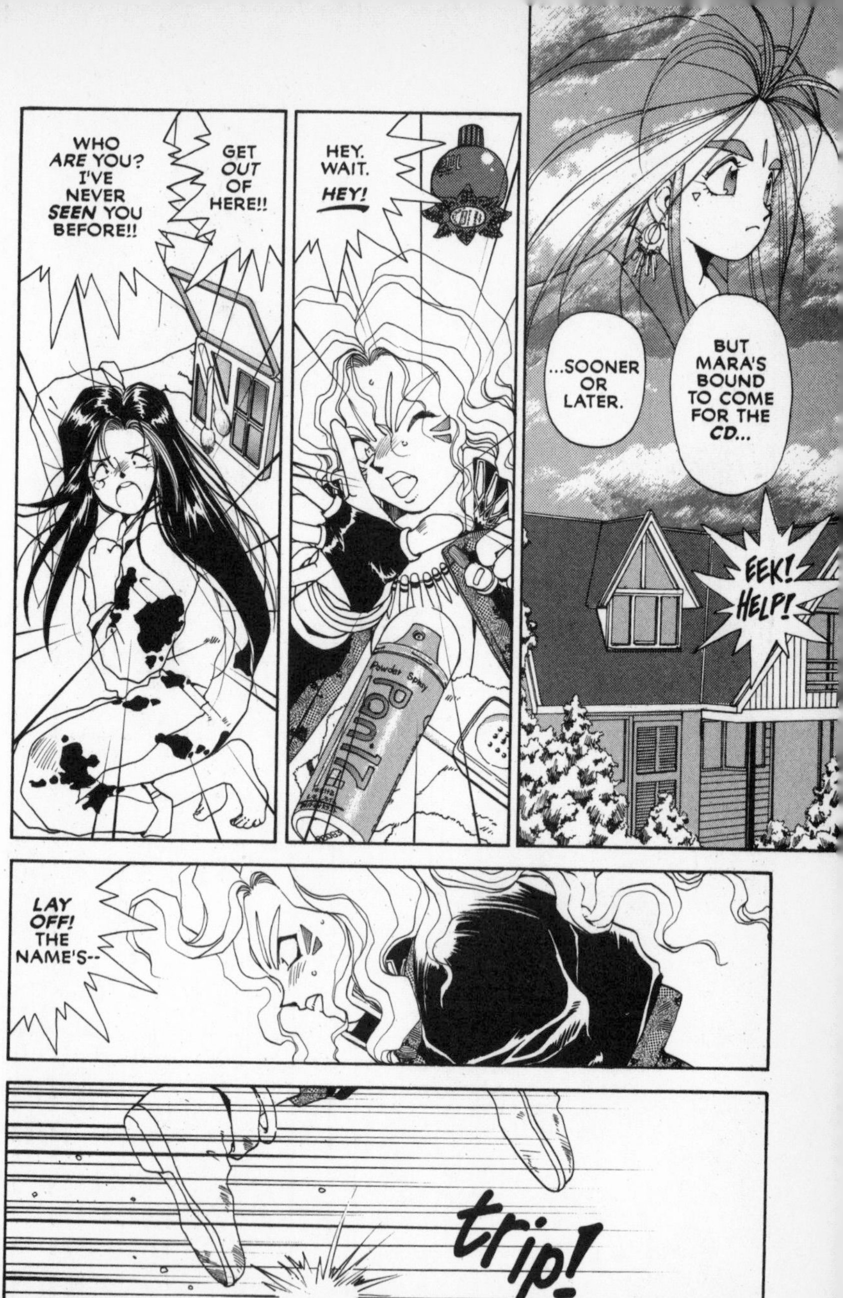
BUT MARA'S BOUND TO COME FOR THE *CD*...
...SOONER OR LATER.
EEK! HELP!
HEY. WAIT. ***HEY!***
GET *OUT* OF HERE!!
WHO *ARE* YOU? I'VE NEVER *SEEN* YOU BEFORE!!
Powder Spray
LAY OFF! THE NAME'S--
trip!

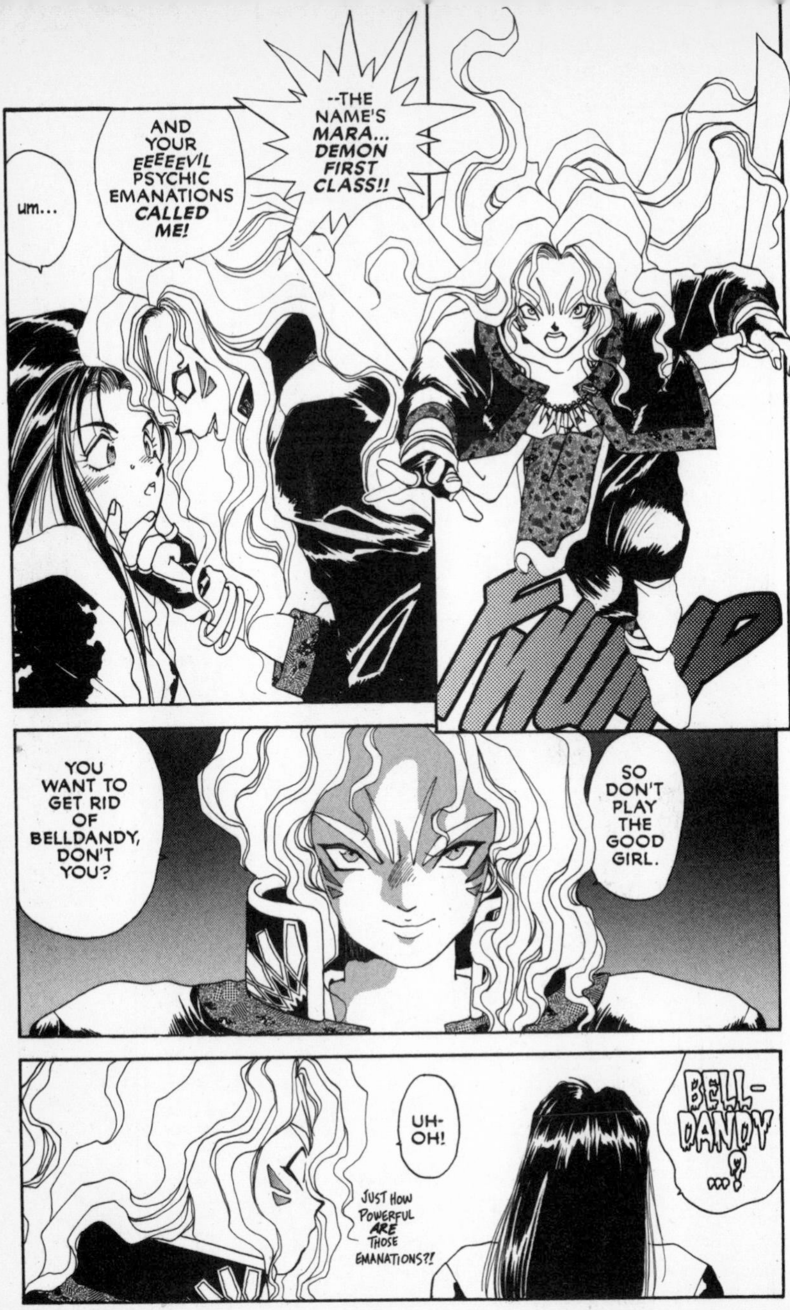
--THE NAME'S MARA... DEMON FIRST CLASS!!
AND YOUR EEEEEVIL PSYCHIC EMANATIONS CALLED ME!
um...
SO DON'T PLAY THE GOOD GIRL.
YOU WANT TO GET RID OF BELLDANDY, DON'T YOU?
BELL-DANDY...?!
UH-OH!
JUST HOW POWERFUL ARE THOSE EMANATIONS?!

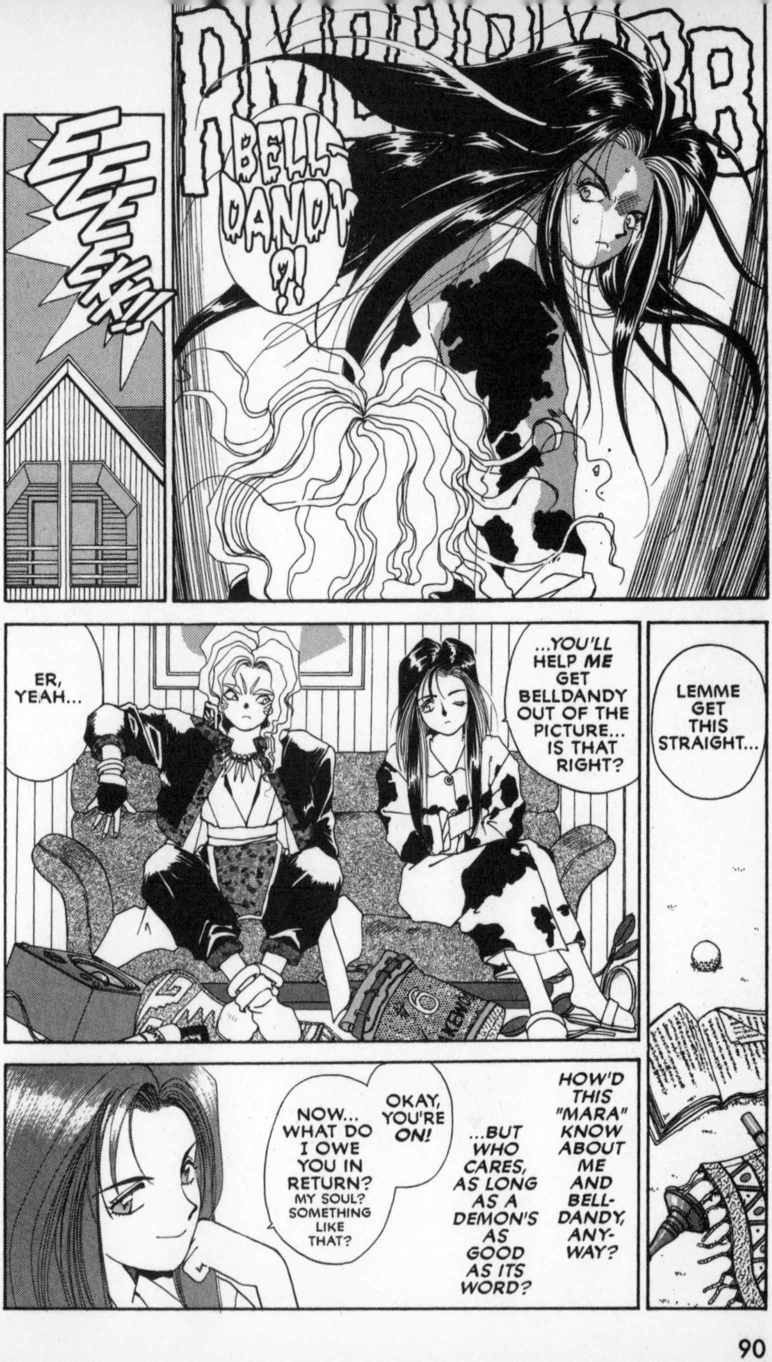
BELL-DANDY?!
EEEEEKK!!
LEMME GET THIS STRAIGHT...
...YOU'LL HELP ME GET BELLDANDY OUT OF THE PICTURE... IS THAT RIGHT?
ER, YEAH...
HOW'D THIS "MARA" KNOW ABOUT ME AND BELL-DANDY, ANY-WAY?
...BUT WHO CARES, AS LONG AS A DEMON'S AS GOOD AS ITS WORD?
OKAY, YOU'RE ON!
NOW... WHAT DO I OWE YOU IN RETURN? MY SOUL? SOMETHING LIKE THAT?

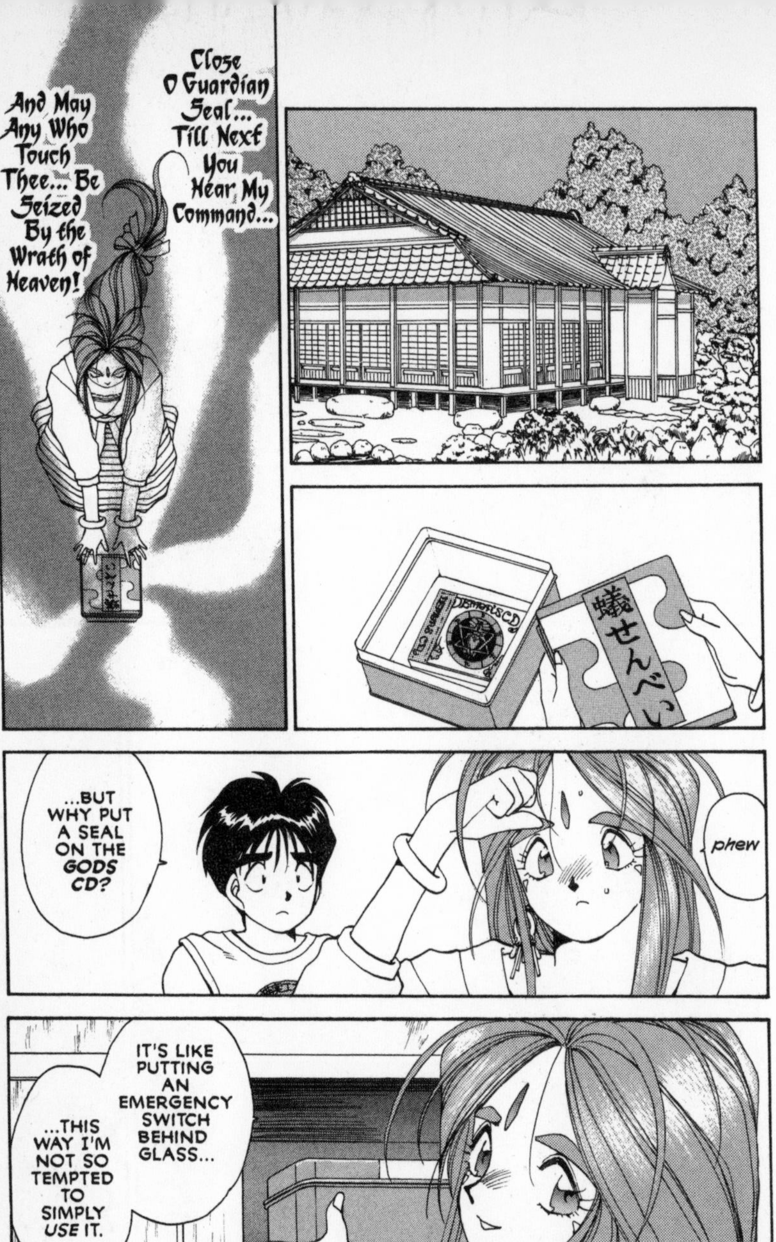
DEMONS CD
蟻せんべい
Close O Guardian Seal... Till Next You Hear My Command...
And May Any Who Touch Thee... Be Seized By the Wrath of Heaven!
phew
...BUT WHY PUT A SEAL ON THE GODS CD?
IT'S LIKE PUTTING AN EMERGENCY SWITCH BEHIND GLASS...
...THIS WAY I'M NOT SO TEMPTED TO SIMPLY USE IT.

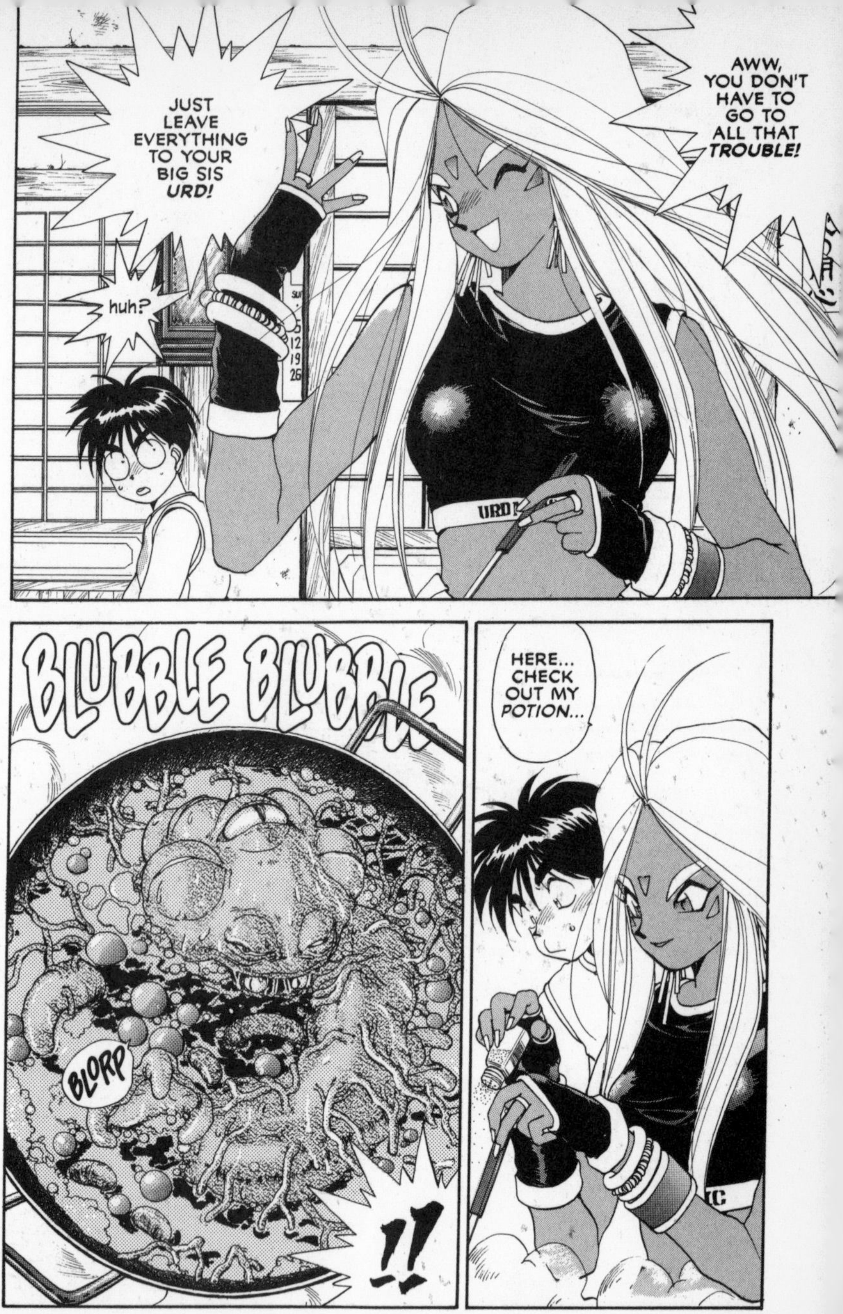
AWW, YOU DON'T HAVE TO GO TO ALL THAT *TROUBLE!*
JUST LEAVE EVERYTHING TO YOUR BIG SIS *URD!*
huh?
HERE... CHECK OUT MY *POTION*...
BLUBBLE BLUBBLE
BLORP
!!

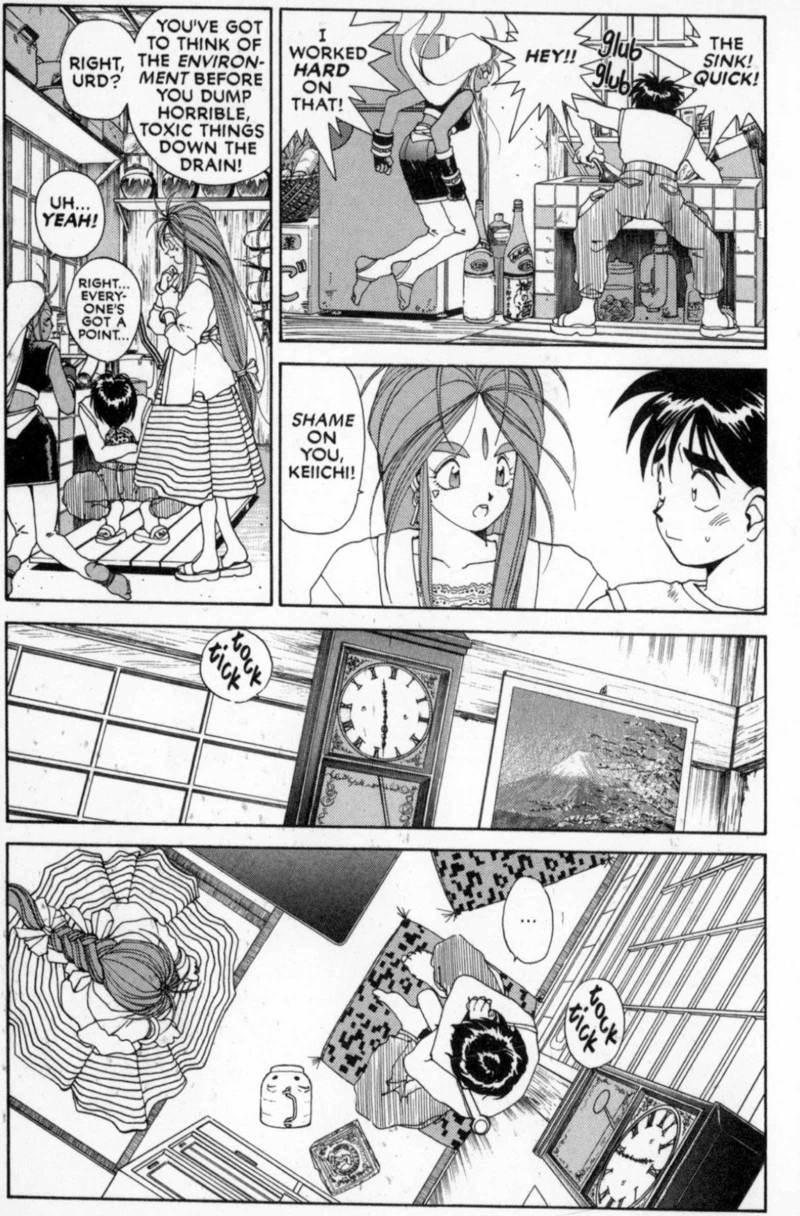
THE SINK! QUICK!
glub glub
HEY!!
I WORKED HARD ON THAT!
SHAME ON YOU, KEIICHI!
YOU'VE GOT TO THINK OF THE ENVIRONMENT BEFORE YOU DUMP HORRIBLE, TOXIC THINGS DOWN THE DRAIN!
RIGHT, URD?
UH... YEAH!
RIGHT... EVERYONE'S GOT A POINT...
tock tick
...
tock tick

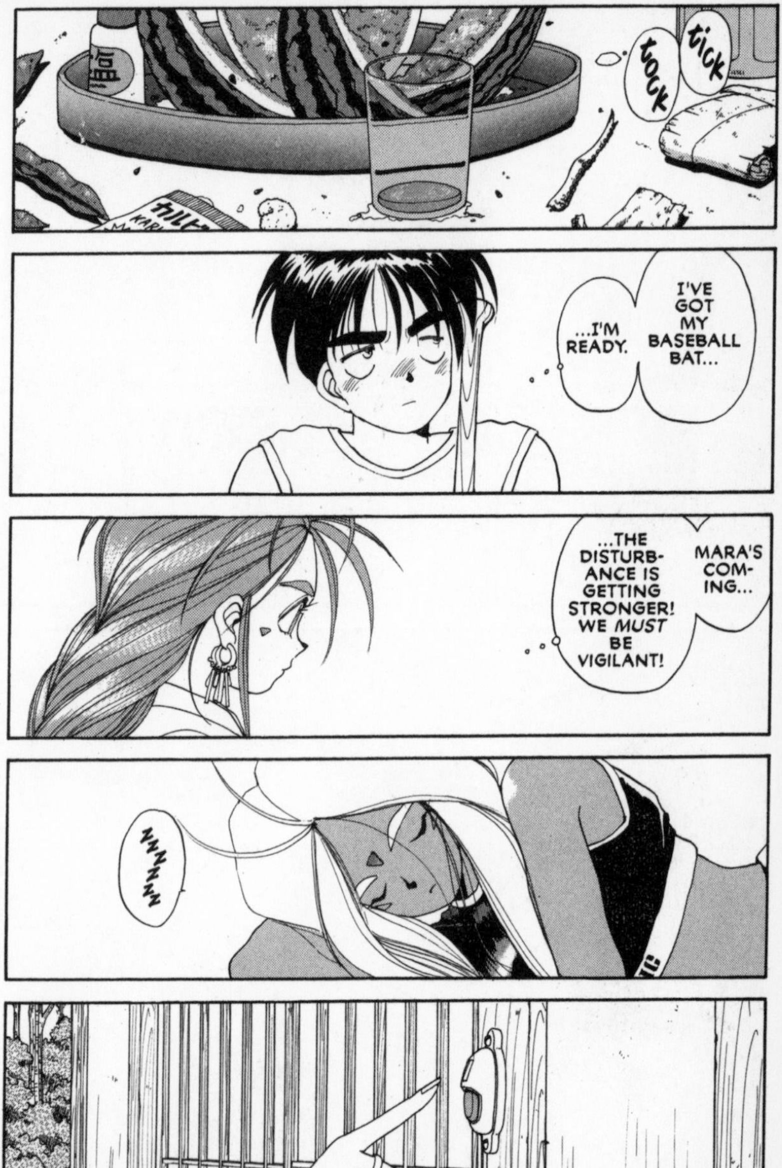

tick
tock
I'VE GOT MY BASEBALL BAT...
...I'M READY.
MARA'S COMING...
...THE DISTURBANCE IS GETTING STRONGER! WE *MUST* BE VIGILANT!
NNNNN

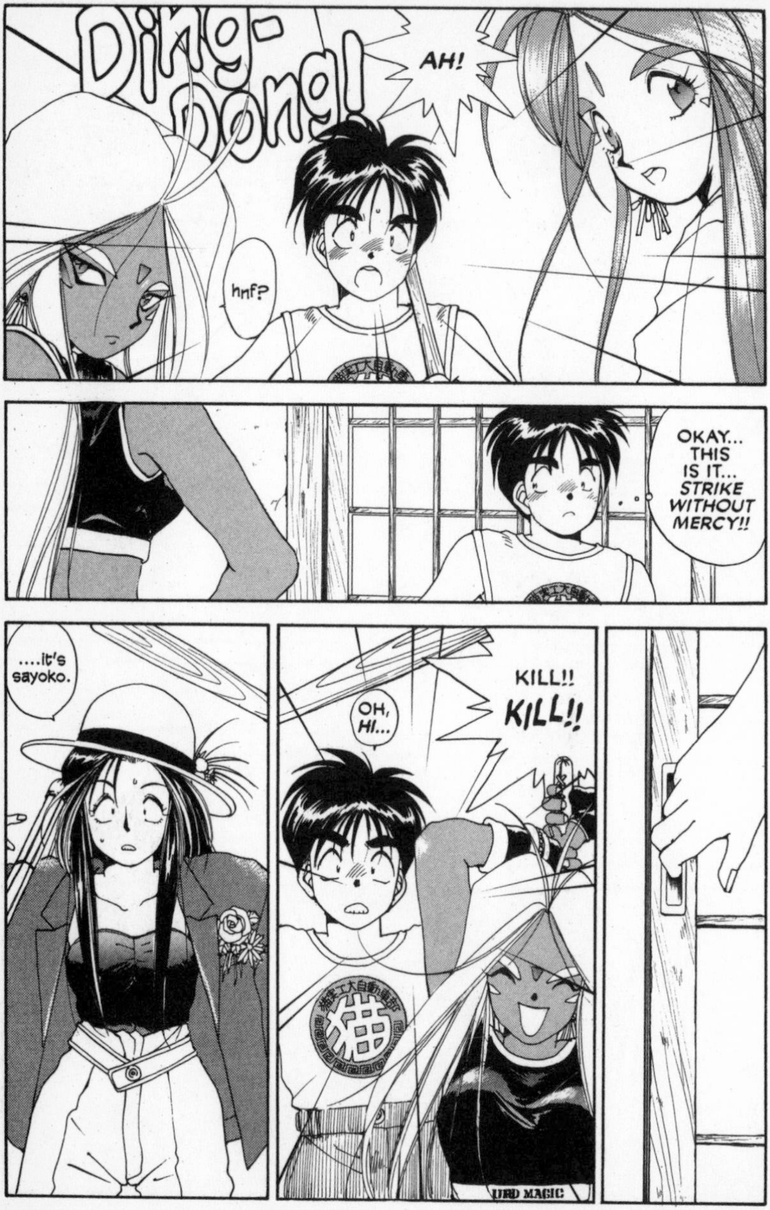
AH!
Ding-Dong!
hnf?
OKAY... THIS IS IT... STRIKE WITHOUT MERCY!!
KILL!! KILL!!
OH, HI...
URD MAGIC
....it's sayoko.

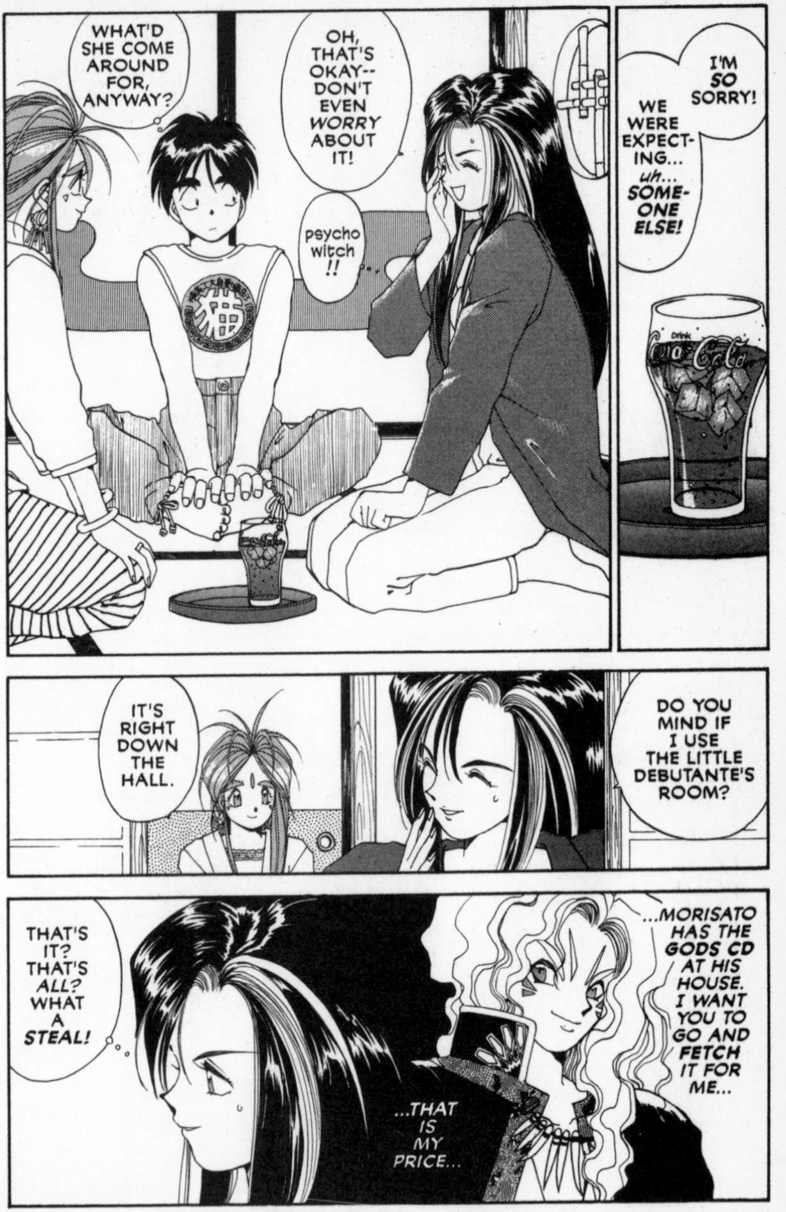
I'M *SO* SORRY!
WE WERE EXPECTING... *uh...* SOMEONE ELSE!
Drink Coca-Cola
OH, THAT'S OKAY-- DON'T EVEN *WORRY* ABOUT IT!
WHAT'D SHE COME AROUND FOR, ANYWAY?
psycho witch!!
DO YOU MIND IF I USE THE LITTLE DEBUTANTE'S ROOM?
IT'S RIGHT DOWN THE HALL.
...MORISATO HAS THE GODS CD AT HIS HOUSE. I WANT YOU TO GO AND FETCH IT FOR ME...
...THAT IS MY PRICE...
THAT'S IT? THAT'S *ALL?* WHAT A *STEAL!*

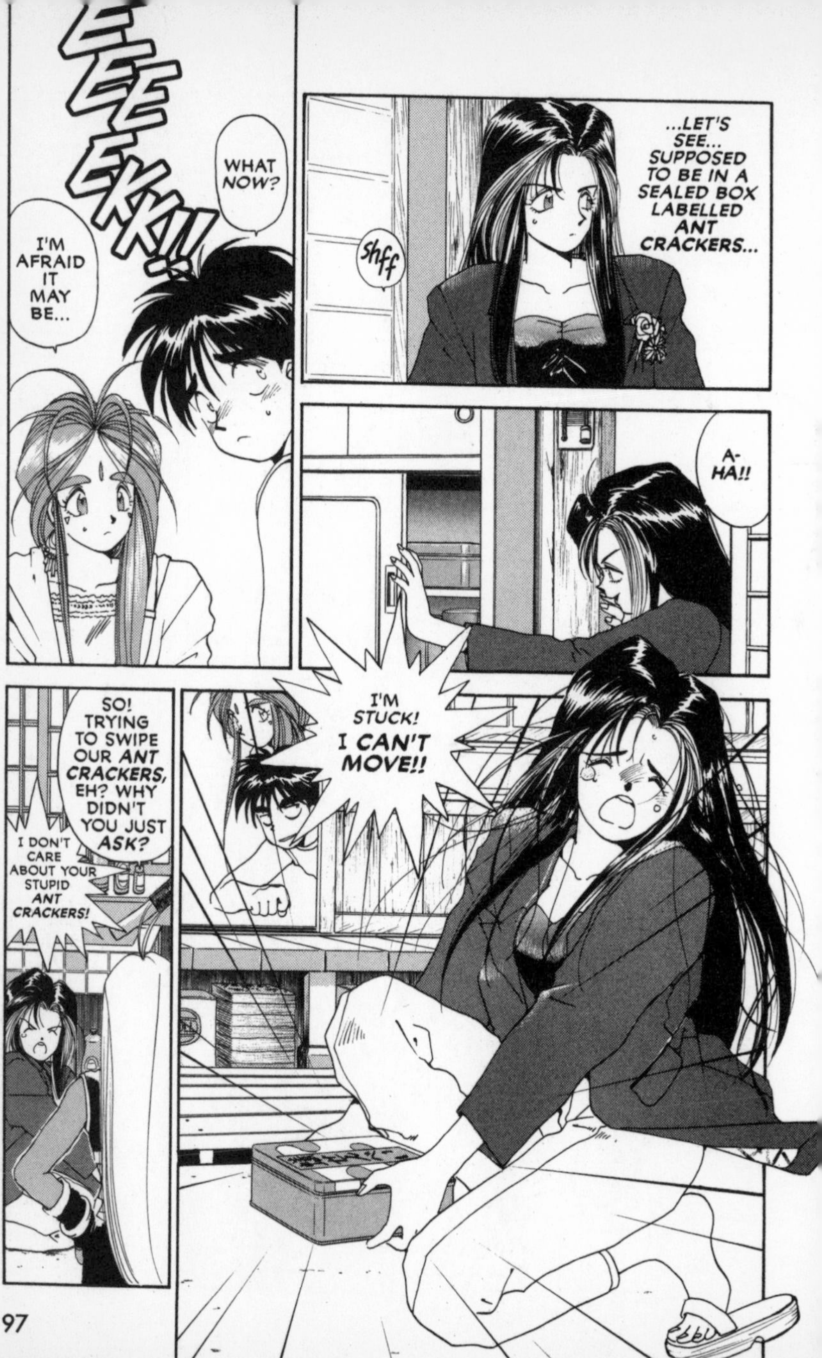
...LET'S SEE... SUPPOSED TO BE IN A SEALED BOX LABELLED ANT CRACKERS...
shff
A-HA!!
EEEEKK!!
WHAT NOW?
I'M AFRAID IT MAY BE...
I'M STUCK! I CAN'T MOVE!!
SO! TRYING TO SWIPE OUR ANT CRACKERS, EH? WHY DIDN'T YOU JUST ASK?
I DON'T CARE ABOUT YOUR STUPID ANT CRACKERS!

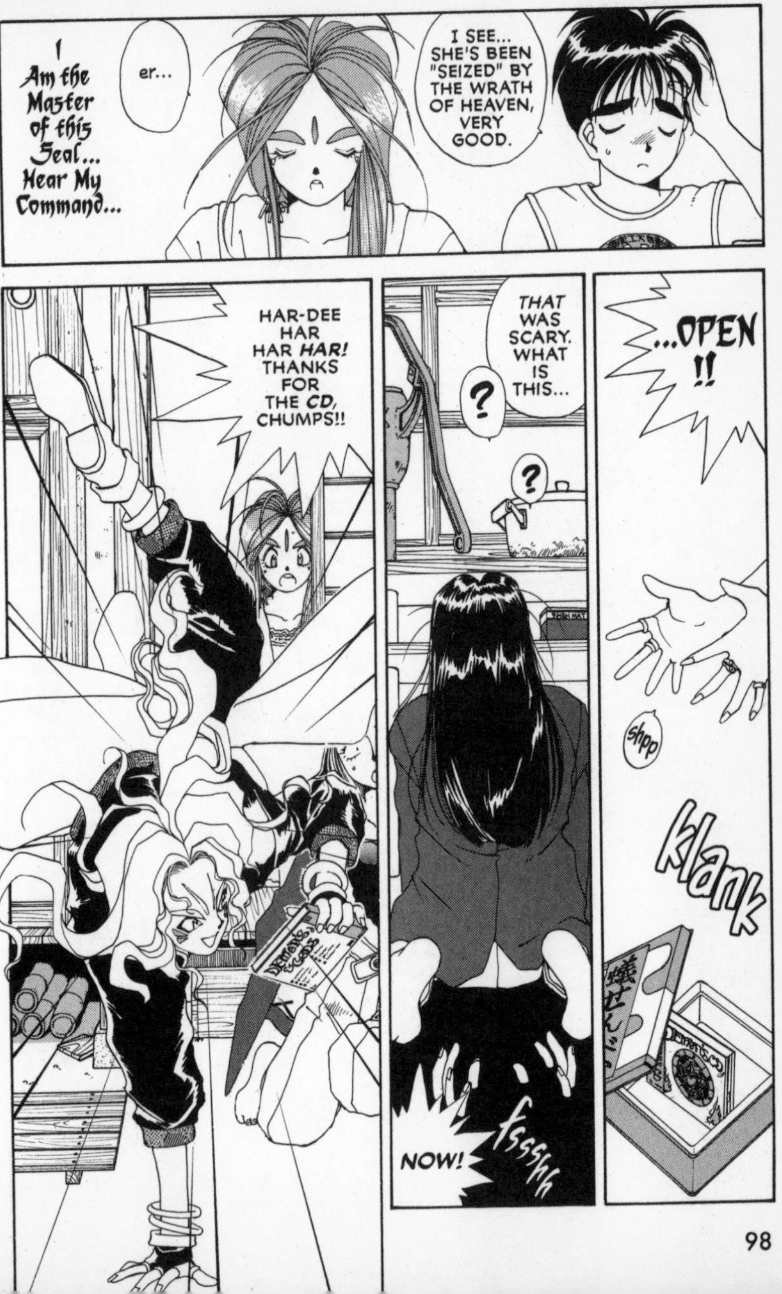
I SEE... SHE'S BEEN "SEIZED" BY THE WRATH OF HEAVEN, VERY GOOD.
er...
I Am the Master of this Seal... Hear My Command...
...OPEN !!
shpp
klank
THAT WAS SCARY. WHAT IS THIS...
?
?
NOW!
fsssshh
HAR-DEE HAR HAR *HAR!* THANKS FOR THE *CD,* CHUMPS!!

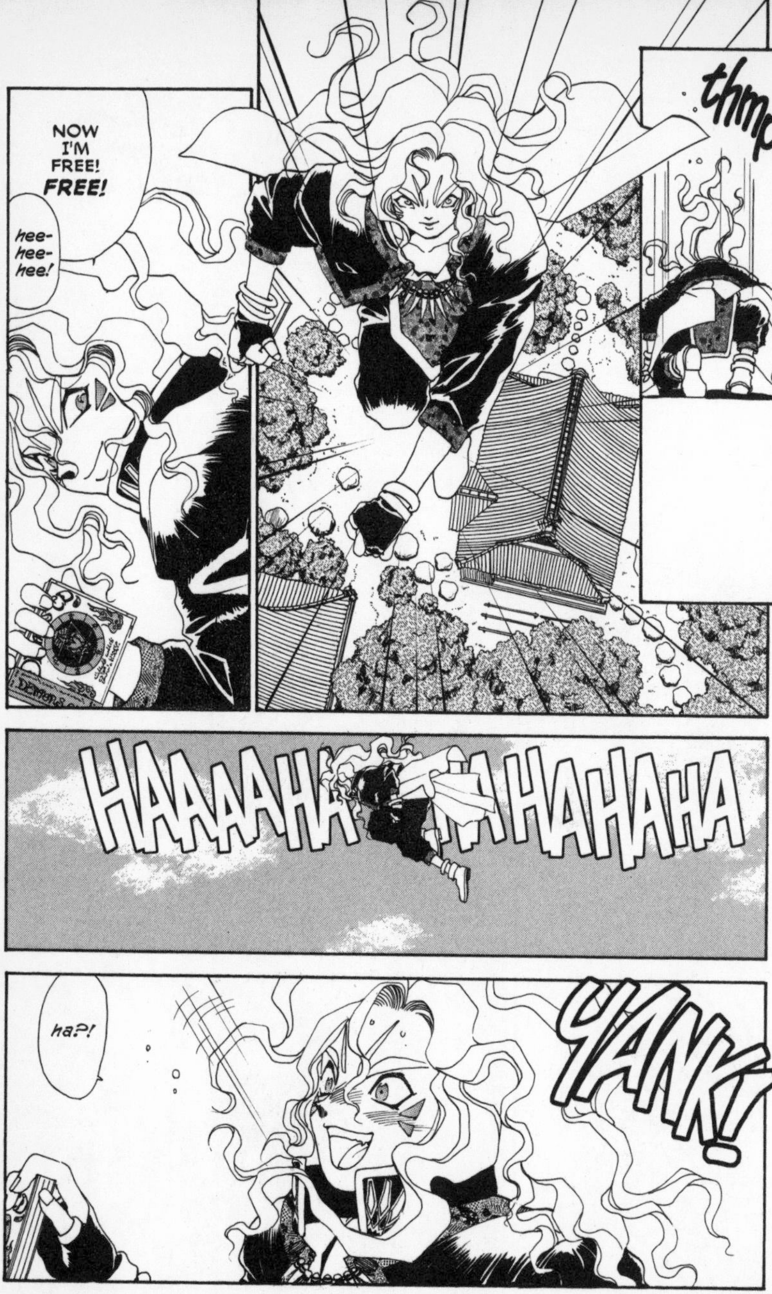
thmp
NOW I'M FREE! FREE!
hee-hee-hee!
HAAAAHA AHAHAHA
YANK!
ha?!

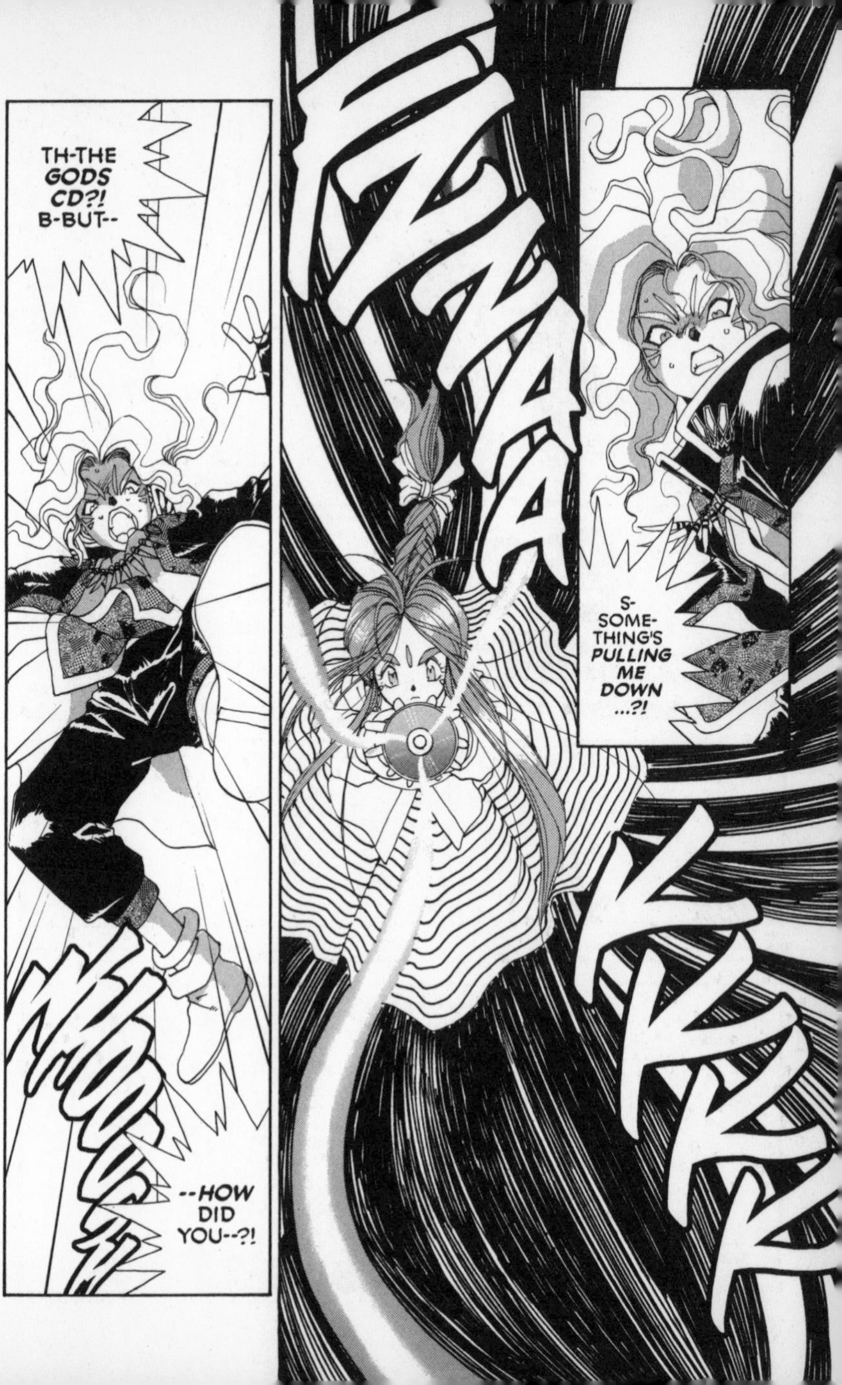
S-SOMETHING'S *PULLING* ME *DOWN*...?!
TH-THE *GODS CD?!* B-BUT--
--*HOW* DID YOU--?!

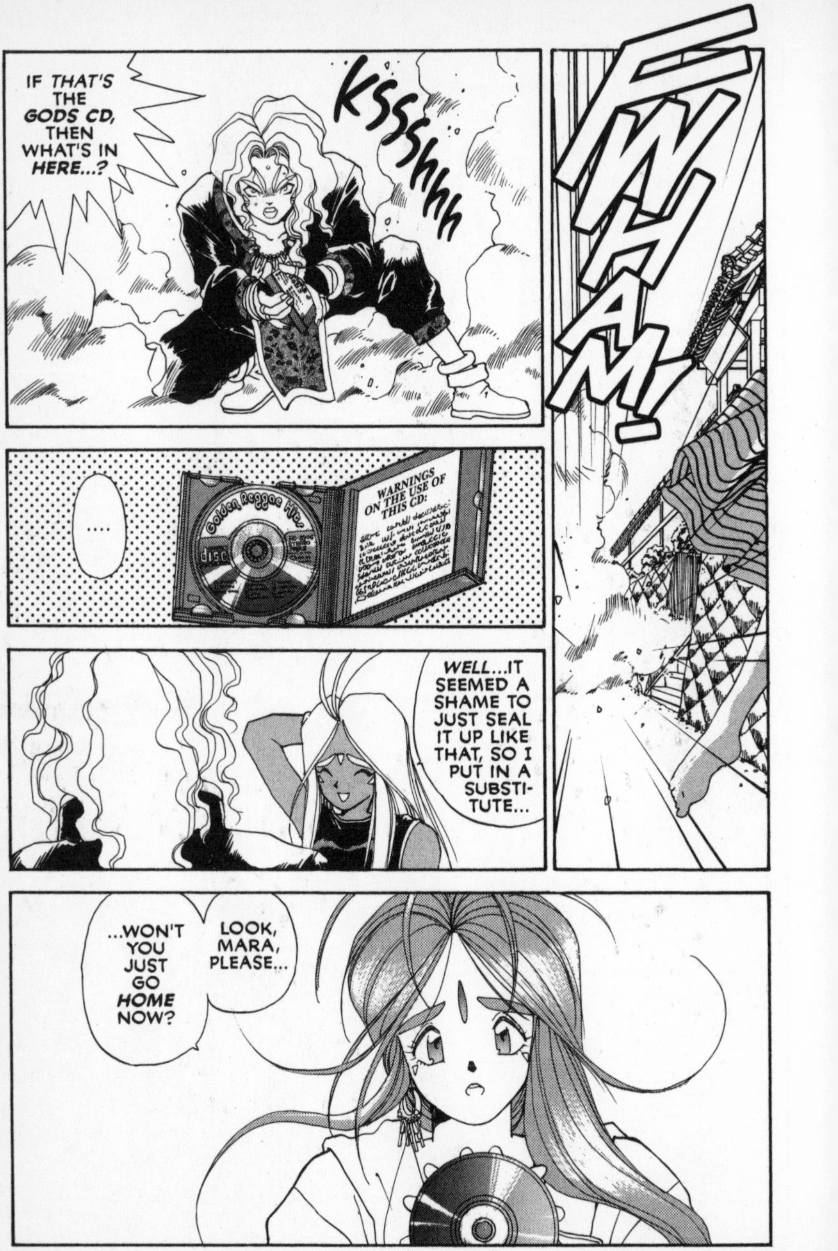
FWHAM!
IF THAT'S THE GODS CD, THEN WHAT'S IN HERE...?
KSSSHHH
....
Golden Reggae Hits
disc
WARNINGS ON THE USE OF THIS CD:
WELL...IT SEEMED A SHAME TO JUST SEAL IT UP LIKE THAT, SO I PUT IN A SUBSTITUTE...
LOOK, MARA, PLEASE...
...WON'T YOU JUST GO HOME NOW?

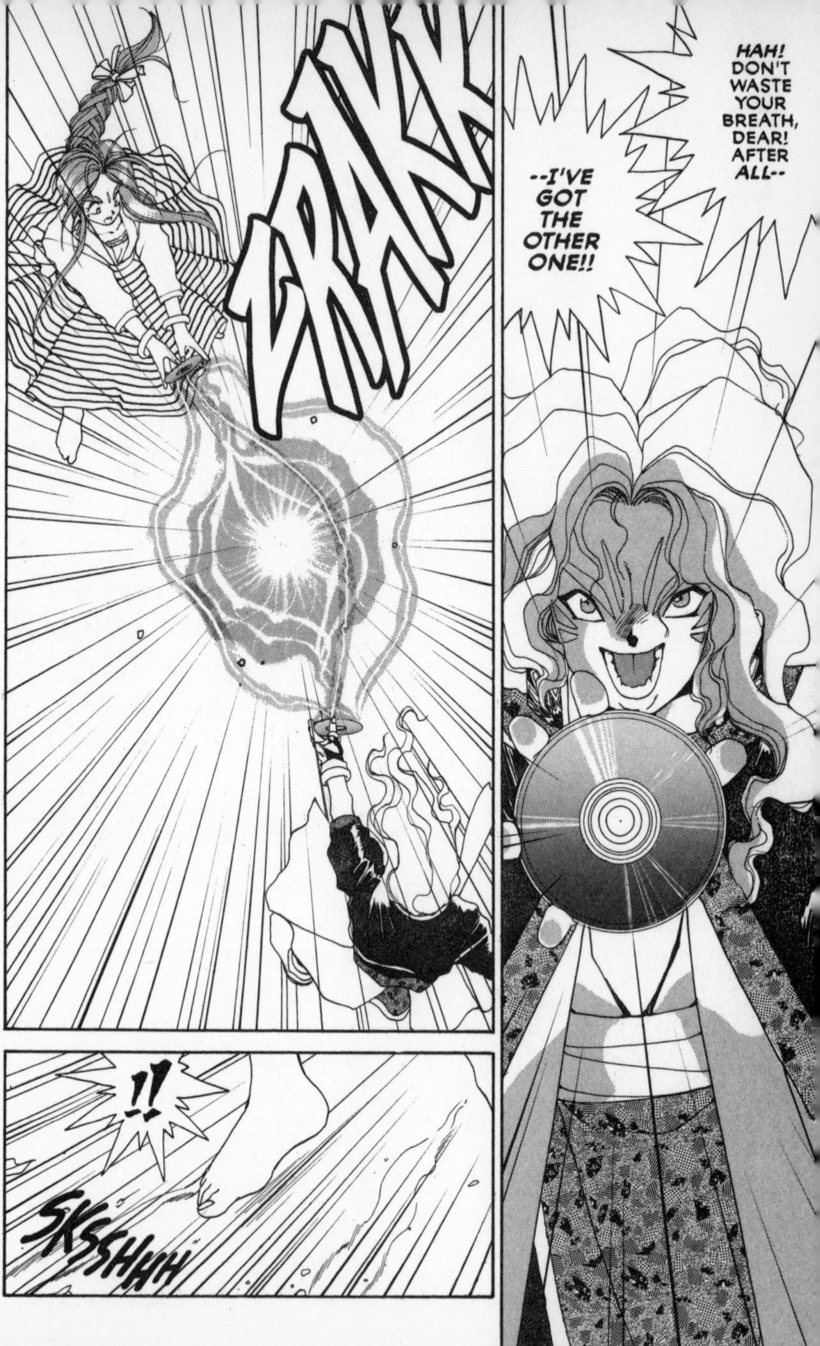
HAH! DON'T WASTE YOUR BREATH, DEAR! AFTER ALL--
--I'VE GOT THE OTHER ONE!!
!!
SKSSHHH

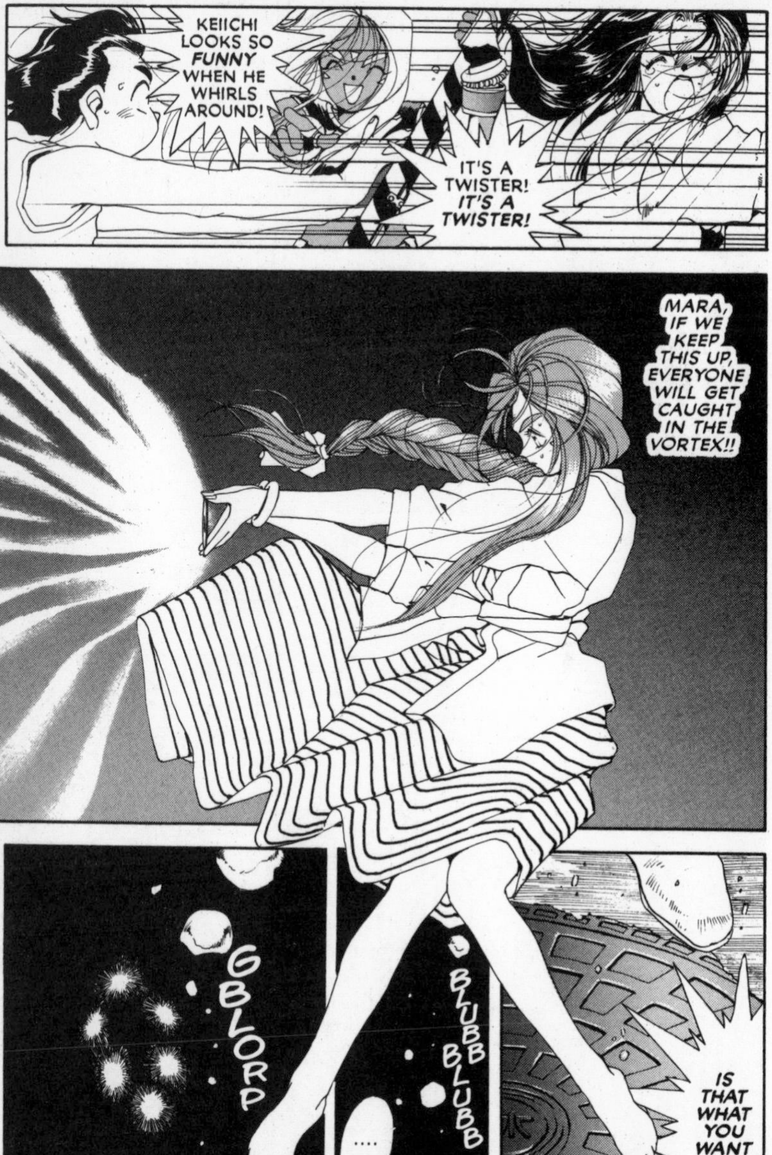
IT'S A TWISTER! IT'S A TWISTER!
KEIICHI LOOKS SO FUNNY WHEN HE WHIRLS AROUND!
MARA, IF WE KEEP THIS UP, EVERYONE WILL GET CAUGHT IN THE VORTEX!!
IS THAT WHAT YOU WANT ?!
BLUBB BLUBB
....
GBLORP

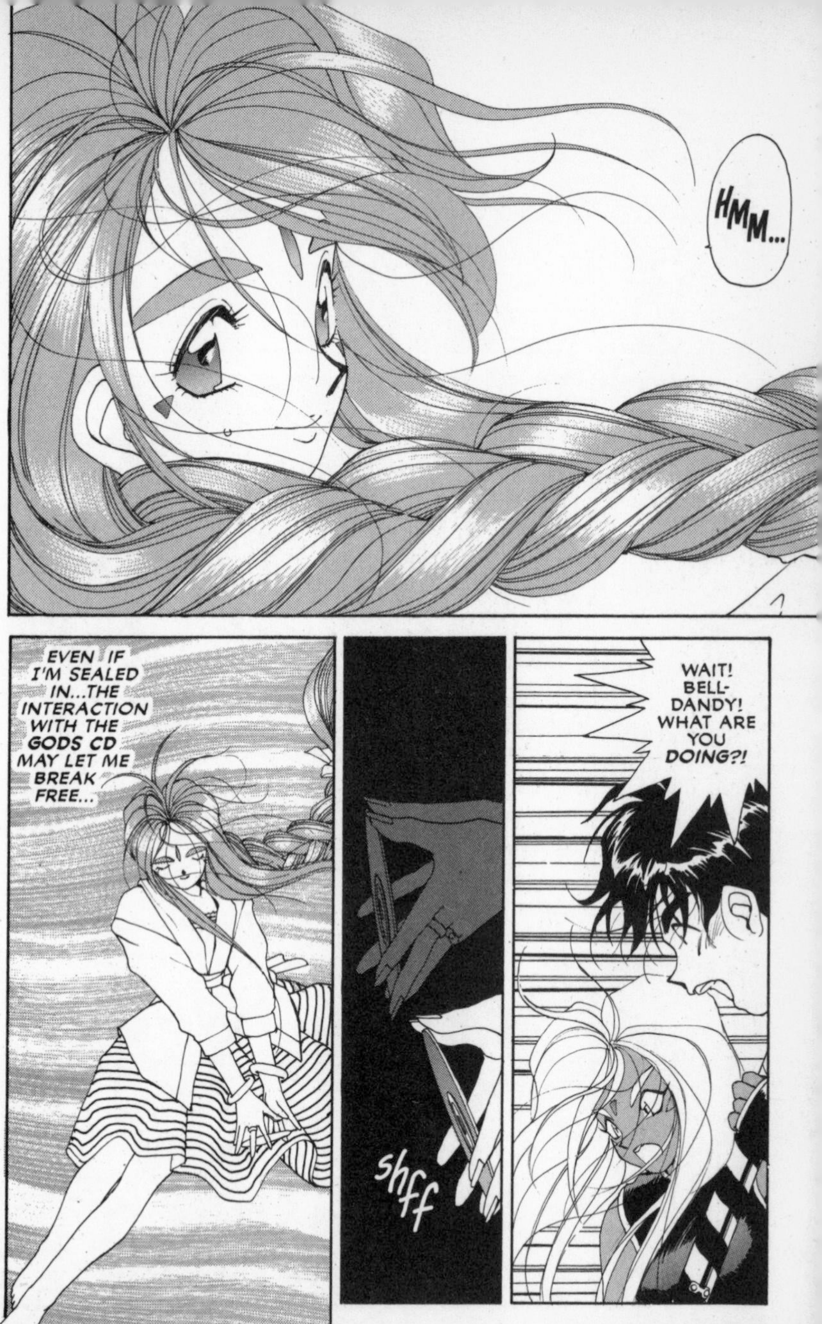
HMM...
WAIT! BELL-DANDY! WHAT ARE YOU DOING?!
shff
EVEN IF I'M SEALED IN...THE INTERACTION WITH THE GODS CD MAY LET ME BREAK FREE...

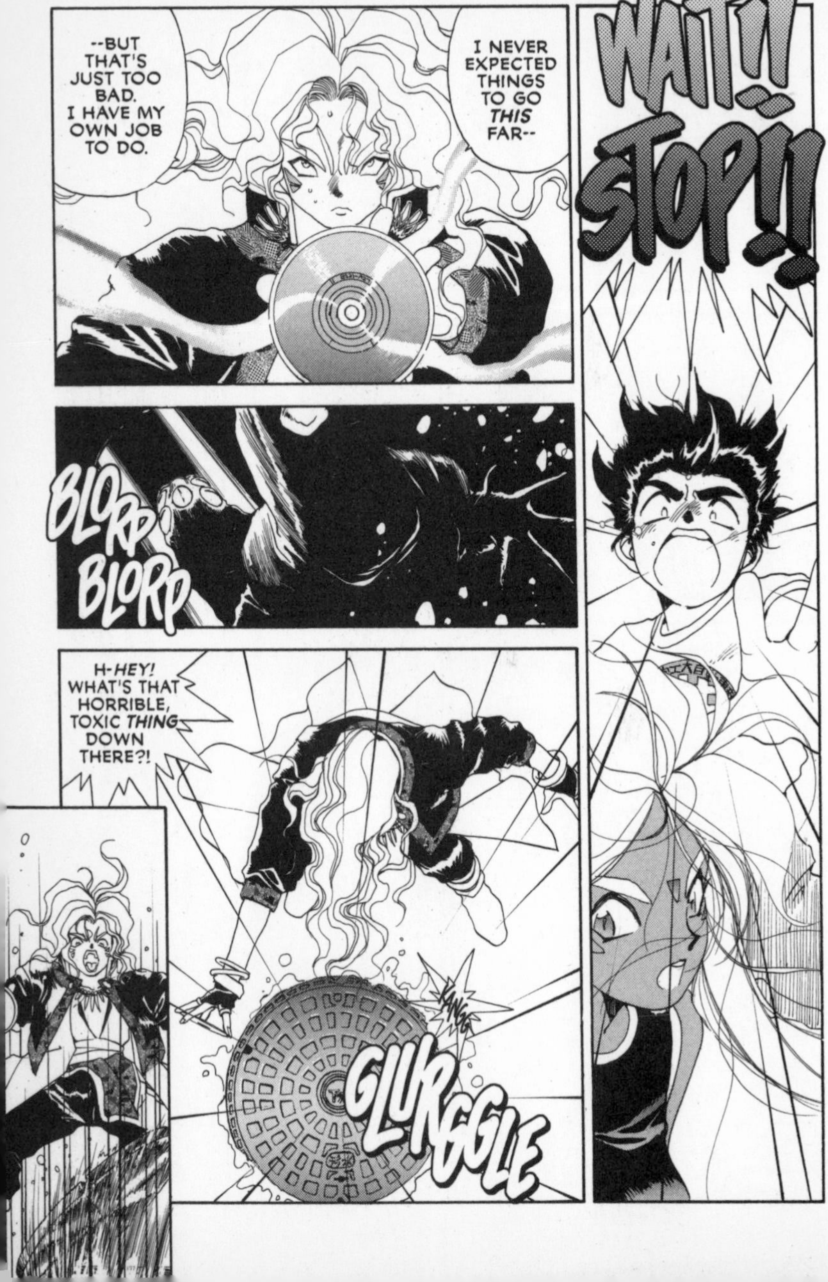
WAIT!! STOP!!
I NEVER EXPECTED THINGS TO GO *THIS* FAR--
--BUT THAT'S JUST TOO BAD. I HAVE MY OWN JOB TO DO.
BLORP BLORP
H-*HEY!* WHAT'S THAT HORRIBLE, TOXIC *THING* DOWN THERE?!
KANG
GLURGGLE

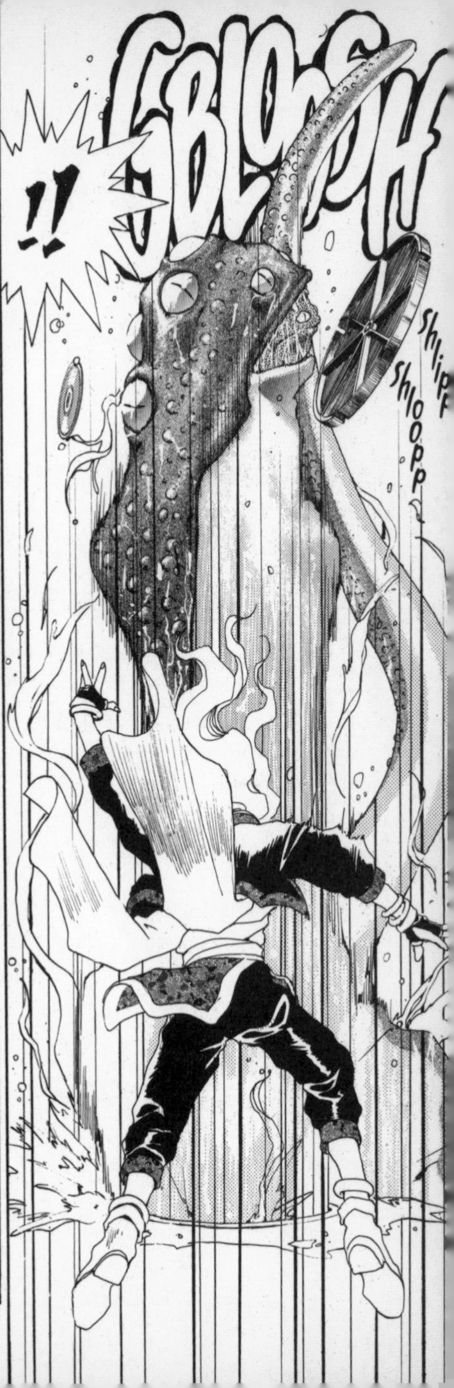
!!
GBLOOSH
SHLIPP
SHLOOOPP

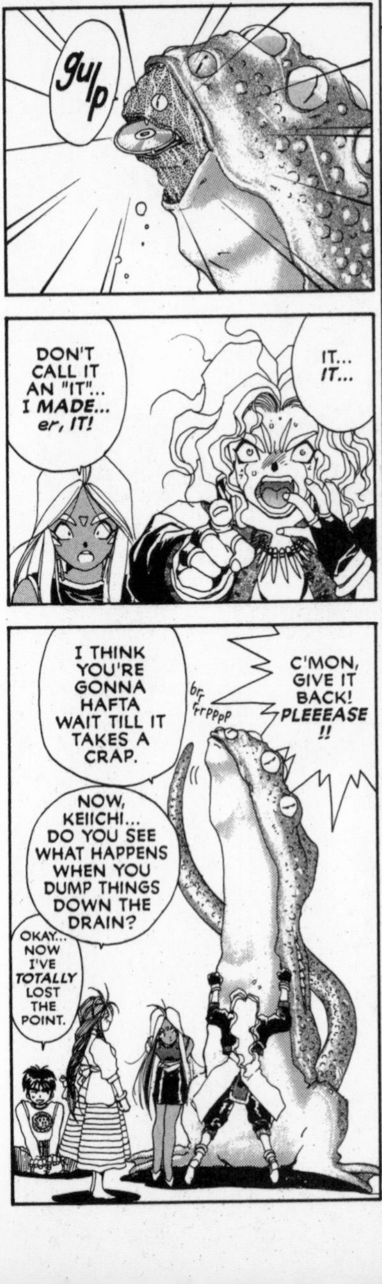
gulp
IT... *IT...*
DON'T CALL IT AN "IT"... I *MADE...* *er, IT!*
C'MON, GIVE IT BACK! ***PLEEEASE !!***
brr rrrpppp
I THINK YOU'RE GONNA HAFTA WAIT TILL IT TAKES A CRAP.
NOW, KEIICHI... DO YOU SEE WHAT HAPPENS WHEN YOU DUMP THINGS DOWN THE DRAIN?
OKAY... NOW I'VE ***TOTALLY*** LOST THE POINT.

CHAPTER 28

Balance-Ball Amour

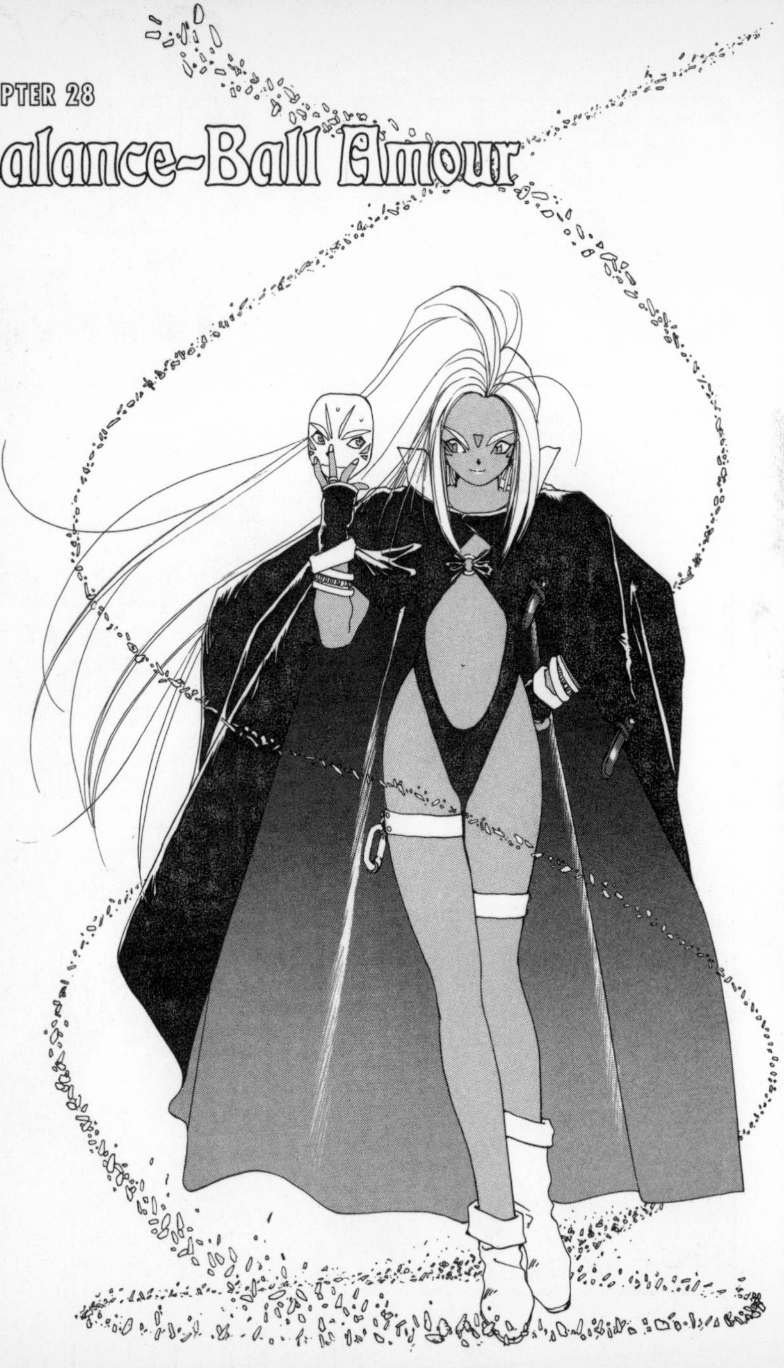

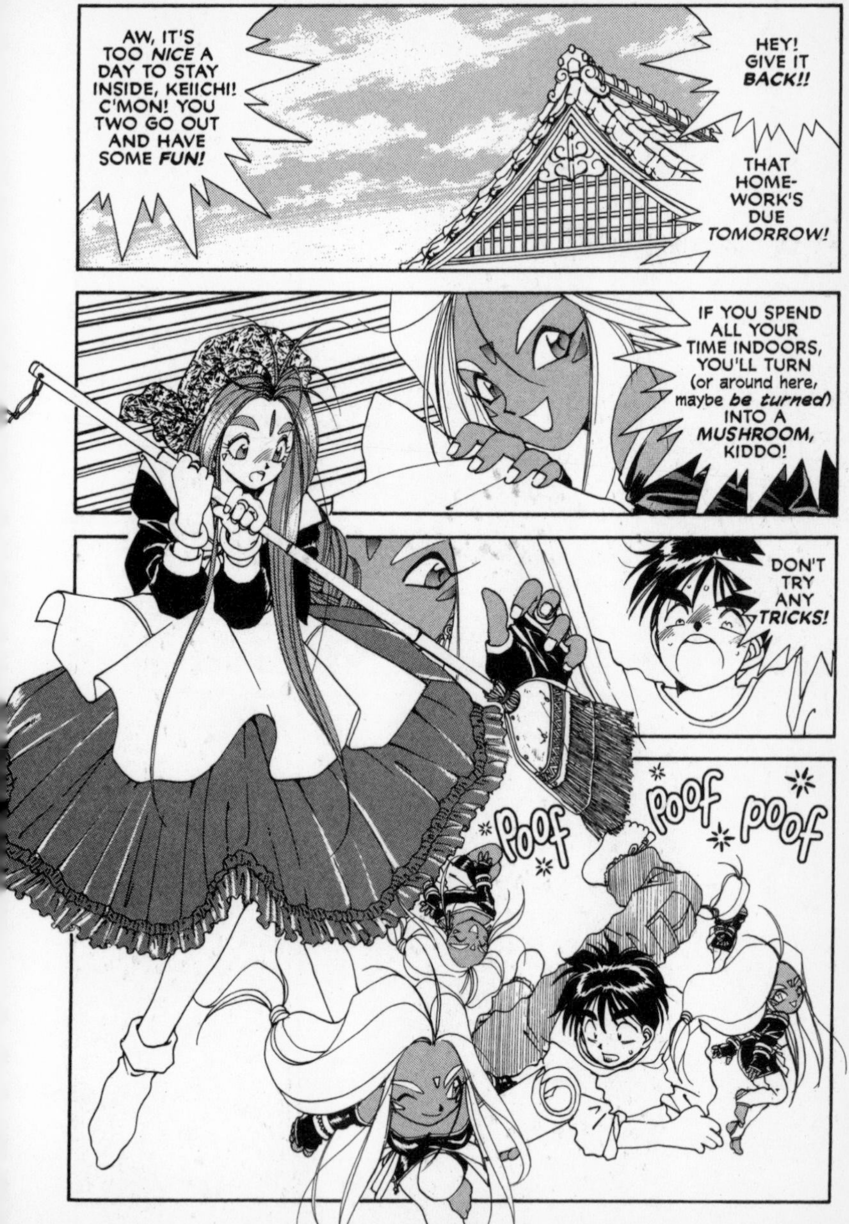
HEY! GIVE IT *BACK!!*
THAT HOME-WORK'S DUE *TOMORROW!*
AW, IT'S TOO *NICE* A DAY TO STAY INSIDE, KEIICHI! C'MON! YOU TWO GO OUT AND HAVE SOME *FUN!*
IF YOU SPEND ALL YOUR TIME INDOORS, YOU'LL TURN (or around here, maybe *be turned*) INTO A *MUSHROOM,* KIDDO!
DON'T TRY ANY *TRICKS!*
poof poof poof

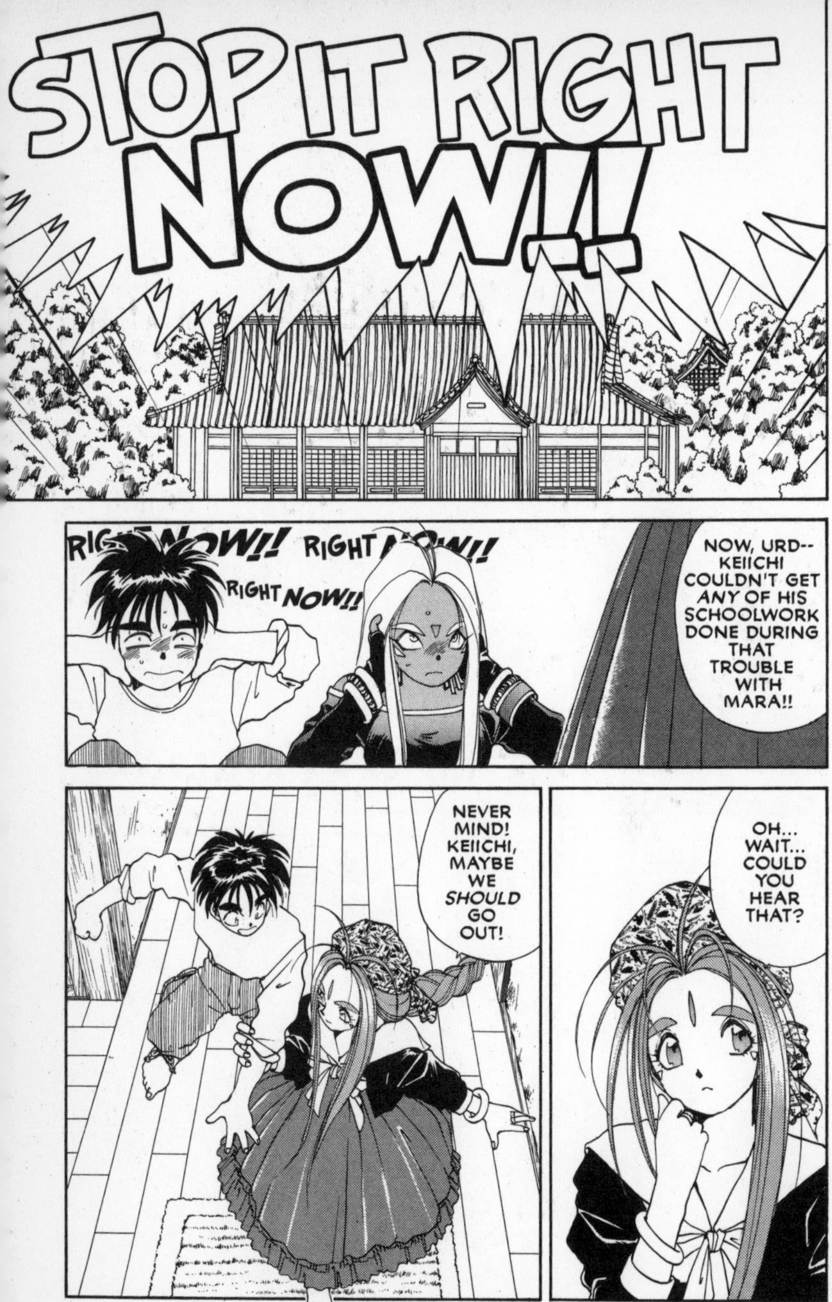
STOP IT RIGHT NOW!!
NOW, URD-- KEIICHI COULDN'T GET ANY OF HIS SCHOOLWORK DONE DURING THAT TROUBLE WITH MARA!!
RIGHT NOW!!
RIGHT NOW!!
OH... WAIT... COULD YOU HEAR THAT?
NEVER MIND! KEIICHI, MAYBE WE SHOULD GO OUT!

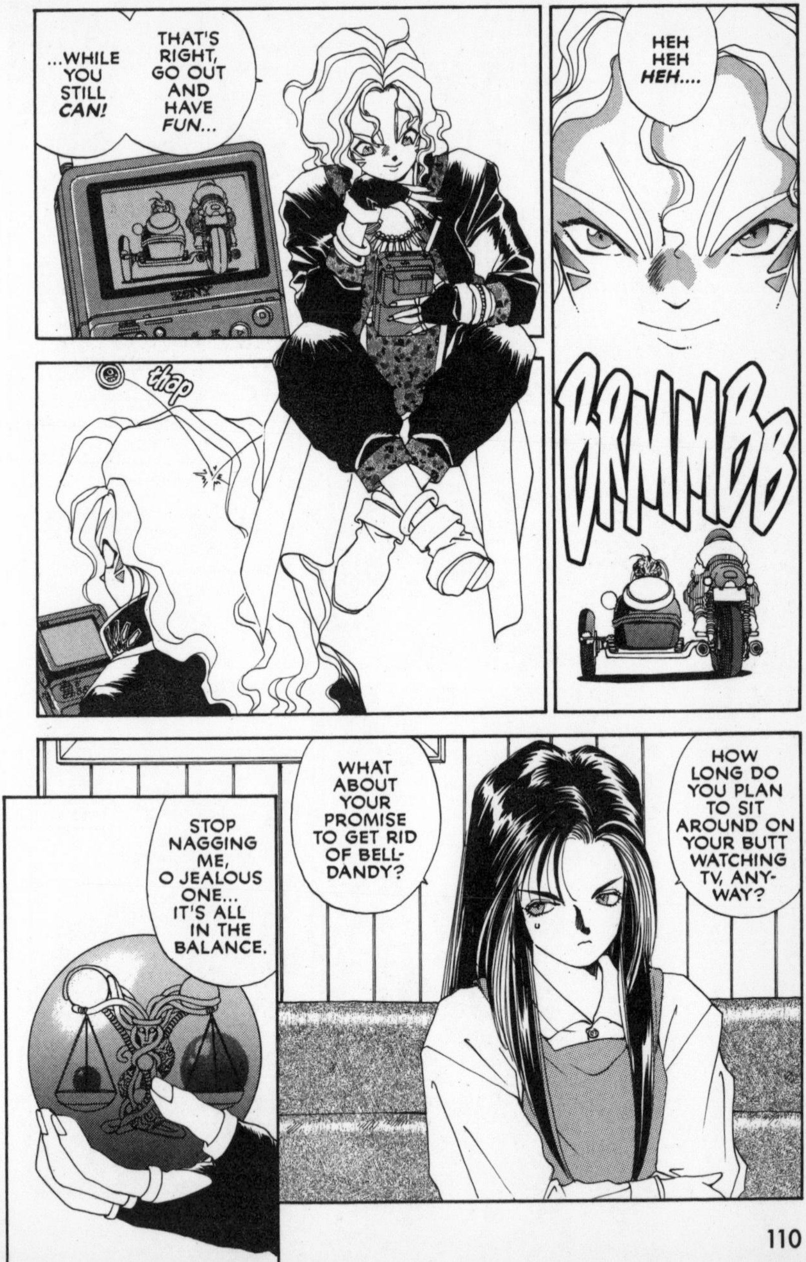
HEH HEH *HEH*....
BRMMBB
THAT'S RIGHT, GO OUT AND HAVE *FUN*...
...WHILE YOU STILL *CAN!*
thap
HOW LONG DO YOU PLAN TO SIT AROUND ON YOUR BUTT WATCHING TV, ANYWAY?
WHAT ABOUT YOUR PROMISE TO GET RID OF BELLDANDY?
STOP NAGGING ME, O JEALOUS ONE... IT'S ALL IN THE BALANCE.

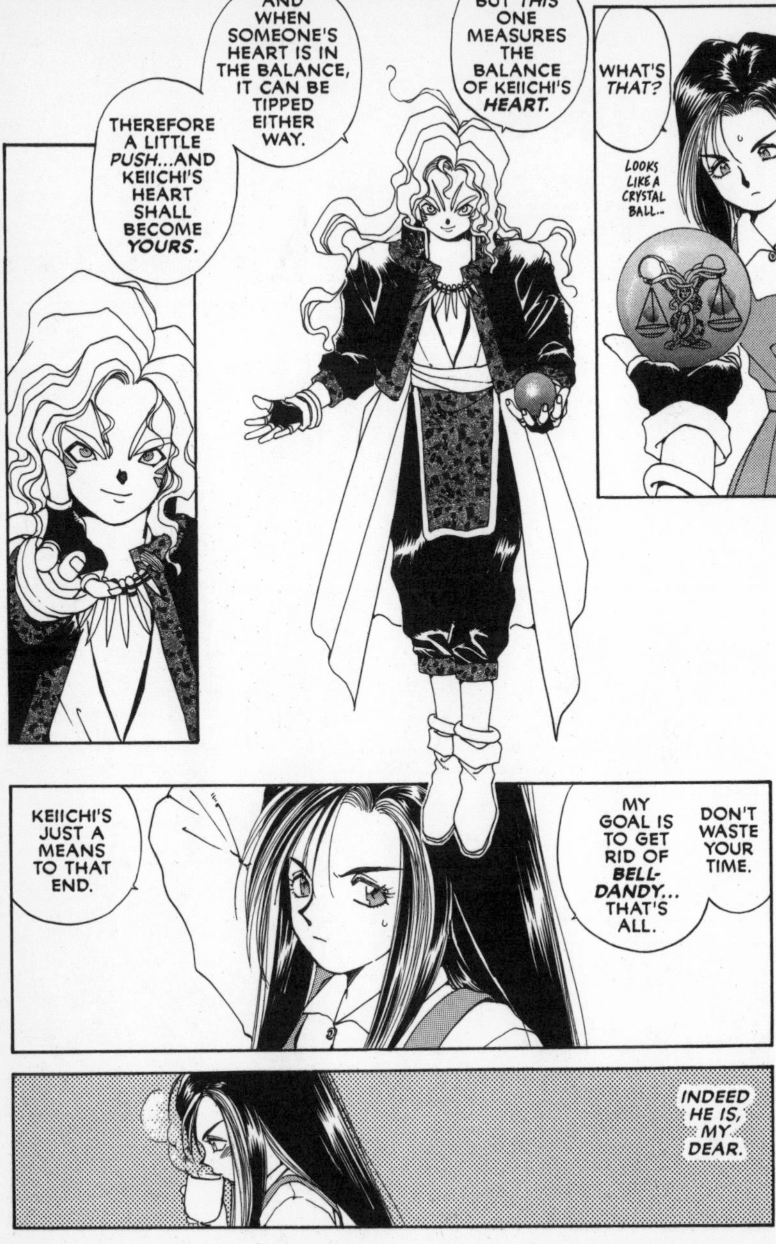
WHAT'S *THAT?*
LOOKS LIKE A CRYSTAL BALL...
INDEED! BUT *THIS* ONE MEASURES THE BALANCE OF KEIICHI'S ***HEART.***
AND WHEN SOMEONE'S HEART IS IN THE BALANCE, IT CAN BE TIPPED EITHER WAY.
THEREFORE A LITTLE *PUSH*...AND KEIICHI'S HEART SHALL BECOME ***YOURS.***
DON'T WASTE YOUR TIME.
MY GOAL IS TO GET RID OF ***BELL-DANDY...*** THAT'S ALL.
KEIICHI'S JUST A MEANS TO THAT END.
INDEED HE IS, MY DEAR.

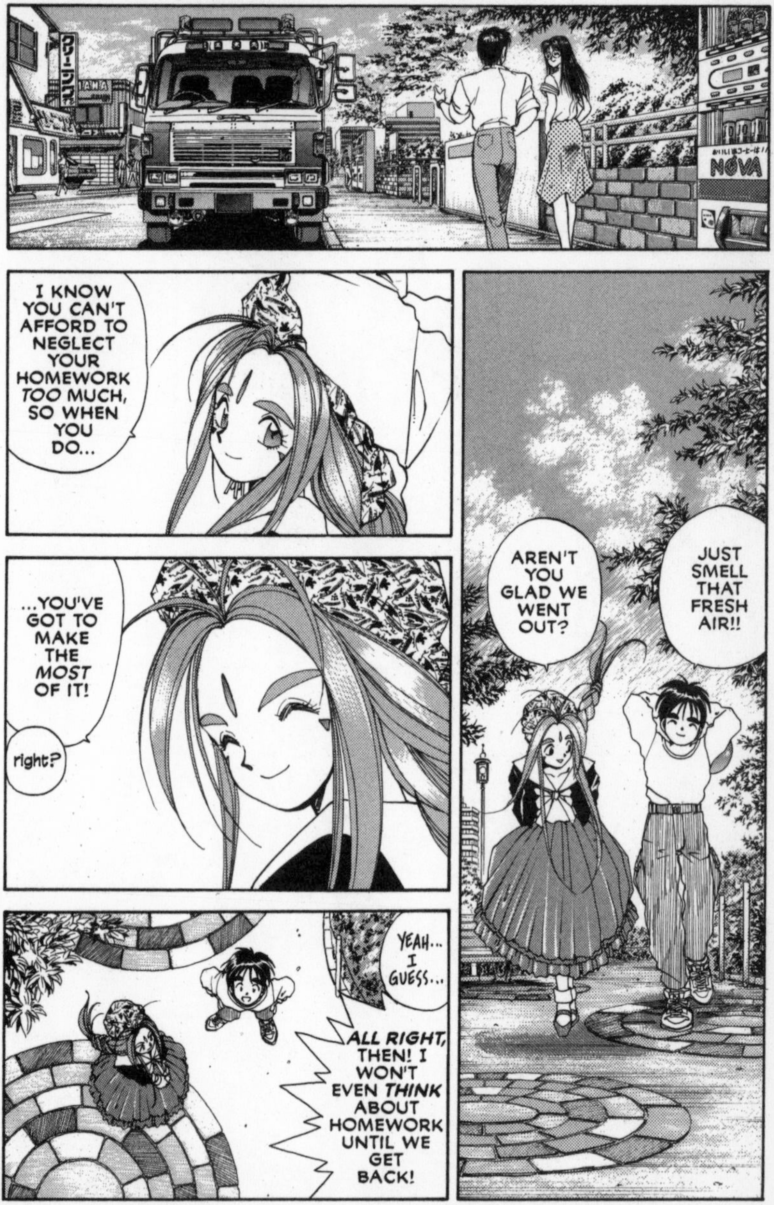
NOVA
JUST SMELL THAT FRESH AIR!!
AREN'T YOU GLAD WE WENT OUT?
I KNOW YOU CAN'T AFFORD TO NEGLECT YOUR HOMEWORK *TOO* MUCH, SO WHEN YOU DO...
...YOU'VE GOT TO MAKE THE *MOST* OF IT!
right?
YEAH... I GUESS...
ALL RIGHT, THEN! I WON'T EVEN ***THINK*** ABOUT HOMEWORK UNTIL WE GET BACK!

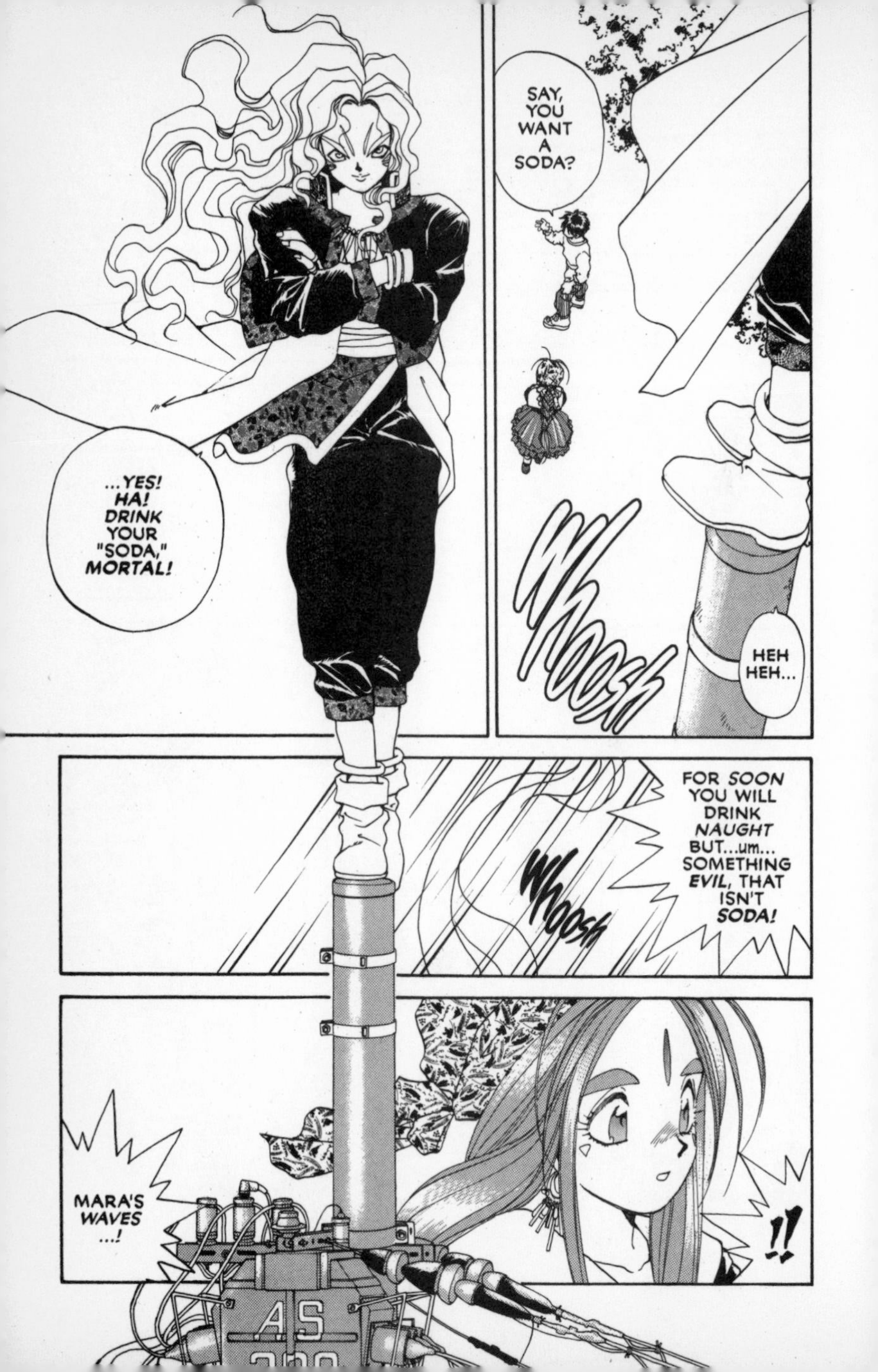
SAY, YOU WANT A SODA?
WHOOSH
HEH HEH...
...YES! HA! DRINK YOUR "SODA," MORTAL!
FOR SOON YOU WILL DRINK NAUGHT BUT...um... SOMETHING EVIL, THAT ISN'T SODA!
Whoosh
!!
MARA'S WAVES ...!

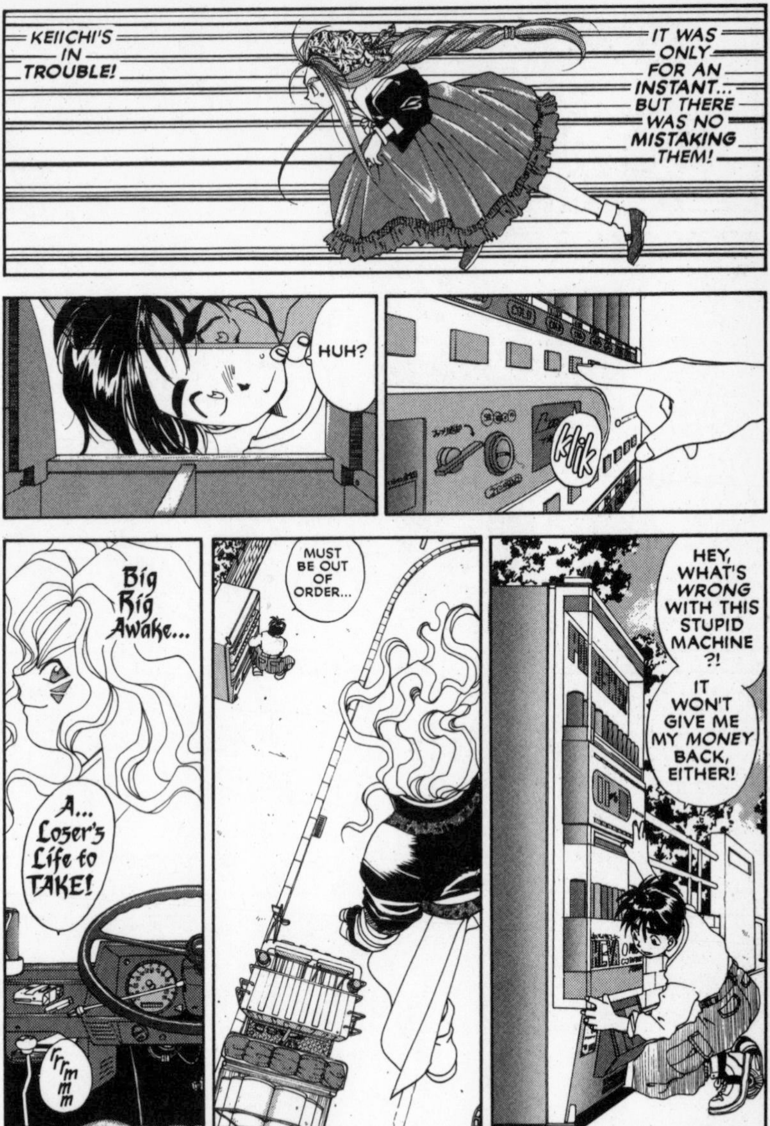
IT WAS ONLY FOR AN INSTANT... BUT THERE WAS NO MISTAKING THEM!
KEIICHI'S IN TROUBLE!
klik
HUH?
HEY, WHAT'S WRONG WITH THIS STUPID MACHINE?!
IT WON'T GIVE ME MY MONEY BACK, EITHER!
MUST BE OUT OF ORDER...
Big Rig Awake...
A... Loser's Life to TAKE!
rrrmmm

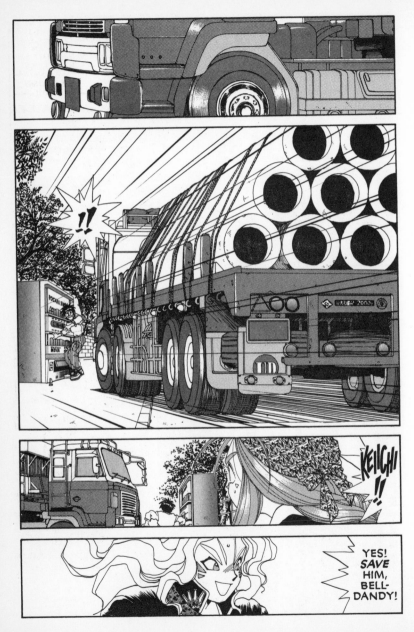

KEIICHI!!

YES! *SAVE* HIM, BELLDANDY!

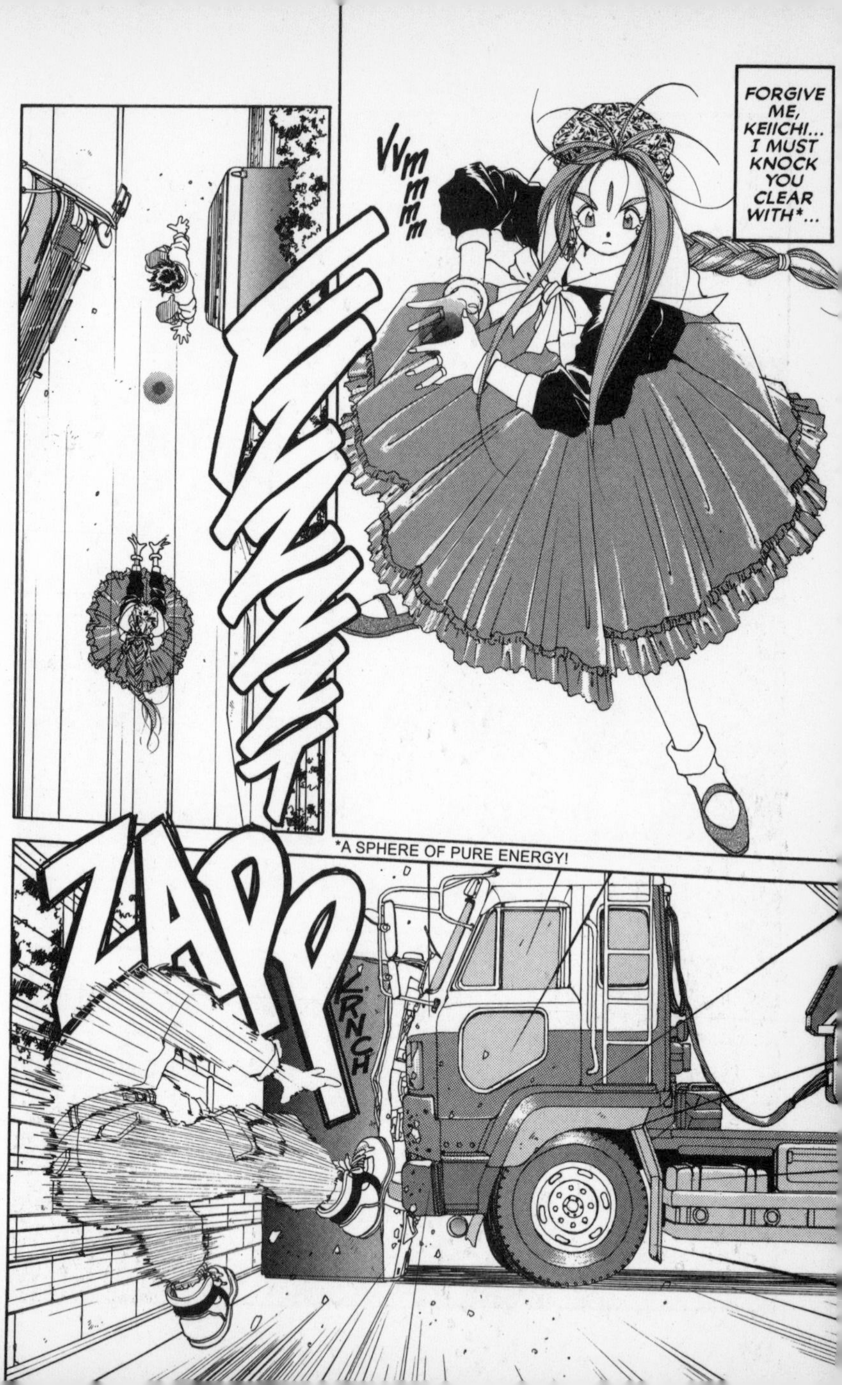
FORGIVE ME, KEIICHI... I MUST KNOCK YOU CLEAR WITH*...
VVmmmmm
ZAP
KRNCH
*A SPHERE OF PURE ENERGY!

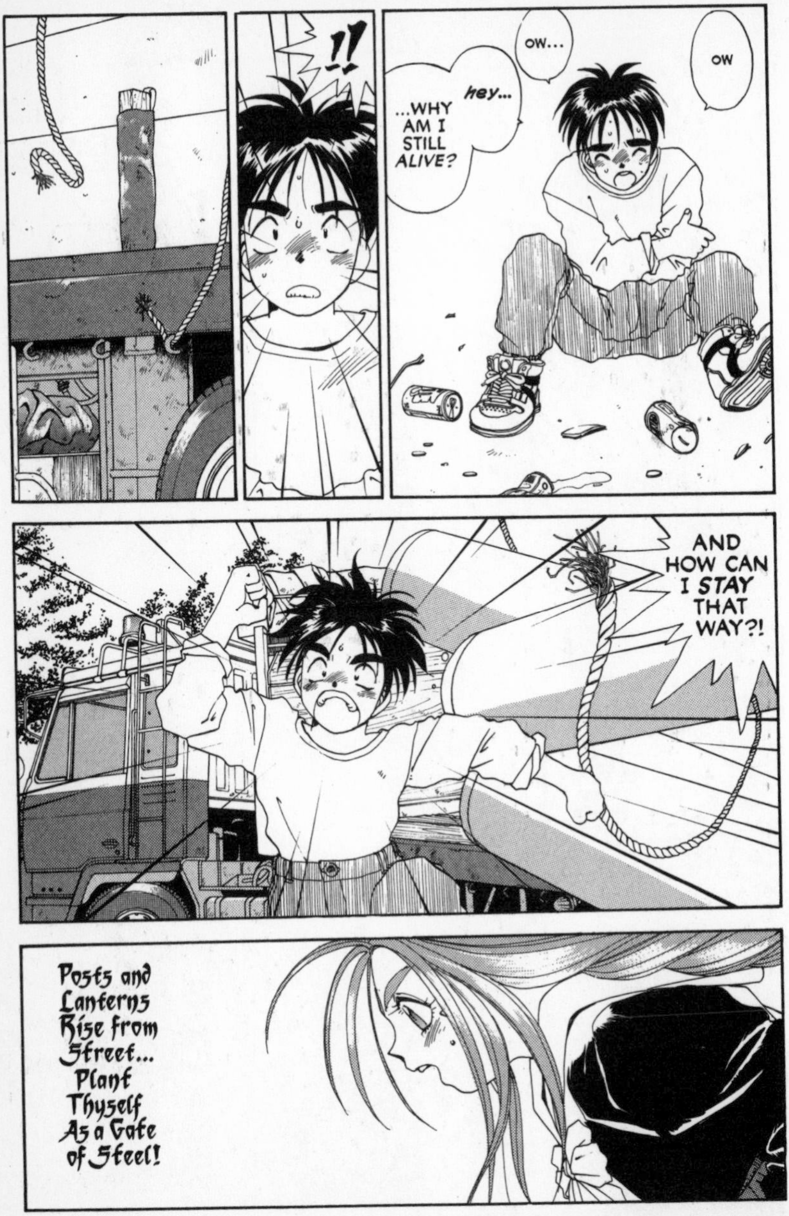
OW
OW...
hey...
...WHY AM I STILL ALIVE?
!!
AND HOW CAN I STAY THAT WAY?!
Posts and Lanterns Rise from Street... Plant Thyself As a Gate of Steel!

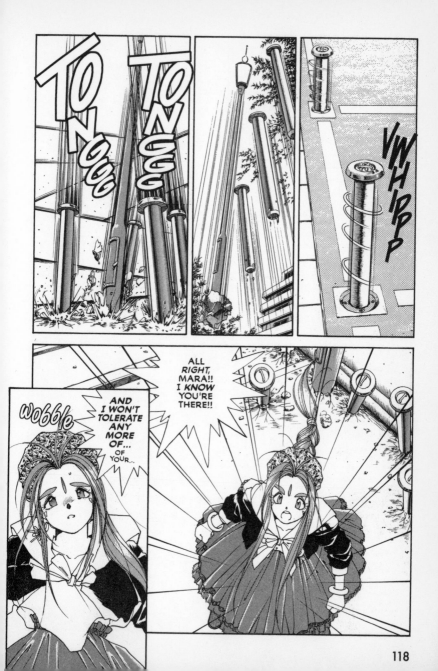

TONGGG

TONGGG

VWHIPP

ALL *RIGHT*, MARA!! I *KNOW* YOU'RE THERE!!

wobble

AND I WON'T TOLERATE ANY MORE OF... OF YOUR...

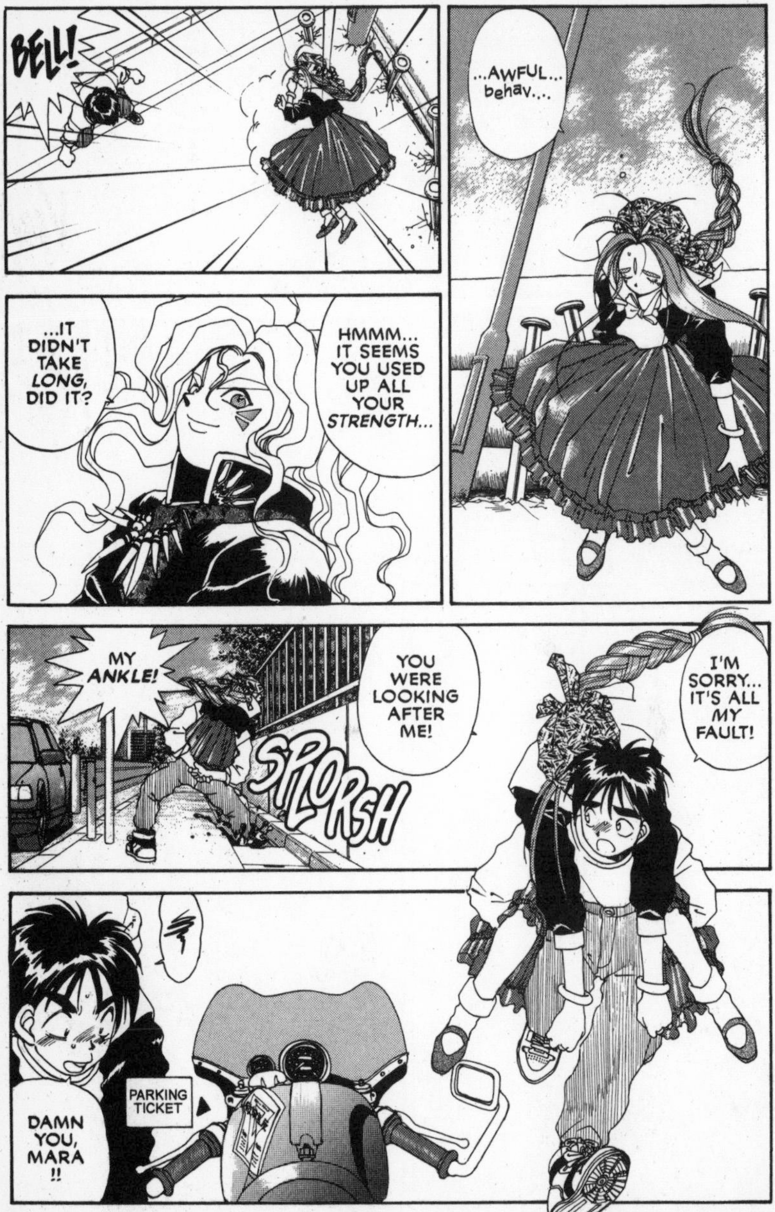
...AWFUL... behav...
BELL!
HMMM... IT SEEMS YOU USED UP ALL YOUR STRENGTH...
...IT DIDN'T TAKE LONG, DID IT?
I'M SORRY... IT'S ALL MY FAULT!
YOU WERE LOOKING AFTER ME!
MY ANKLE!
SPLORSH
PARKING TICKET
DAMN YOU, MARA!!

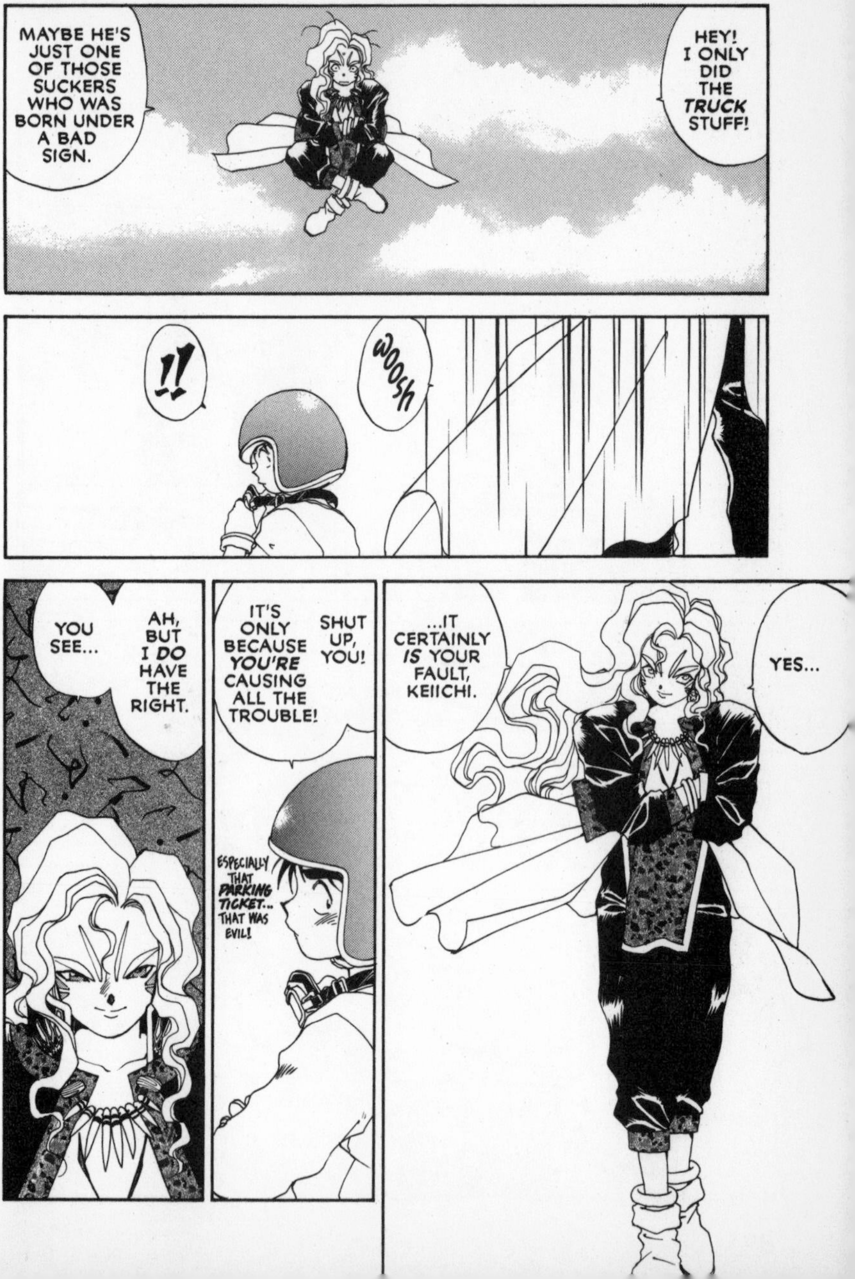
HEY! I ONLY DID THE *TRUCK* STUFF!
MAYBE HE'S JUST ONE OF THOSE SUCKERS WHO WAS BORN UNDER A BAD SIGN.
WOOSH
!!
YES...
...IT CERTAINLY *IS* YOUR FAULT, KEIICHI.
SHUT UP, YOU!
IT'S ONLY BECAUSE *YOU'RE* CAUSING ALL THE TROUBLE!
ESPECIALLY THAT *PARKING TICKET*... THAT WAS EVIL!
AH, BUT I *DO* HAVE THE RIGHT.
YOU SEE...

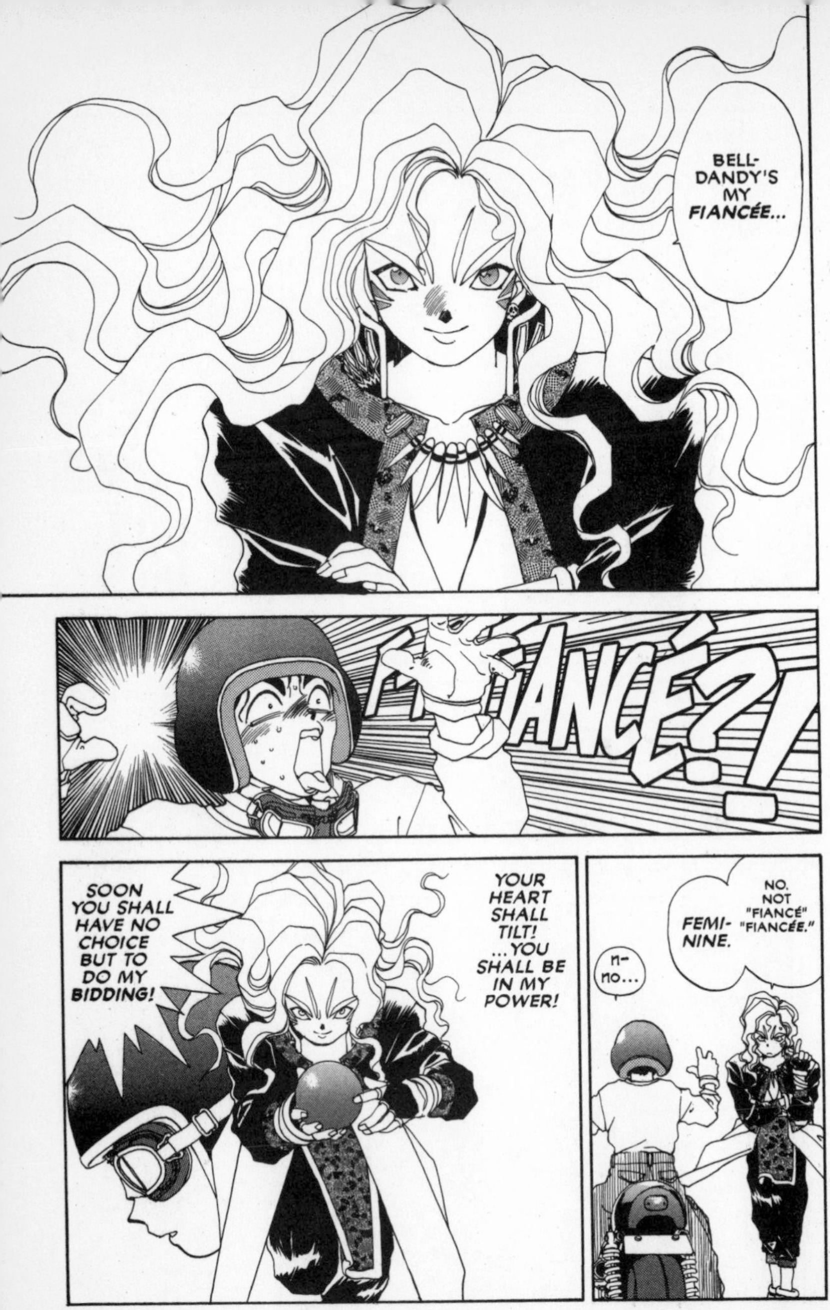
BELL-DANDY'S MY *FIANCÉE...*
ANCÉ?!
NO. NOT "FIANCÉ" "FIANCÉE."
FEMI-NINE.
n-no...
YOUR HEART SHALL TILT! ...YOU SHALL BE IN MY POWER!
SOON YOU SHALL HAVE NO CHOICE BUT TO DO MY BIDDING!

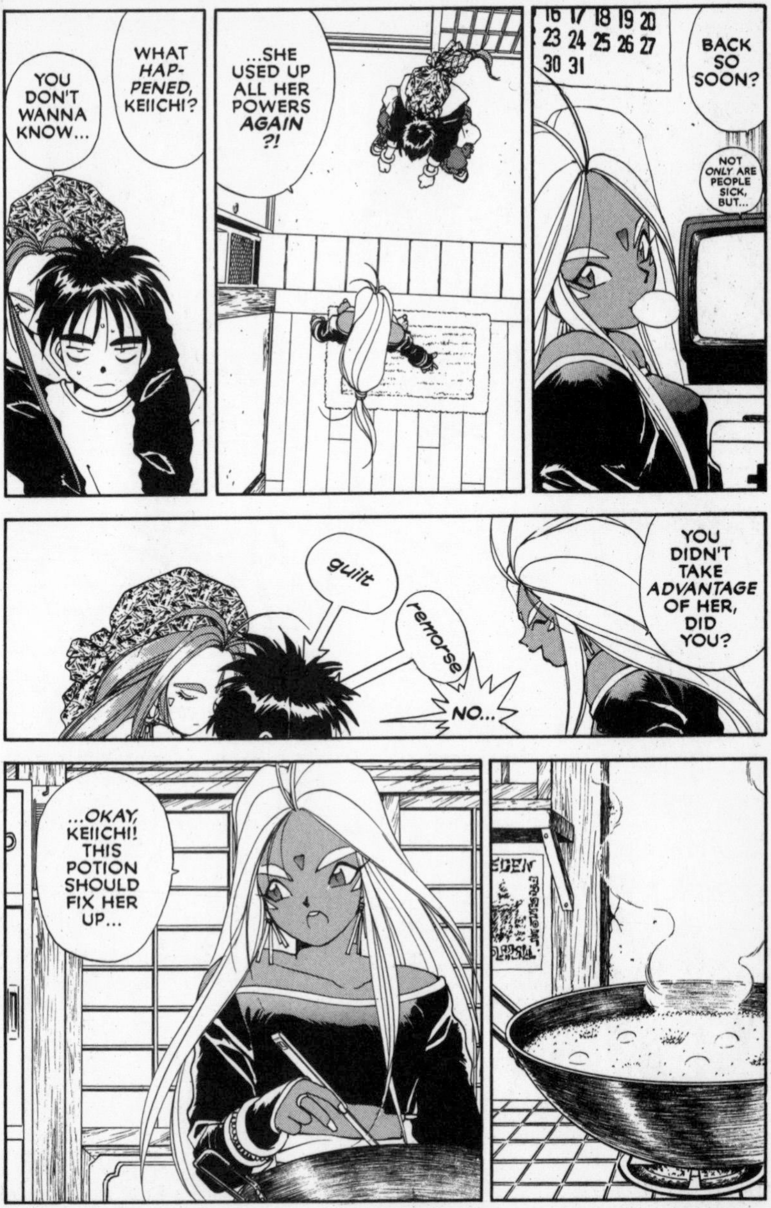
16 17 18 19 20
23 24 25 26 27
30 31
BACK SO SOON?
NOT ONLY ARE PEOPLE SICK, BUT...
...SHE USED UP ALL HER POWERS *AGAIN* ?!
WHAT *HAP-PENED,* KEIICHI?
YOU DON'T WANNA KNOW...
YOU DIDN'T TAKE *ADVANTAGE* OF HER, DID YOU?
NO...
remorse
guilt
EDEN
...*OKAY,* KEIICHI! THIS POTION SHOULD FIX HER UP...

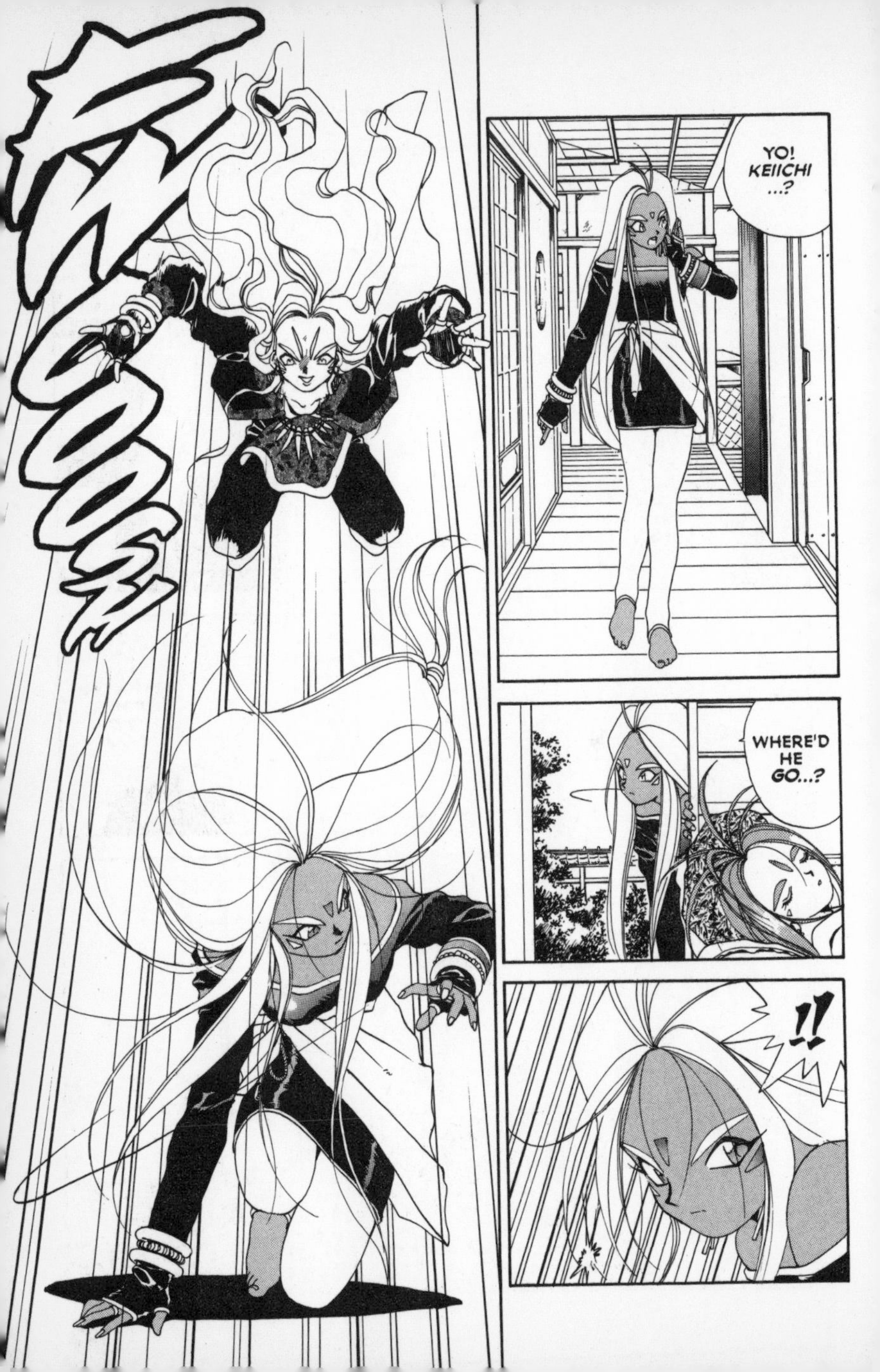
YO! KEIICHI ...?
WHERE'D HE GO...?
!!

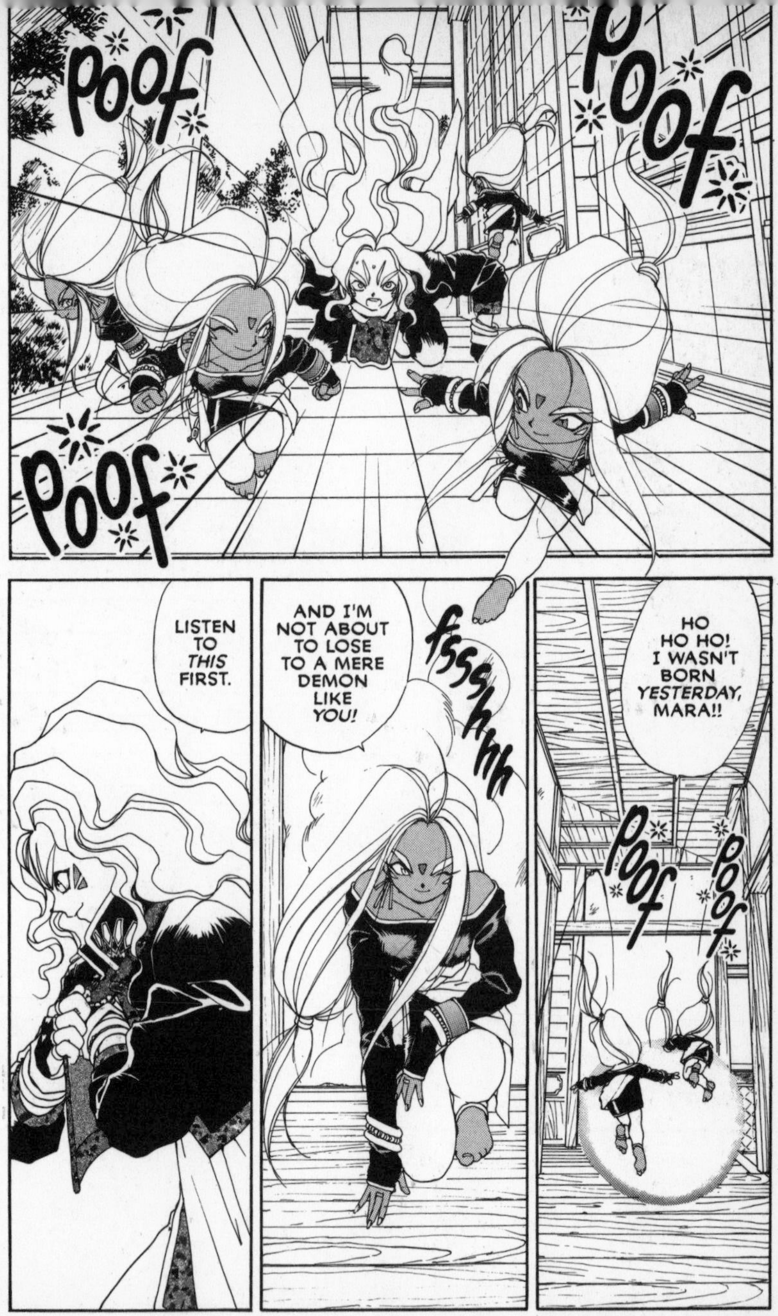
POOF
POOF
POOF
HO HO HO! I WASN'T BORN *YESTERDAY*, MARA!!
POOF
POOF
AND I'M NOT ABOUT TO LOSE TO A MERE DEMON LIKE *YOU!*
fssshhhh
LISTEN TO *THIS* FIRST.

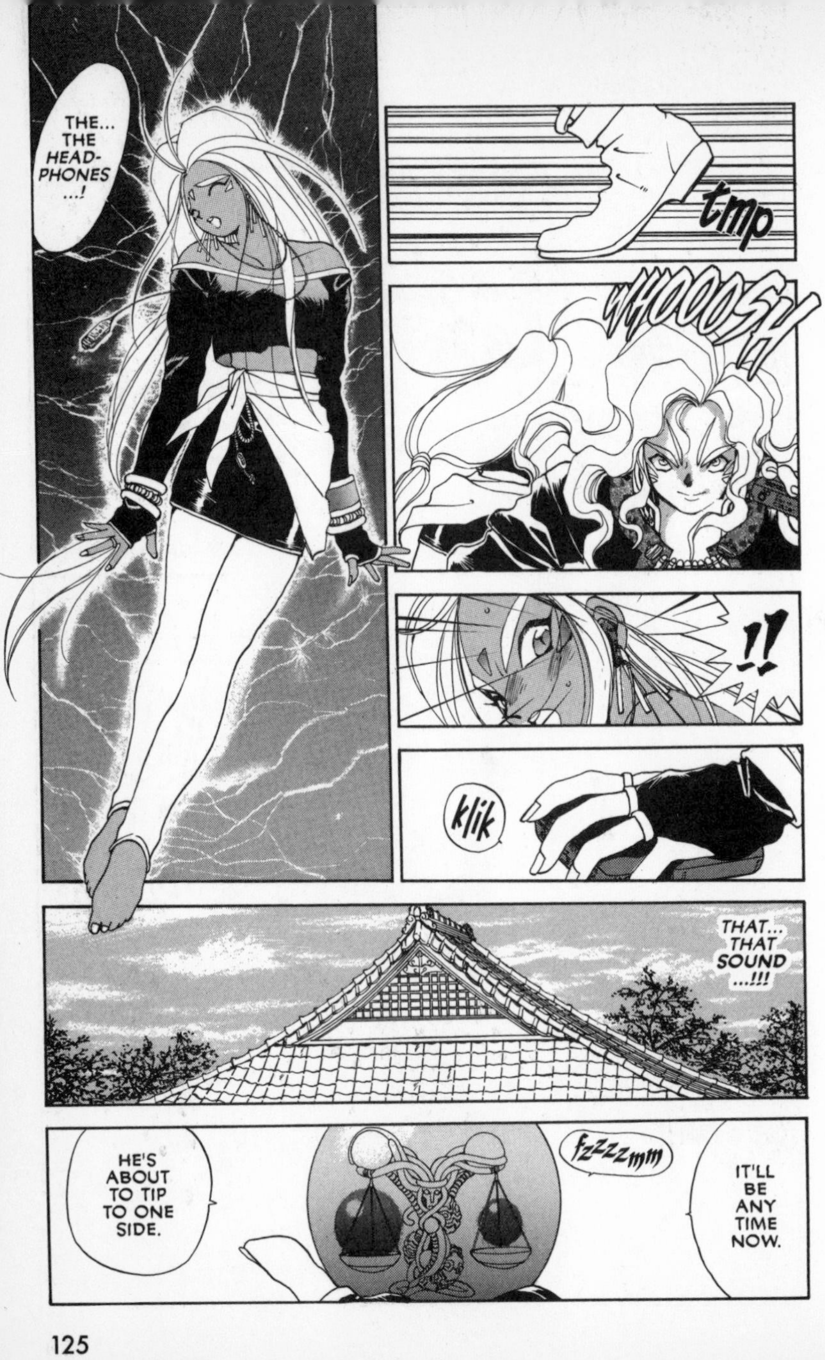
tmp
WHOOOSH
!!
klik
THE... THE HEAD-PHONES ...!
THAT... THAT SOUND ...!!!
IT'LL BE ANY TIME NOW.
fzzzzmm
HE'S ABOUT TO TIP TO ONE SIDE.

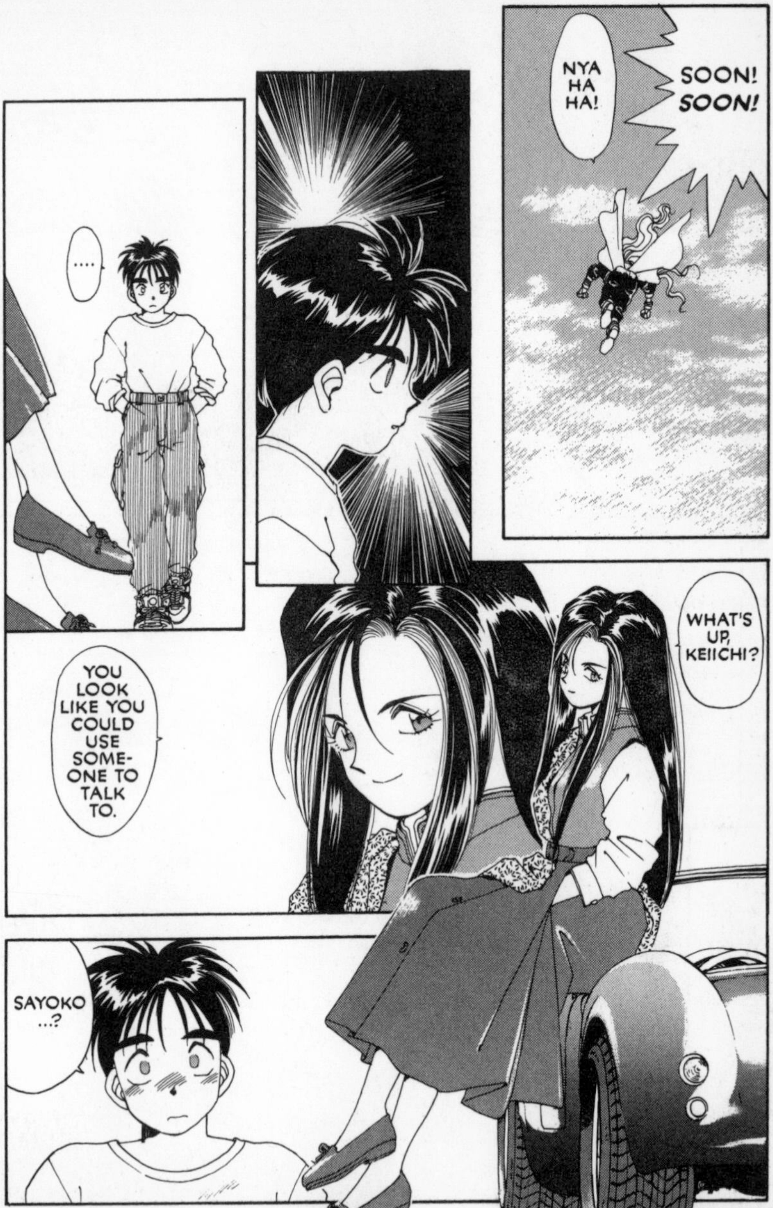
SOON! SOON!
NYA HA HA!
....
WHAT'S UP, KEIICHI?
YOU LOOK LIKE YOU COULD USE SOME-ONE TO TALK TO.
SAYOKO ...?

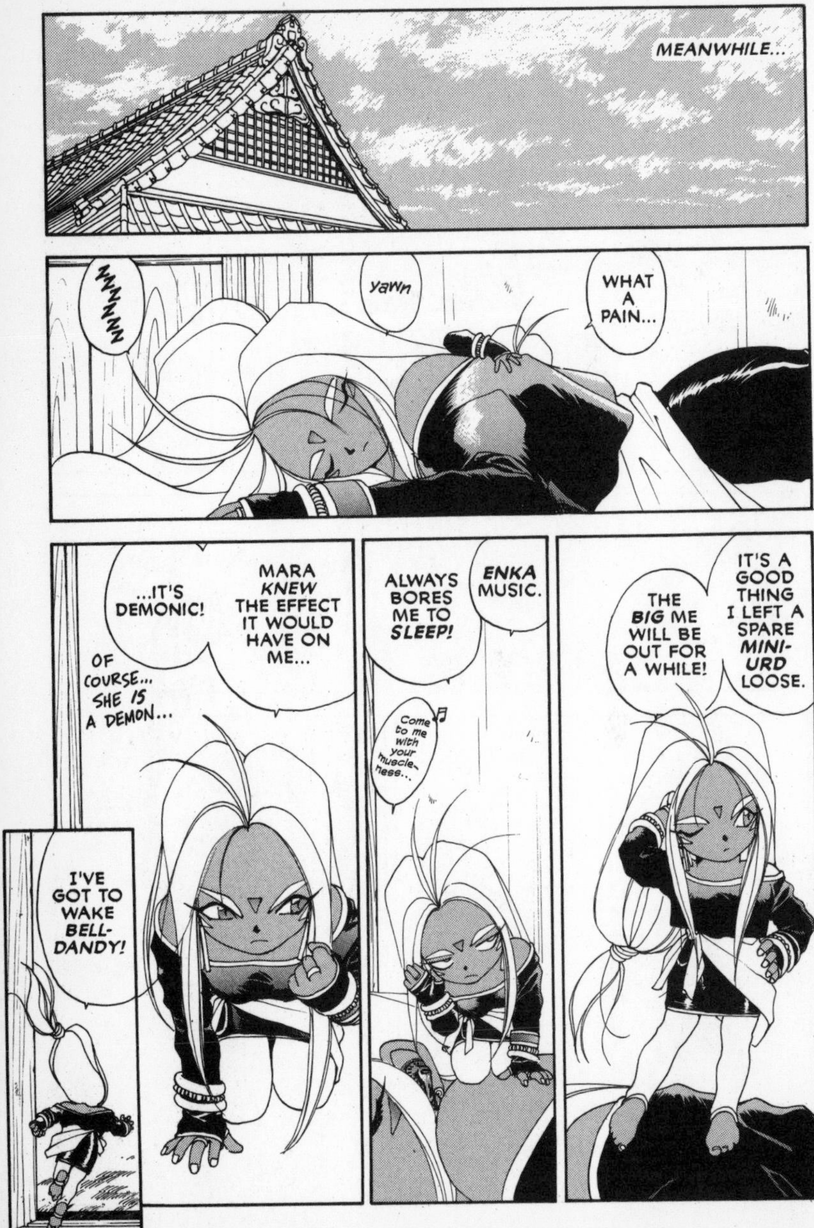
MEANWHILE...
WHAT A PAIN...
yawn
ZZZZZ
IT'S A GOOD THING I LEFT A SPARE MINI-URD LOOSE.
THE BIG ME WILL BE OUT FOR A WHILE!
ENKA MUSIC.
ALWAYS BORES ME TO SLEEP!
Come to me with your muscle-ness...
MARA KNEW THE EFFECT IT WOULD HAVE ON ME...
...IT'S DEMONIC!
OF COURSE... SHE IS A DEMON...
I'VE GOT TO WAKE BELL-DANDY!

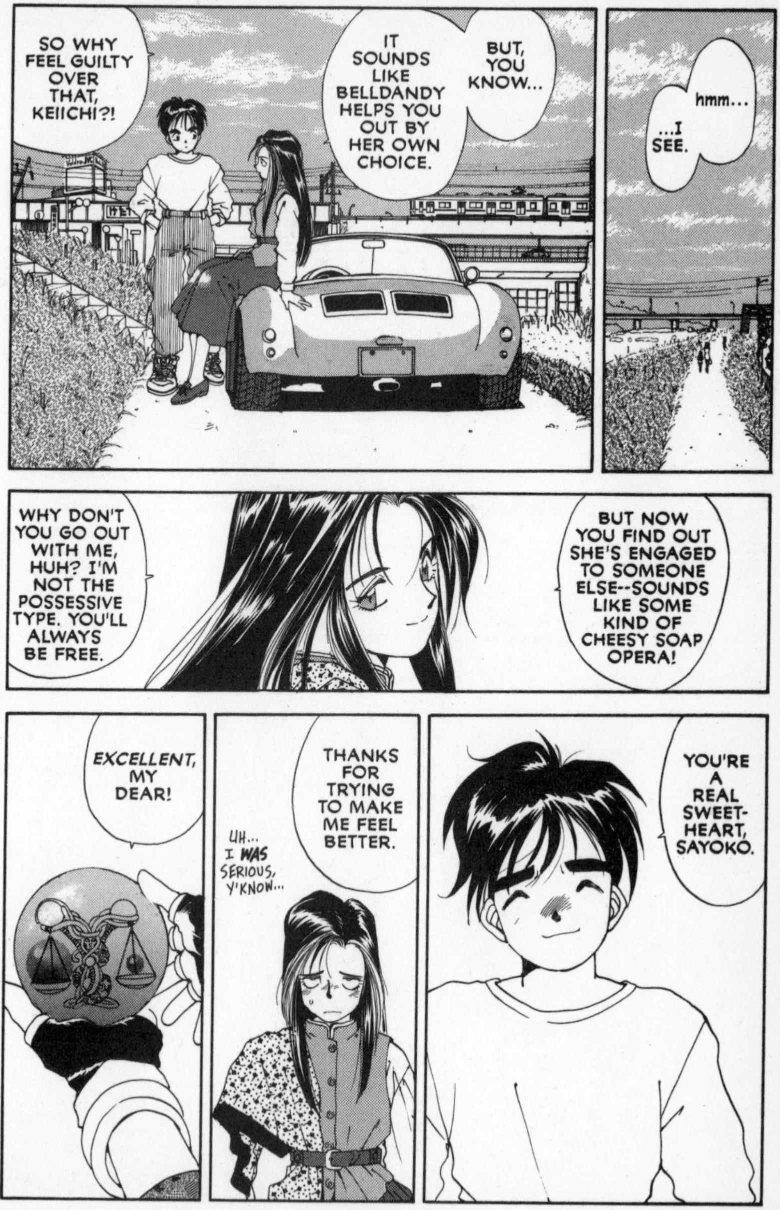
hmm...
...I SEE.
BUT, YOU KNOW...
IT SOUNDS LIKE BELLDANDY HELPS YOU OUT BY HER OWN CHOICE.
SO WHY FEEL GUILTY OVER THAT, KEIICHI?!
BUT NOW YOU FIND OUT SHE'S ENGAGED TO SOMEONE ELSE--SOUNDS LIKE SOME KIND OF CHEESY SOAP OPERA!
WHY DON'T YOU GO OUT WITH ME, HUH? I'M NOT THE POSSESSIVE TYPE. YOU'LL ALWAYS BE FREE.
YOU'RE A REAL SWEET-HEART, SAYOKO.
THANKS FOR TRYING TO MAKE ME FEEL BETTER.
UH... I *WAS* SERIOUS, Y'KNOW...
EXCELLENT, MY DEAR!

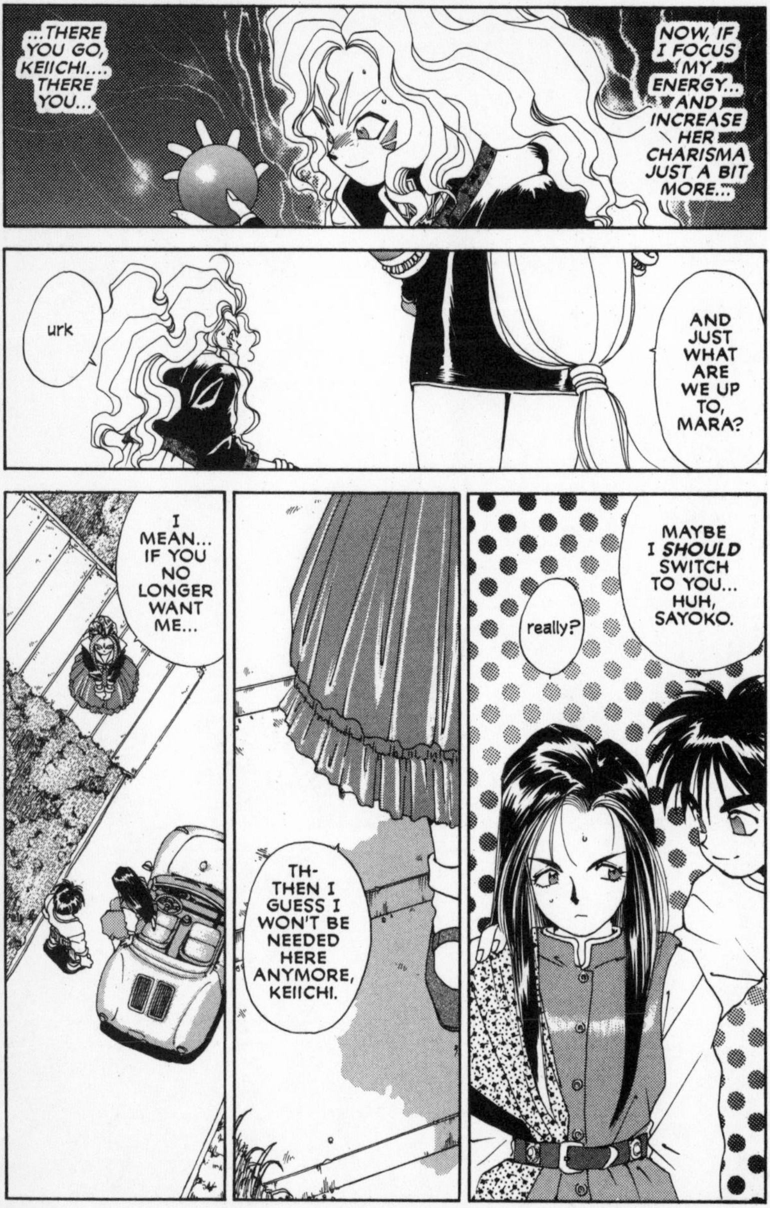
NOW, IF I FOCUS MY ENERGY... AND INCREASE HER CHARISMA JUST A BIT MORE...
...THERE YOU GO, KEIICHI.... THERE YOU...
AND JUST WHAT ARE WE UP TO, MARA?
urk
MAYBE I *SHOULD* SWITCH TO YOU... HUH, SAYOKO.
really?
TH-THEN I GUESS I WON'T BE NEEDED HERE ANYMORE, KEIICHI.
I MEAN... IF YOU NO LONGER WANT ME...

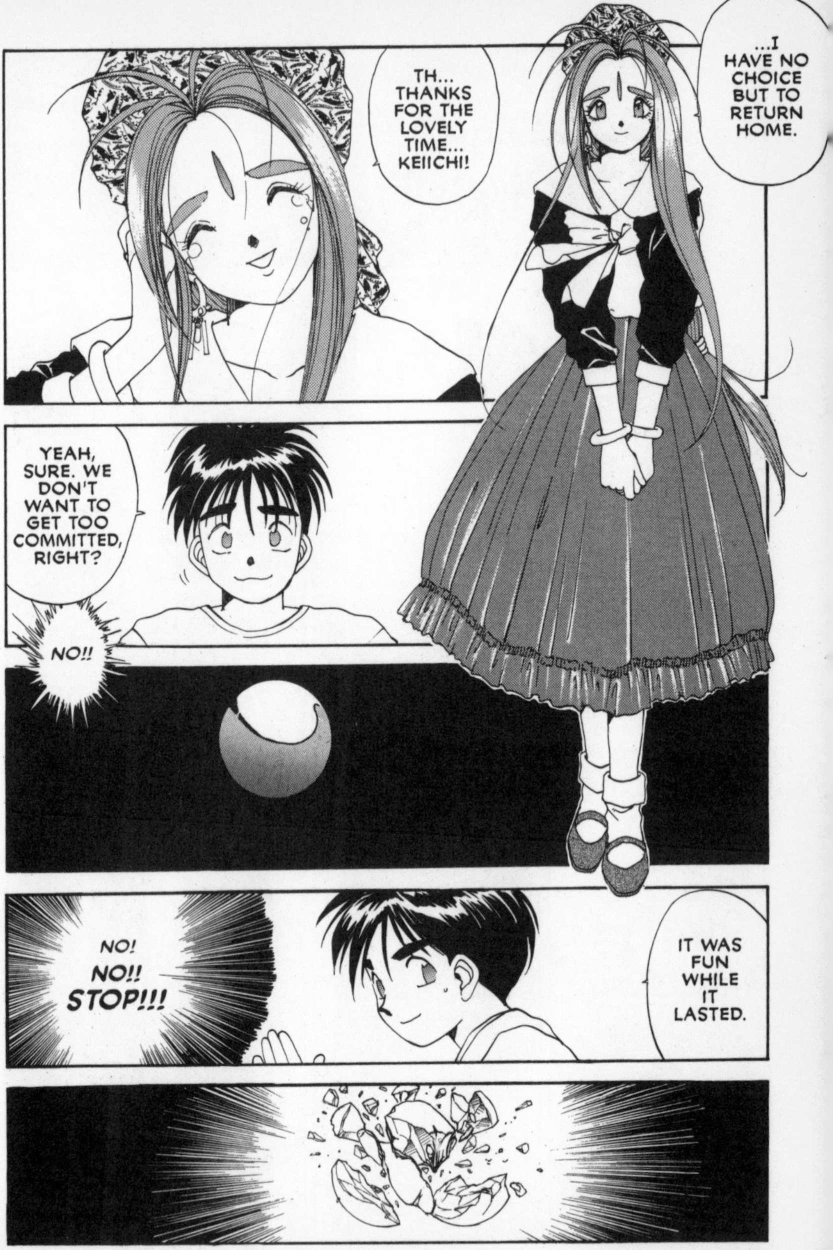
...I HAVE NO CHOICE BUT TO RETURN HOME.
TH... THANKS FOR THE LOVELY TIME... KEIICHI!
YEAH, SURE. WE DON'T WANT TO GET TOO COMMITTED, RIGHT?
NO!!
IT WAS FUN WHILE IT LASTED.
NO! NO!! STOP!!!

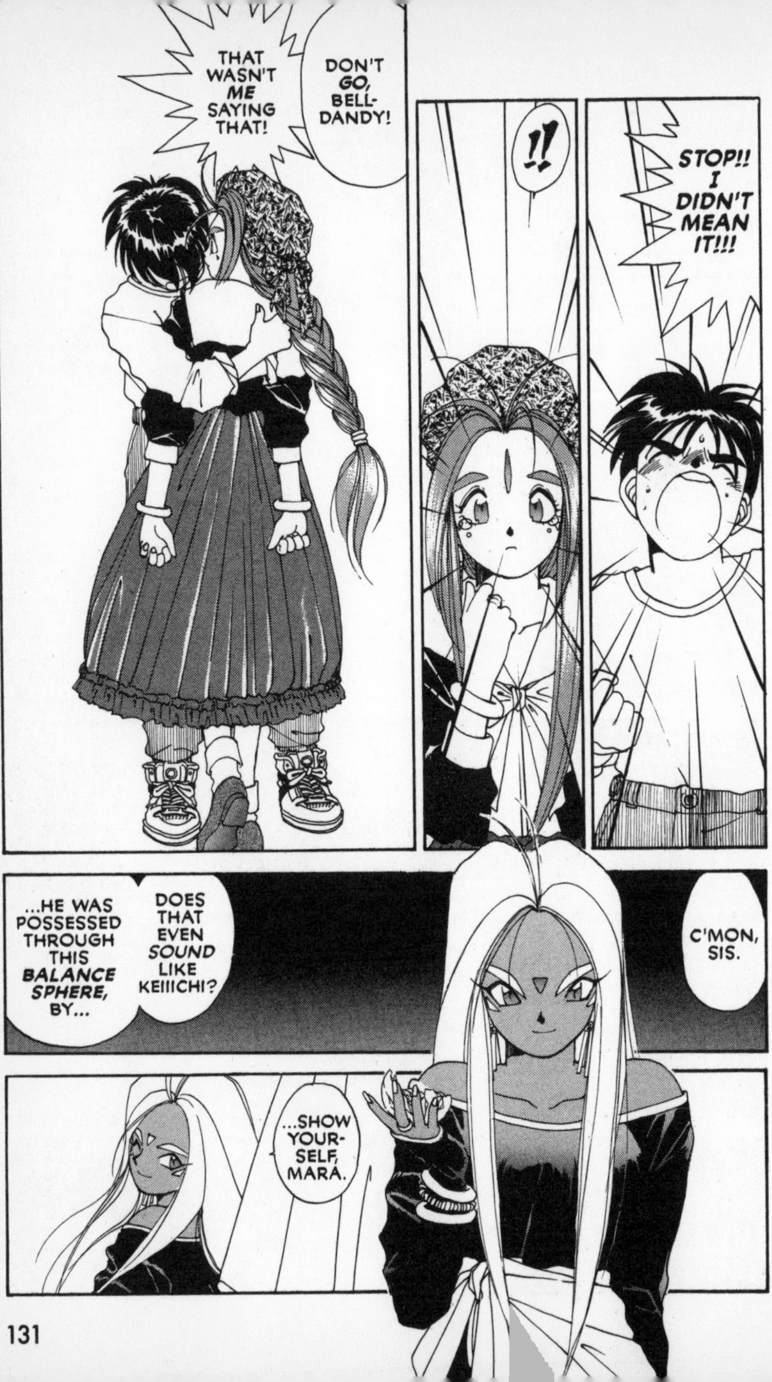
STOP!! I DIDN'T MEAN IT!!!
!!
DON'T GO, BELL-DANDY!
THAT WASN'T ME SAYING THAT!
C'MON, SIS.
DOES THAT EVEN SOUND LIKE KEIIICHI?
...HE WAS POSSESSED THROUGH THIS BALANCE SPHERE, BY...
...SHOW YOURSELF, MARA.

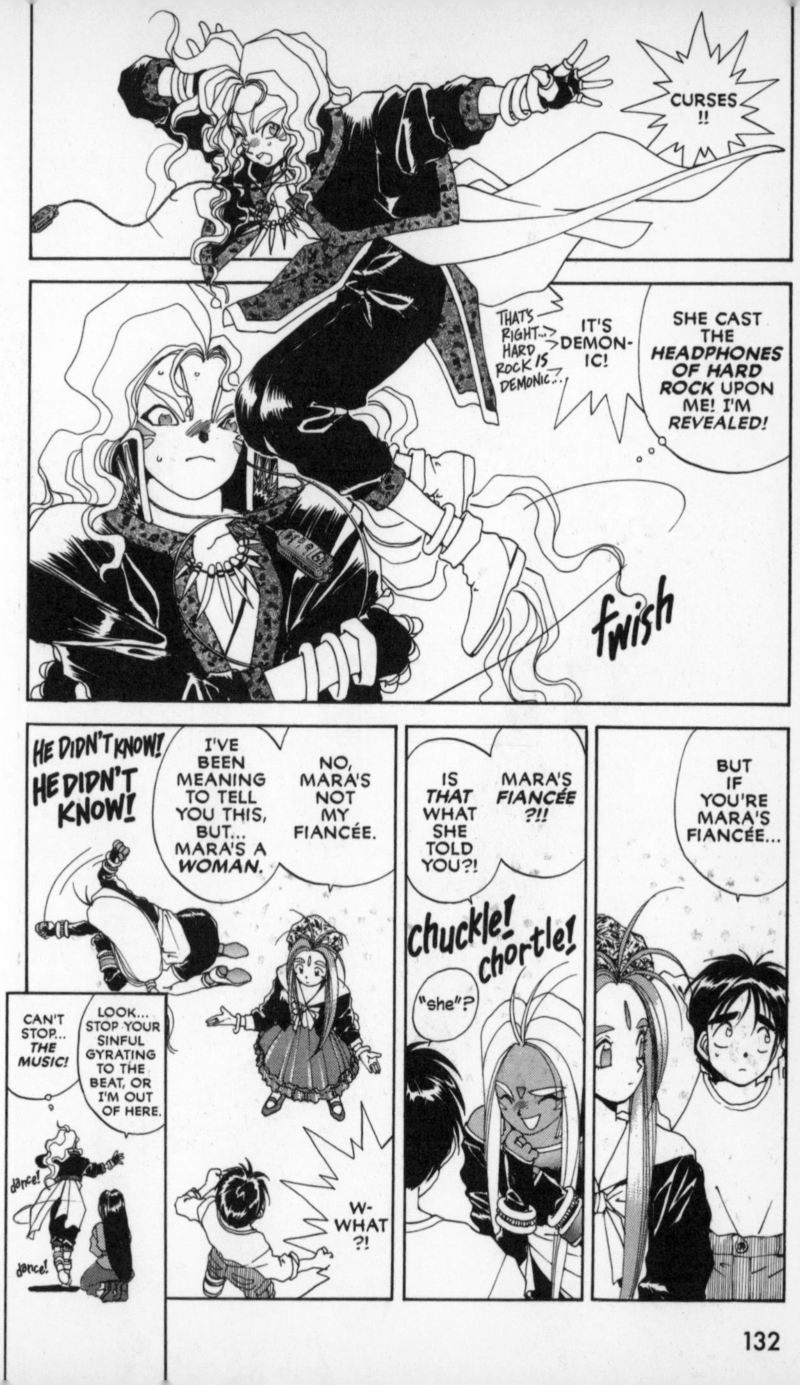

CURSES!!
SHE CAST THE HEADPHONES OF HARD ROCK UPON ME! I'M REVEALED!
IT'S DEMON-IC!
THAT'S RIGHT... HARD ROCK IS DEMONIC...
fwish
BUT IF YOU'RE MARA'S FIANCÉE...
MARA'S FIANCÉE?!!
IS THAT WHAT SHE TOLD YOU?!
chuckle! chortle!
"she"?
NO, MARA'S NOT MY FIANCÉE.
I'VE BEEN MEANING TO TELL YOU THIS, BUT... MARA'S A WOMAN.
HE DIDN'T KNOW! HE DIDN'T KNOW!
W-WHAT?!
LOOK... STOP YOUR SINFUL GYRATING TO THE BEAT, OR I'M OUT OF HERE.
CAN'T STOP... THE MUSIC!
dance!
dance!

CHAPTER 29

The Worst Day of a Demon

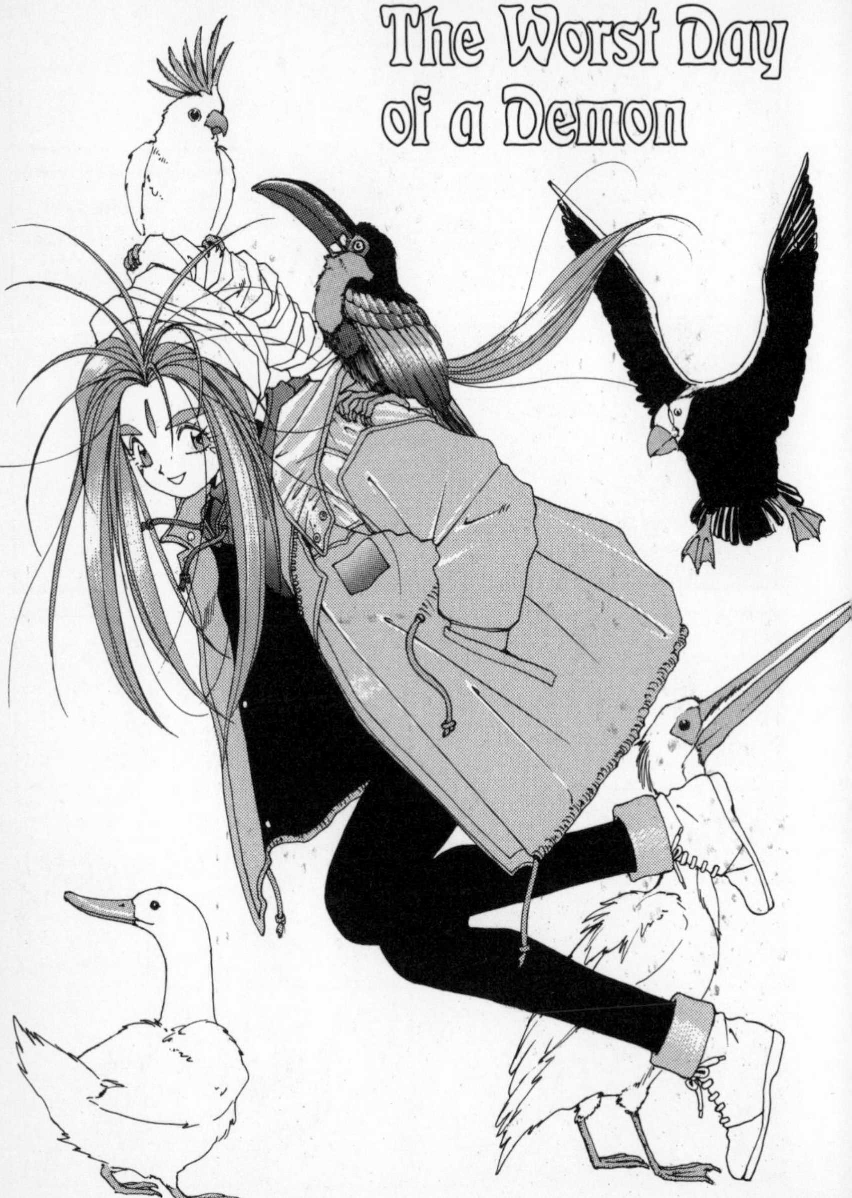

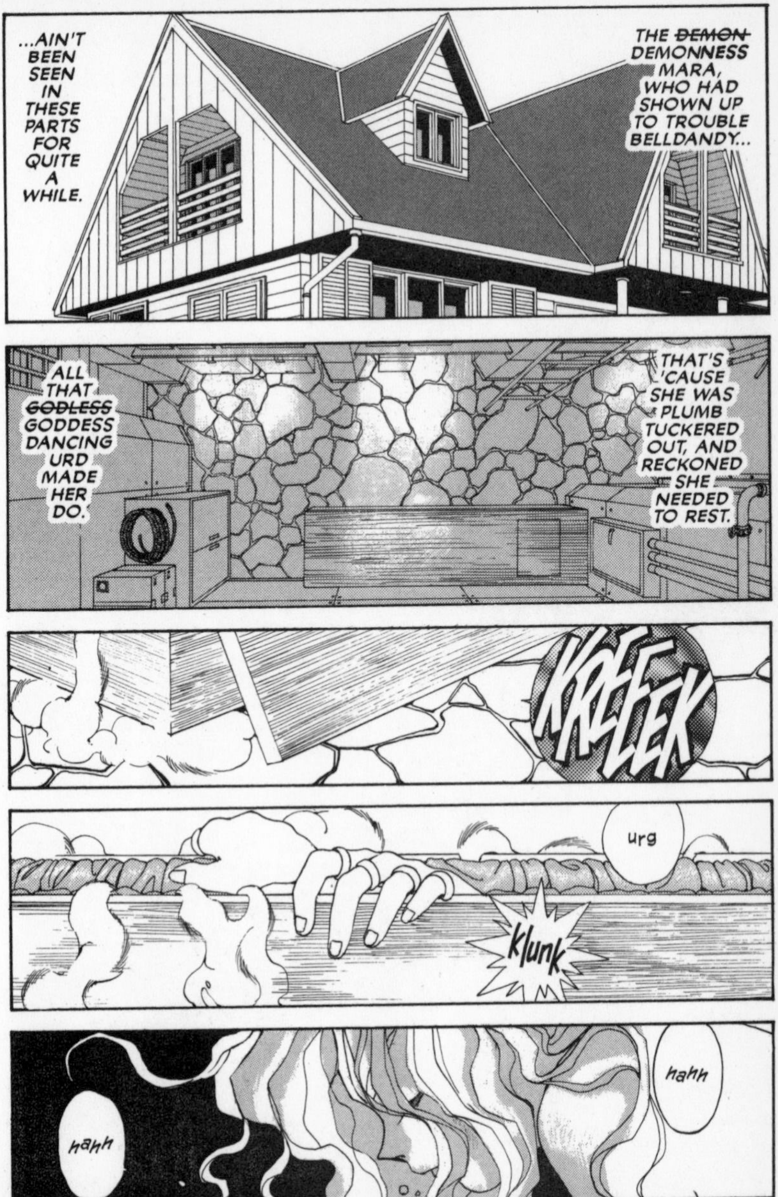
THE ~~DEMON~~ DEMONNESS MARA, WHO HAD SHOWN UP TO TROUBLE BELLDANDY...
...AIN'T BEEN SEEN IN THESE PARTS FOR QUITE A WHILE.
THAT'S 'CAUSE SHE WAS PLUMB TUCKERED OUT, AND RECKONED SHE NEEDED TO REST.
ALL THAT ~~GODLESS~~ GODDESS DANCING URD MADE HER DO.
KREEEK
urg
klunk
hahh
hahh

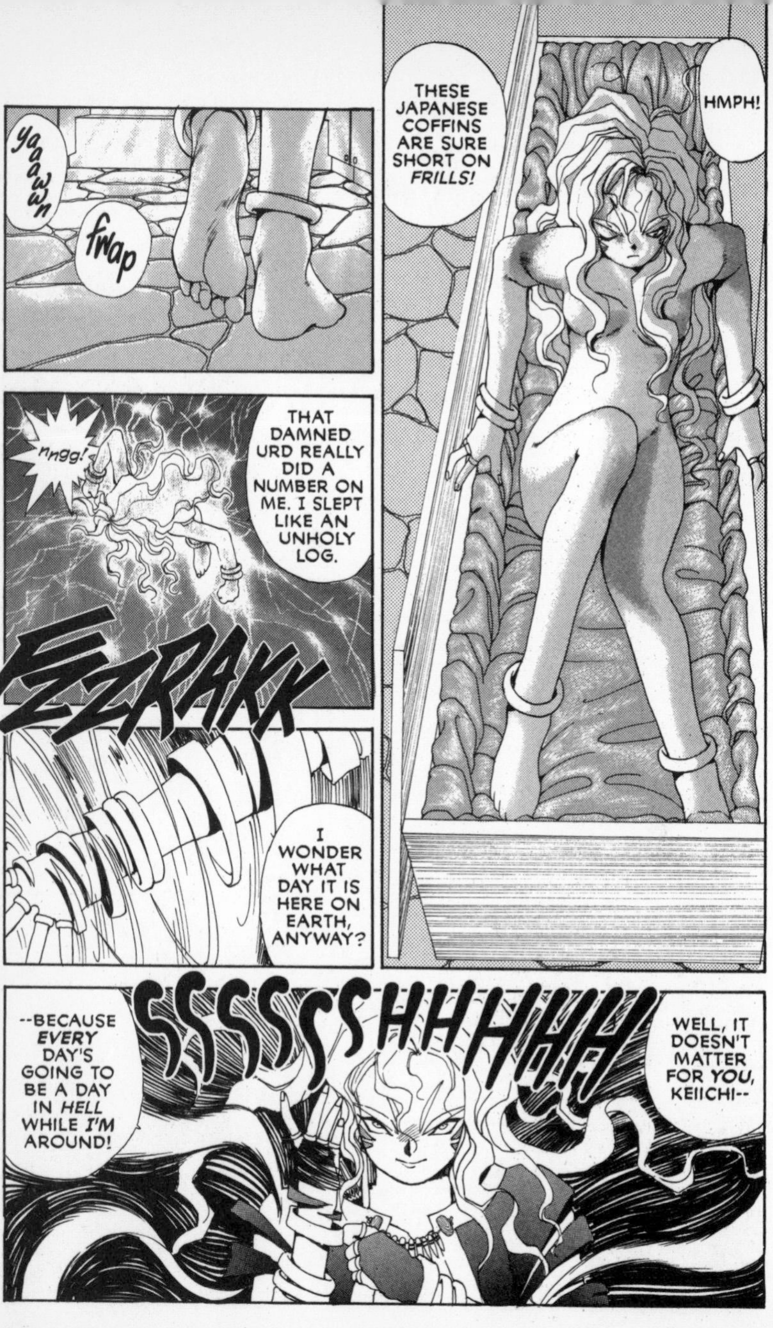
HMPH!
THESE JAPANESE COFFINS ARE SURE SHORT ON *FRILLS!*
yaaawn
fwap
THAT DAMNED URD REALLY DID A NUMBER ON ME. I SLEPT LIKE AN UNHOLY LOG.
nngg!
FZZRAKK
I WONDER WHAT DAY IT IS HERE ON EARTH, ANYWAY?
WELL, IT DOESN'T MATTER FOR *YOU,* KEIICHI--
SSSSSSHHHHHH
--BECAUSE *EVERY* DAY'S GOING TO BE A DAY IN *HELL* WHILE *I'M* AROUND!

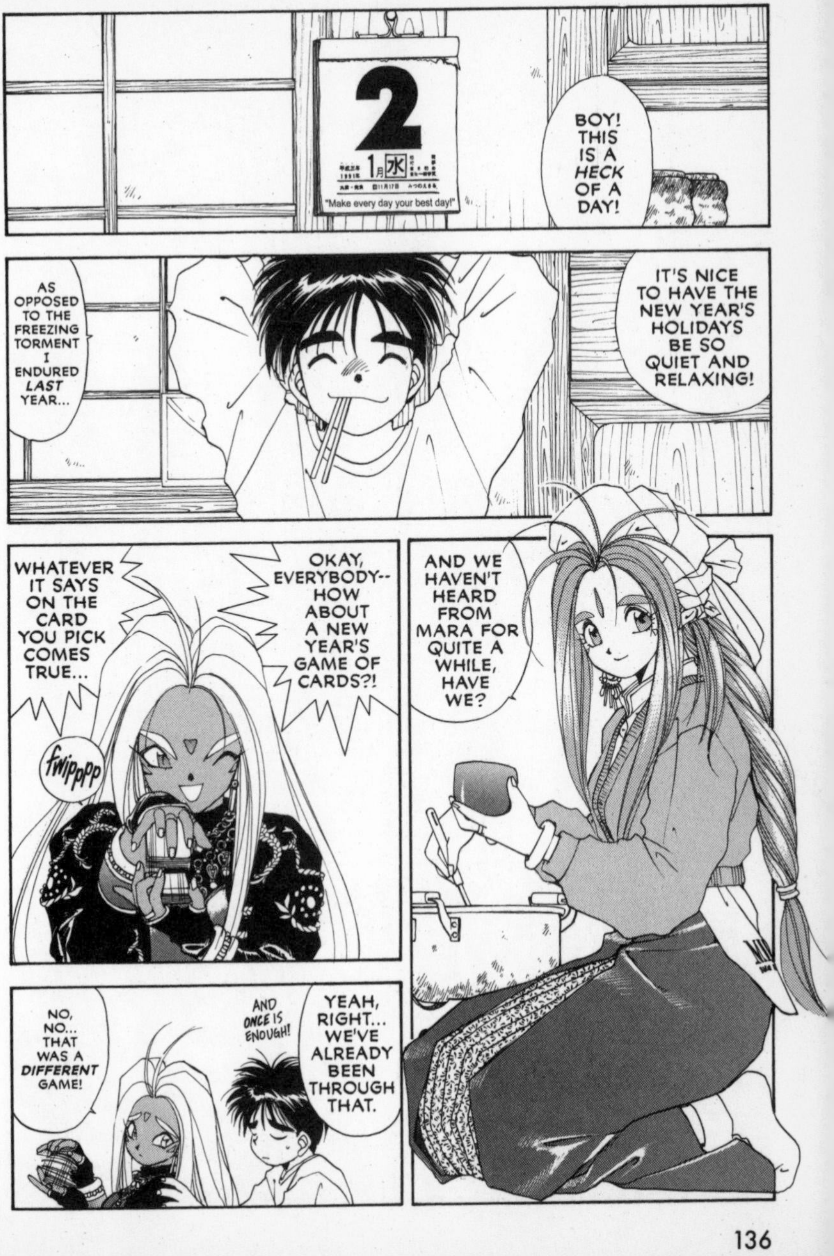
2
1月 水
"Make every day your best day!"
BOY! THIS IS A HECK OF A DAY!
IT'S NICE TO HAVE THE NEW YEAR'S HOLIDAYS BE SO QUIET AND RELAXING!
AS OPPOSED TO THE FREEZING TORMENT I ENDURED LAST YEAR...
AND WE HAVEN'T HEARD FROM MARA FOR QUITE A WHILE, HAVE WE?
OKAY, EVERYBODY-- HOW ABOUT A NEW YEAR'S GAME OF CARDS?!
WHATEVER IT SAYS ON THE CARD YOU PICK COMES TRUE...
fwipppp
YEAH, RIGHT... WE'VE ALREADY BEEN THROUGH THAT.
AND ONCE IS ENOUGH!
NO, NO... THAT WAS A DIFFERENT GAME!

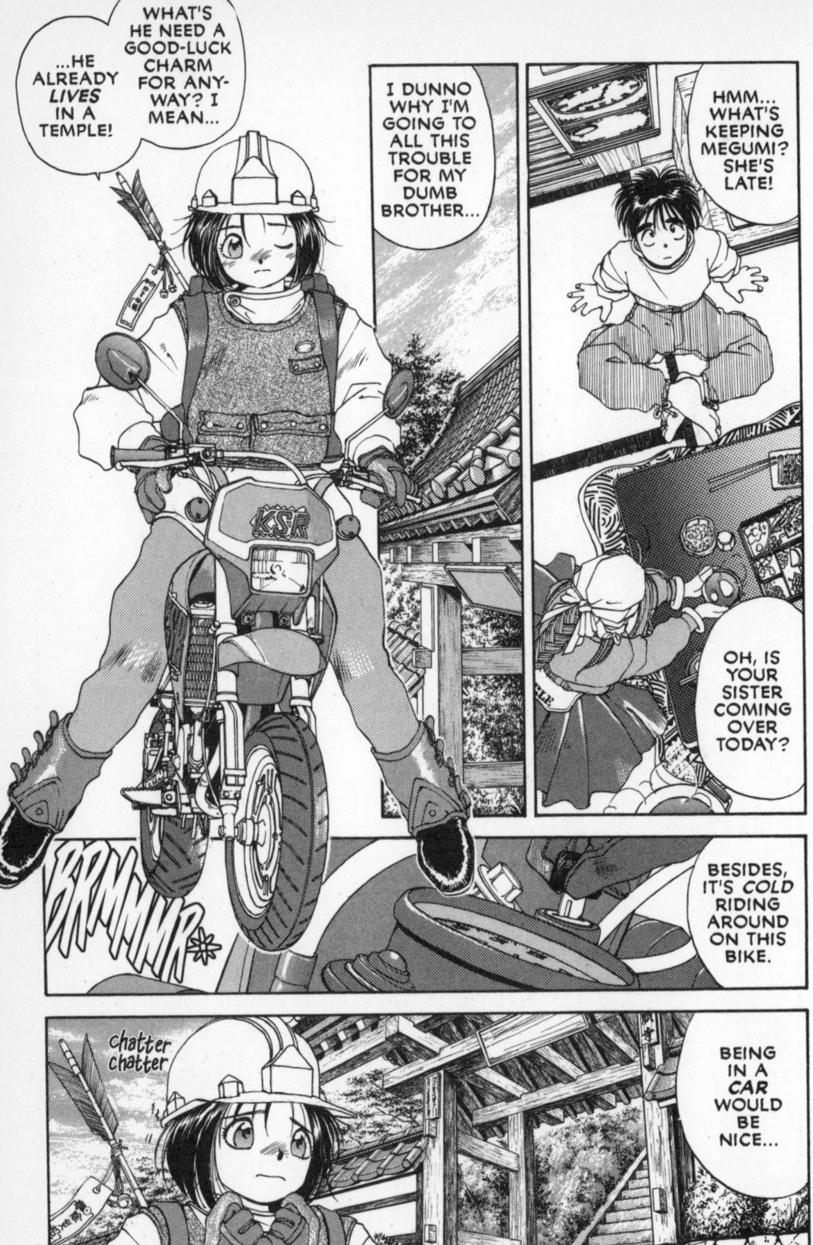
HMM... WHAT'S KEEPING MEGUMI? SHE'S LATE!
OH, IS YOUR SISTER COMING OVER TODAY?
I DUNNO WHY I'M GOING TO ALL THIS TROUBLE FOR MY DUMB BROTHER...
WHAT'S HE NEED A GOOD-LUCK CHARM FOR ANYWAY? I MEAN...
...HE ALREADY *LIVES* IN A TEMPLE!
BESIDES, IT'S *COLD* RIDING AROUND ON THIS BIKE.
BRMMMR
BEING IN A *CAR* WOULD BE NICE...
chatter chatter

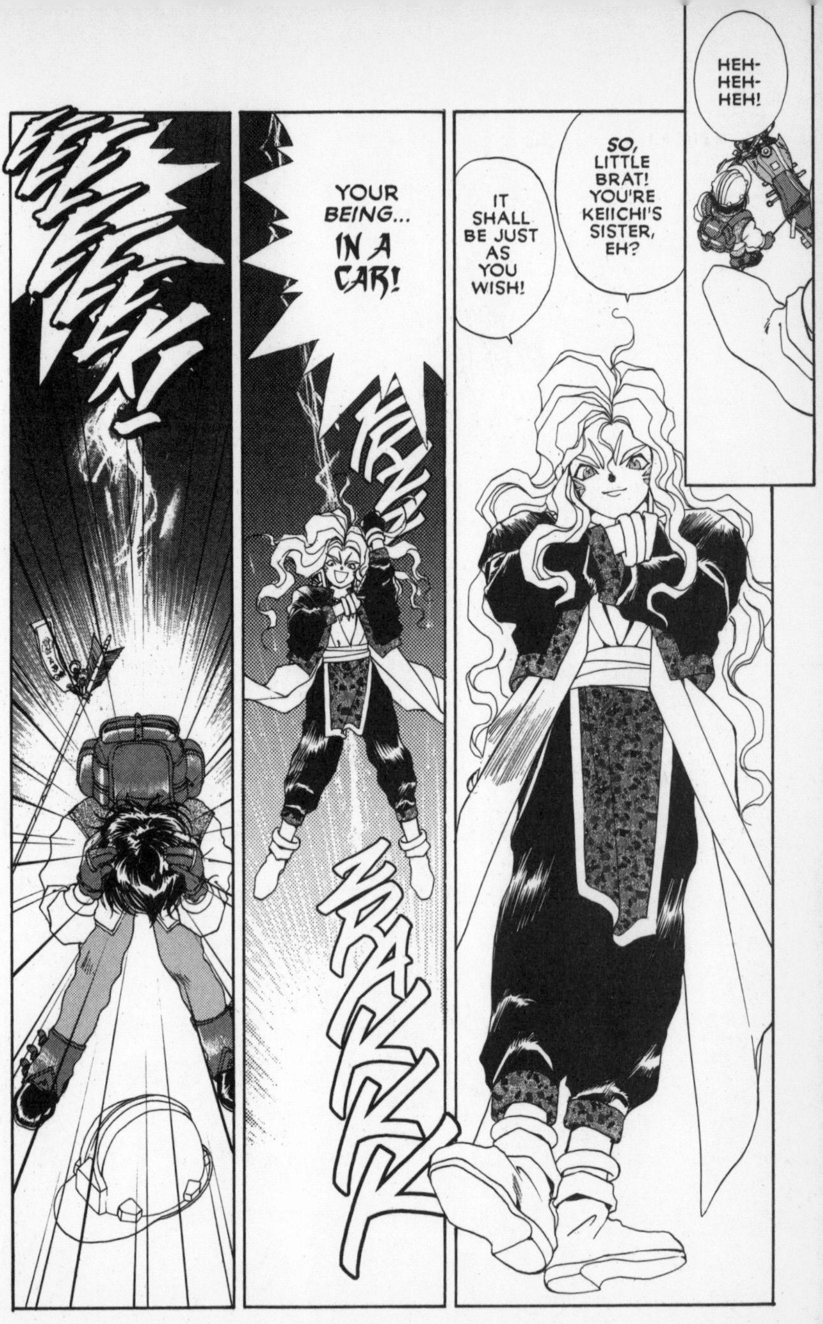
HEH-HEH-HEH!
SO, LITTLE BRAT! YOU'RE KEIICHI'S SISTER, EH?
IT SHALL BE JUST AS YOU WISH!
YOUR BEING... IN A CAR!

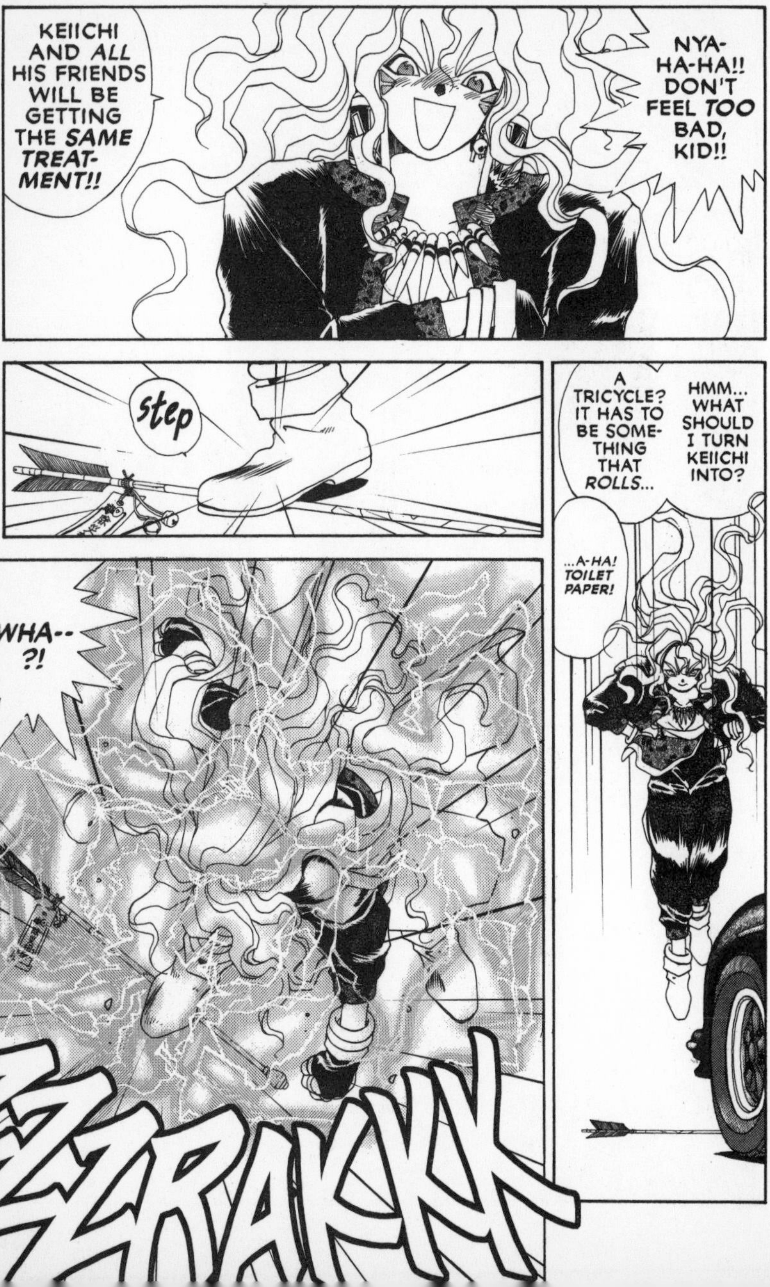
NYA-HA-HA!! DON'T FEEL *TOO* BAD, KID!!
KEIICHI AND *ALL* HIS FRIENDS WILL BE GETTING THE *SAME TREATMENT!!*
HMM... WHAT SHOULD I TURN KEIICHI INTO?
A TRICYCLE? IT HAS TO BE SOMETHING THAT *ROLLS*...
...*A-HA! TOILET PAPER!*
step
WHA-- ?!
ZZRAKKK

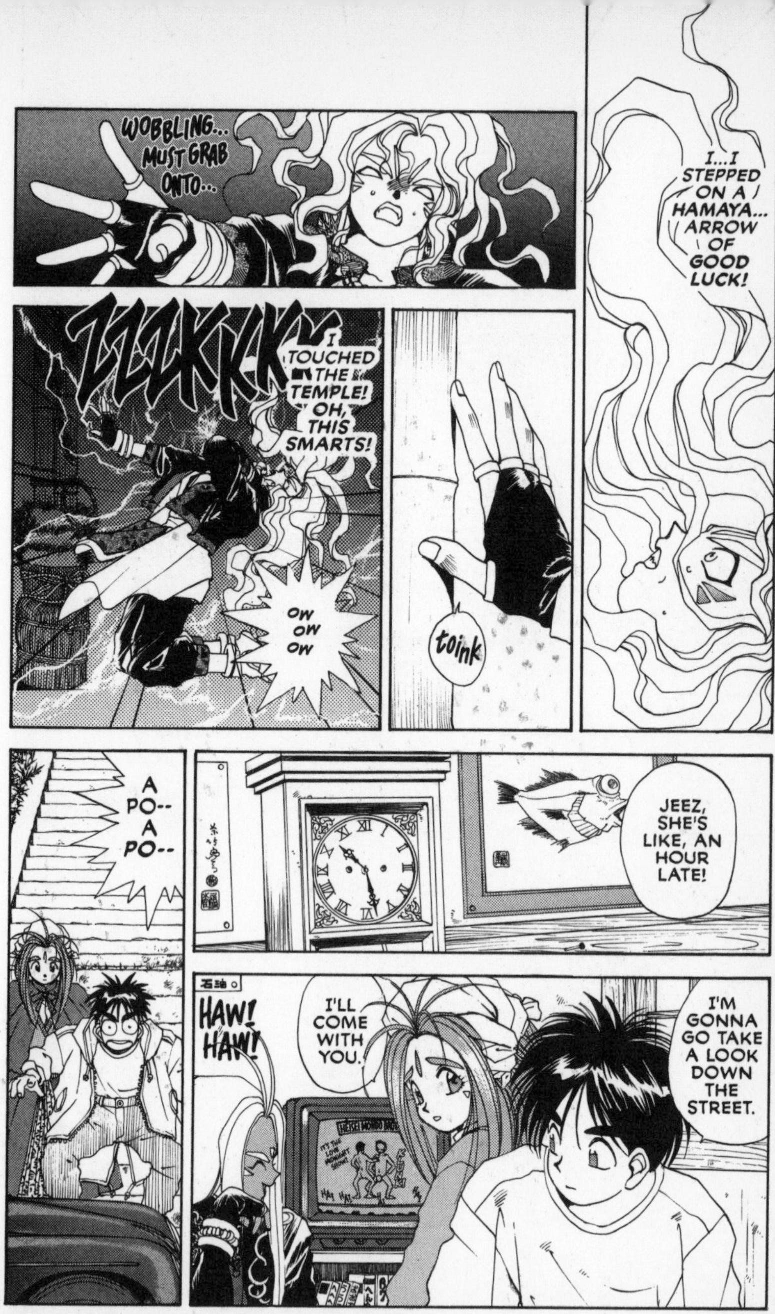

I...I STEPPED ON A HAMAYA... ARROW OF GOOD LUCK!
WOBBLING... MUST GRAB ONTO...
toink
ZZZKKKK
I TOUCHED THE TEMPLE! OH, THIS SMARTS!
OW OW OW
JEEZ, SHE'S LIKE, AN HOUR LATE!
I'M GONNA GO TAKE A LOOK DOWN THE STREET.
I'LL COME WITH YOU.
HAW! HAW!
A PO-- A PO--

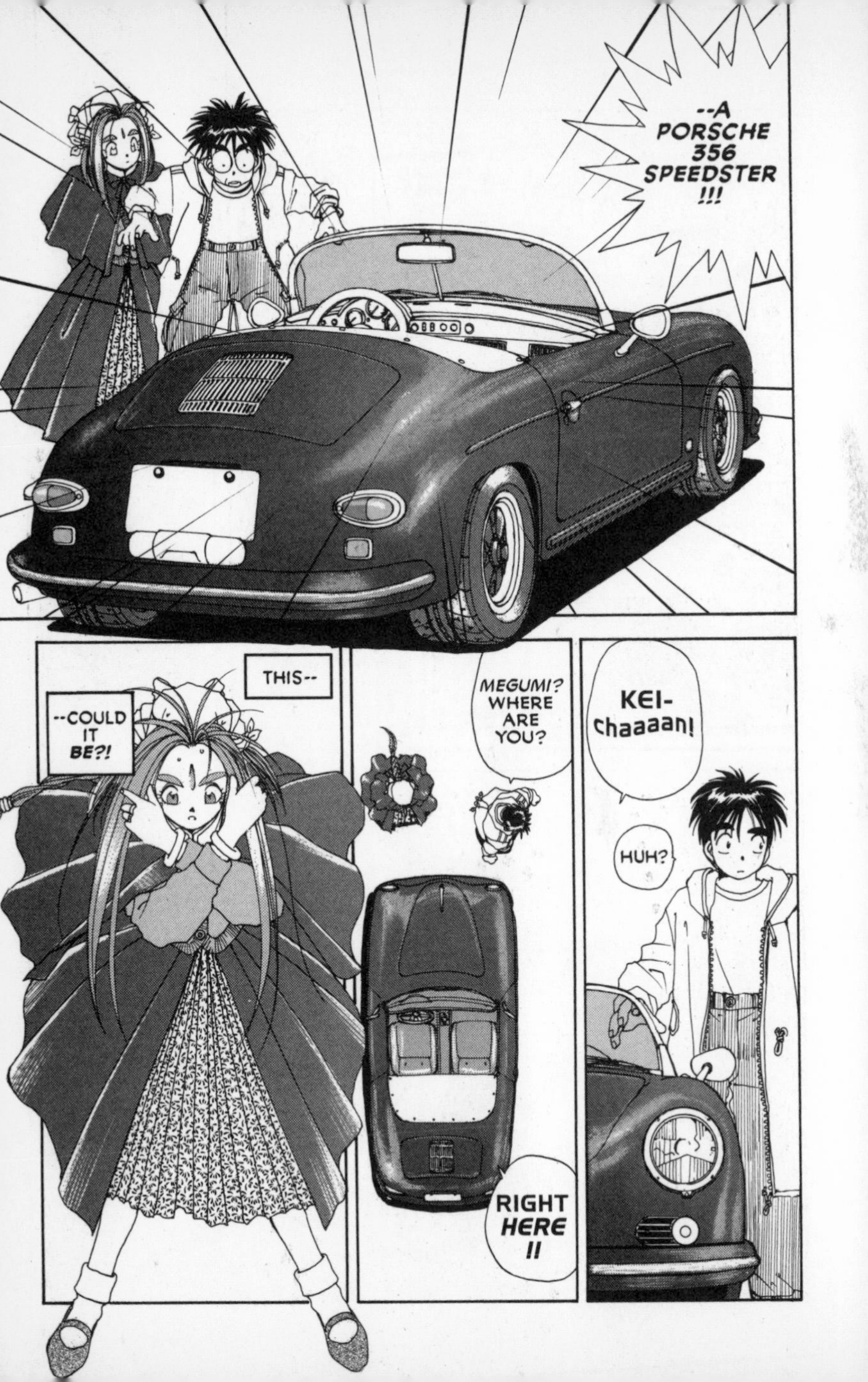
--A PORSCHE 356 SPEEDSTER !!!
KEI-chaaaan!
HUH?
MEGUMI? WHERE ARE YOU?
RIGHT HERE !!
THIS--
--COULD IT BE?!

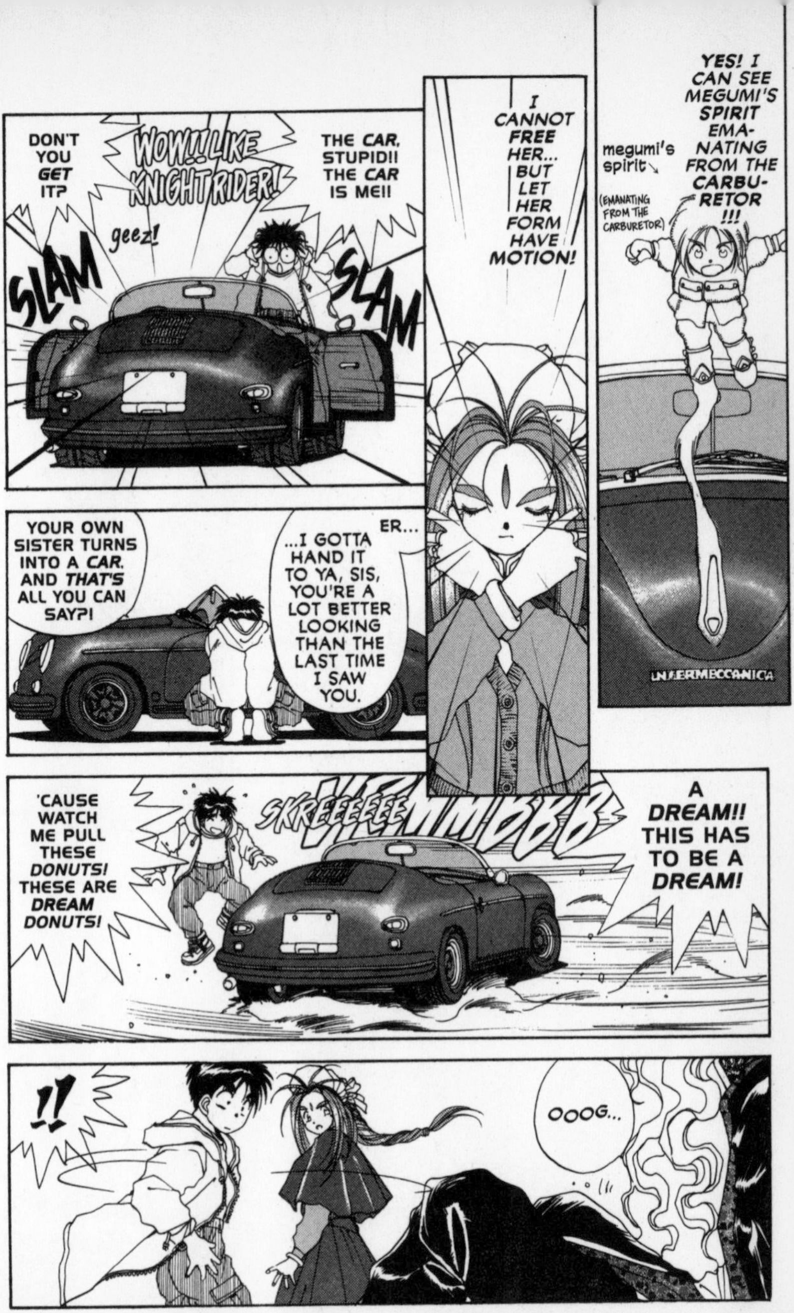
YES! I CAN SEE MEGUMI'S SPIRIT EMANATING FROM THE CARBURETOR !!!
megumi's spirit
(EMANATING FROM THE CARBURETOR)
I CANNOT FREE HER... BUT LET HER FORM HAVE MOTION!
THE CAR, STUPID!! THE CAR IS ME!!
WOW!! LIKE KNIGHT RIDER!
DON'T YOU GET IT?
geez!
SLAM
SLAM
ER...
...I GOTTA HAND IT TO YA, SIS, YOU'RE A LOT BETTER LOOKING THAN THE LAST TIME I SAW YOU.
YOUR OWN SISTER TURNS INTO A CAR, AND THAT'S ALL YOU CAN SAY?!
A DREAM!! THIS HAS TO BE A DREAM!
SKREEEEEEE
'CAUSE WATCH ME PULL THESE DONUTS! THESE ARE DREAM DONUTS!
OOOG...
!!

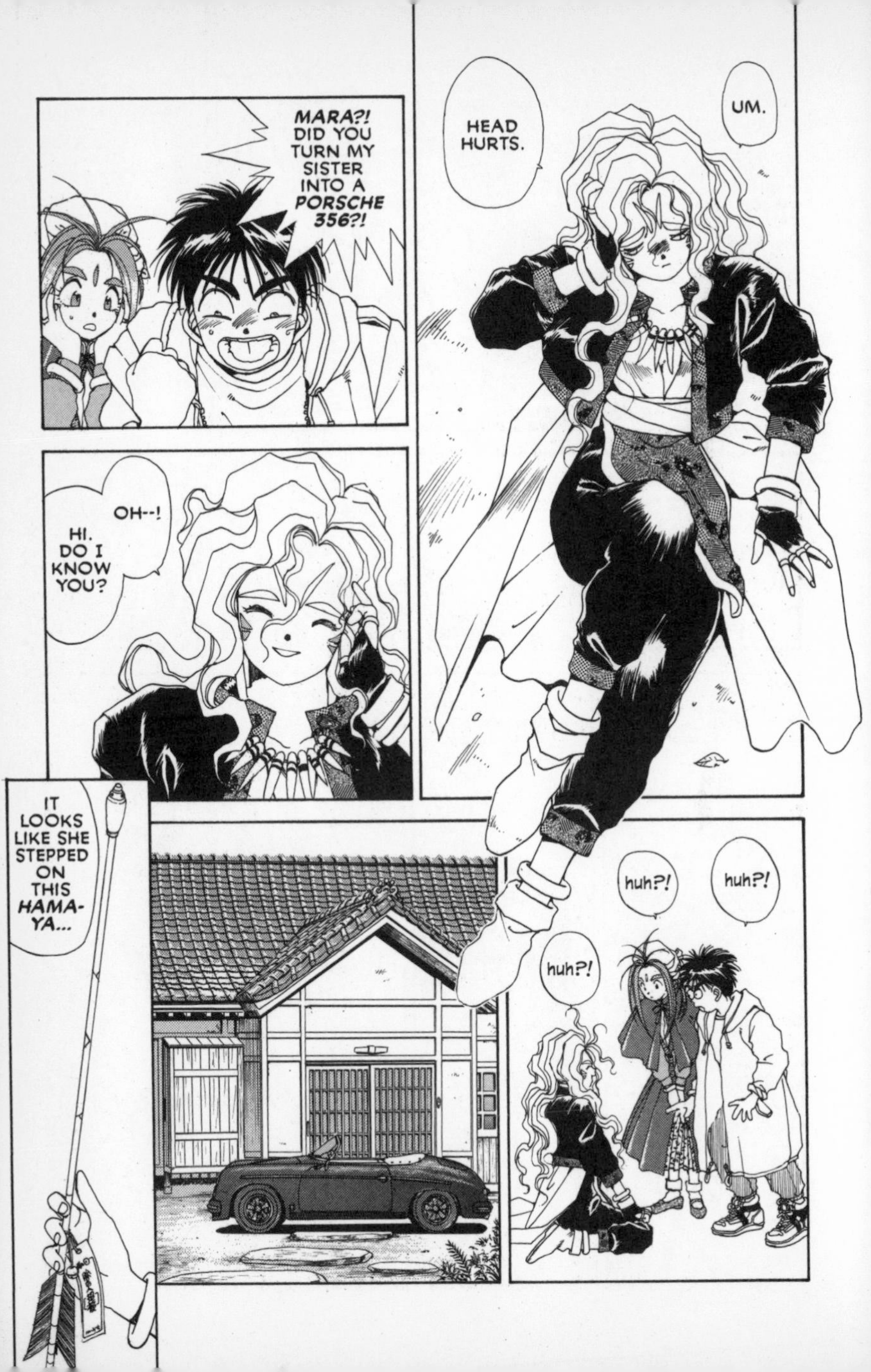
UM.
HEAD HURTS.
MARA?! DID YOU TURN MY SISTER INTO A PORSCHE 356?!
OH--!
HI. DO I KNOW YOU?
huh?!
huh?!
huh?!
IT LOOKS LIKE SHE STEPPED ON THIS HAMA-YA...

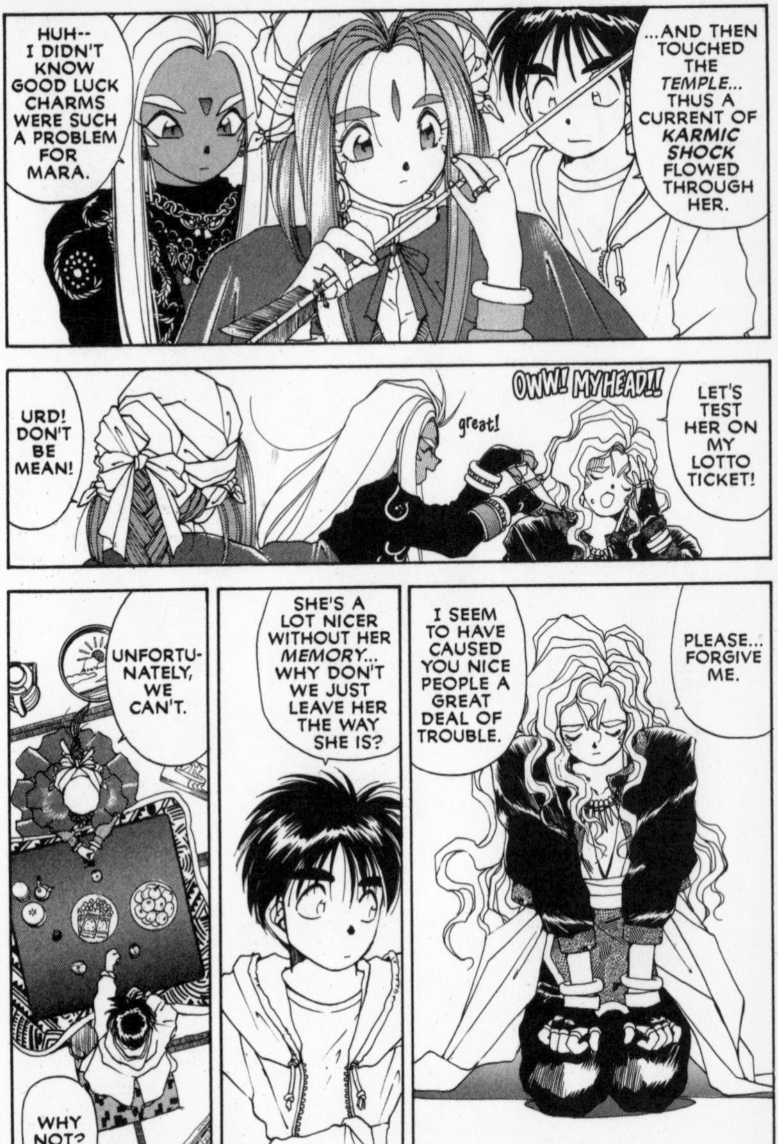
...AND THEN TOUCHED THE *TEMPLE*... THUS A CURRENT OF ***KARMIC SHOCK*** FLOWED THROUGH HER.
HUH-- I DIDN'T KNOW GOOD LUCK CHARMS WERE SUCH A PROBLEM FOR MARA.
LET'S TEST HER ON MY LOTTO TICKET!
OWW! MY HEAD!!
great!
URD! DON'T BE MEAN!
PLEASE... FORGIVE ME.
I SEEM TO HAVE CAUSED YOU NICE PEOPLE A GREAT DEAL OF TROUBLE.
SHE'S A LOT NICER WITHOUT HER *MEMORY*... WHY DON'T WE JUST LEAVE HER THE WAY SHE IS?
UNFORTU-NATELY, WE CAN'T.
WHY NOT?

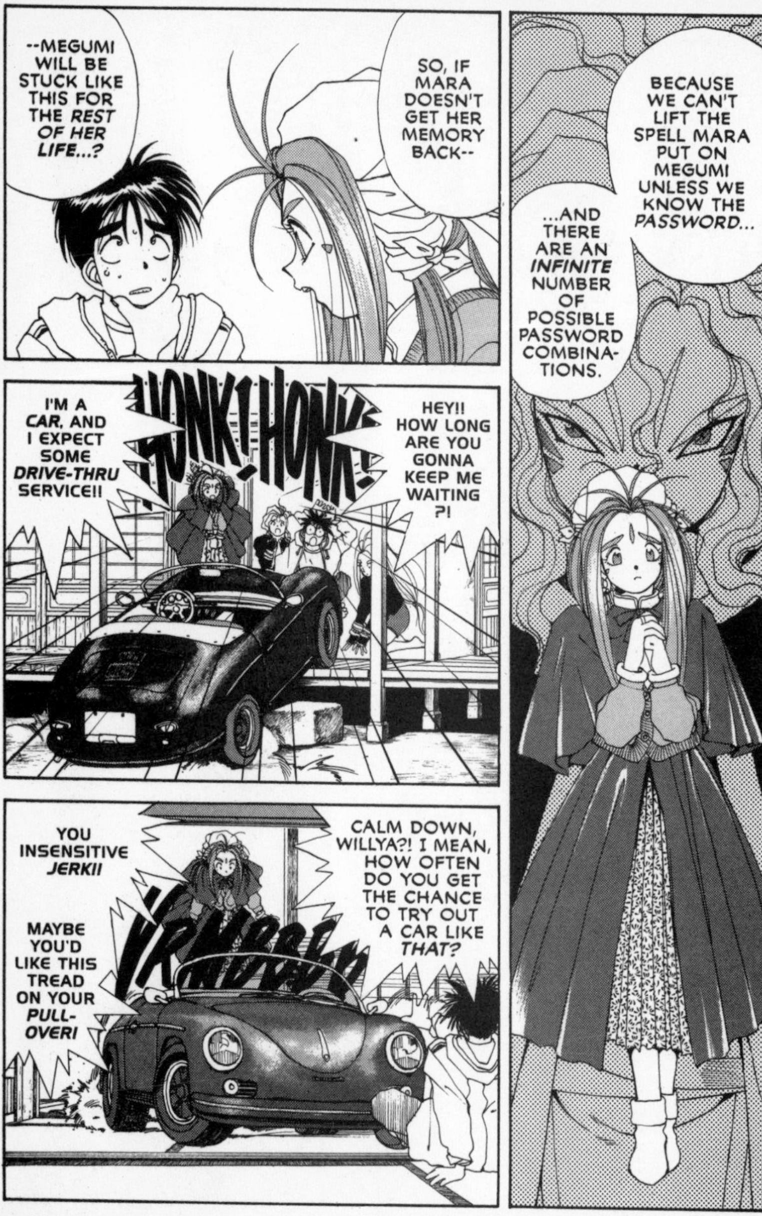
BECAUSE WE CAN'T LIFT THE SPELL MARA PUT ON MEGUMI UNLESS WE KNOW THE *PASSWORD*...
...AND THERE ARE AN *INFINITE* NUMBER OF POSSIBLE PASSWORD COMBINATIONS.
SO, IF MARA DOESN'T GET HER MEMORY BACK--
--MEGUMI WILL BE STUCK LIKE THIS FOR THE *REST OF HER LIFE*...?
HEY!! HOW LONG ARE YOU GONNA KEEP ME WAITING ?!
HONK! HONK!
I'M A *CAR*, AND I EXPECT SOME *DRIVE-THRU* SERVICE!!
CALM DOWN, WILLYA?! I MEAN, HOW OFTEN DO YOU GET THE CHANCE TO TRY OUT A CAR LIKE *THAT?*
YOU INSENSITIVE *JERK!!*
MAYBE YOU'D LIKE THIS TREAD ON YOUR *PULL-OVER!*

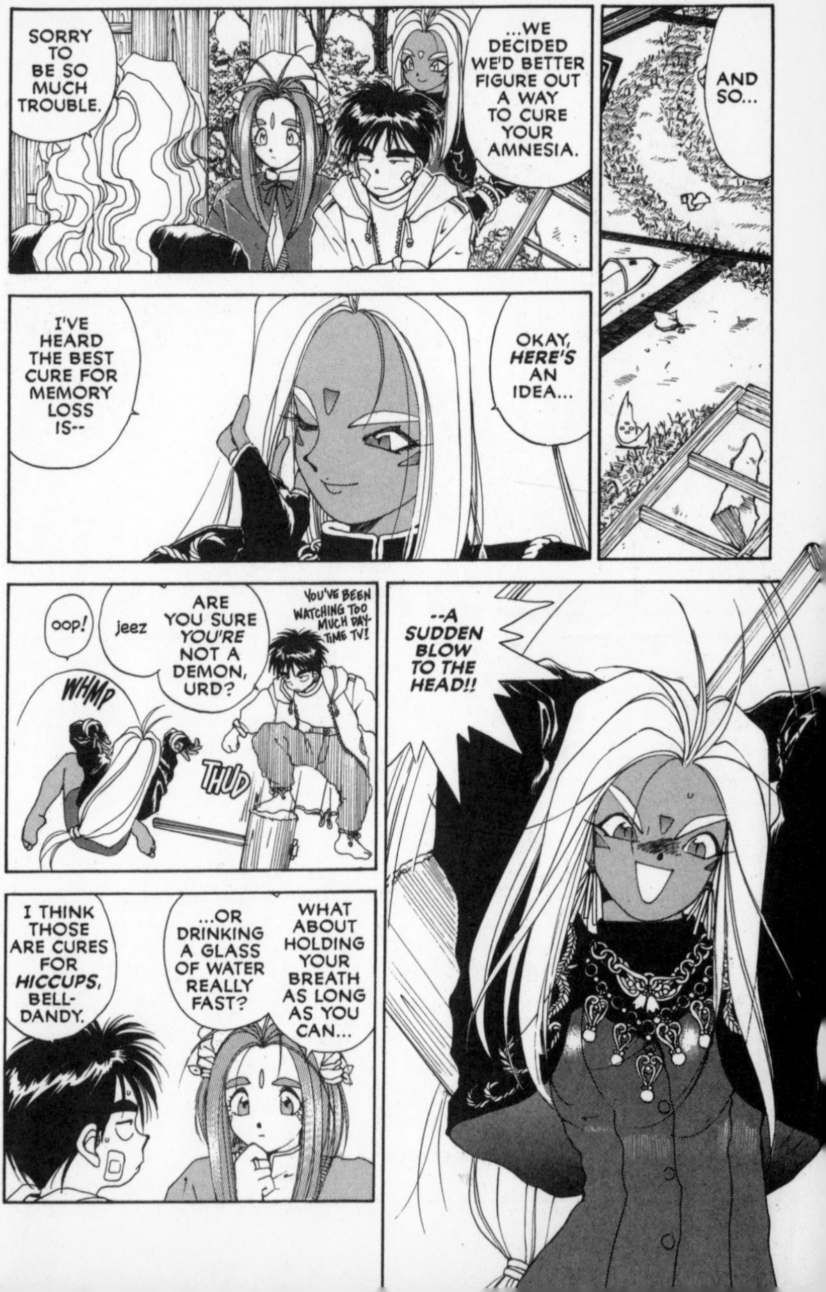
AND SO...
...WE DECIDED WE'D BETTER FIGURE OUT A WAY TO CURE YOUR AMNESIA.
SORRY TO BE SO MUCH TROUBLE.
OKAY, *HERE'S* AN IDEA...
I'VE HEARD THE BEST CURE FOR MEMORY LOSS IS--
--A *SUDDEN BLOW TO THE HEAD!!*
YOU'VE BEEN WATCHING TOO MUCH DAY-TIME TV!
ARE YOU SURE *YOU'RE* NOT A DEMON, URD?
jeez
oop!
WHMP
THUD
WHAT ABOUT HOLDING YOUR BREATH AS LONG AS YOU CAN...
...OR DRINKING A GLASS OF WATER REALLY FAST?
I THINK THOSE ARE CURES FOR *HICCUPS,* BELL-DANDY.

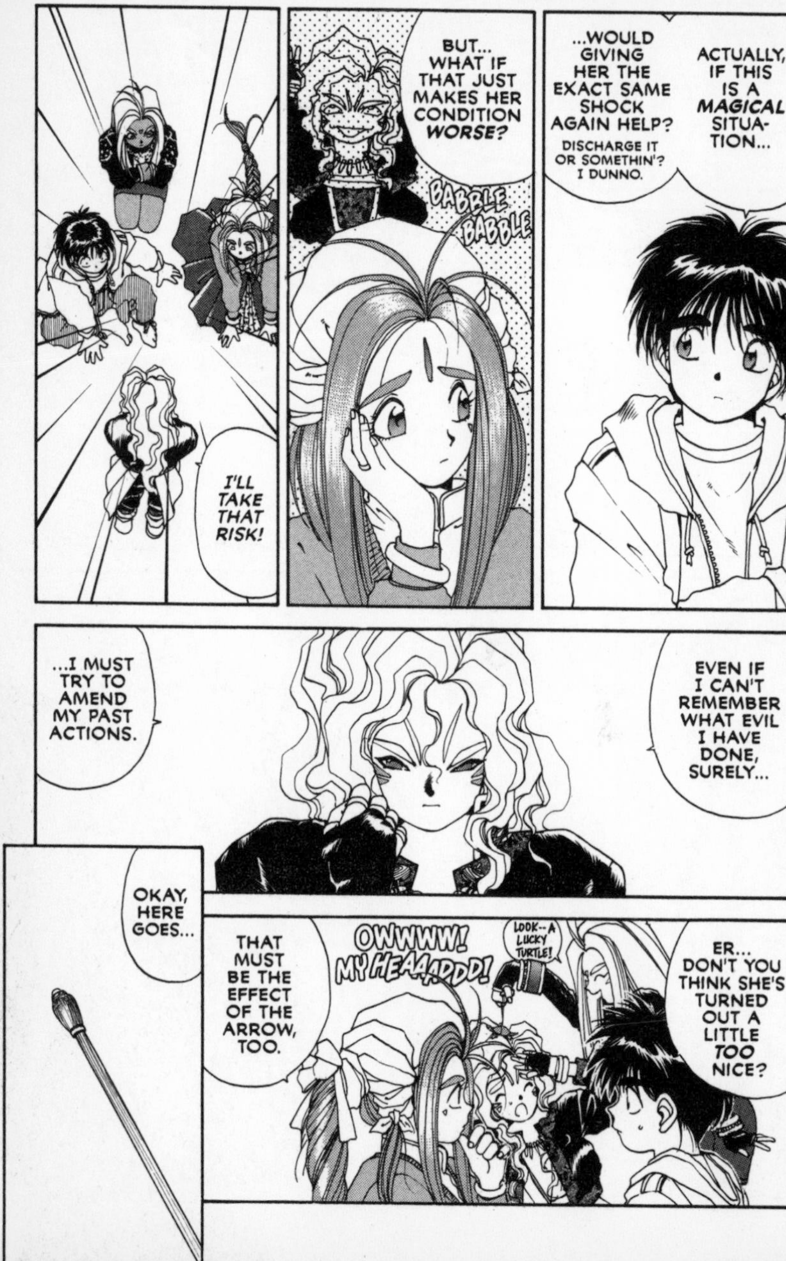
ACTUALLY, IF THIS IS A *MAGICAL* SITUATION...
...WOULD GIVING HER THE EXACT SAME SHOCK AGAIN HELP?
DISCHARGE IT OR SOMETHIN'? I DUNNO.
BUT... WHAT IF THAT JUST MAKES HER CONDITION *WORSE?*
BABBLE BABBLE
I'LL TAKE THAT RISK!
EVEN IF I CAN'T REMEMBER WHAT EVIL I HAVE DONE, SURELY...
...I MUST TRY TO AMEND MY PAST ACTIONS.
ER... DON'T YOU THINK SHE'S TURNED OUT A LITTLE *TOO* NICE?
LOOK-- A LUCKY TURTLE!
OWWWW! MY HEAAADDD!
THAT MUST BE THE EFFECT OF THE ARROW, TOO.
OKAY, HERE GOES...

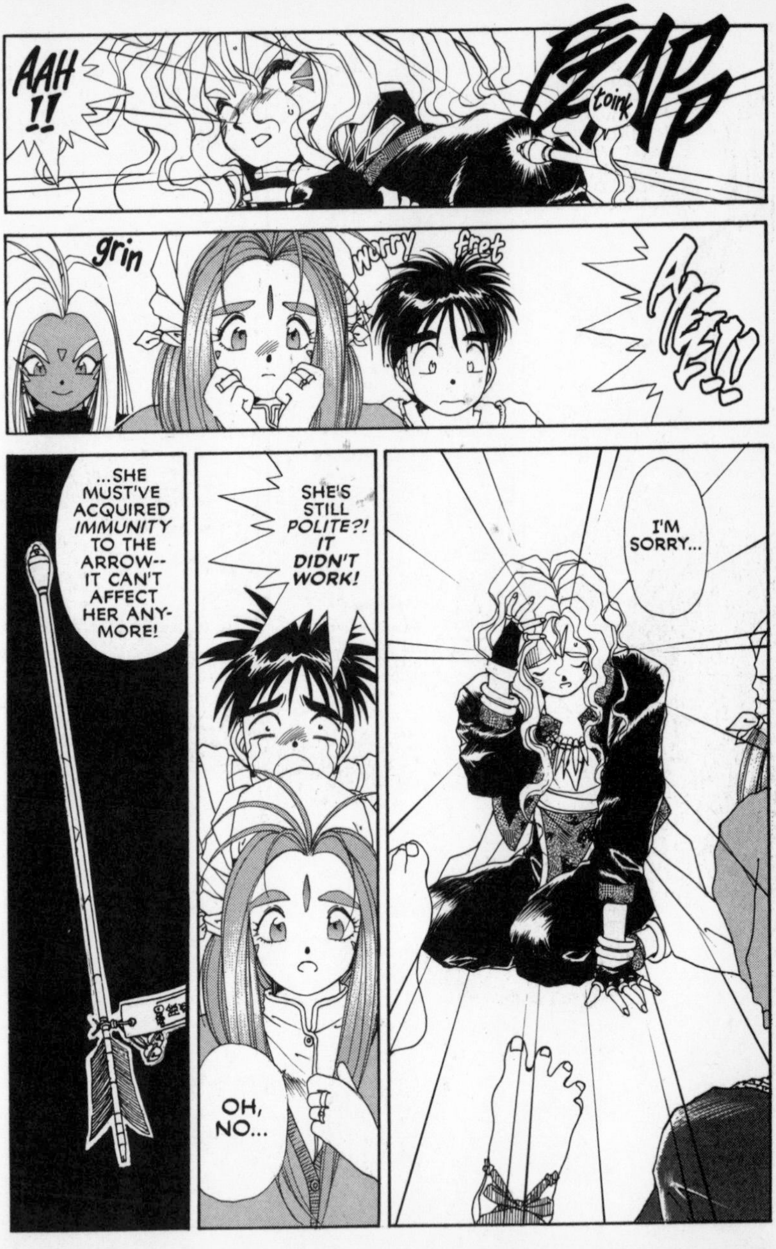
FZAPP
toink
AAH!!
AIEE!!
fret
worry
grin
I'M SORRY...
SHE'S STILL *POLITE*?! IT DIDN'T WORK!
OH, NO...
...SHE MUST'VE ACQUIRED *IMMUNITY* TO THE ARROW-- IT CAN'T AFFECT HER ANYMORE!

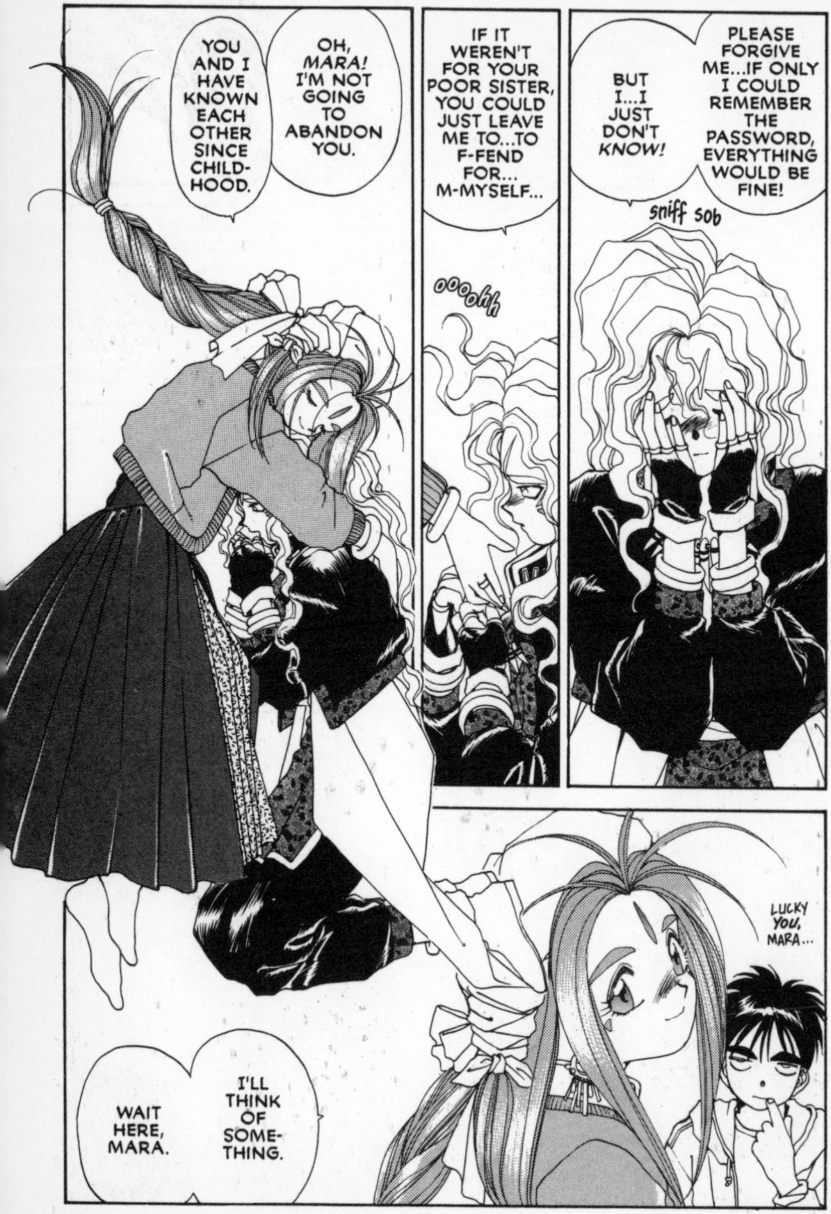
PLEASE FORGIVE ME...IF ONLY I COULD REMEMBER THE PASSWORD, EVERYTHING WOULD BE FINE!
BUT I...I JUST DON'T *KNOW!*
sniff sob
IF IT WEREN'T FOR YOUR POOR SISTER, YOU COULD JUST LEAVE ME TO...TO F-FEND FOR... M-MYSELF...
oooohh
OH, *MARA!* I'M NOT GOING TO ABANDON YOU.
YOU AND I HAVE KNOWN EACH OTHER SINCE CHILD-HOOD.
LUCKY *YOU,* MARA...
I'LL THINK OF SOME-THING.
WAIT HERE, MARA.

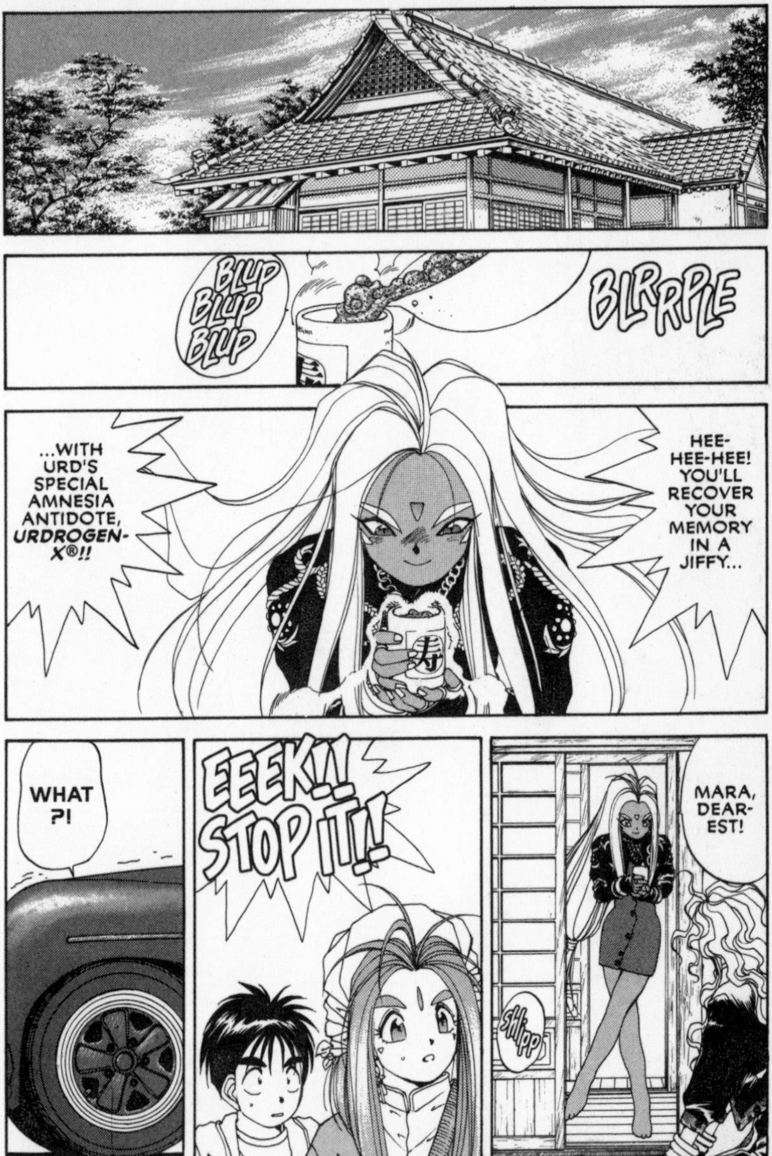
BLRRPLE
BLUP BLUP BLUP
HEE-HEE-HEE! YOU'LL RECOVER YOUR MEMORY IN A JIFFY...
...WITH URD'S SPECIAL AMNESIA ANTIDOTE, URDROGEN-X®!!
MARA, DEAR-EST!
SHIPP
EEEK!! STOP IT!!
WHAT?!

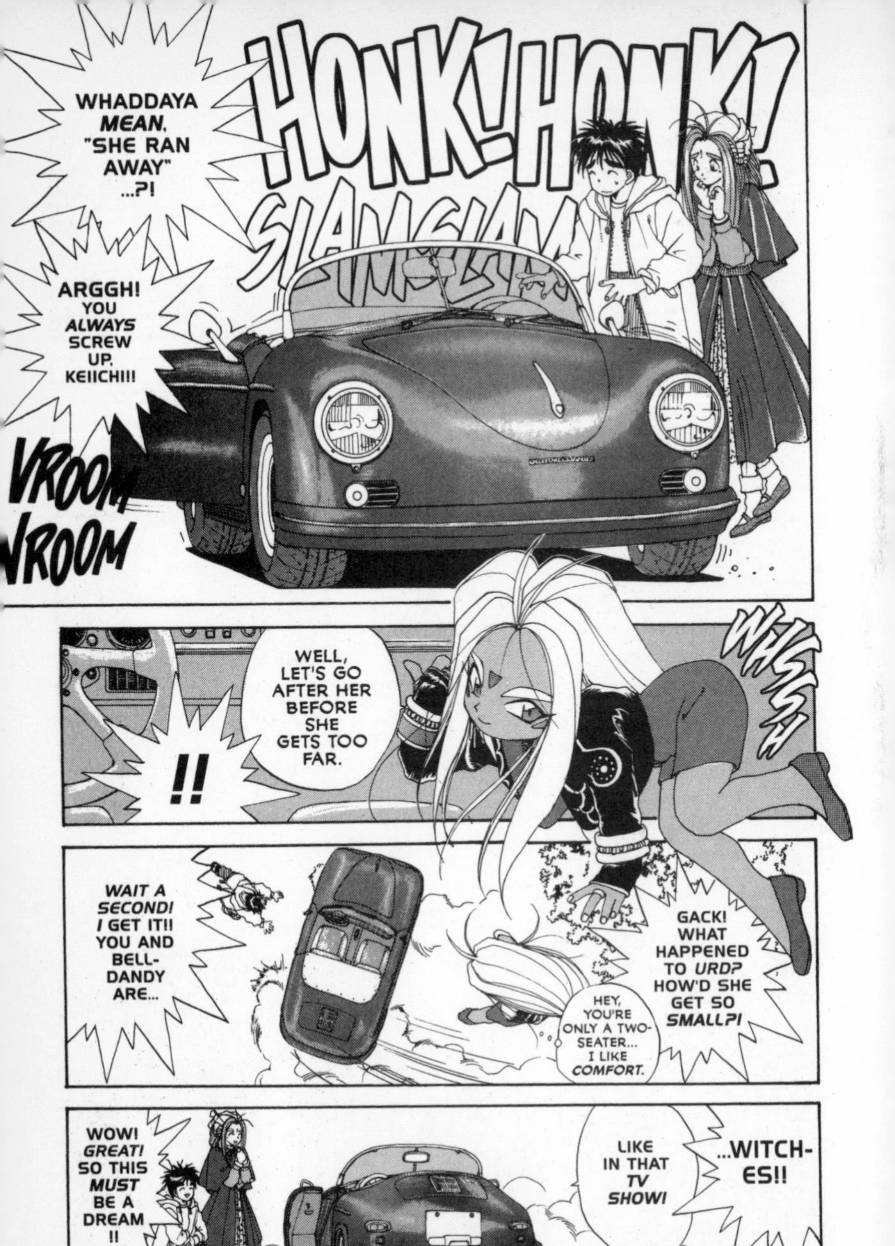
HONK! HONK!
SLAMSLAM
WHADDAYA *MEAN*, "SHE RAN AWAY" ...?!
ARGGH! YOU *ALWAYS* SCREW UP, KEIICHI!!
VROOM VROOM
WELL, LET'S GO AFTER HER BEFORE SHE GETS TOO FAR.
!!
GACK! WHAT HAPPENED TO *URD?* HOW'D SHE GET SO *SMALL?!*
HEY, YOU'RE ONLY A TWO-SEATER... I LIKE *COMFORT.*
WAIT A SECOND! I GET IT!! YOU AND BELL-DANDY ARE...
...WITCH-ES!!
LIKE IN THAT *TV SHOW!*
WOW! *GREAT!* SO THIS *MUST* BE A DREAM !!

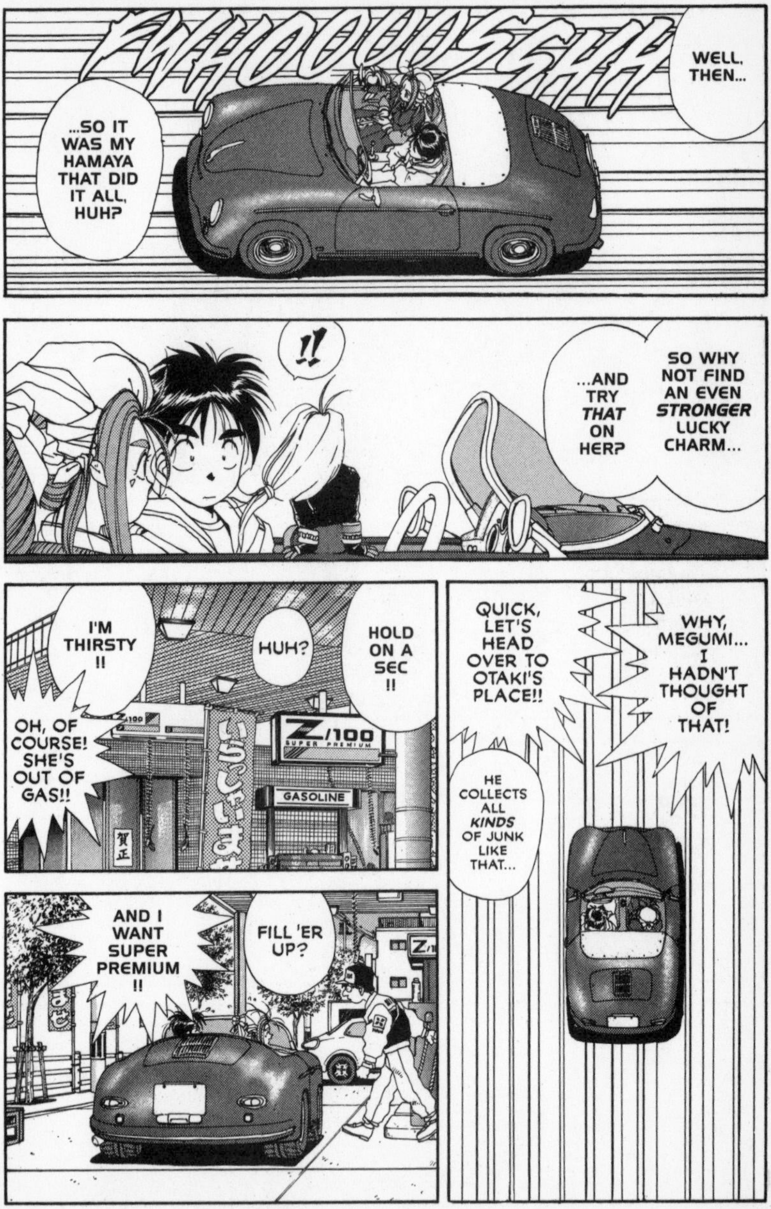
WELL, THEN...
...SO IT WAS MY HAMAYA THAT DID IT ALL, HUH?
SO WHY NOT FIND AN EVEN *STRONGER* LUCKY CHARM...
...AND TRY *THAT* ON HER?
!!
WHY, MEGUMI... I HADN'T THOUGHT OF THAT!
QUICK, LET'S HEAD OVER TO OTAKI'S PLACE!!
HE COLLECTS ALL *KINDS* OF JUNK LIKE THAT...
HOLD ON A SEC !!
HUH?
I'M THIRSTY !!
Z/100 SUPER PREMIUM
GASOLINE
賀正
OH, OF COURSE! SHE'S OUT OF GAS!!
FILL 'ER UP?
AND I WANT SUPER PREMIUM !!

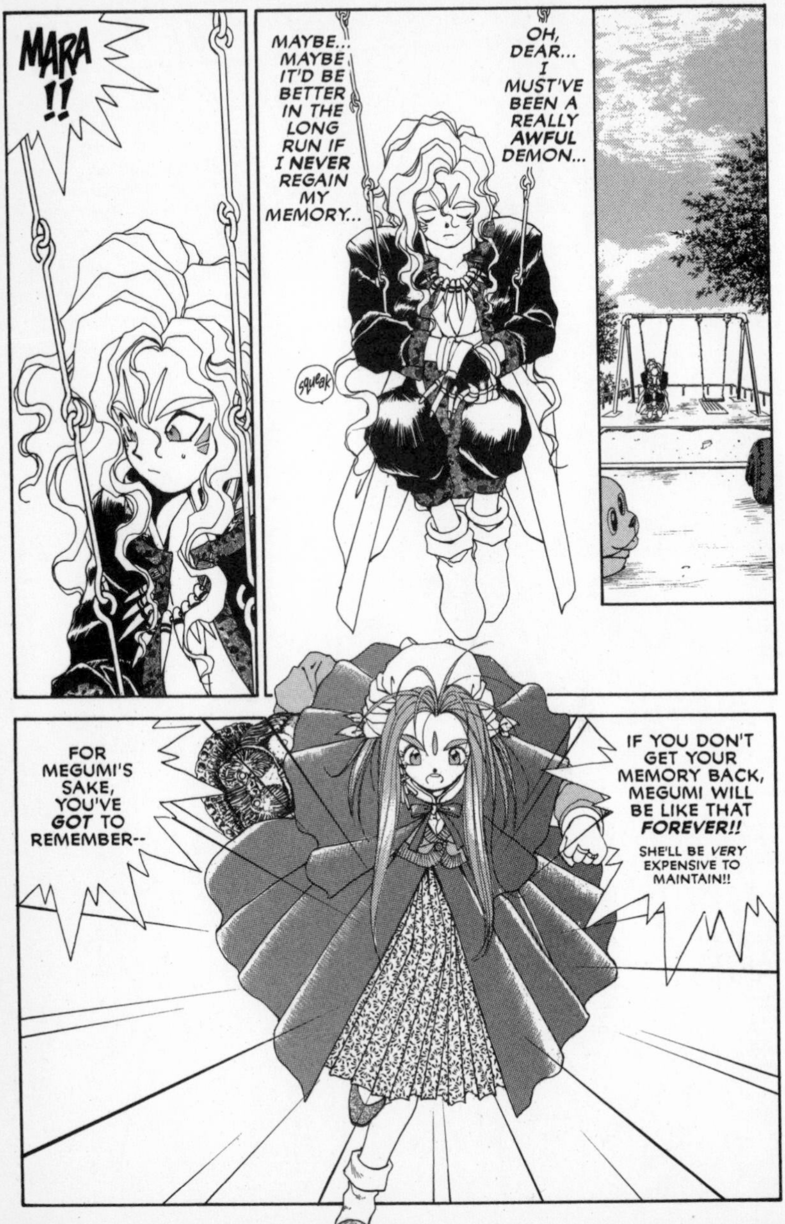

OH, DEAR... I MUST'VE BEEN A REALLY AWFUL DEMON...
MAYBE... MAYBE IT'D BE BETTER IN THE LONG RUN IF I NEVER REGAIN MY MEMORY...
squeak
MARA !!
IF YOU DON'T GET YOUR MEMORY BACK, MEGUMI WILL BE LIKE THAT FOREVER!!
SHE'LL BE VERY EXPENSIVE TO MAINTAIN!!
FOR MEGUMI'S SAKE, YOU'VE GOT TO REMEMBER--

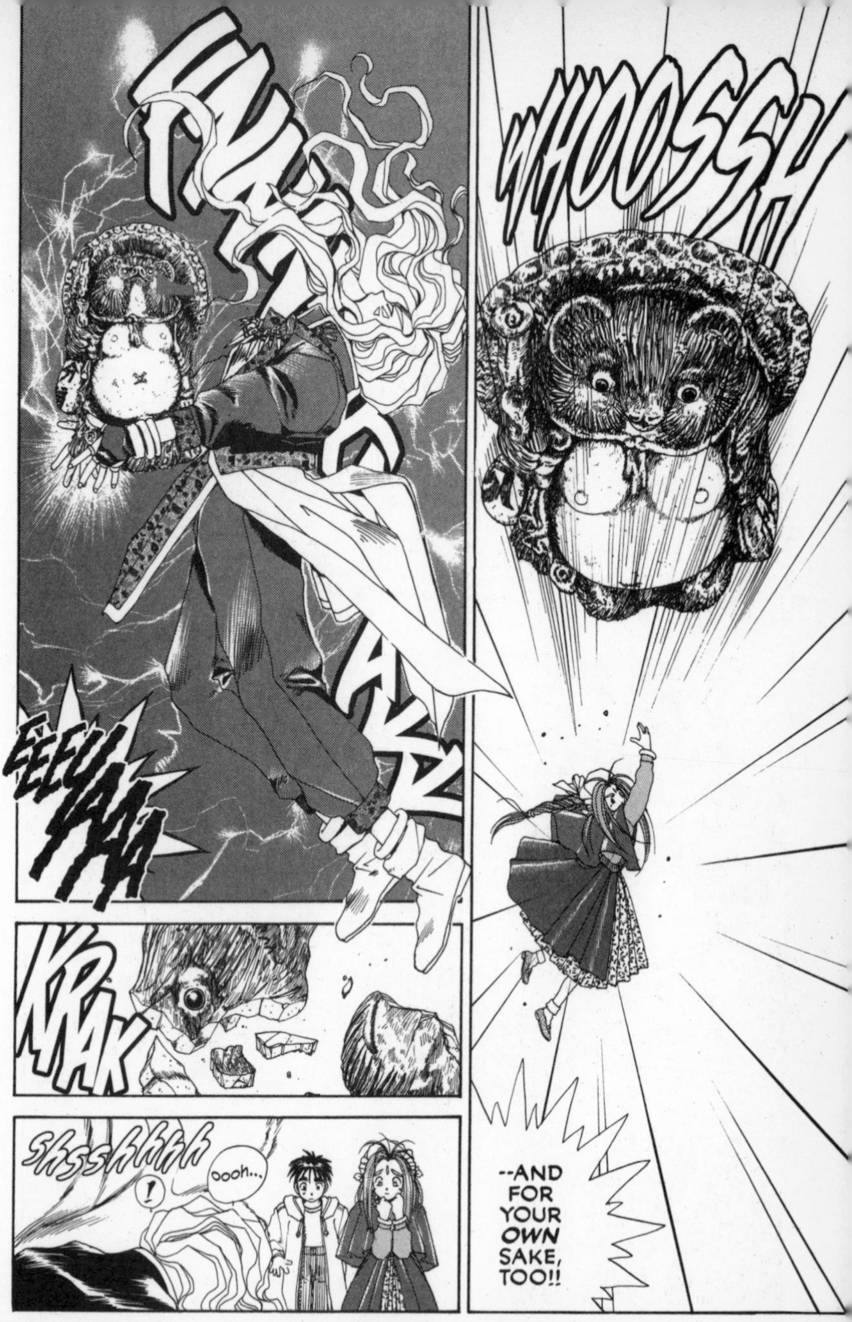
WHOOSSH
--AND FOR YOUR OWN SAKE, TOO!!
KRAK
Shsshhhh
!
oooh...

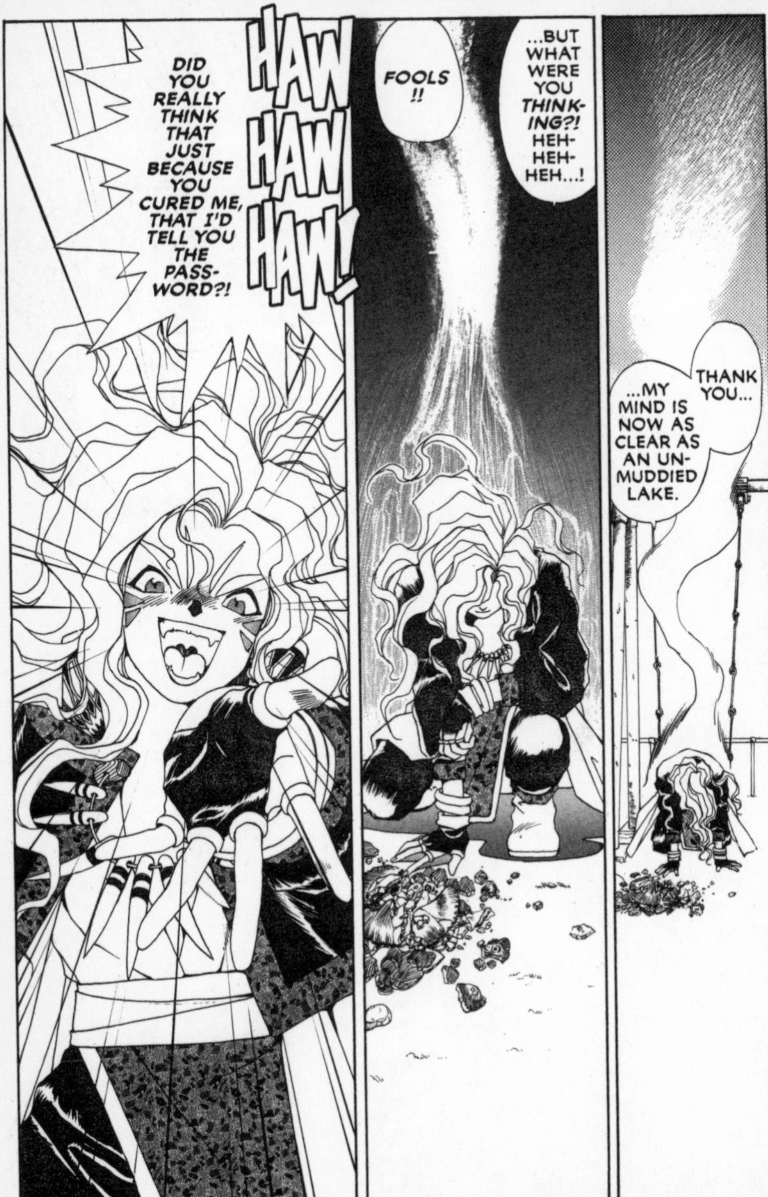
THANK YOU...
...MY MIND IS NOW AS CLEAR AS AN UN-MUDDIED LAKE.
...BUT WHAT WERE YOU *THINKING?!* HEH-HEH-HEH...!
FOOLS !!
HAW HAW HAW!
DID YOU REALLY THINK THAT JUST BECAUSE YOU CURED ME, THAT I'D TELL YOU THE PASS-WORD?!

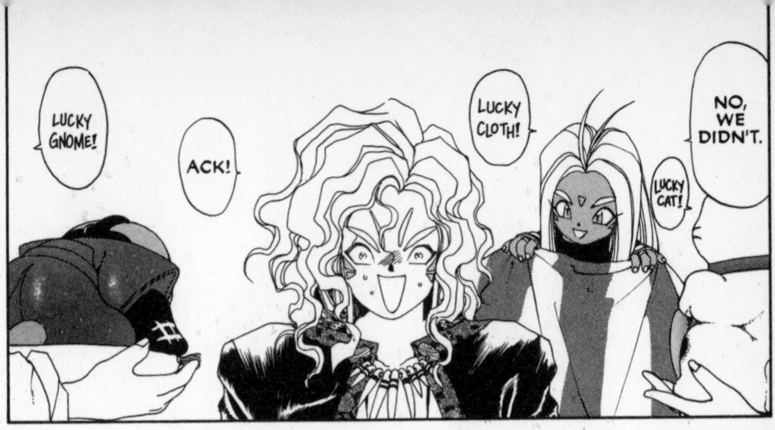
NO, WE DIDN'T.
LUCKY CAT!
LUCKY CLOTH!
ACK!
LUCKY GNOME!

ONE PASSWORD LATER

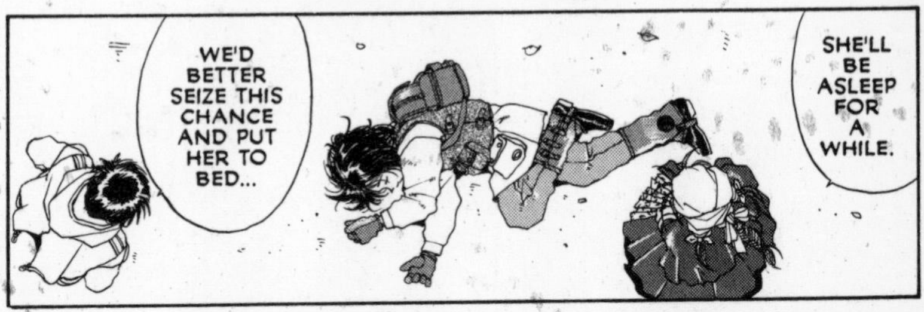
SHE'LL BE ASLEEP FOR A WHILE.
WE'D BETTER SEIZE THIS CHANCE AND PUT HER TO BED...

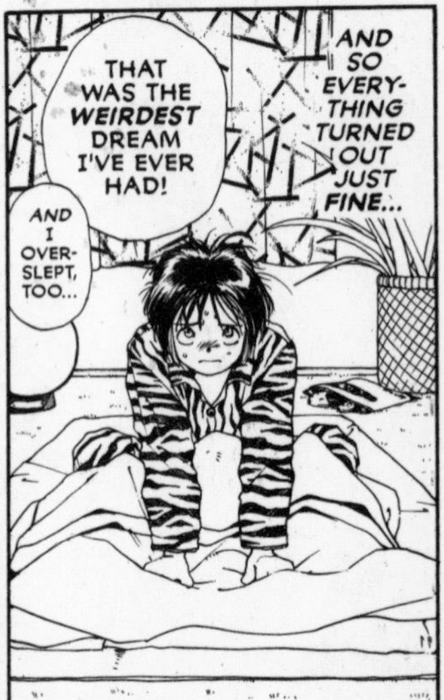
AND SO EVERY-THING TURNED OUT JUST FINE...
THAT WAS THE WEIRDEST DREAM I'VE EVER HAD!
AND I OVER-SLEPT, TOO...

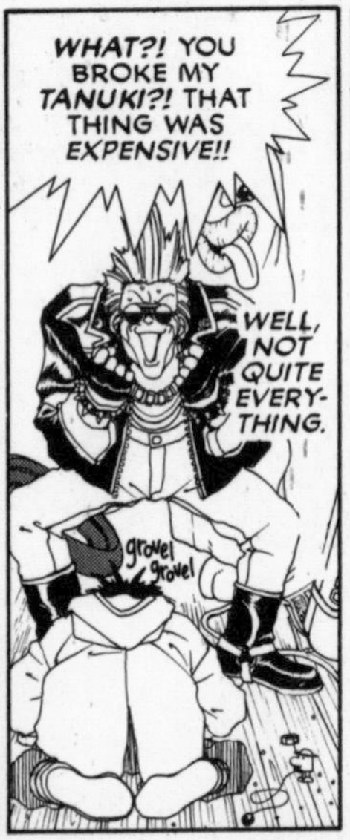
WHAT?! YOU BROKE MY TANUKI?! THAT THING WAS EXPENSIVE!!
WELL, NOT QUITE EVERY-THING.
grovel grovel

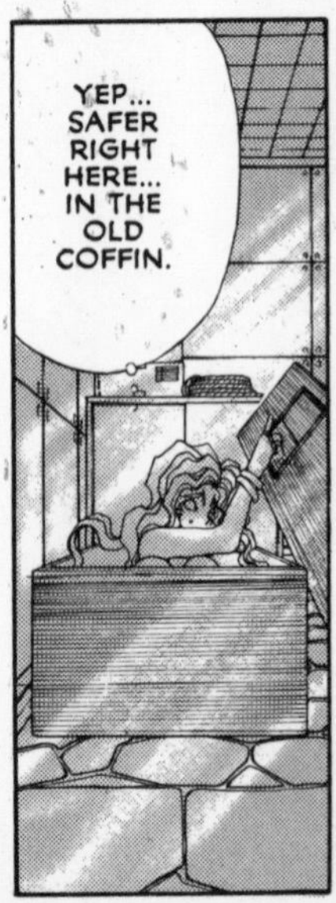
YEP... SAFER RIGHT HERE... IN THE OLD COFFIN.

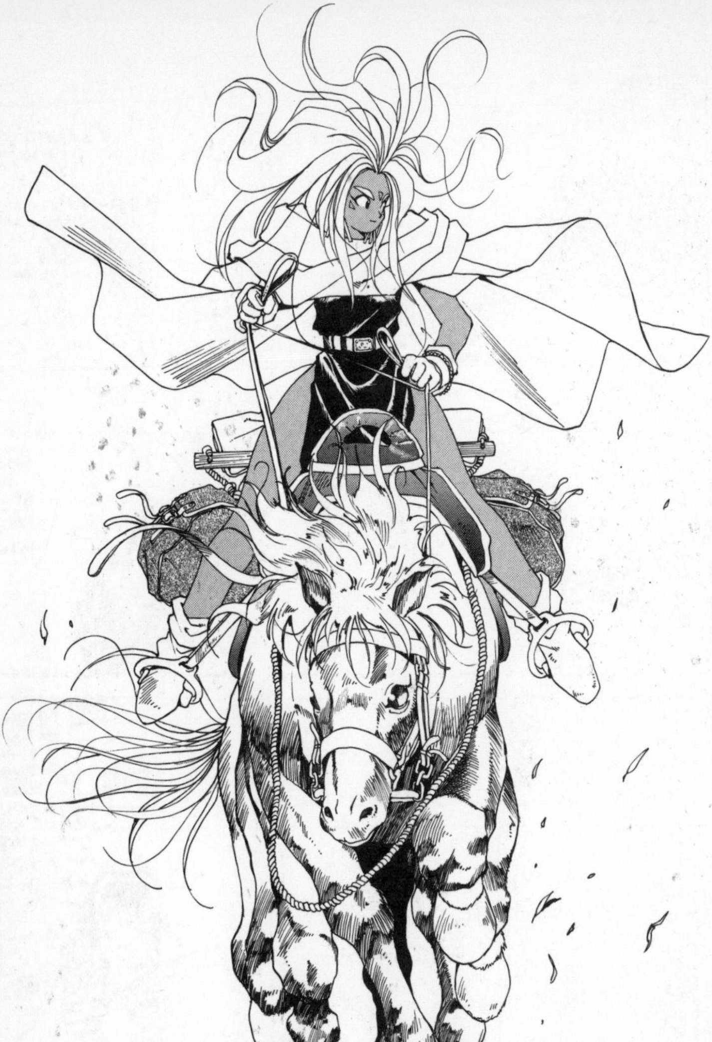

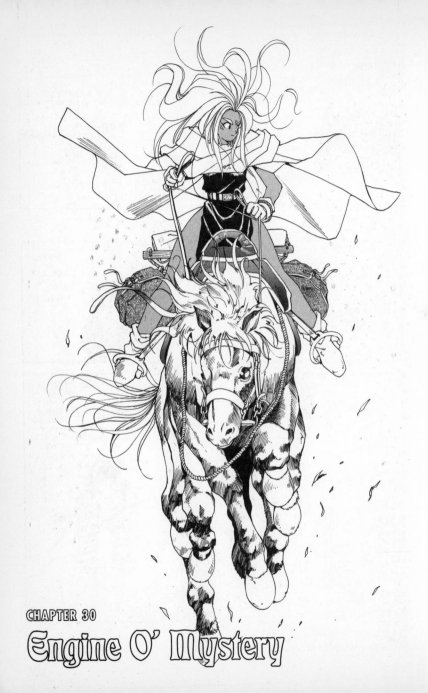

CHAPTER 30

Engine O' Mystery

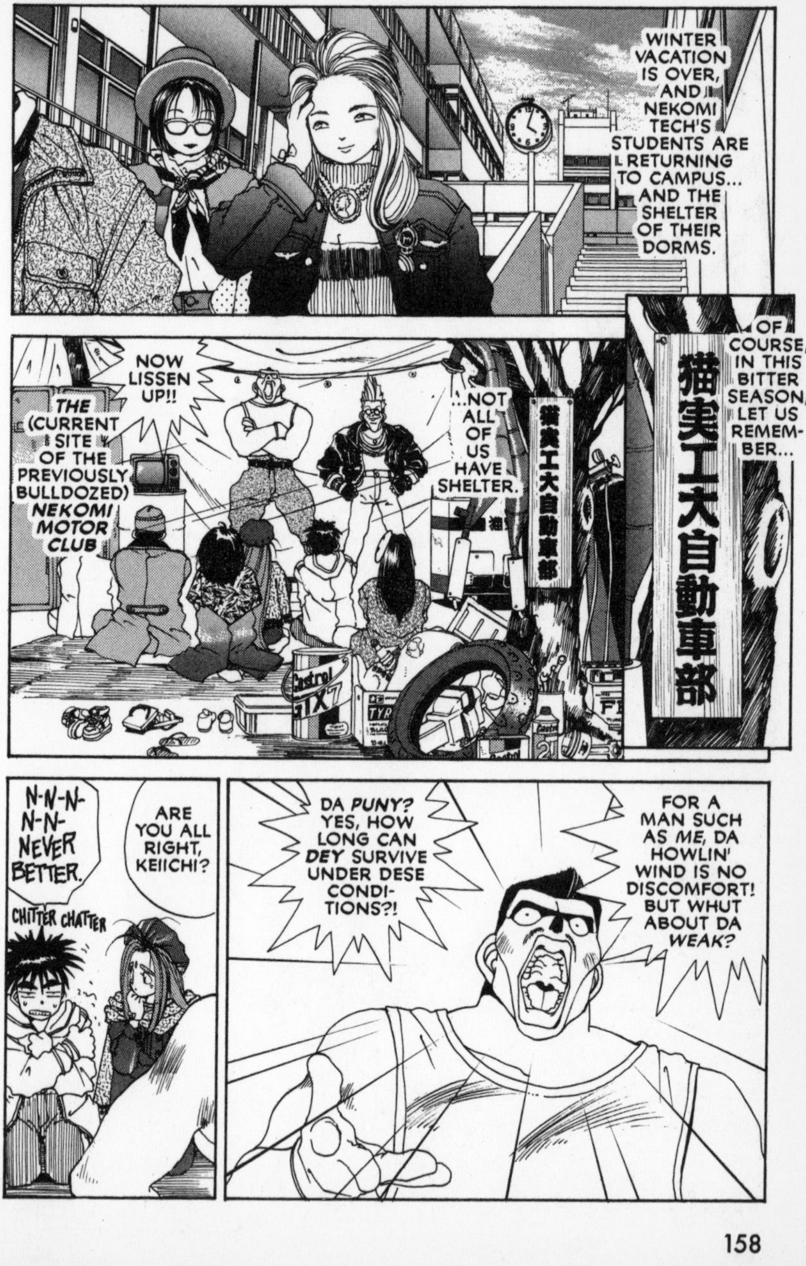

WINTER VACATION IS OVER, AND NEKOMI TECH'S STUDENTS ARE RETURNING TO CAMPUS... AND THE SHELTER OF THEIR DORMS.
猫実工大自動車部
OF COURSE, IN THIS BITTER SEASON, LET US REMEMBER...
...NOT ALL OF US HAVE SHELTER.
猫実工大自動車部
NOW LISSEN UP!!
THE (CURRENT SITE OF THE PREVIOUSLY BULLDOZED) *NEKOMI MOTOR CLUB*
FOR A MAN SUCH AS *ME*, DA HOWLIN' WIND IS NO DISCOMFORT! BUT WHUT ABOUT DA *WEAK*?
DA *PUNY*? YES, HOW LONG CAN *DEY* SURVIVE UNDER DESE CONDI-TIONS?!
ARE YOU ALL RIGHT, KEIICHI?
N-N-N-N-N-NEVER BETTER.
CHITTER CHATTER

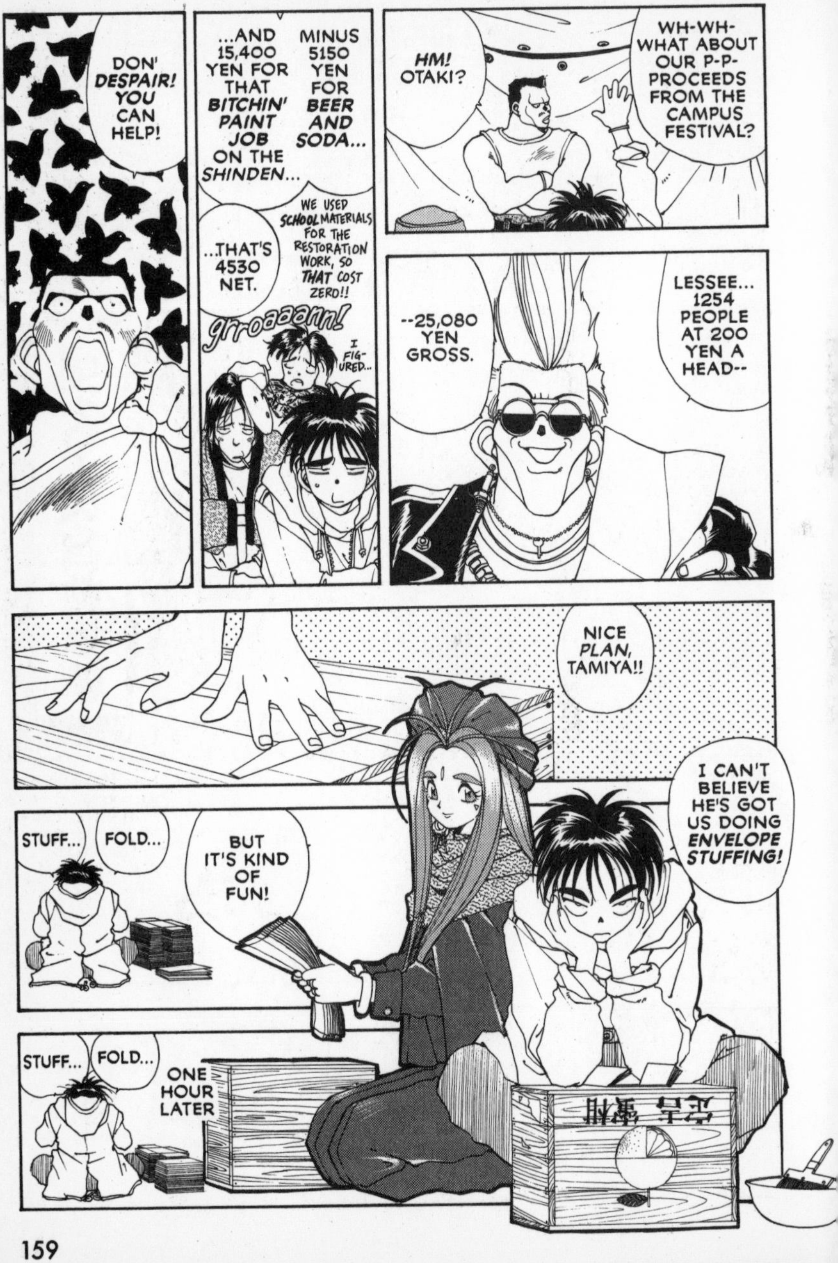
WH-WH-WHAT ABOUT OUR P-P-PROCEEDS FROM THE CAMPUS FESTIVAL?
HM! OTAKI?
LESSEE... 1254 PEOPLE AT 200 YEN A HEAD--
--25,080 YEN GROSS.
MINUS 5150 YEN FOR BEER AND SODA...
...AND 15,400 YEN FOR THAT BITCHIN' PAINT JOB ON THE SHINDEN...
WE USED SCHOOL MATERIALS FOR THE RESTORATION WORK, SO THAT COST ZERO!!
...THAT'S 4530 NET.
grroaaann!
I FIGURED...
DON' DESPAIR! YOU CAN HELP!
NICE PLAN, TAMIYA!!
I CAN'T BELIEVE HE'S GOT US DOING ENVELOPE STUFFING!
BUT IT'S KIND OF FUN!
FOLD...
STUFF...
ONE HOUR LATER
FOLD...
STUFF...

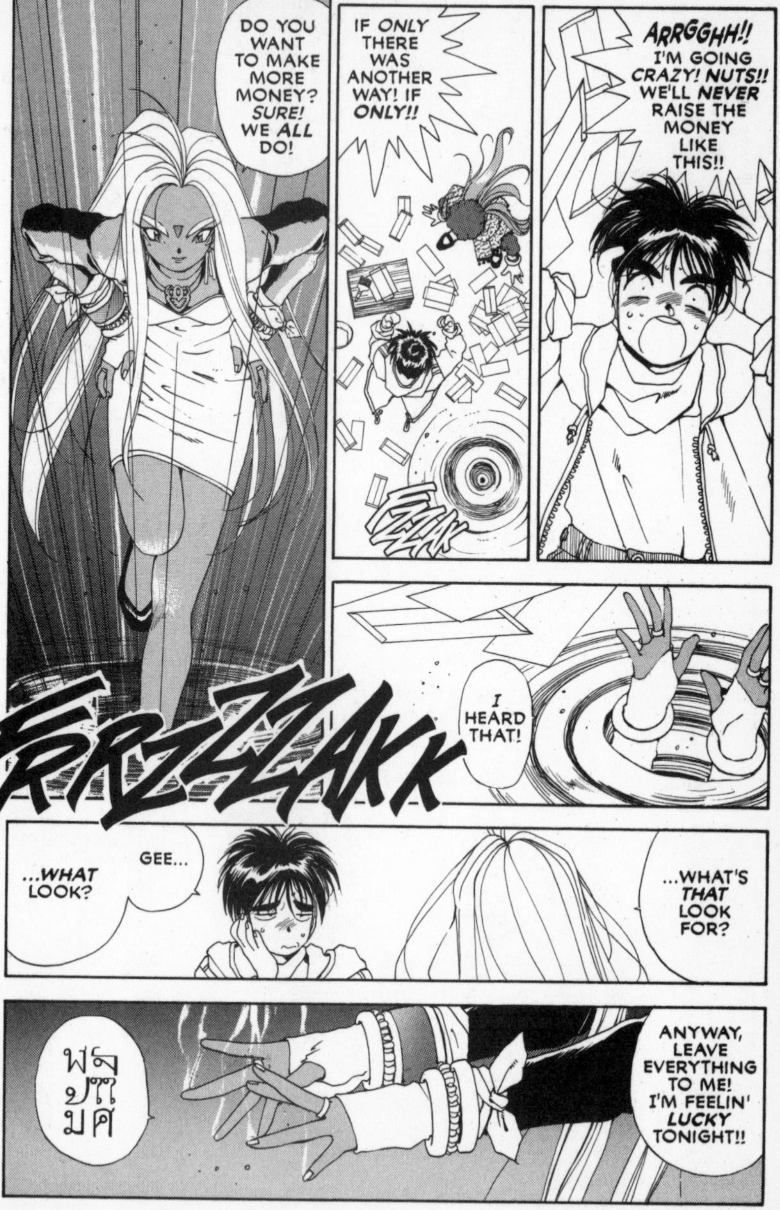
ARRGGHH!! I'M GOING CRAZY! NUTS!! WE'LL NEVER RAISE THE MONEY LIKE THIS!!
IF ONLY THERE WAS ANOTHER WAY! IF ONLY!!
FZZAK
I HEARD THAT!
DO YOU WANT TO MAKE MORE MONEY? SURE! WE ALL DO!
FRRZZZAKK
...WHAT'S THAT LOOK FOR?
GEE...
...WHAT LOOK?
ANYWAY, LEAVE EVERYTHING TO ME! I'M FEELIN' LUCKY TONIGHT!!

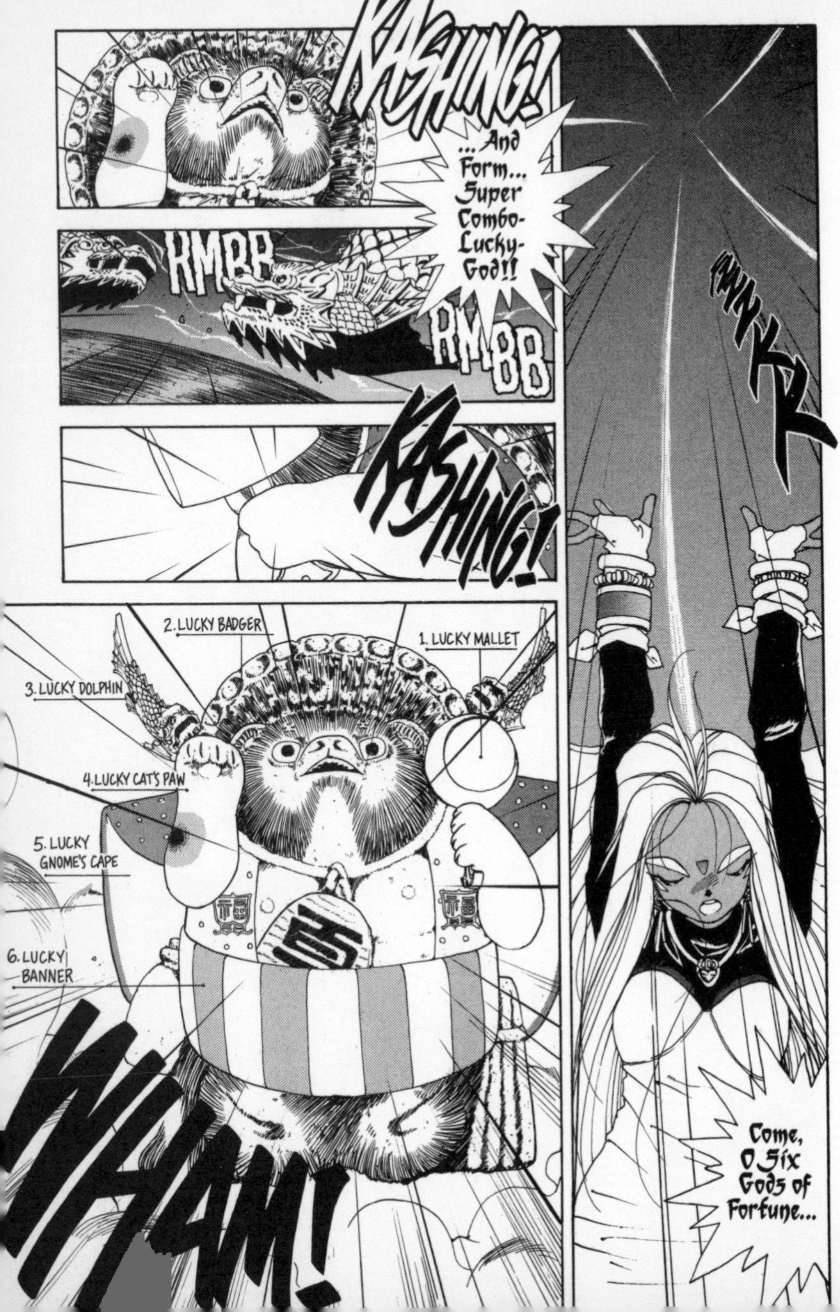
Come, O Six Gods of Fortune...
KASHING!
...And Form... Super Combo-Lucky-God!!
RMBB
RMBB
KASHING!
1. LUCKY MALLET
2. LUCKY BADGER
3. LUCKY DOLPHIN
4. LUCKY CAT'S PAW
5. LUCKY GNOME'S CAPE
6. LUCKY BANNER
WHAM!

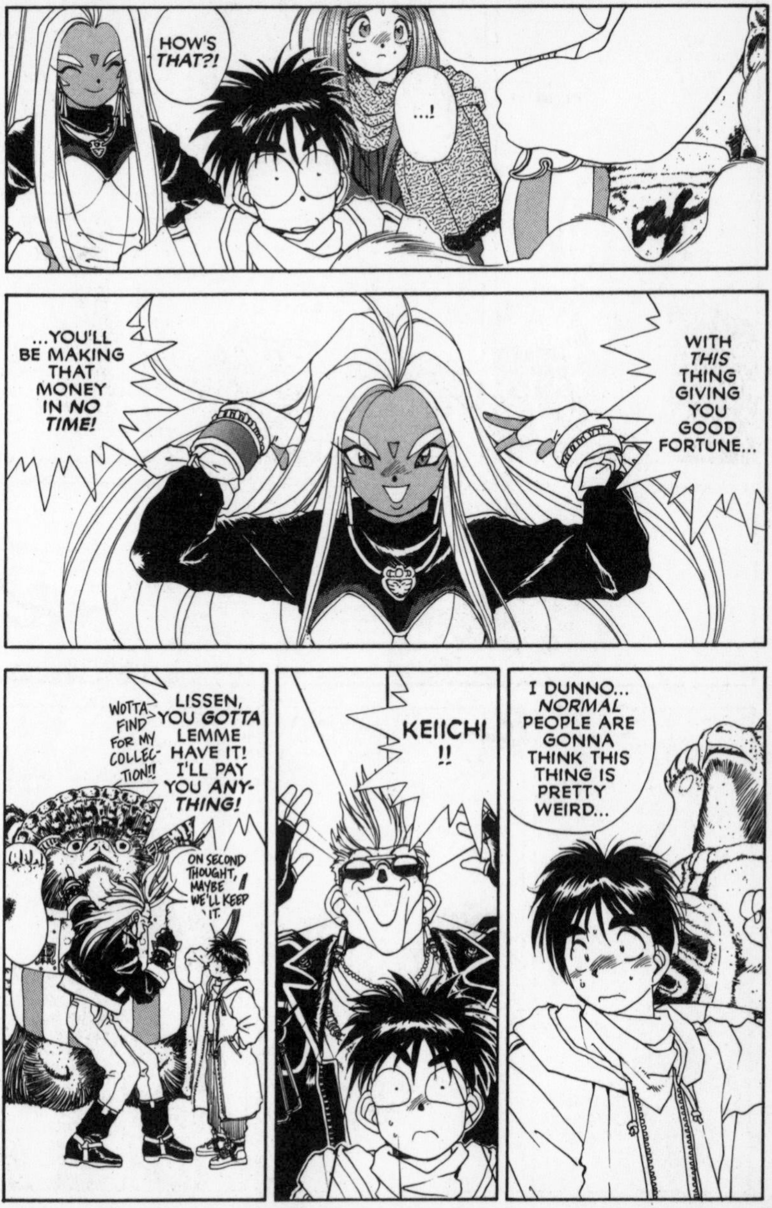
HOW'S THAT?!
...!
WITH THIS THING GIVING YOU GOOD FORTUNE...
...YOU'LL BE MAKING THAT MONEY IN NO TIME!
I DUNNO... NORMAL PEOPLE ARE GONNA THINK THIS THING IS PRETTY WEIRD...
KEIICHI !!
LISSEN, YOU GOTTA LEMME HAVE IT! I'LL PAY YOU ANYTHING!
WOTTA FIND FOR MY COLLECTION!!
ON SECOND THOUGHT, MAYBE WE'LL KEEP IT.

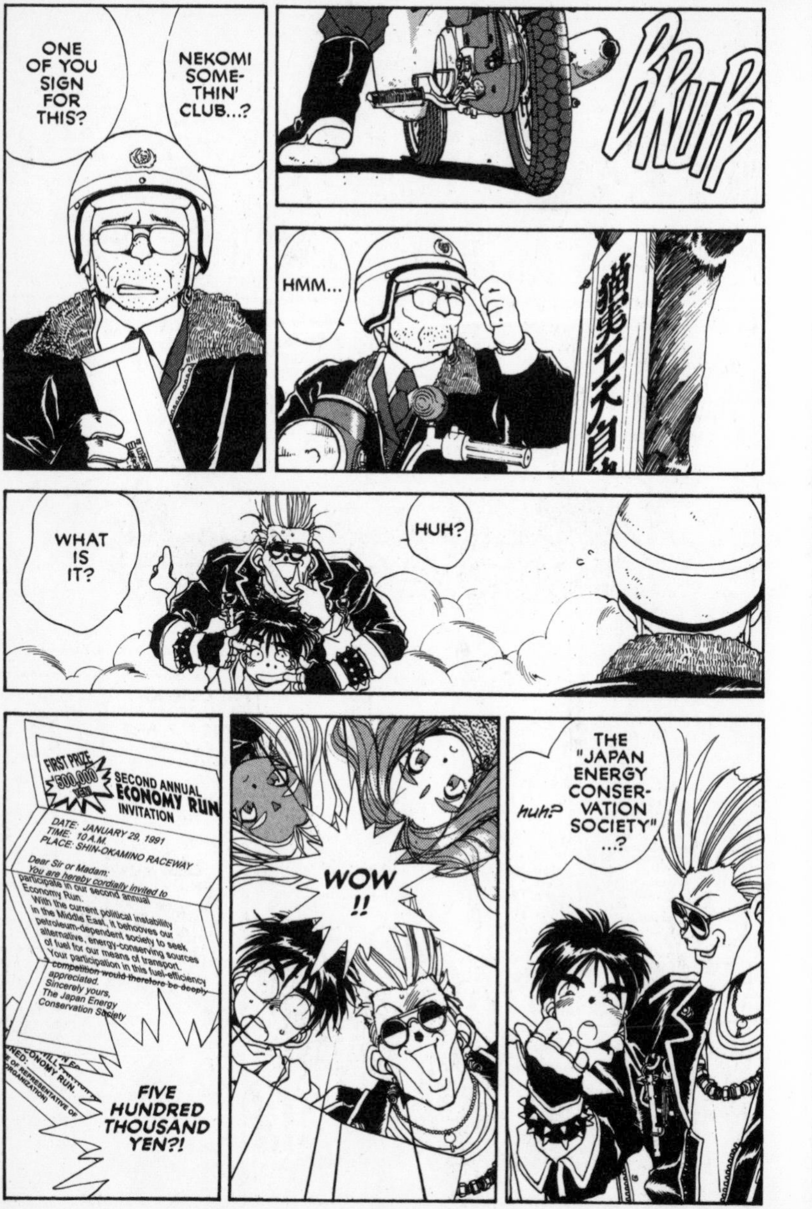
BRUP
HMM...
NEKOMI SOMETHIN' CLUB...?
ONE OF YOU SIGN FOR THIS?
HUH?
WHAT IS IT?
THE "JAPAN ENERGY CONSERVATION SOCIETY" ...?
huh?
WOW !!
FIRST PRIZE 500,000 YEN
SECOND ANNUAL ECONOMY RUN INVITATION
DATE: JANUARY 29, 1991
TIME: 10 A.M.
PLACE: SHIN-OKAMINO RACEWAY
Dear Sir or Madam:
You are hereby cordially invited to participate in our second annual Economy Run.
With the current political instability in the Middle East, it behooves our petroleum-dependent society to seek alternative, energy-conserving sources of fuel for our means of transport.
Your participation in this fuel-efficiency competition would therefore be deeply appreciated.
Sincerely yours,
The Japan Energy Conservation Society
FIVE HUNDRED THOUSAND YEN?!

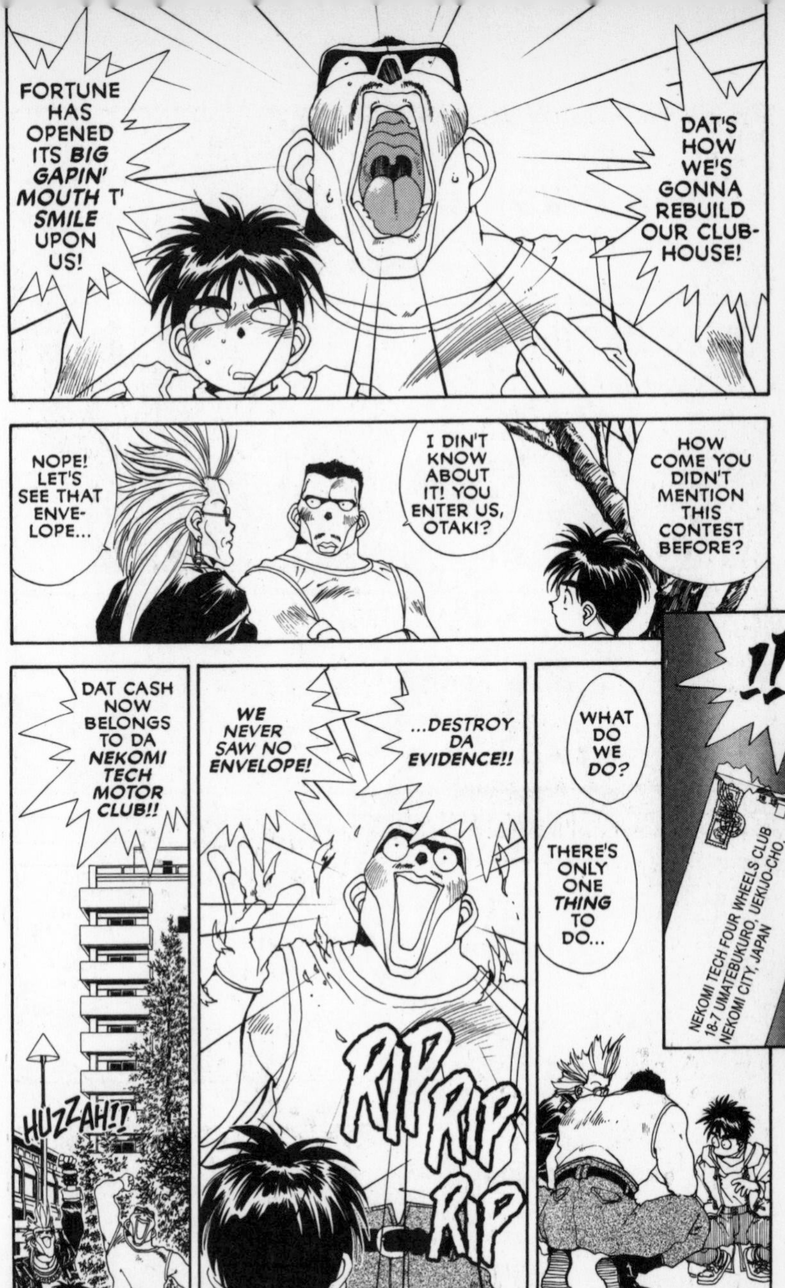
DAT'S HOW WE'S GONNA REBUILD OUR CLUB-HOUSE!
FORTUNE HAS OPENED ITS BIG GAPIN' MOUTH T' SMILE UPON US!
HOW COME YOU DIDN'T MENTION THIS CONTEST BEFORE?
I DIN'T KNOW ABOUT IT! YOU ENTER US, OTAKI?
NOPE! LET'S SEE THAT ENVE-LOPE...
!!
NEKOMI TECH FOUR WHEELS CLUB
18-7 UMATEBUKURO, UEKIJO-CHO,
NEKOMI CITY, JAPAN
WHAT DO WE DO?
THERE'S ONLY ONE THING TO DO...
...DESTROY DA EVIDENCE!!
WE NEVER SAW NO ENVELOPE!
RIP RIP RIP
DAT CASH NOW BELONGS TO DA NEKOMI TECH MOTOR CLUB!!
HUZZAH!!

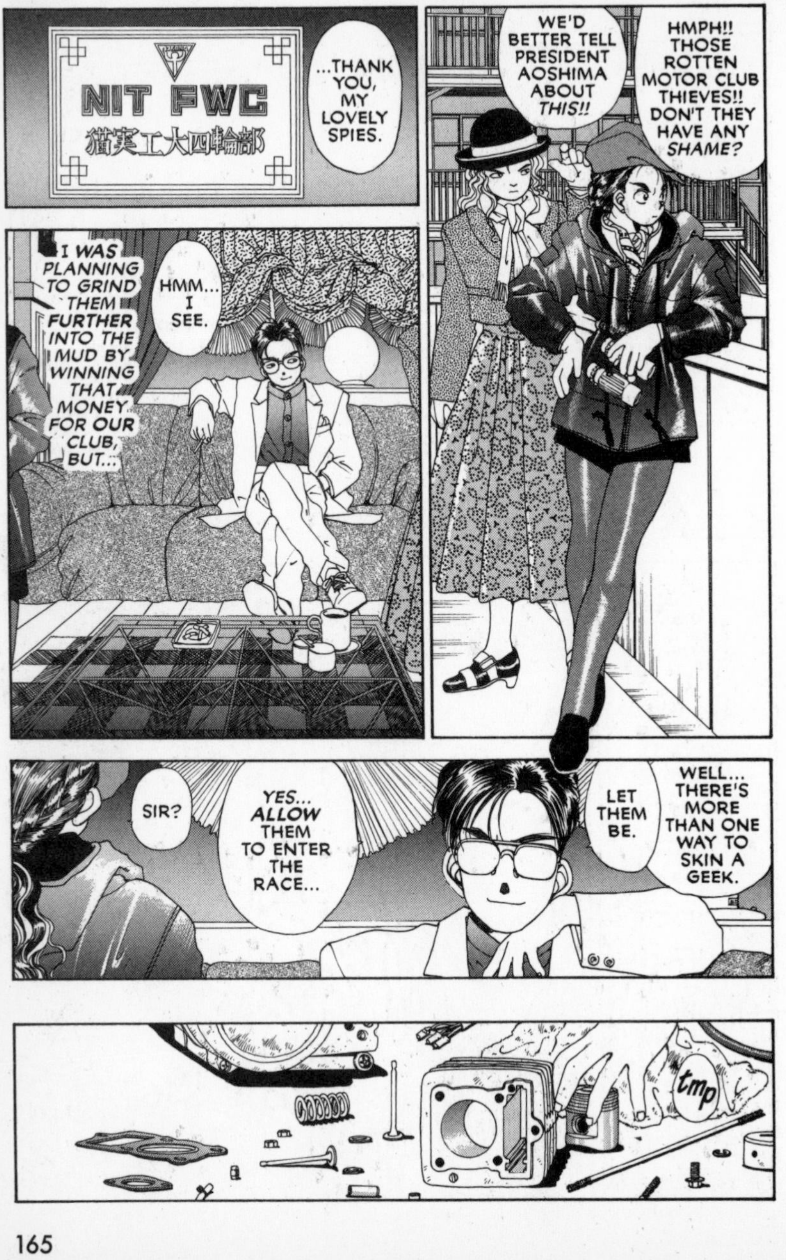
HMPH!! THOSE ROTTEN MOTOR CLUB THIEVES!! DON'T THEY HAVE ANY *SHAME?*
WE'D BETTER TELL PRESIDENT AOSHIMA ABOUT *THIS!!*
...THANK YOU, MY LOVELY SPIES.
NIT FWC
猫実工大四輪部
HMM... I SEE.
I WAS PLANNING TO GRIND THEM FURTHER INTO THE MUD BY WINNING THAT MONEY FOR OUR CLUB, BUT...
WELL... THERE'S MORE THAN ONE WAY TO SKIN A GEEK.
LET THEM BE.
YES... ***ALLOW*** THEM TO ENTER THE RACE...
SIR?
tmp

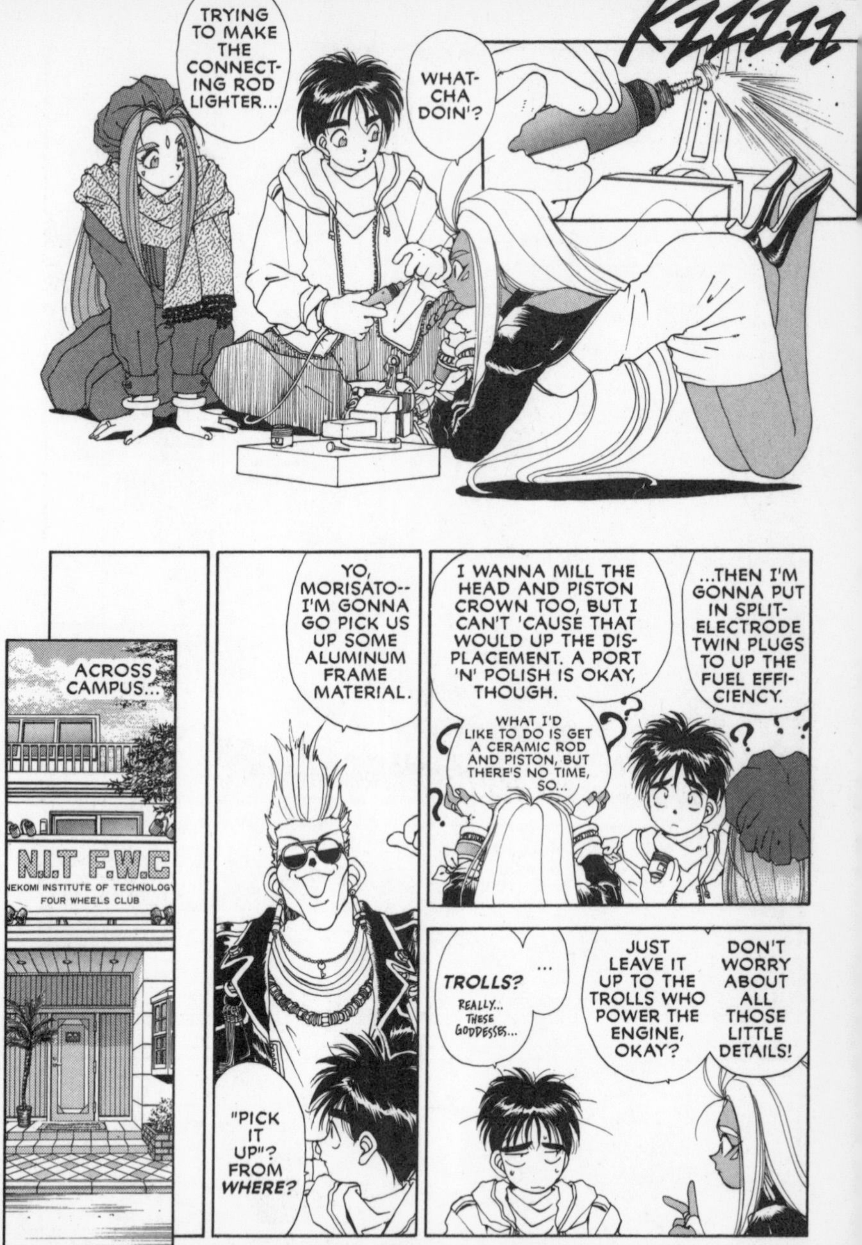
KZZZZZ
WHAT-CHA DOIN'?
TRYING TO MAKE THE CONNECTING ROD LIGHTER...
...THEN I'M GONNA PUT IN SPLIT-ELECTRODE TWIN PLUGS TO UP THE FUEL EFFICIENCY.
I WANNA MILL THE HEAD AND PISTON CROWN TOO, BUT I CAN'T 'CAUSE THAT WOULD UP THE DISPLACEMENT. A PORT 'N' POLISH IS OKAY, THOUGH.
WHAT I'D LIKE TO DO IS GET A CERAMIC ROD AND PISTON, BUT THERE'S NO TIME, SO...
DON'T WORRY ABOUT ALL THOSE LITTLE DETAILS!
JUST LEAVE IT UP TO THE TROLLS WHO POWER THE ENGINE, OKAY?
...
TROLLS?
REALLY... THESE GODDESSES...
YO, MORISATO-- I'M GONNA GO PICK US UP SOME ALUMINUM FRAME MATERIAL.
"PICK IT UP"? FROM *WHERE?*
ACROSS CAMPUS...
N.I.T F.W.C
NEKOMI INSTITUTE OF TECHNOLOGY
FOUR WHEELS CLUB

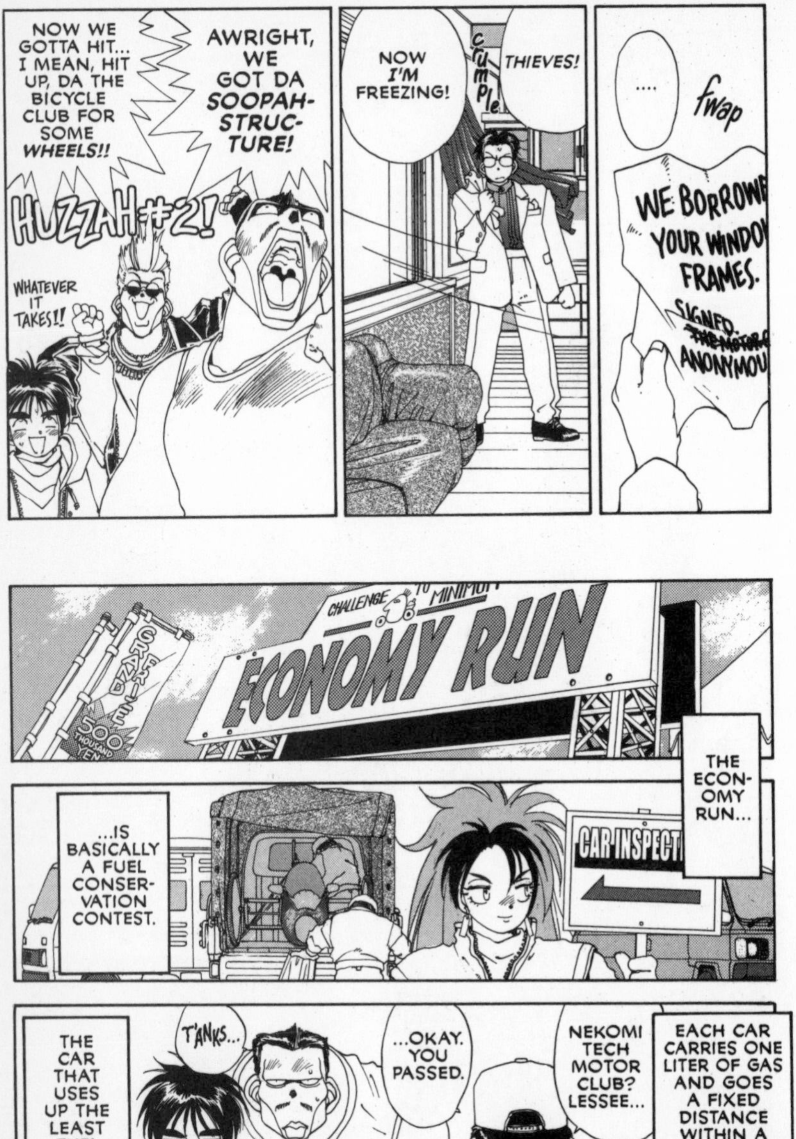
....
fwap
WE BORROWE YOUR WINDO FRAMES.
SIGNED, THE MOTOR C ANONYMOU
THIEVES!
crumple
NOW I'M FREEZING!
AWRIGHT, WE GOT DA SOOPAH-STRUC-TURE!
NOW WE GOTTA HIT... I MEAN, HIT UP, DA THE BICYCLE CLUB FOR SOME WHEELS!!
HUZZAH #2!
WHATEVER IT TAKES!!
THE ECONOMY RUN...
CHALLENGE TO MINIMUM
ECONOMY RUN
500 THOUSAND YEN
CAR INSPECTI
...IS BASICALLY A FUEL CONSERVATION CONTEST.
EACH CAR CARRIES ONE LITER OF GAS AND GOES A FIXED DISTANCE WITHIN A FIXED PERIOD OF TIME.
NEKOMI TECH MOTOR CLUB? LESSEE...
...OKAY. YOU PASSED.
T'ANKS...
THE CAR THAT USES UP THE LEAST FUEL WINS.

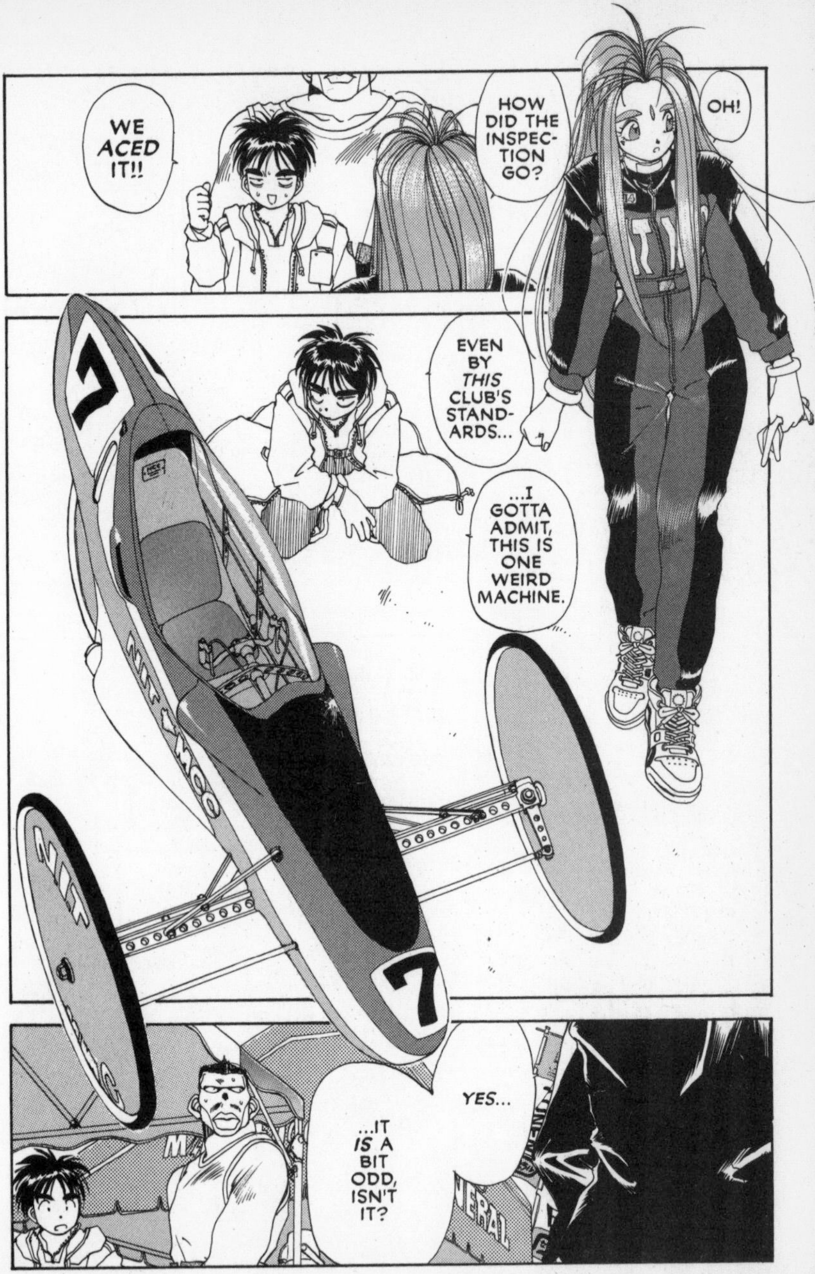
OH!
HOW DID THE INSPECTION GO?
WE *ACED* IT!!
EVEN BY *THIS* CLUB'S STANDARDS...
...I GOTTA ADMIT, THIS IS ONE WEIRD MACHINE.
YES...
...IT *IS* A BIT ODD, ISN'T IT?

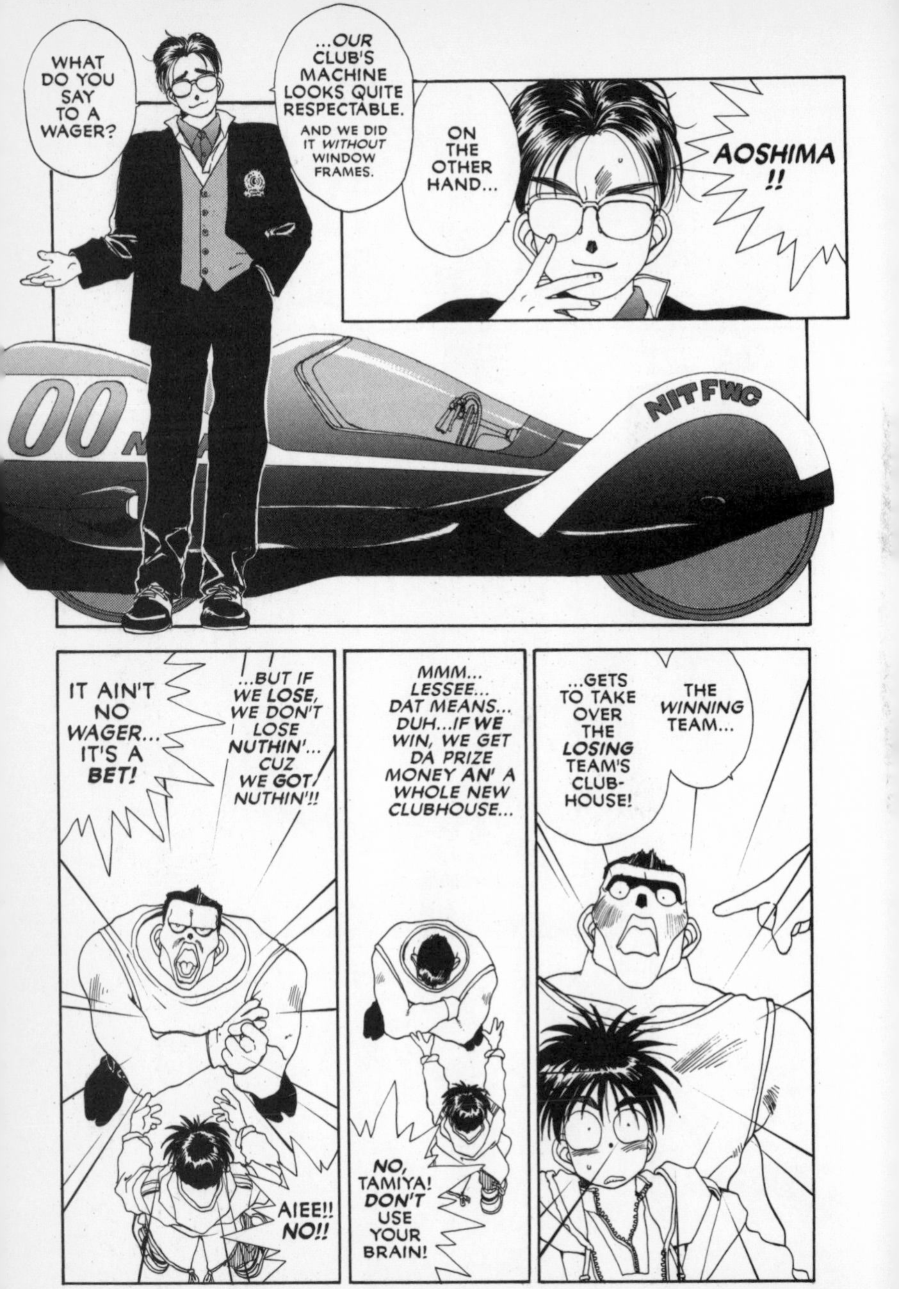
AOSHIMA !!
ON THE OTHER HAND...
...OUR CLUB'S MACHINE LOOKS QUITE RESPECTABLE.
AND WE DID IT WITHOUT WINDOW FRAMES.
WHAT DO YOU SAY TO A WAGER?
00
NITFWC
THE WINNING TEAM...
...GETS TO TAKE OVER THE LOSING TEAM'S CLUB-HOUSE!
MMM... LESSEE... DAT MEANS... DUH...IF WE WIN, WE GET DA PRIZE MONEY AN' A WHOLE NEW CLUBHOUSE...
NO, TAMIYA! DON'T USE YOUR BRAIN!
...BUT IF WE LOSE, WE DON'T LOSE NUTHIN'... CUZ WE GOT NUTHIN'!!
IT AIN'T NO WAGER... IT'S A BET!
AIEE!! NO!!

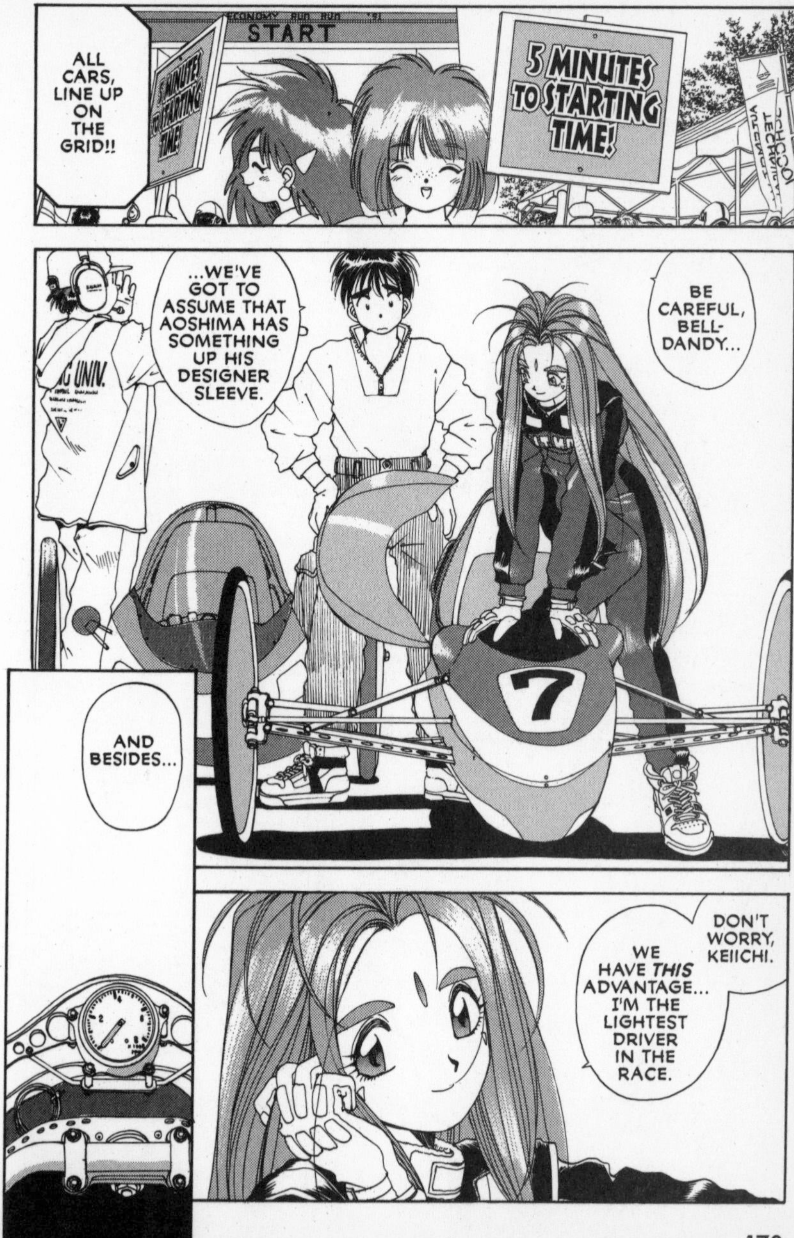

5 MINUTES TO STARTING TIME!
START
5 MINUTES TO STARTING TIME!
ALL CARS, LINE UP ON THE GRID!!
BE CAREFUL, BELL-DANDY...
...WE'VE GOT TO ASSUME THAT AOSHIMA HAS SOMETHING UP HIS DESIGNER SLEEVE.
AND BESIDES...
DON'T WORRY, KEIICHI.
WE HAVE *THIS* ADVANTAGE... I'M THE LIGHTEST DRIVER IN THE RACE.

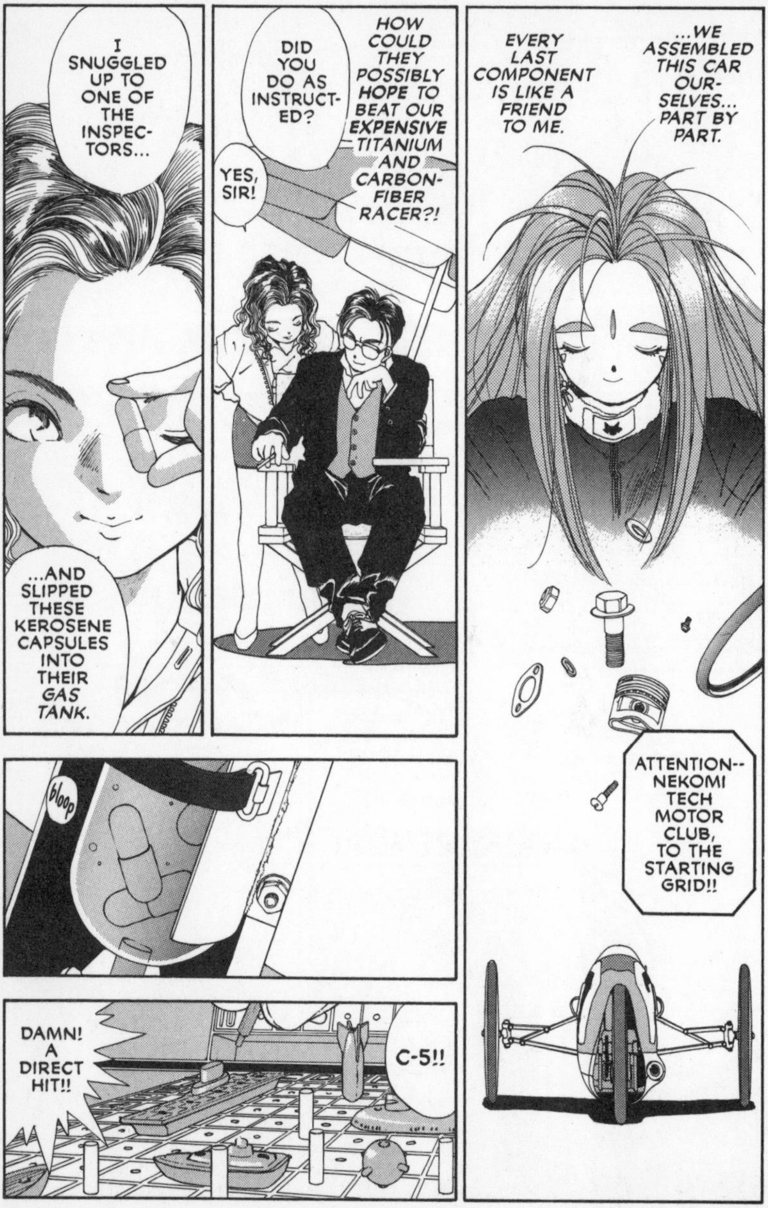
...WE ASSEMBLED THIS CAR OUR-SELVES... PART BY PART.
EVERY LAST COMPONENT IS LIKE A FRIEND TO ME.
ATTENTION-- NEKOMI TECH MOTOR CLUB, TO THE STARTING GRID!!
HOW COULD THEY POSSIBLY HOPE TO BEAT OUR EXPENSIVE TITANIUM AND CARBON-FIBER RACER?!
DID YOU DO AS INSTRUCT-ED?
YES, SIR!
I SNUGGLED UP TO ONE OF THE INSPEC-TORS...
...AND SLIPPED THESE KEROSENE CAPSULES INTO THEIR GAS TANK.
bloop
C-5!!
DAMN! A DIRECT HIT!!

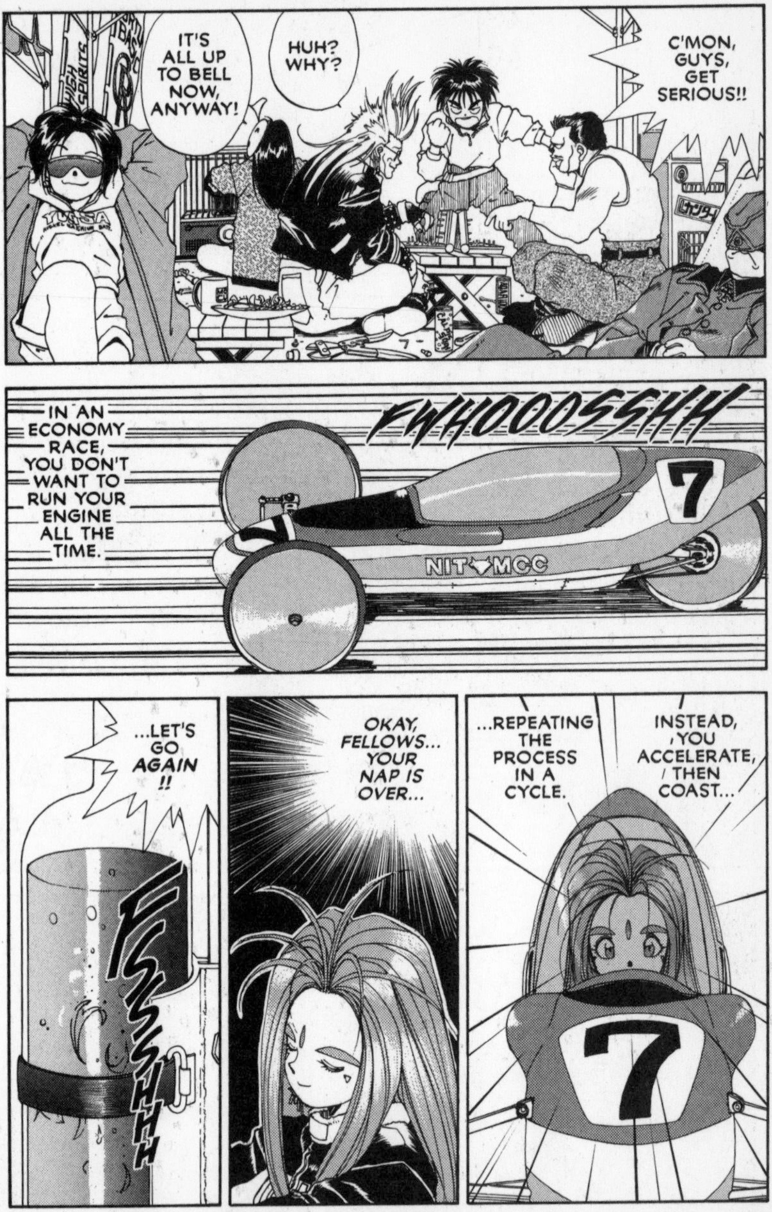
C'MON, GUYS, GET SERIOUS!!
HUH? WHY?
IT'S ALL UP TO BELL NOW, ANYWAY!
FWHOOOSSHH
IN AN ECONOMY RACE, YOU DON'T WANT TO RUN YOUR ENGINE ALL THE TIME.
NIT MCC
INSTEAD, YOU ACCELERATE, THEN COAST...
...REPEATING THE PROCESS IN A CYCLE.
OKAY, FELLOWS... YOUR NAP IS OVER...
...LET'S GO AGAIN!!
FSSSHHHH

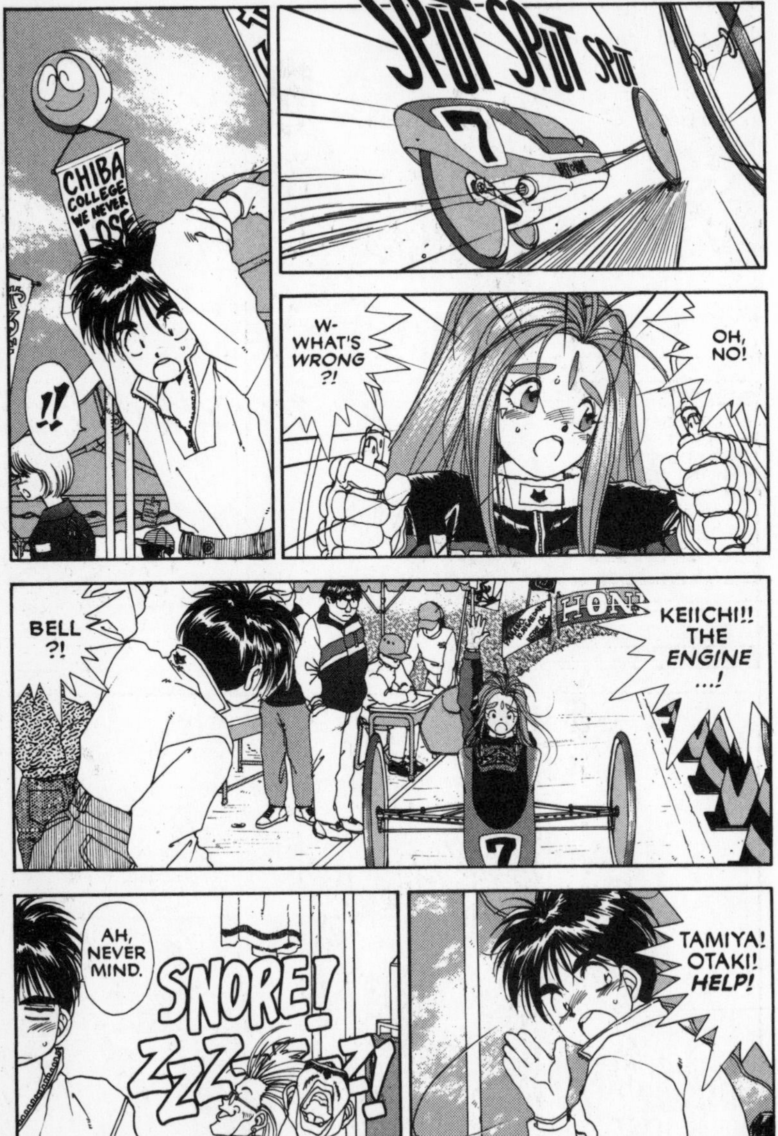
SPUT SPUT SPUT
OH, NO!
W-WHAT'S WRONG ?!
CHIBA COLLEGE WE NEVER LOSE
!!
KEIICHI!! THE ENGINE ...!
BELL ?!
TAMIYA! OTAKI! HELP!
AH, NEVER MIND.
SNORE!
ZZZ-Z-Z!

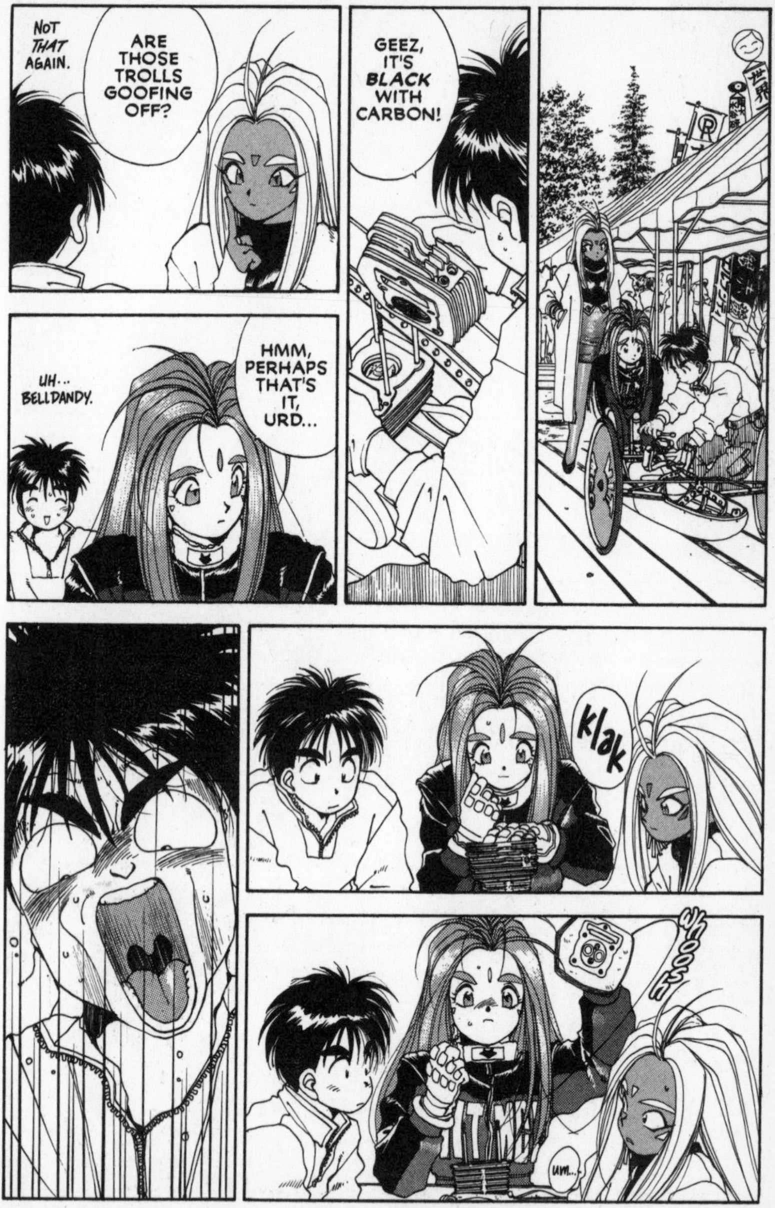
GEEZ, IT'S BLACK WITH CARBON!
ARE THOSE TROLLS GOOFING OFF?
NOT THAT AGAIN.
HMM, PERHAPS THAT'S IT, URD...
UH... BELLDANDY.
klak
WHOOSH
um...

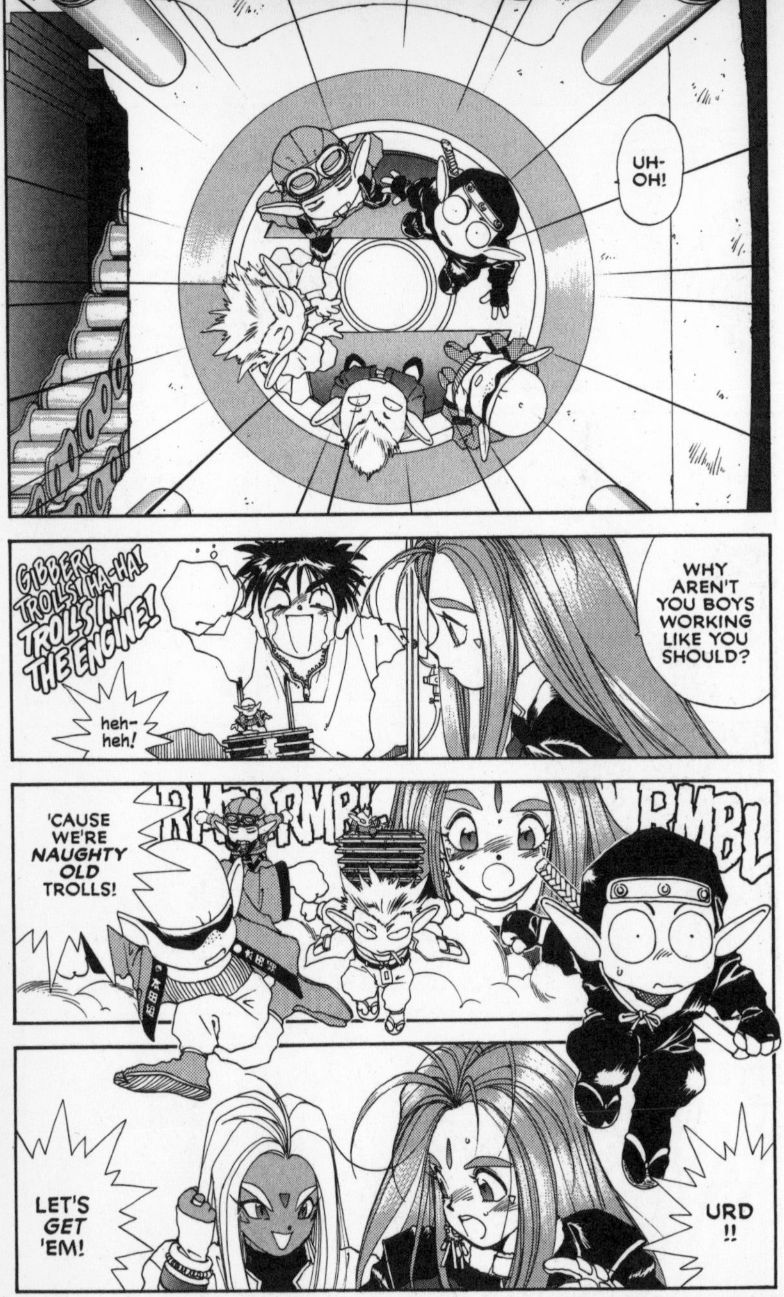

UH-OH!
WHY AREN'T YOU BOYS WORKING LIKE YOU SHOULD?
GIBBER! TROLLS! HA-HA! TROLL'S IN THE ENGINE!
heh-heh!
RMBL
'CAUSE WE'RE NAUGHTY OLD TROLLS!
URD !!
LET'S GET 'EM!

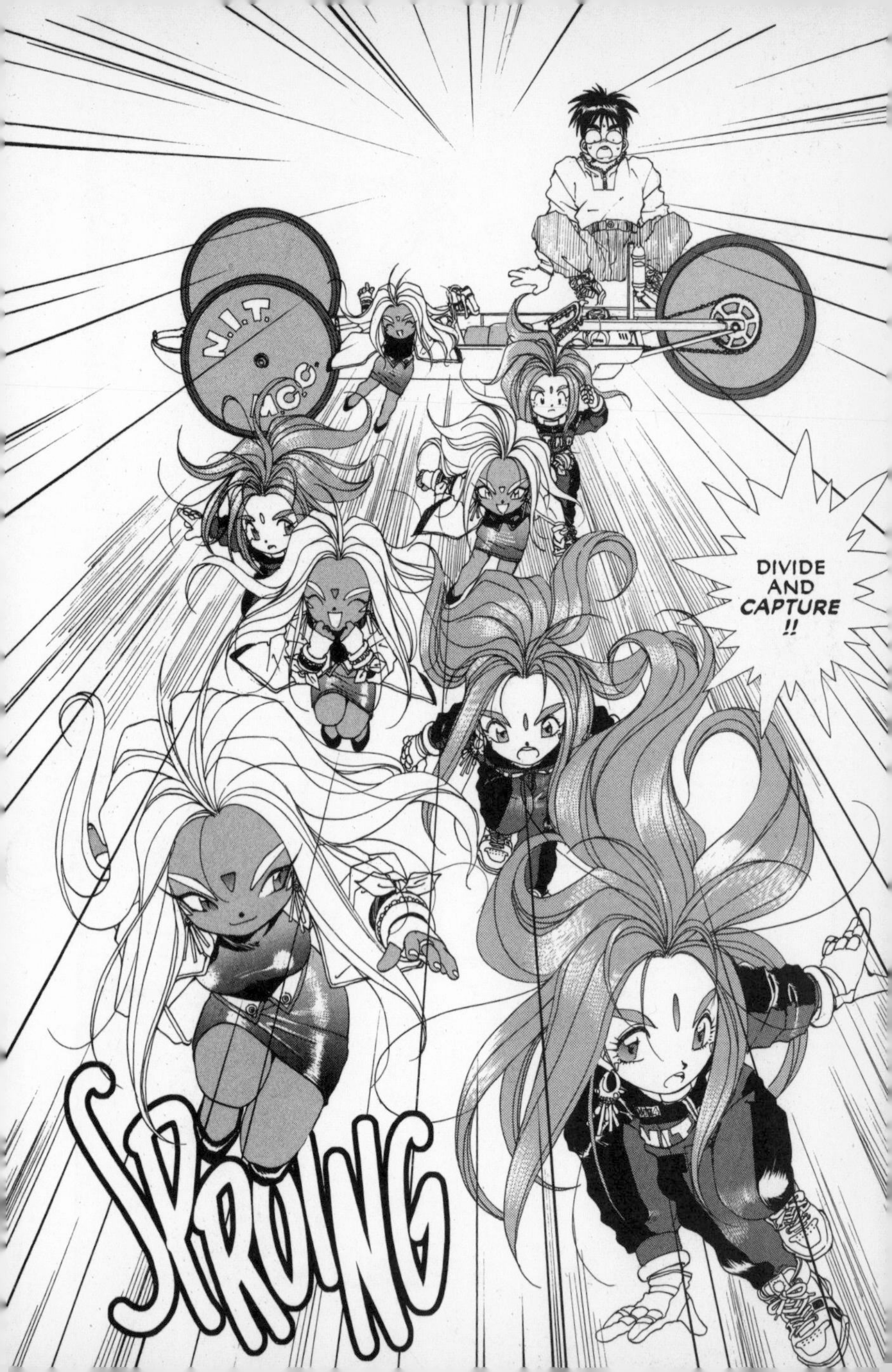
DIVIDE AND CAPTURE !!
SPROING

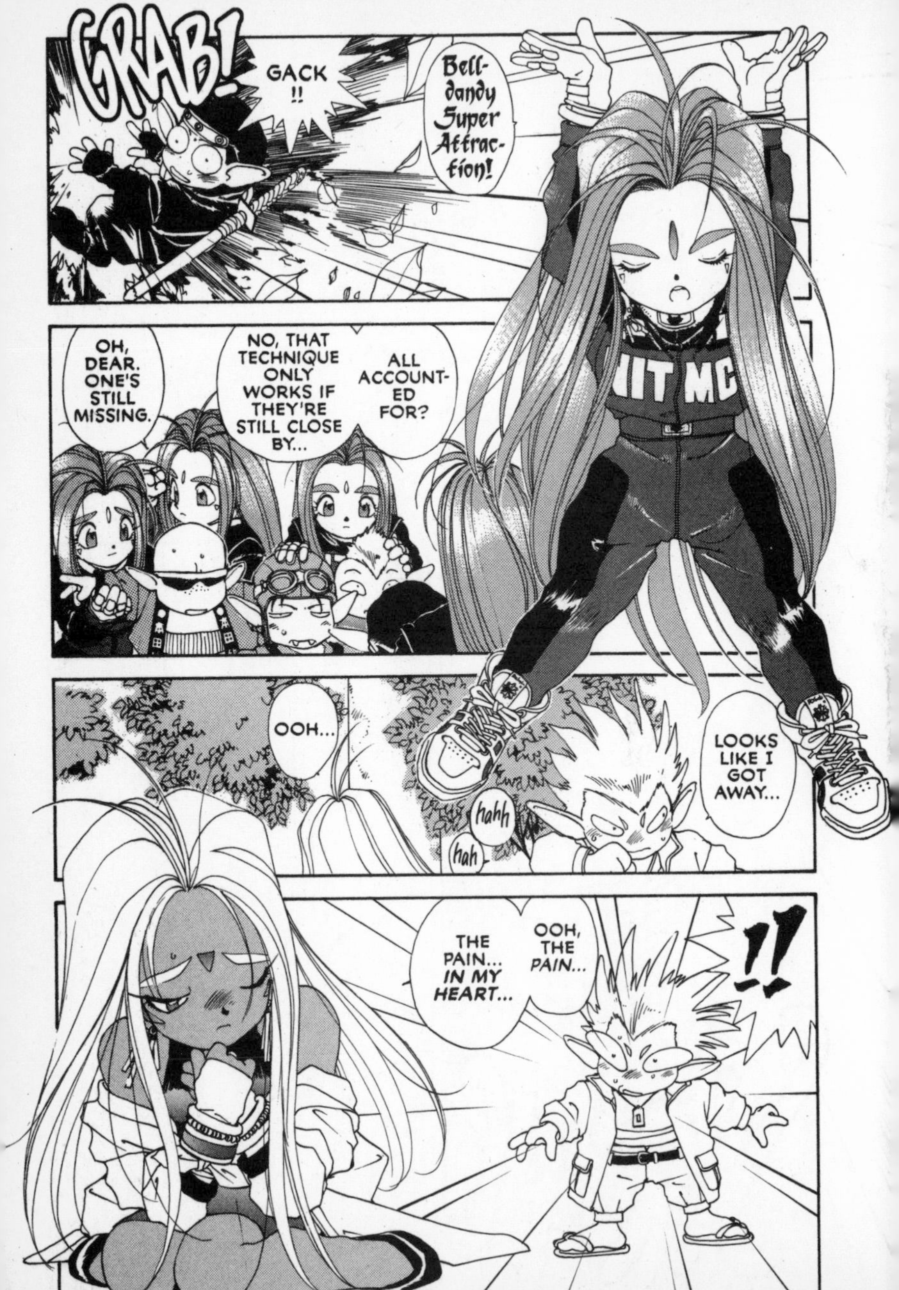
Bell-dandy Super Attrac-tion!
GRAB!
GACK !!
ALL ACCOUNT-ED FOR?
NO, THAT TECHNIQUE ONLY WORKS IF THEY'RE STILL CLOSE BY...
OH, DEAR. ONE'S STILL MISSING.
LOOKS LIKE I GOT AWAY...
hahh
hah
OOH...
!!
OOH, THE *PAIN*...
THE PAIN... *IN MY HEART*...

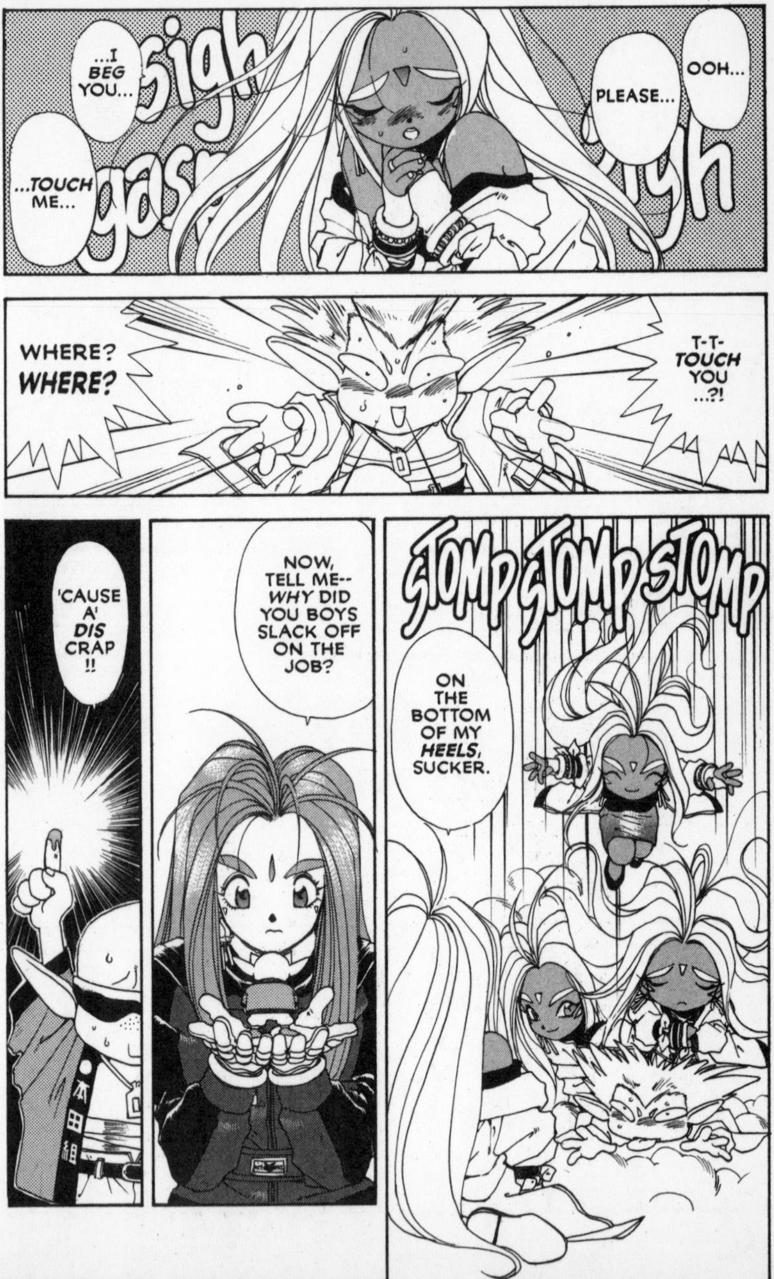
OOH...
PLEASE...
sigh
...I BEG YOU...
sigh
...TOUCH ME...
gasp
T-T-*TOUCH* YOU ...?!
WHERE? **WHERE?**
STOMP STOMP STOMP
ON THE BOTTOM OF MY *HEELS*, SUCKER.
NOW, TELL ME-- *WHY* DID YOU BOYS SLACK OFF ON THE JOB?
'CAUSE A' *DIS* CRAP !!
本田組

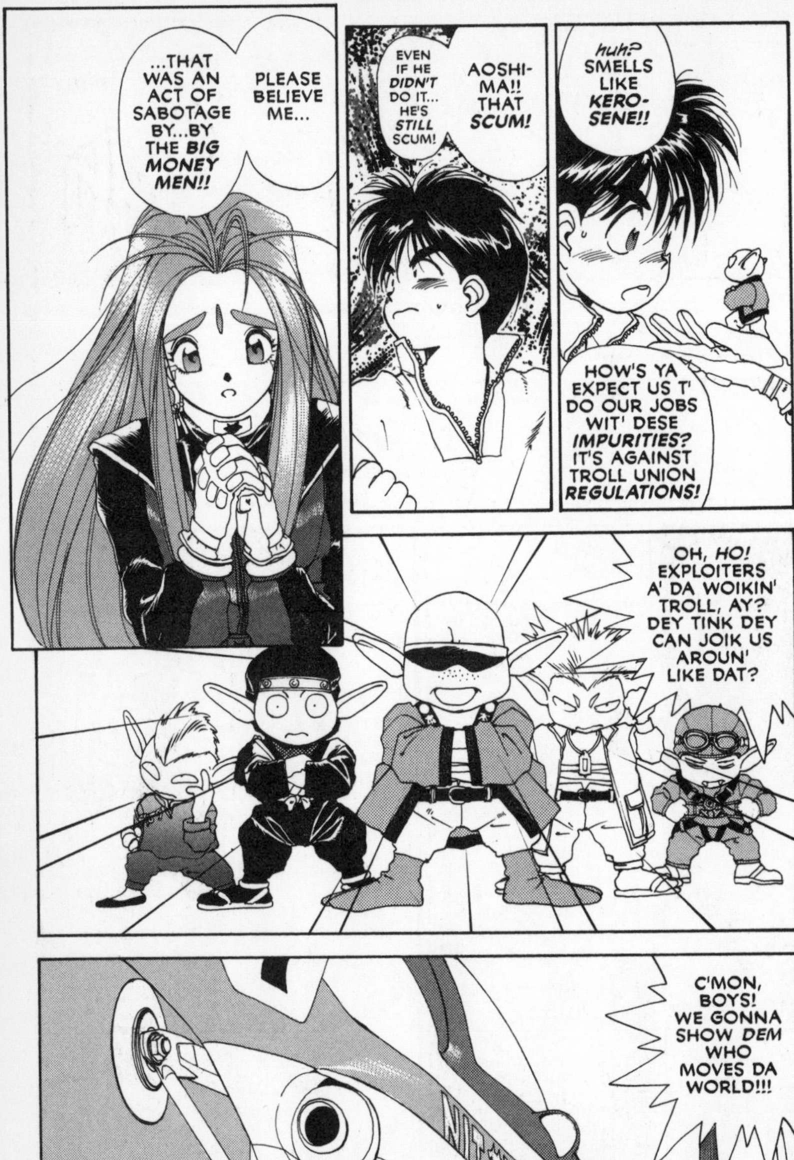
huh? SMELLS LIKE KERO-SENE!!
HOW'S YA EXPECT US T' DO OUR JOBS WIT' DESE IMPURITIES? IT'S AGAINST TROLL UNION REGULATIONS!
AOSHIMA!! THAT SCUM!
EVEN IF HE DIDN'T DO IT... HE'S STILL SCUM!
PLEASE BELIEVE ME...
...THAT WAS AN ACT OF SABOTAGE BY...BY THE BIG MONEY MEN!!
OH, HO! EXPLOITERS A' DA WOIKIN' TROLL, AY? DEY TINK DEY CAN JOIK US AROUN' LIKE DAT?
C'MON, BOYS! WE GONNA SHOW DEM WHO MOVES DA WORLD!!!

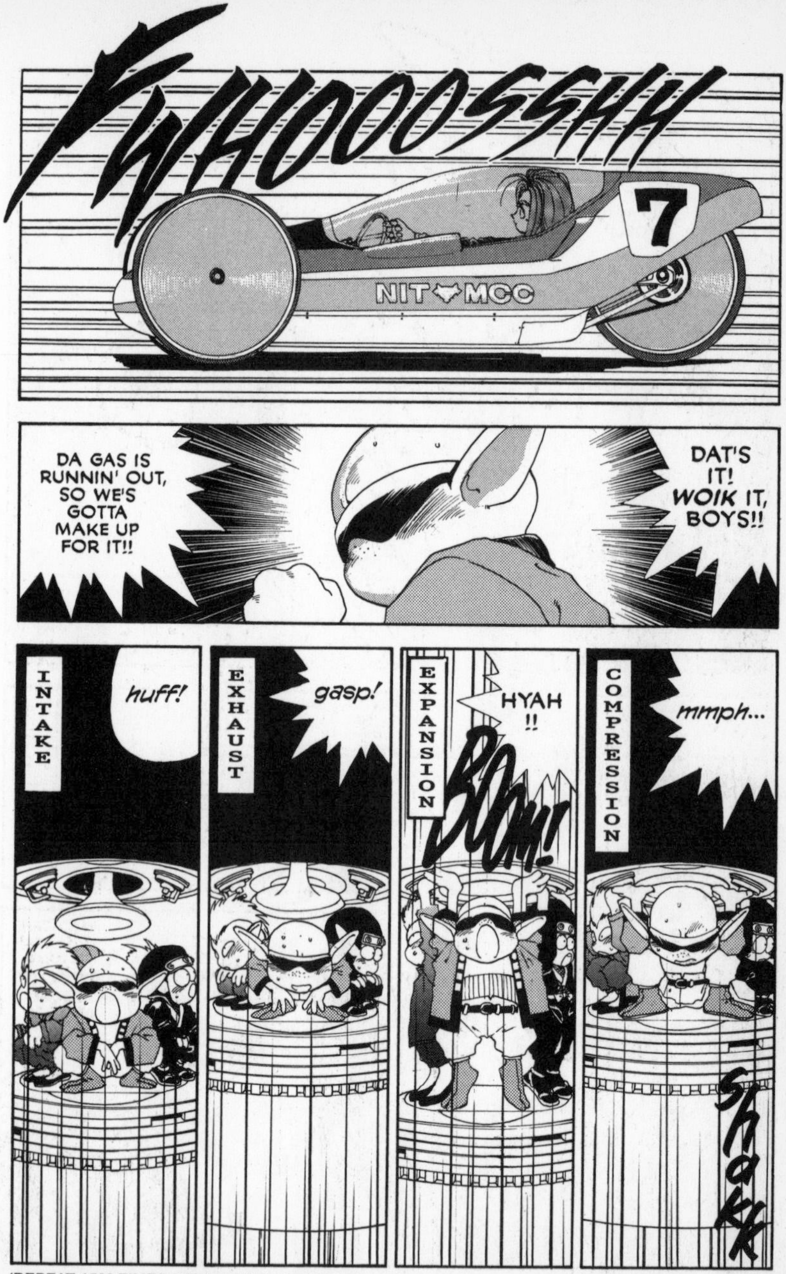
FWHOOOSSHH
7
NIT MCC
DAT'S IT! WOIK IT, BOYS!!
DA GAS IS RUNNIN' OUT, SO WE'S GOTTA MAKE UP FOR IT!!
COMPRESSION
mmph...
SHAKK
EXPANSION
HYAH !!
BOOM!
EXHAUST
gasp!
INTAKE
huff!

(REPEAT 1500 TIMES PER MINUTE = 3000RPM)

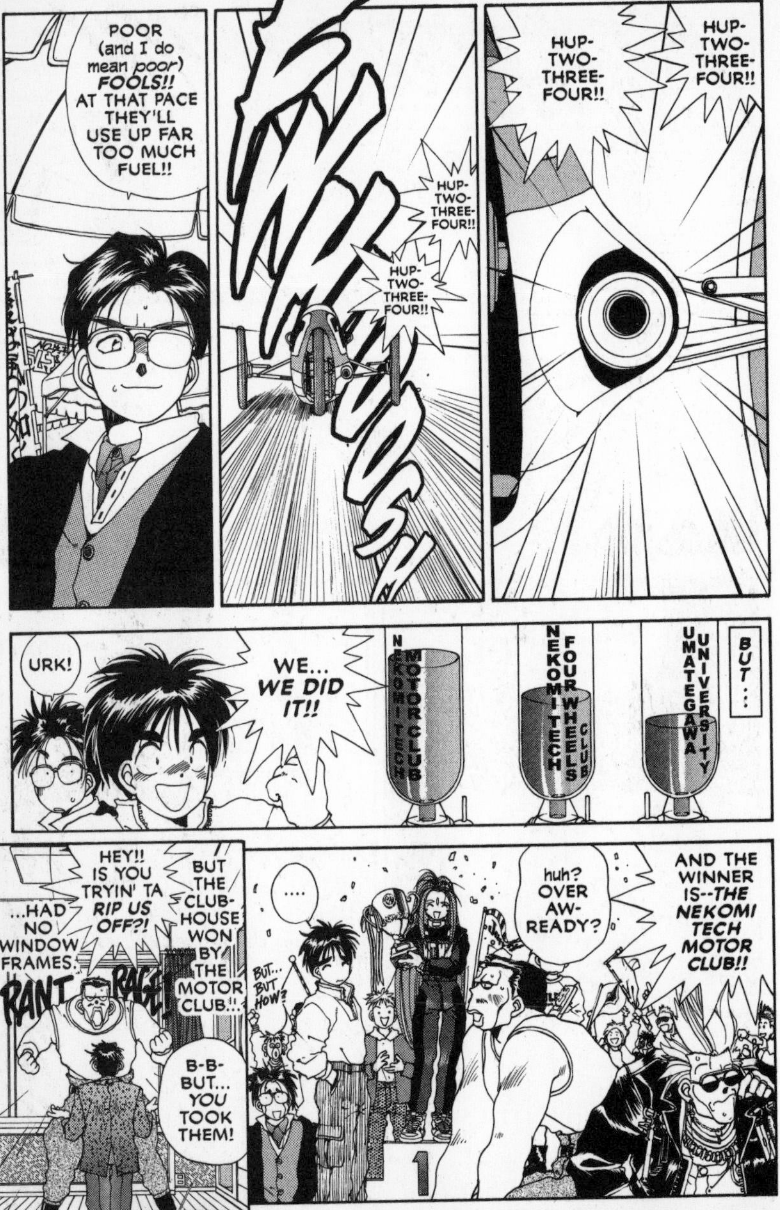
HUP-TWO-THREE-FOUR!!
HUP-TWO-THREE-FOUR!!
HUP-TWO-THREE-FOUR!!
HUP-TWO-THREE-FOUR!!
POOR (and I do mean *poor*) ***FOOLS!!*** AT THAT PACE THEY'LL USE UP FAR TOO MUCH FUEL!!
BUT...
UMATEGAWA UNIVERSITY
NEKOMI TECH FOUR WHEELS CLUB
NEKOMI TECH MOTOR CLUB
WE... ***WE DID IT!!***
URK!
AND THE WINNER IS--***THE NEKOMI TECH MOTOR CLUB!!***
huh? OVER AW-READY?
....
BUT... BUT *HOW?*
BUT THE CLUB-HOUSE WON BY THE MOTOR CLUB...
...HAD NO WINDOW FRAMES.
HEY!! IS YOU TRYIN' TA ***RIP US OFF?!***
RANT
RAGE!
B-B-BUT... *YOU* TOOK THEM!

EDITOR
Carl Gustav Horn

DESIGNER
Scott Cook

EDITORIAL ASSISTANT
Rachel Miller

ART DIRECTOR
Lia Ribacchi

PUBLISHER
Mike Richardson

English-language version
produced by Dark Horse Comics

OH MY GODDESS! Vol. 4
©2006 by Kosuke Fujishima. All rights reserved. First published in Japan in 1991 by Kodansha, Ltd., Tokyo. Publication rights
for this English edition arranged through Kodansha, Ltd. This English-
language edition ©2006 by Dark Horse Comics, Inc. All other material
©2006 by Dark Horse Comics, Inc. All rights reserved. No portion of this
publication may be reproduced or transmitted, in any form or by any
means, without the express written permission of the copyright holders.
Names, characters, places, and incidents featured in this publication are
either the product of the author's imagination or are used fictitiously. Any
resemblance to actual persons (living or dead), events, institutions, or
locales, without satiric intent, is coincidental. Dark Horse Manga™ is a
trademark of Dark Horse Comics, Inc. Dark Horse Comics® is a trademark
of Dark Horse Comics, Inc., registered in various categories and
countries. All rights reserved.

Published by Dark Horse Manga
A division of Dark Horse Comics, Inc.
10956 SE Main Street
Milwaukie, OR 97222
www.darkhorse.com

To find a comics shop in your area,
call the Comic Shop Locator Service
toll-free at 1-888-266-4226

First edition: January 2007
ISBN-10: 1-59307-623-1
ISBN-13: 978-1-59307-623-8

1 3 5 7 9 10 8 6 4 2

Printed in Canada

letters to the
ENCHANTRESS

10956 SE Main Street, Milwaukie, Oregon 97222
omg@darkhorse.com • www.darkhorse.com

NOTE: Full addresses and e-mail addresses will not be printed, unless you ask! All fan artwork, letters, and e-mails submitted become the property of Dark Horse Comics.

Welcome back! Once again, we present an economy-size letter that rules "Enchantress" like a tyrant. As with Ms. Swain from Vol. 24, it's nice to hear from a local reader. The "Powell's" to which our latest correspondent refers is a strong supporter of Dark Horse Manga—its main store in downtown Portland is perhaps the largest used bookstore in the world. It's exactly the kind of place you would find Yomiko Readman. But unfortunately, I never have.

Hello!

I've been teaching myself Japanese for a while now. Manga and anime are very much part of that effort, and I love *AMS/OMG!* [*Aa Megamisama/Oh My Goddess!*—the Japanese and English versions of the title—CGH] It's a great story with great visuals. (One image I wish they'd used in the anime was when Belldandy sat on the bottom edge of the mirror as if it was a windowsill.) And, I'm enough of a purist to prefer unflipped manga like your latest volumes and reissues.

Actually, I've had better luck tracking down *AMS/OMG!* in audiovisual formats than in print. I have your reissues of volumes 1 and 2; volume 22 is set aside. Between Powell's and Kinokuniya, I also got the first three tankoubon in Japanese, plus the semi-encyclopedic *AMS Collection*, covering the series through 2004. In contrast, I have the first five DVDs of the TV anime, the complete OAV series, the movie, the movie soundtrack, and the *AMS Singles* CD. (It's not exactly a hardship to hear Kikuko Inoue saying or singing Belldandy's lines.) [Kikuko Inoue also played Yoshiko Ueno, Kubo's girlfriend in *Otaku no Video*. So he ends up not only being dumped, but dumped by Belldandy. For an otaku, that's truly adding insult to injury. A rarely-remarked upon fact is that Ms. Inoue *also* played Super Idol Misty May. Considering the circumstances, you then begin to realize a new, psychologically disturbing level to *ONV*. Who knew there could be yet another level?—CGH]

In his letter in Volume 2, Timotheus was trying to work out a timeline. Let's look at the clues we've been given.

The calendar on Sada's kitchen wall (chapter 2) shows the month of October, and the pattern of days matches 1988. That matches with Belldandy sweeping leaves at the temple (which was more conspicuous in the anime). In chapter 16, Keiichi reminds himself that it was the 25th. So, Belldandy came into Keiichi's life on 25 October 1988. (The moon was full, by the way.) [I note with interest that in the Catholic Mass, the scripture reading for October 25, 1988 was Ephesians 5: 21-23, which has an odd resonance with *Oh My Goddess!*—CGH]

The splash page for chapter 4 shows Belldandy walking in snow, but there's no snow in the actual story until the end of chapter 5, when we see a Christmas tree in Sayoko's apartment. Deciduous trees are still bare in chapter 6. It's not clear if the greenery in chapter 7 is all evergreen, or if some deciduous trees are coming back.

After Megumi has passed her entrance exam, we learn (chapter 9) that there are just two weeks left before classes start. (Isn't that sorta last minute for entrance exams?) Since the traditional start of the Japanese school year is 1 April, that puts the exam in mid-March. In the anime, she'd already passed the entrance exam when she showed up just before White Day. **[In Japan, Valentine's Day is customarily for girls to give chocolates to boys; the boys reciprcate one month later with white chocolate; hence "White Day"—CGH]** That's 14 March, so the timing matches. Megumi entered the picture (chapter 8) on about 7 March 1989, at which point Belldandy and Keiichi had been living alone together for about four-and-a-half months without even kissing once. **[April 1, 1988 was a Friday; I understand that school in Japan usually begins on the first Monday in April, which would have been the 4th—CGH]**

Timotheus misunderstood the postmark date. In the Japanese calendar, 1989 started out as Showa 64; the sixty-fourth year of the reign of Emperor Hirohito. Then, Hirohito died of cancer only a week into the new year, on 7 January 1989. Suddenly, 1989 became Heisei 1, the first year of the reign of Emperor Akihito. The postmark date is Heisei 1, February 4. I'm guessing that the letter gave the actual dates of Megumi's visit, and Keiichi interpreted it as "this week" while he was reading aloud.

The beach retreat (chapter 13) is apparently during the short summer vacation which interrupts a school year rather than separating them. Urd shows up (chapter 14) soon after. The festival and . . . uh . . . pageant (chapter 15) . . . happen in late summer, which brings it back to their first anniversary, in October '89 (chapter 16).

(By the way, I suggest the word "meniversary" for a monthly milestone.)

One aspect of language and culture that I pay a lot of attention to is names. (What can I say, I'm an SCA herald.) **[When I lived in the Bay Area, I met a mead distiller, Mike Faul, who was doing a good trade with the SCA. I was dubious, because I was never a big fan of honey, but it's really quite a refined drink. Check out www.rabbitsfootmeadery.com. But only if you're Urd's age or older—CGH]**

As can be seen by the sign on Keiichi's bedroom door, the surname Morisato is typical of the peasant-type locatives created in 1870, when the 94% of the populace who'd been forbidden to have surnames were suddenly required to have them. It simply describes where his ancestors were living at the time, or had come from: *mori* "forest" + *sato* "village" = Morisato, "forest village."

(I haven't read anything that explicitly says so, but I can picture swarms of bureaucrats going out across the countryside. It would be at least as challenging a task as the Domesday Book in medieval England.) **[People take having a last name for granted, but it was also uncommon for the average person (i.e., a peasant) in early medieval Europe to have a last name—CGH]**

I was surprised when his personal name didn't show up until Sada spoke it, in chapter 2. As expected, the *ichi* part is "1," as in "firstborn." The *kei* kanji that his parents chose means "firefly." I think that fits in with a lot of other Japanese names that are variations on "bright," including most of the 250+ names that are pronounced "Akira." (The *bert* or *berto* element in some Western names of Germanic origin also means "bright," but the Europeans meant it as a metaphor for "famous"; I suspect the Japanese mean "lively.") **[I just checked the original Japanese again, and yes, it does appear Sada is the first to use "Keiichi." Otaku seem to be very familiar with him—CGH]**

Oh, and K1 isn't a nickname for Keiichi; it's shorthand. It's quick and easy to write, and most Japanese will pronounce it "Keiichi," the same as if it was written in ideographic kanji or phonetic hiragana. Also, its clear and simple lines are easily distinguishable from a distance, making it a good choice to emblazon on his racing coveralls, as in the movie.

The name Belldandy has such an Anglo-French flavor that I never would have guessed that it's a cognate of the modern German word *werden*. Thanks for reprinting Toren Smith's essay.

The name of the temple they live in is Tariki Hongan. That's a phrase that can be translated as "salvation solely by divine benevolence." **[It should be noted that just like the Christian doctrine of "salvation by grace," there is a vast body of writing in Buddhism about what *tariki-hongan* actually means, and what it implies for the believer. However, in colloquial use in Japan, it definitely has the connotation of being saved by others, rather than by your own efforts—CGH]**

"Megumi" is written in hiragana instead of kanji. That option eliminates the common guessing game of choosing from among multiple pronunciations, but leaves the issue of meaning wide open to speculation. The *Collection* shows it as a single-kanji name that means "blessed" or "blessing" (or maybe "she blesses us").

Sayoko is *sa* "sand" + *yo* "night" + *ko* "child/girl," whatever that combination means. Mishima is *mi* "3" (or "third") + *shima* "island." Aoshima is "blue/green island." Toshiyuki is *toshi* "narrative" + *yuki* "origin."

Sada is "help" + "field." Kakuta is "corner field." Ozawa is *o* "big" + *sawa* "swamp."

In the original, Tamiya and Otaki aren't actually named until chapters 12 and 18, respectively. They were usually *sempai* ("upperclassman") or *ano hito* ("that person") or some such. Tamiya is *ta* "field" + *miya* "palace." His personal name is Toraichi; the *tora* is "first horary sign: tiger." It implies that he's not only firstborn, but he was born in a Year of the Tiger, like 1962. Otaki is "big waterfall." His personal name is never given.

I don't know yet if it ever shows up in the manga, but the anime has Tamiya and Otaki calling each other "Den-chan" and "Dai-chan." At first, those cutesy nicknames confused me. Then I realized that "den" is an alternate pronunciation of the "field" kanji, and "dai" is an alternate pronunciation of the "big" kanji. **[As a matter of fact, they *do* use those nicknames in the manga, as early as Vol. 3. In Vol. 14 (called "Queen Sayoko" or the original English version of the *OMG!* manga—they were rendered as "Tammy" (^_^) and "Ottie")—CGH]**

At the very beginning of the original manga, Keiichi is taking a message for "Aoyama-sempai" ("upperclassman Aoyama"), not Tamiya. In the one-frame flashback, Tamiya didn't tell him whom to take messages for, displaying the classic Japanese assumption that context is enough. Aoyama is apparently one of the other sempai in the Motor Club. But, since none of them are actually named any time soon, even Japanese readers may have been confused into thinking that Tamiya's name was Aoyama.

The translator seems to have tried to avoid that confusion by glossing over the mention of Aoyama's name. In the anime, which was also written after that confusion was resolved, Tamiya is identified early on; one of the chores he leaves Keiichi is to wait for a call that Aoyama "blue/green mountain") is expecting. **[The mysterious Aoyama is discussed a bit further in *Oh My Goddess! Colors*—CGH]**

Satoko is *sato* "village/hometown" + *ko* "child/girl." Yamano, in this case, is *ya* "arrow" + *ma* "pause" + *no* "valley"; a valley where you can pause between the arrows of war? From the attitude of Satoko's father, I wonder if it's a samurai name rather than a peasant name.

The most intriguing name is bound up with the setting: Nekomi. The kanji are clearly *neko* "cat" + *mi* "fruit." I can't find any such term as "cat-fruit" in any of my dictionaries or idiom guides. One interpretation might be "kitten," but that's just wild speculation. Scattered throughout the manga and anime, there are feline logos obviously inspired by the name. One of those can be found on a bank in a recurring anime locale, the Nekomidouri Shoutengai, or Nekomi Street Shopping Area.

As to where Nekomi is: according to the address on the letter that Megumi delivers to Keiichi, Nekomi is a city in Chiba Prefecture. (Most of Chiba is a peninsula that encloses the eastern side of Tokyo Bay.) The weather report at the end of chapter 5 refers to snow blanketing Kanto, which is the "Eastern Region" that might also be thought of as Greater Tokyo. That's no help here; all of Chiba is included in Kanto. It's hard to be sure, but Nekomi doesn't seem to be on the shore of either the bay or the ocean. Other clues to narrow down the location will probably show up.

Obviously a college town, Nekomi is a (presumably fictional) outlying "suburb" of Tokyo, something like Forest Grove is to Portland, Oregon. But a "suburb" of one of the two largest cities in the world can be pretty large itself. Nekomi seems closer in size to Portland than Forest Grove.

One last topic is the placement of products and brand names that you've already pointed out some of. There are a lot of them, especially on Megumi's shirts. That's one more difference from the anime, which uses a widespread process I call "product *displacement*." Familiar brand names and their logos are slightly altered into parodies of themselves. For example, there are Somy TV & VCR, NacDonald's restaurant, a Country 13 realtor, and Dack Daniel's whiskey. The only two product categories that seem immune to the process are weapons and vehicles. (For weapons, look at *City Hunter* or *Gunsmith Cats.*) Keiichi's motorcycle remains a BMW in the anime. Sayoko's Beemer becomes a Mercedes, but it's still a real brand.

Looking forward to the next volume,

Vincent Burch
Portland, OR

P.S. You said that *OMG!* is the second-longest-running manga in the U.S. I'm guessing the longest-running one was created by Rumiko Takahashi.

That's exactly right. The longest-running manga in the U.S. was Rumiko Takahashi's *Ranma 1/2*, published by Viz. It has had a production history very similar to that of *Oh My Goddess!*—it first ran as a Western-style monthly comic book in 1992, and was collected into many graphic novels (in *Ranma's* case, up to Vol. 22) until in 2003 the monthly comic was cancelled and it switched starting with Vol. 23 to Japanese orientation, while at the same time going back and re-releasing the early volumes unflopped. The final volume of *Ranma 1/2* came out just recently; now the honor has passed to *Oh My Goddess!*

Speaking of 1994 (and of Viz), in lieu of our regular notes on old school *OMG!*, we have a special treat . . . with that same classic flavor! Thanks to the kind permission of Viz Media, LLC, we are reprinting the interview with Kosuke Fujishima that appeared in the February 1994 issue of *Animerica* magazine. Beginning in 1993 until the end of its run in 2005, *Animerica*, under the editorship of Trish Ledoux and later Julie Davis, was the first regular monthly professional anime and manga magazine in the United States.

Note that bracketed comments in bold are new for this 2006 re-printing, whereas the regular bracketed comments were from the original 1994 *Animerica* interview.

ANIMERICA: What made you decide to become a manga artist? Did you start as an assistant to anyone?

KOSUKE FUJISHIMA: I started because I love manga—or rather, I liked to draw and create stories. Actually, I think that manga was just the most familiar type of art to me, easily accessible to study and create. That may be closer to the truth. I think I could have gotten into animation just as easily. I was an assistant to Tatsuya Egawa for about a year and a half.

A: What was your debut work?
KF: When Mr. Egawa's *Be Free!* manga was going to be made into a live-action movie, I drew the "making of" movie story, called *Making Be Free!!* That was actually my debut work. But essentially, my first original work was *You're Under Arrest!* (*Taiho Shichauzo*). **[*Be Free!* was my favorite manga in high school. None of Egawa's manga have ever been published in English, but the anime *Golden Boy* is based on his manga of the same name. Note that Dark Horse published two volumes of *You're Under Arrest* in English. A police action-comedy, *YUA!* has a different feel from *OMG!*, but if you're a Fujishima fan you should definitely check it out—CGH]**

A: What's the good part of being a manga artist? And what's the not-so-good part?
KF: I can draw what I want to express and have that seen by many people. I've become what I most wanted to be, and there's nothing happier than that. On the other hand, the tough part about being a pro is that I have to go on doing it whether I feel like it or not. You can't always do what you want to do when you want to do it. Also, this might not be as important as other reasons but . . . well, manga artists don't have to commute to work [laughs].

A: If you hadn't become a manga artist, what do you think you might have become?
KF: I think I still would have become an artist. I don't think I could have gotten away from the fields of design and art. At this point, I can't think of anything else I would have done except become a manga artist.

A: Where did you get the inspiration for *Oh My Goddess!*?
KF: I thought it might be an interesting idea if being a goddess was a job, an occupation. I based it on Norse mythology, which is relatively unknown in Japan.

A: Do you have any spelling preferences for rendering the names of goddesses in English? I understand that in the United States, there's been some confusion . . .
KF: Well, Belldandy is spelled with a "B," even though the proper spelling in the actual Norse mythology is "Verdandi." Then there's Urd and Skuld; the spelling of those two names are unchanged.

A: Where do you stand on the animated version of *Oh! My Goddess*? What do you think of the quality of the OAV series? **[The original five-volume anime version of *OMG!*, currently available from www.animeigo. com. It shares the same director and character designer as the current TV series, but the characters in the OAV naturally appear different from the TV series, reflecting how Fujishima's style has changed over the past decade—CGH]**
KF: Well, it's based on my drawings, of course, so there are always going to be suggestions I could make as the author to improve it, to create new ideas, and to point out exactly where the animation deviates from my original ideas. But animation is the product of the animators, after all, so I just keep quiet so long as their creative intentions are obvious. Even if it's just a *little* different from the manga . . . well, let's just say that if the animation is going to end up being exactly the same as the manga, there's no point in animating it. I think the function of animation is best served when a work with a flavor different from the original comic

emerges, even though both the animation and the comic share the same universe. Quality-wise, I think the level of the *Oh My Goddess!* animation is considerably high. I worked on the storyboards for parts of the opening and parts of the ending of the third OAV volume, so I feel as though the animation is another part of me.

A: It's looking like the English versions of both the animation and the manga are going to be released soon. Do you have any thoughts on your work being seen in the U.S.?

KF: I don't know how well they'll be received, but I hope that the fans will support them. I never intended to create the story for an international audience, so I'm curious to see how people overseas will perceive it.

A: The number of anime and manga overseas is on the rise. Does this come as a surprise to you?

KF: The development of Japanese anime and manga is itself unique, and there are quite a few high-quality works, so I'd like to see them get greater circulation overseas. It would be nice if my works were included among them.

A: When the U.S. company releasing the animation announced their intention to call it "Oh My Goddess!" rather than "Ah! My Goddess," as had been printed in the manga all these years, a great debate started among fans over what the title should be. Which one best reflects your intentions, "Ah!" or "Oh". . . ?

KF: In terms of nuance, I think "Oh" probably comes closer. However it ends up, I think it should be rendered to make better sense in the language of the target country.

A: That's what usually has to happen when titles are brought over to another language. Kishiro's *Gunnm*, for example, became *Battle Angel Alita* in its English version. What about your own works? Do you have a preference

one way or the other? How would you feel if the comic and animated versions came out with different titles overseas?

KF: If there's something that fits well in that language, I wouldn't complain. After all, there are movie titles that work much better once they're changed . . . although there are also those that *don't* work [laughs]. I would like to see that the titles of the comics and the animation stay consistent, however.

A: Since we're already on the general topic . . . how do you feel about flopped artwork? It seems as though this has become the standard for publications of manga in America.

KF: It's painful. I'm not that skilled an artist, and so when the artwork is flipped, all the shortcomings in my drawings become obvious. There's also an artistic consideration. Some panels lose the balance of their composition when they're flopped. If it were possible, I would prefer for everyone to be able to see the original version, the way I intended my artwork to be seen in the first place.

A: Is there anything in particular about the American fans of both your animated and manga work that you would like to know?

KF: Actually, I'd like to know what aspects of my work American fans are attracted to. I'm sure they must have a different perspective than Japanese fans. Cultural differences, most likely.

A: Let's talk a little about the *Oh My Goddess!* series. Which goddess is your favorite? Are there any aspects of their character, style, or fashion that you are particularly fond of?

KF: I don't really have a favorite, but . . . well, Urd is always outspoken and has more mature sensibilities, so I like her.

A: Speaking of fashion, your characters are always so beautifully dressed. Where do you get the ideas for the fashions in your comics?

KF: I study fashion quite a lot. Often, I find surprises in children's clothes. I'm always ready for a chance to study children and women's clothes at department stores.

A: As a manga artist, what are your work habits like? Do you work every day of the month? Are you a morning person? A night person . . .?
KF: I work almost every day, and I'm usually a night person. I don't pull that many all-nighters, however. I find that my drawing skills start going down the drain if I pull too many of those [laughs]. I try to leave a little free time in my schedule when I can help it.

A: How many assistants do you have?
KF: Six.

A: Do you ever have times when being a professional manga artist seems more trouble than it's worth, times when you feel discouraged?
KF: When I can't think up a story. When I can't draw the way I want to.

A: And what do you do to comfort yourself?
KF: I talk on the phone with friends. Talking to someone in the same business is best. When I see others going through the same thing, I'm comforted that I'm not alone, and I find courage in that.

A: Do you have any advice for fans who want to draw their own manga?
KF: Everyone's goals are different, so I can't make a blanket comment, but an artist basically draws manga to communicate an idea to others. The idea won't be communicated if the work is understandable only to its creator. It just won't work. I think the meaning of manga is to have it understood by as many people as possible.

A: It won't surprise you to hear that there are several publications devoted to comics journalism in America. Do you have your own "theory of manga"?
KF: As far as a theory goes, I guess I've already said it. To be successful, manga needs to be understood by as many people as possible. I have a certain interest in the nature of comics journalism, but I don't have a particular theory other than what I've already expressed.

A: In Japan, manga with highly violent and sexual content is often the target of criticism. Your manga doesn't come under this sort of scrutiny, however, perhaps because the stories are more "pure" and tend to revolve around adolescents What are your thoughts on sex and violence in manga? **[Although hardly extreme material, You're Under Arrest was definitely more fan-service oriented than Oh My Goddess!. Since YUA! was a seven-volume series, and at the time of the interview OMG! was only up to Vol. 9, it would have been perhaps more fair to say that Fujishima had moved in the direction of "pure" stories, rather than to suggest they were entirely representative of him—CGH]**
KF: One way of looking at it is that I haven't drawn any explicit sex and violence because it hasn't been necessary. It happens often enough in real life and besides, sex isn't something evil. I think pretending sex and violence doesn't exist only breeds ignorance. There are stories that actually require a certain amount of it to be successfully told. Of course, this is all assuming that the sex and violence isn't done gratuitously.

A: Is there something you keep in mind when you draw manga?
KF: I try to express at least one definite idea clearly. That's my goal.

A: What about the future? What kind of stories would you like to draw?
KF: Right now, for the indefinite future, I'm tied up with Oh My Goddess! After that,

who knows? I may end up continuing to draw adolescent stories. I'm also interested in stories which explore "male-bonding" friendships and situations.

A: Of all your other works, are there any in particular that you'd like your American fans to read?

KF: I only have two other works. *You're Under Arrest!* and *Striker*, so I guess the choice isn't too difficult. And even though I drew it from a different perspective, *Striker* was created with American comics in mind. Naturally, I'm interested in an American reaction. **[Since 1997, Fujishima has also become known for his character designs in the *Sakura Taisen* series. *Striker*, which apparently has never been collected in Japan, is understood to be a gonzo baseball story that ran occasionally in the weekly Kodansha magazine *Morning*—CGH]**

A: Let's talk about your hobbies. What sort of things do you enjoy doing? Do you have any favorite music, or favorite films?

KF: My favorite things are motorcycles, automobiles, airplanes, the sea. Reading. Plastic models. My favorite activities are sleeping, riding motorcycles, drawing pictures, and talking on the phone. My favorite music . . . well, I listen to everything. My favorite movies are *Streets of Fire*, *Blues Brothers*, *Das Boot*, *The Hidden*, and *Terminator 2*. I've also been getting into *Memphis Belle* a lot recently. I bought a sidecar recently—a German sidecar by the name Krauser Domani—and I'm pretty infatuated with that at the moment.

A: Are there any foreign countries you'd like to visit?

KF: Australia. America. Germany. But I'm most comfortable with Japan. I would like to see drag racing and air racing in America someday. The only problem is that I can't speak English [laughs].

A: Are you interested in mecha and robots? They don't appear much in your work, but . . .

KF: Sure, I like them very much. Real-life robots are doing wonderful things, and it's fun watching them do their work.

A: Any future plans relating to your leisure time?

KF: I'd like to become a pilot and fly by myself, but that's just not possible with the time I have. The sky is right there, but it's so far away. So I just lie down and watch the sky.

A: As we discussed a little earlier, anime and manga are becoming very popular overseas. There are even anime and manga conventions. Would you be interested in attending one day . . . ?

KF: Hmm, I wonder what sort of things they do there? I only hear rumors . . .

A: In closing, do you have a message for your English-speaking fans?

KF: If there's anyone out there who reads my manga and is inspired to become a comics artist because of it, then I would really be pleased. I wonder if there is anyone . . . ? [laughs]. One of my dreams is to become a world-class manga artist someday. If by some chance I ever achieve that, I would like my fans to be proud and say "I knew him when." You can count on me to try my best for both our sakes.

Special thanks to Syrian otaku Wa-L Masri, who explains that the Arabic on the cover of the Demons CD (p.60) is a conjugation of the verb "to do." The Arabic on the Gods CD (p.77) is just random letters, and the "Arabic" on the inside of the case (p.101) is just squiggles ^_^.

–CGH

Creator Kosuke Fujishima in 1991!

His message to fans in the original Japanese *Oh My Goddess!* Vol. 4:

"Thank you so much for all your support! It's already been two years into the manga, and here I am at the fourth volume. Since I began I've moved from Higashi-Nakano to Kawasaki. I've exchanged my Suzuki GSX-R for a Harley. But one thing that hasn't changed is that I still don't get any bodily exercise. My only physical recreation is to walk around my apartment. With one of those step counters."

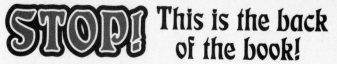

STOP! This is the back of the book!

This manga collection is translated into English, but arranged in right-to-left reading format to maintain the artwork's visual orientation as originally drawn and published in Japan. If you've never read comics this way before, take a look at the diagram below to give yourself an idea of how to go about it. Basically, you'll be starting in the upper right-hand corner, and will read each word balloon and panel moving right-to-left. It may take a little getting used to, but you should get the hang of it very quickly. Have fun! If this is the millionth manga you've read this way, never mind. ^_^

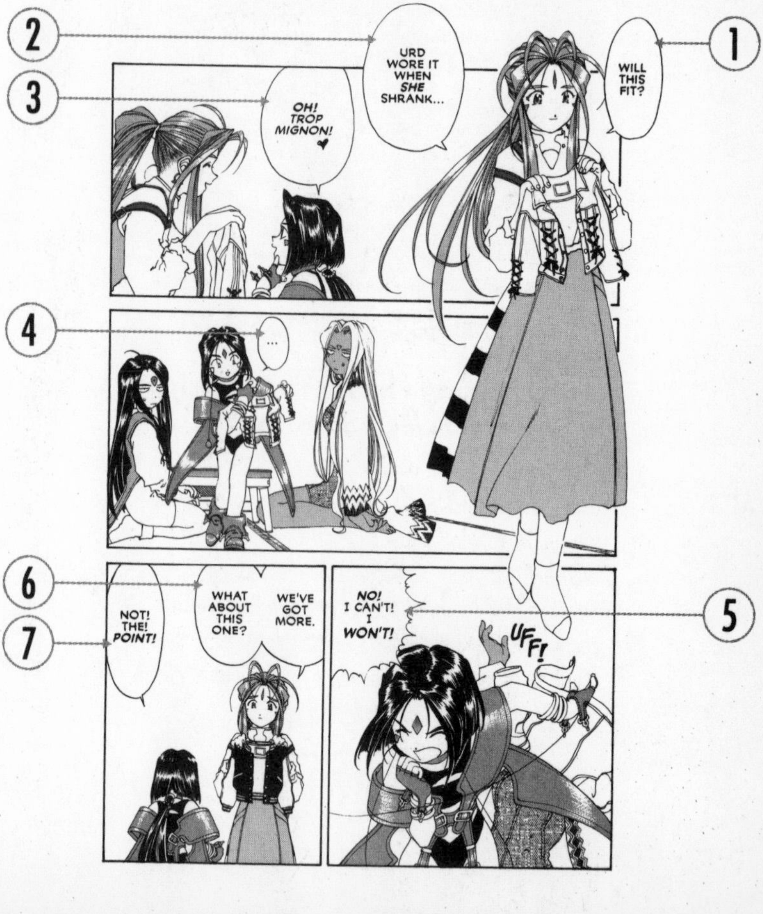
1
WILL THIS FIT?
2
URD WORE IT WHEN SHE SHRANK...
3
OH! TROP MIGNON!
4
...
5
NO! I CAN'T! I WON'T!
UFF!
6
WE'VE GOT MORE.
WHAT ABOUT THIS ONE?
7
NOT! THE! POINT!